Stories from the

OLD SQUIRE'S FARM

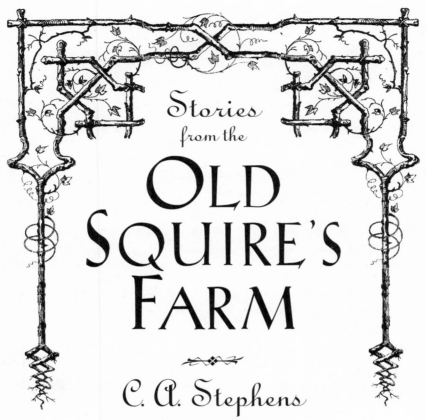

Stories
from the
OLD SQUIRE'S FARM

C. A. Stephens

COMPILED AND EDITED BY

Charles G. Waugh and Eric-Jon Waugh

RUTLEDGE HILL PRESS
Nashville, Tennessee

Published by Rutledge Hill Press
211 Seventh Avenue North, Nashville, Tennessee 37219.

Distributed in Canada by H. B. Fenn & Company, Ltd., 34 Nixon Road, Bolton, Ontario L7E 1W2.

Typography by D&T/Bailey Typesetting, Inc., Nashville, Tennessee
Design by Bruce Gore, Gore Studio, Inc., Nashville, Tennessee

Acknowledgments: For help in obtaining original periodicals, Rutledge Hill Press is grateful to Ed Todd at the Ben West Library in Nashville and to Jim Toplin, MaryBeth Blalock, and Gokhan Gunay at the Vanderbilt University Library.

Illustration Credits: All drawings are from *The Youth's Companion*. Photographs on pp. 402 and 407 are used by permission of Down East Enterprises, Camden, Maine.

Library of Congress Cataloging-in-Publication Data

Stephens, C. A. (Charles Asbury), 1844–1931.
    Stories from the Old Squire's Farm / C. A. Stephens : compiled and edited by Charles G. Waugh and Eric-Jon Waugh.
      p. cm.
    ISBN 1-55853-334-6
    1. Maine—Social life and customs—Fiction. 2. Grandparents—Maine—Fiction. 3. Domestic fiction, American. 4. Farm life—Maine—Fiction. 5. Children—Maine—Fiction. 6. Orphans—Maine—Fiction. 7. Family—Maine—Fiction. I. Waugh, Charles G. II. Waugh, Eric-Jon, 1978– III. Title.
    PS3537.T3533S75   1995
    974.1'009734—dc20   95–5299
                                                      CIP

Printed in the United States of America
3 4 5 6 7 — 99 98 97

CONTENTS

Contents

Stories from the
OLD SQUIRE'S
FARM

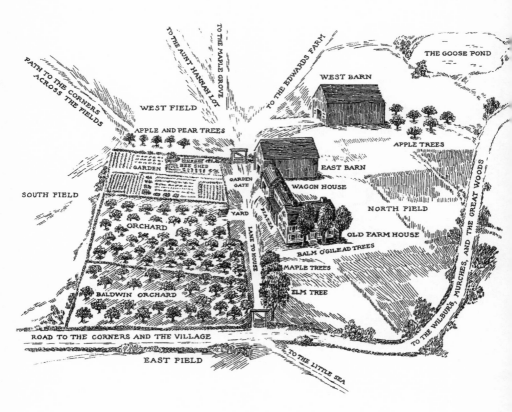

THE GOOSE POND

TO THE EDWARDS FARM

WEST BARN

TO THE AUNT HANNAH LOT

TO THE MAPLE GROVE

PATH TO THE CORNERS
ACROSS THE FIELDS

WEST FIELD

APPLE TREES

APPLE AND PEAR TREES

GARDEN

BEE SHED

GARDEN
GATE

EAST BARN

WAGON HOUSE

SOUTH FIELD

YARD

PIAZZA

NORTH FIELD

TO THE WILBURS, MURCHES, AND THE GREAT WOODS

ORCHARD

LANE TO HOUSE

OLD FARM HOUSE

BALM O'GILEAD TREES

MAPLE TREES

BALDWIN ORCHARD

ELM TREE

ROAD TO THE CORNERS AND THE VILLAGE

EAST FIELD

TO THE LITTLE SEA

MAP OF
THE OLD SQUIRE'S FARM

INTRODUCTION

AWAY DOWN EAST IN THE PINE TREE STATE, there is a lake dearer to my heart than all the other waters of this fair earth, for its shores were the scenes of my boyhood, when life was young and the world a romance still unread.

The white settlers called it the Great Pond; but long before they came to Maine, the Indians had named it Pennesseewassee (pronounced *Penny-see-was-see*), the lake-where-the-women-died, from the Abnaki words, *penem-pegouas-abem*, in memory, perhaps, of some unhistoric tragedy.

From their villages on the upper Saco waters, the Pequawkets were accustomed to cross over to the Androscoggin and often stopped at this lake, midway, to fish in the spring, and again in winter to hunt for moose, then snowbound in their "yards." On snowshoes, or paddling their birch canoes along the pine-shadowed streams, these tawny, pre-Columbian warriors came and camped on the Pennesseewassee; we still pick up their flint arrowheads along the shore, and it may even be that the short, brown Skraellings were here before them, in Neolithic days.

There are two ponds, or lakes, of this name, the Great and the Little Pennesseewassee, the latter lying a mile and a half to the west of the larger expanse and connected to it by a brook.

To the northeast, north, and west, the land rises in long, picturesque ridges and mountains of medium altitude; and still beyond and above these, in the west and northwest, loom Mt. Washington, Madison, Kearsarge, and other White Mountain peaks.

The larger lake is a fine sheet of water, five miles in length, containing four dark green islets, and the view from its bosom is one of the most beautiful in this our State of Lakes.

Hither, shortly after the "Revolution," came the writer's great-grandfather, poor in purse, for he had served throughout that long and at times hopeless struggle for liberty. In payment he had received a large roll of "Continental Money," all of which would at that time have sufficed, scarcely, to procure him a tavern dinner. No "bounties," no "pensions," then stimulated the citizen soldiery. With little to aid him save his ax on his shoulder, the unremunerated patriot made a clearing on the slopes, looking southward upon the lake; and here, after some weeks, or months, of toil, he brought his young family, consisting of my great-grandmother and two children. They came up the lake in a skiff, fashioned from a pine log. Landing on a still-remembered rock, it is said that the ex-soldier turned about and, taking the roll of Continental scrip from his pocket, threw it far out into the water, exclaiming, "So much for soldiering! But here, by the blessing of God, we will have a home yet!"

While going through the forest from the lake up to the clearing, a distance of a mile or more, they lost their way, for night had fallen and, after wandering for an hour, were obliged to sleep in the woods beneath the boughs of a pine; and it was not till the next forenoon that they found the clearing and the little log house in which my great-grandmother began her humble housekeeping.

Other settlers made their way hither, and other farms were cleared. Indians and moose departed and came no more. Then followed half a century of robust, agricultural life on a virgin soil. The boys grew large and tall; the girls were strong and handsome. It was a hearty and happy era.

But no happy era is enduring; the young men began to take what was quaintly called "the western fever" and leave the home country for greater opportunities in Illinois, Wisconsin, and Iowa. The young women, too, went away in numbers to work in the cotton factories at

Lowell, Lawrence, and Biddeford; few of them came back, or if they returned, they were not improved in health, or otherwise.

Joseph, the third son of the Revolutionary soldier and pioneer, remained at the old farm and lived on alone there with his wife, Ruth, after his own sons had left home to enter other and less certain avocations than farming.

Then came war again, the terrible Civil War, when every one of these sons, true to their soldier ancestry, entered the army of the Republic. Of the five not one survived that murderous conflict. And so it happened that we, the grandchildren, war waifs and orphaned, came back from 1861 to 1864, to live at Grandfather's old farm on the Pennesseewassee.

When I arrived in 1864, Uncle William's son, Addison, and Uncle Coville's son, Halstead, were both fourteen. Uncle Robert's daughter, Theodora, was thirteen and Uncle Charles's daughters, Ellen and Wealthy, were twelve and nine.

We were, of course, a great burden on the old folks, who were compelled to begin life over again, so to speak, on our account. At the age of sixty-five, Grandfather, who was known as the Old Squire, set himself to till the farm on a larger scale and to renew his lumbering operations, winters. Grandmother, too, was constrained to increase her dairy, her flocks of geese and other poultry, and to begin anew the labor of spinning and knitting.

It is but fair to say, however, that we all—with one exception, perhaps—had a decent sense of the obligations we incurred, and on most occasions, I believe, we did what we could to aid in the labors of the farm.

Much as we added to the burdens of our grandparents, I can now see that our coming lent fresh zest to their lives: they had something new to live for; they took hold of life again for another fifteen years.

Fifteen years of youth.

It was life's happy era with us, full of hopes and plans for the future, full too of those many jolts that young folks get from inexperience, nor yet free from those mistakes that all of us make when we first set off on life's journey. Like some bright panorama it passes on memory's walls, so many pictures of that hopeful young life of ours at the old farm as we grew up together, getting an education, or the rudiments of one, at the district school, and later at the village academy, Kent's Hill Seminary, Bowdoin College, and Harvard University.

The five of us who survived gradually left home—without a thought, as it seemed, of the old nest or of the old birds—to become a professor, a teacher, a rancher, a businessman, and a writer.

But after discovering how lonely the Old Squire and Gram had become, we arranged a second homecoming and together decided on a course of action that was to provide them with renewed excitement and add, we believe, another fifteen years to their lives.

C. A. Stephens

1

The Vermifuge Bottle

AT THE CLOSE OF THE CIVIL WAR, WHICH WROUGHT sad havoc in our family, it became necessary that several of us of the younger generation should go to live at the home of our grandparents in Maine. There were six of us, all first cousins, ranging in age from nine to fifteen, who were thus brought under one roof; and our grandparents, for the second time in their lives, were obliged to undertake the care and support of a young family.

We came from five different states of the Union, and two of us had never before even seen the others. It is, therefore, not remarkable that at first there were some small disagreements, due to our different ideas of things. On the whole, however, we got on very well together.

The quaint, rural life had many charms for us, and after recovering from our bereavement and homesickness we enjoyed it immensely. We were, of course, a great burden on the old people, who were compelled to begin life over again on our account. At the age of sixty-five Grandfather set himself to till the farm on a larger scale and to renew his lumbering operations in the winter. Grandmother, too, was constrained to increase her dairy and her flocks of geese and other poultry, and to begin anew the labor of spinning and knitting.

It is but fair to say, however, that we all—with one exception, perhaps—had a decent sense of the obligations we incurred, and on most occasions, I believe, we did what we could to aid in all the labors of the farm.

It was a cozy old farmhouse, filled with everything that New England people accumulated in the mid-nineteenth century, and we were not long in taking full possession of it in the name of home. Much as we added to the burdens of our grandparents, I can now see that our coming lent fresh zest to their lives; they had something new to live for.

Of course everything did not always go smoothly; we often had our small rights and wrongs to think about. Grievances arose now and then, and one of them was the black bottle of vermifuge.

Now Gram was a dear old soul, but she had certain fixed ideas as to the ailments of youngsters and the appropriate remedies therefore. Whenever any one of us had taken cold or committed youthful indiscretions in diet, she was always persuaded that we were suffering from an attack of Worms—which I am spelling with a big "W" because it was a very large ailment in her eyes. To her mind, and in all honesty, the average child was a kind of walking helminthic menagerie, a thin shell of flesh and skin, enclosing hundreds, if not thousands, of Worms! And drastic measures were necessary to keep this raging internal population down to the limits where a child could properly live.

For this bane of juvenile existence, Gram had one constant sovereign in which she reposed implicit faith, and that was a great spoonful of Van Tassel's Vermifuge, followed four hours later by two great spoonfuls of castor oil. Be it said, too, that the castor oil of that period was the genuine oily, rank abomination, crude from the bean, and not the "Castoria" of present times, which children are alleged to cry for! And as for Van Tassel's Vermifuge, it resembled raw petroleum, and of all greenish-black, loathly nostrums was the most nauseous to swallow. It was my fixed belief and hope in those youthful years that if anywhere in the next world there were a deep, dark, super-heated compartment far below all others, it would be reserved expressly for Van Tassel and his anthelminthic.

Whenever, therefore, any one of us put in an appearance at the breakfast table, looking a little rusty and "pindling," without appetite, Gram would survey the unfortunate critically, with commiseration on her placid countenance, and exclaim, "Those Worms are at work again! Poor child, you are all eaten up by Worms! You must take a dose of vermifuge."

This diagnosis once made, excuses, prayers, sudden assumptions of liveliness, or pseudo exhibitions of ravenous appetite, availed nothing. Gram would rise from the table, walk calmly to the medicine cupboard, and fetch out that awful bottle and spoon.

With a species of fascination, the Worm suspect would then watch Gram turn out the hideous, sticky liquid, till the tablespoon was full and crowning over the brim of it all around. Why, even to this day, as the picture rises in memory, I feel my stomach roll and see the hard, wild grin on the face of Halstead as he watched the ordeal approach me.

"Now shut your eyes and open your mouth," Gram would say and, when the awful dose was in, "Swallow! Swallow hard!" Then up would come her soft, warm hand under my chin, tilting my head back like a chicken's. There was no escape.

On one occasion Halstead bolted while the vermifuge was being poured out for him, and escaped to the barn. But he had to go without his breakfast that forenoon, and when he appeared at the dinner table, bottle, spoon, and Gram—with a severe countenance—were waiting for him.

Theodora used to try to take hers without murmuring, although convinced that it was a mere whim, stipulating only that she might go out in the kitchen to swallow it. But with Wealthy, who was younger, the ingestion of vermifuge was usually preceded by an orgy of tears and supplications. Addison, who was older and generally well, long smiled in a superior way at the grimaces of us who were more "Wormy." But shortly after our first Thanksgiving Day at the farm he, too, fell ill and failed to come down to breakfast. On his absence being noted, Gram went upstairs to inquire into his plight; and it was with a sense of exultation rather than proper pity, I fear, that Halse and I saw the old lady come down presently and get the vermifuge bottle. We heard Addison expostulating and arguing in rebuttal for some minutes, but he lost the case. Wealthy, who had stolen upstairs on tiptoe to view the denouement, informed us later, in great glee, that Addison had attempted by a sudden movement to eject the nauseous mouthful, but that Gram had clapped one hand under his chin and pinched his nose with the thumb and finger of the other, till he was compelled to swallow in order to breathe.

About that time it was hopefully observed that the bottle was nearly empty. A certain cheerfulness sprang up. It proved short-lived. The next time the Old Squire went to the village, Gram sent for two more bottles. The benevolent smile with which she exhibited the fresh supply to us that night caused our hearts to sink. To have it handier, she poured both bottles into an empty demijohn and put the spoon beside it in the cupboard.

Addison, although a pretty good boy in the main, was a crafty one. I never knew, certainly, whether or not Halstead and Ellen had any previous knowledge as to the prank Addison played with the vermifuge, but I rather think not. There was another large flask-shaped bottle in the same cupboard, about half full of elderberry wine, old and quite thick, which Gram had made years before. It was used only "for sickness" and was always kept on the upper shelf. We knew what it was, however; by the time we had been there a year, there were not many bottles in that or any other cupboard that we had not investigated.

The vermifuge and the old elderberry wine looked not a little alike, and what Ad must have done—though he never fairly owned up to it— was to shift the thick, dark liquids from one bottle to the other and restore the bottles to their usual places in the cupboard. Time went on and I think that it was Ellen who had next to take a dose from the bottle. It was then remarked that she neither shed tears nor made the usual wry faces. Nor yet did she appear in haste to seize and swallow the draught of consolatory coffee from the Old Squire's sympathetic hand. "Why, Nellie girl, you are getting to be quite brave," was his approving comment, and Ellen, with a puzzled glance around the table, laughed, looked earnestly at Gram but said nothing; I think she had caught Addison's eye fixed meaningfully on her.

If recollection serves me all right, I was the next whose morning symptoms indicated the need of vermifuge; and I remember the thrill of amazement that went through me when the spoon upset its dark contents adown the roots of my tongue and Gram's cozy hand came up under my chin.

"Why, Gram!" I spluttered. "This isn't—!"

"Here, dear boy, take a good swallow of coffee. That'll take the taste out o' your mouth," Gramp interrupted, his own face drawn into a compassionate pucker, and he clapped the cup to my mouth. I drank, but, still wondering, was about to break forth again, when a vigorous kick under the table led me to take second thought. Addison was regarding me in a queer way; so was Ellen. Gram was placidly putting away the bottle and spoon, and something that tingled very agreeably was warming up my stomach. I burst out laughing, but another kick constrained me to preserve silence.

For some reason we did not say anything to each other about this, although I remember feeling very curious concerning that last dose. A species of roguish freemasonry took root among us. Once after that, when vermifuge was mentioned, Addison winked to me; and I think we were pretty well aware that something funny had started, unbeknown to Gram. Theodora, however, knew nothing of it. Whether this reprehensible slyness would have continued among the rest of us until we had taken up the whole of the elderberry wine, I cannot say; but about a month later, a dismal exposé was precipitated one Friday night by the arrival of Elder Witham. There was to be a quarterly meeting at the meeting house Saturday afternoon and Sunday, and the elder came to the Old Squire's to stay till Monday morning.

Elder Witham was getting on in years, and on this occasion he had taken a little cold, and being a lean, tall, atrabilious man, his appetite was affected. Gram, as usual, had prepared a good super, largely on the elder's account; but I remember that after we had sat down and the elder had asked the blessing, he straightened back and said, "Sister Ruth, I see you've got a nice supper. But I don't believe I can eat a mouthful tonight. I'm all out of fix. I'm afraid I shan't be able to preach tomorrow. If you will not think it strange, I want to go back into the sitting room and lie down a bit on your lounge, to see if I can't feel better."

Gram was much disturbed; she followed the elder from the table and we overheard her speak of sending for a doctor, but the elder said no, he guessed that he should soon feel better.

"Well, but Elder Witham, isn't there something I can give you to take?" Gram asked. "Some Jamaica ginger, or something like that?"

"Oh, that is rather too fiery for me," we heard the elder say.

"Then how would a few swallows of my elderberry wine do?" queried Gram.

"But you know, Sister Ruth, that I don't much approve of such things," the elder replied.

"Still, I think really that it would do you good," urged Gram.

"Perhaps," assented the elder, for, truth to say, this was not his first introduction to the elderberry bottle; and we heard Gram go to the medicine cupboard.

And "about this time," as the old almanac used to have it, several of us youngsters at the supper table began to feel strangely interested. Addison glanced across at Ellen, then jumped up suddenly and took a step or two toward the sitting room, but changed his mind and went hastily out through the kitchen into the woodshed. After a moment or two, Ellen stole out after him. As for myself, mental confusion had fallen on me; I looked at Halse, but he was eating very fast.

The trouble culminated speedily, for it does not take long to turn out a small glass of elderberry wine, or drink it, for that matter. The elder did not drink it all, however; he took one good swallow, then jumped to his feet and ran to the woodbox. "Sins of Judas! What? What? What stuff's this?" he spluttered, clearing his mouth as energetically as possible. "You've given me bug pizen by mistake! And I've swallered a lot of it!"

Inexpressibly shocked and alarmed, Gram could hardly trust the evidence of her senses. She stared helplessly, at first, then all in a tremble, snatched up the bottle, smelled of it, then tasted it.

"My sakes, Elder Witham!" she cried, "but don't be scared, it's only vermifuge, such as I give the children for Worms!"

"Tsssauh!" coughed the elder. "But it's nasty stuff, ain't it?"

By this time, Gramp had appeared on the scene, and he fetched a cup of tea to take the taste out of the elder's mouth. Halstead snatched a handful of cookies off the table and decamped. I could not find anything of Addison or Ellen, and so ventured into the sitting room with Theodora and Wealthy.

Gram, the Old Squire, and Elder Witham were now holding a species of first-aid council. The elder had taken a full swallow of vermifuge, and after reading the "Directions," they all came to the conclusion that the only safe and proper thing to do was for him to take two tablespoonfuls of castor oil. This was accomplished during the evening, but it was a strangely hushed and completely overawed household. Gram, indeed, was nearly prostrated with mortification. How the Old Squire felt was not quite so clear; as we milked that night, I thought once that I saw him shaking strangely as he sat at his cow that stood next to mine, but I was so shocked myself that I could hardly believe, then, that he was laughing.

Addison helped milk, but immediately disappeared again, and Halse soon retired to bed. Ellen, too, had gone to bed.

Next morning, affairs had not brightened much. Nobody spoke at the breakfast table. The elder's breakfast was carried in to him, and the net result was that he did not preach that afternoon, as was expected; another minister occupied the pulpit.

Gram gave up going to that quarterly meeting altogether. Shame was near making her ill, and the clouds of chagrin hung low for several days.

It was not till Thursday, following, that Gram recovered her spirits and temper sufficiently to inquire into it. Thursday morning she questioned the whole of us with severity.

Little actual information was elicited, however, for the reason that most of us knew but little about it. We confessed what we knew unless, perhaps, Ad kept back something. We all—all except Theodora—knew that we had previously taken elderberry instead of Van Tassel, and Gram gave us an earnest lecture on the meanness of such concealments of facts. The Old Squire said nothing at the time, but I think that he had some private conversation with Addison concerning the matter.

The episode put a damper on the vermifuge bottle, however, as it was never quite so prominent afterward. But I have digressed and gone in advance of my narrative of events at the old farm that season.

A Fight with Hornets

WE HAD TWO TERRIBLE BUGBEARS TO BRAVE MY FIRST summer at the Old Squire's, and they were by no means imaginary ones.

There were six, including myself, who went to school together on that road—Ellen and Wealthy, Kate Edwards, and Georgie and Edson Wilbur. None of us were more than ten or eleven years old, except myself, who was twelve.

In the country, especially in backwoods districts, boys are not generally allowed to go to school in the summer after they are ten or eleven years old. There is always too much hoeing and haying to be done on their fathers' farms. In my case, however, the Old Squire wanted Miss Willy, the teacher, to figure out what lesson groups to place me in for winter school.

It was nearly a mile down to the red schoolhouse that stood at the Corners. The road ran along the side of a long ridge of pasture land between pole and brush fences, which were rather low and poor, and bushes grew plentifully all along the way.

It was a road but little traveled. We would often scare up partridges between the very wheel ruts, or see hares scudding across it. It was a wonderful place for bluejays. It seems to me now that we never passed without seeing a squad of these noisy birds. Berries, too, were abundant— strawberries in June, and in July and early August, raspberries and blackberries by the bushel.

Ah, those were pleasant times—trudging home from school, berrying, bird's-nesting, and chasing the red squirrels along the fences—or would have been but for the bugbears.

The first and worst of these was Dagon, the second an enormous nest of those great black-banded hornets that are so common in New England. This nest hung from a low branch of a small white maple, one of a clump that stood just inside the pasture fence, two or three rods from the road.

When we first saw it in June, it was not larger than a quart bowl; but it grew and grew, till by the first of August it would have filled a ten-quart bucket. Scores of those great savage hornets would swarm out at the least provocation, even at the sound of our voices. Young fellows passing had thrown stones and sticks at the nest and made the hornets irritable, and, indeed, we boys had frequently stoned it.

First Edson, then Georgie, had been stung as we passed. The hornets would dart at us like bullets. If we came within a hundred feet of their house, we were almost sure to hear a quick, vengeful buzz and feel the long, poisonous stings of these worst of all hornets.

Both Edson and Georgie were stung near the left ear. Within an hour their faces had swollen almost beyond recognition. We used to either run past the nest at full speed, or else get over the fence and pass at a long distance from it.

But Dagon was the larger and far more dangerous object of our daily terrors. Dagon was a three-year-old Herefordshire bull belonging to "Uncle" Billy Murch, as he was called, whose pasture bordered the road.

Well do I remember the great white-faced monster: his short, thick horns, surly pink nose, and wicked, red-ringed eyes. All of this animal, except his broad white face, was a deep chestnut red, glossy and sleek as an otter skin. He was what stock fanciers would deem a beauty but to us schoolchildren a furious beast, lying in wait to rend and gore us. Never were the followers of Cadmus in greater fear of the dragon than we were of Dagon.

Dagon had received his singular name from Elder Witham, the local Methodist minister. Elder Witham, while crossing the pasture, had been attacked by him and had but narrowly escaped severe injuries. The reverend gentleman went gravely to complain to the bull's owner.

"Mr. Murch," he said, "your great Dagon has assaulted me, and but for God's mercy would have trodden me under his feet."

Uncle Billy Murch's reply was characteristic: "Them as is afeard o' my bull had better keep out o' my parster."

But Dagon did not keep in his pasture. The low, weak fence offered little or no obstacle to him. The herd of cattle that Uncle Billy kept there was often in the road, Dagon with them. And then with what terror would we discover his big milk-white face or hear his deep bass notes issuing from a cloud of dust, followed by the sudden outburst of his far resounding tenor! It was skulk and run then, and we made wide detours to avoid giving Mr. Bull offense.

But still we had no relief. Dagon had an uncanny faculty for divining when human beings were afraid of him and took pleasure in the terror he inspired. Again and again he would sally forth to the schoolhouse. He would parade up and down in front of that small shrine of rural education, booing and pawing up dust, well aware that neither the teacher nor the scholars would dare venture forth; and by way of adding to the terror within he would sometimes put his nose up at the front window with a sounding *whoosh* of his breath. On several occasions he had lain down near the door and leisurely chewed his cud. Once he kept us in so late that the teacher put us out quietly at the back window, then managed to follow us herself, and we all had to climb a stone wall and run round through a pasture to escape and come home.

Of course we complained at home. Something was said a number of times to Uncle Billy about the danger of letting so vicious an animal run at large. But the Murches, good neighbors though they were in many respects, were unfortunate, not to say remiss, in properly looking after their domestic animals, which were habitually out of bounds, strolling along the highway or breaking into their neighbors' fields. And none of our folks liked to have trouble with the old man, who was known to be crabbed and revengeful.

As the season advanced, Dagon grew more and more aggressive and noisy. If he saw us passing, he would come to the fence and follow along beside it as we scudded in the road, and if he found a place low enough, over he would leap with a roar.

Then we had to scramble over the fence on the lower side of the road in a hurry. It was a wonder he did not sometimes overhaul us, for the fence was made of brush, and we often stuck in it.

One morning Wealthy had a particularly narrow escape. Dagon was in the road. Some larger boys passing had stoned and enraged him. We came upon him suddenly in a clump of sumac by the roadside.

"Oh Dagon! There's Dagon!" Kate cried, for she had first discovered him.

We turned and fled back up the road. But the bull had seen us, and followed with a fierce snort.

In her terror, Wealthy, encumbered with her books and basket, fell and got behind the rest of us, who were already climbing the fence.

As we tumbled over, we saw to our horror that the infuriated animal was close upon her. Screaming with affright, she jumped down over a great rick of old logs on the lower side of the road. Dagon, not daring to leap on so uncertain a foothold, stood and looked down on her, arching his neck and giving vent to a queer, whining bellow.

Wealthy, crouching between the pile of logs and the fence, durst not stir till Edson and I, stealing along on the lower side of the fence, pulled away the bottom brush and dragged her beneath the poles into the field below.

We dared not go back after her basket and books, which Dagon had trampled under his feet. The poor child could scarcely get over her fright for that whole day. And that very afternoon, when going home from school, she was stung by one of the hornets.

To elude Dagon and dodge the hornets required all our skill. Left to our own resources, we at length hit on a plan to turn our two implacable enemies one against the other. I believe it was Kate who first proposed that we should try to get the bull into the hornets' nest, but we all, girls and boys, helped to carry out the scheme.

First, we looked for a good hole in the fence on the lower side of the road, through which we could beat a hasty retreat to the bushes. As I have said, the hornets' nest was just inside of the pasture where Dagon reigned supreme.

The fence along here chanced to be pretty good, being through bushes where fencing stuff was plenty, and we had not much fear that the bull would leap over it. We waited for an opportunity to draw Dagon into our plot. At length, one Thursday afternoon, we saw him within twenty rods of the hornets' nest.

"Now, ole feller," said Kate, "we'll get you into the limbos!"

First, we sent Wealthy off into the bushes to be out of the way. Kate, Ellen, and I then got old hemlock knots to throw and cautiously posted ourselves in the high brakes, twenty or thirty yards from the hornets' nest.

I well remember what a hot, muggy afternoon it was. Edson now began to stalk along the road and to imitate Dagon's deep, gruff *booings*, while Georgie stood and waved her little hat, trimmed with an old red ribbon.

The sound of this counterfeit challenge soon came to Dagon's jealous ears. He raised his head and glared around, then began to bellow and paw, breaking out at times into a loud, trumpet-like defiance. Catching sight of Georgie's hat, he started for the road at a confident trot. No doubt he meant to teach us a lesson that we should not forget.

"He's coming! He's coming!" Edson and Georgie both cried, and darted through the hole in the lower fence.

We three in the brakes rose and let fly our knots at the hornets' nest.

Whack, whack! They went against it and out poured the hornets with angry hum, just as Dagon, with a menacing bellow, came crashing through the brush down to the fence.

Thanks to our stratagem, he found things ready for him! Kate, Ellen, and I had fled, but we heard the sounds of fearful commotion. Scores of the infuriated hornets darted at Dagon the instant he presented himself. But, long accustomed to frighten and drive everybody and everything, the bull was loath to fly.

He plunged and tore about, uttering some of the oddest bellowings and bawlings that I ever heard. The fence cracked, and we could see the bushes waving and swaying. The more Dagon tore around, the more the hornets stung him. Though we saw little of the tussle, we could hear enough to make sure that Dagon had all he could attend to.

Edson plucked up courage to creep back along the fence, below the road. A minute after, he called out that the bull had run; and then we all saw Dagon going up across the pasture, with tail erect, snorting like twenty bagpipes!

That was sport for us, and we exulted to our hearts' content. But, for good reasons, we each promised to say nothing of our trick.

Next day we saw the other cattle, but not Dagon. That night it was rumored about that the bull was sick—all swelled up—didn't know what ailed him, supposed to be poisoned.

A few days after, it was reported that Murch's bull had somehow got into a hornets' nest, and was stung and injured. Everyone thought it a very singular circumstance.

But Dagon was not killed, though it was nearly a fortnight before he again made his appearance in the pasture, a wiser and a better bull. From that day he never took any notice of us children.

Meanwhile, Uncle Billy had come by at night with a huge bundle of straw and burned out the hornets' nest. So that one and the same stroke of mother-wit ridded us of both our bugbears, and we had nothing more to molest us on our way to school that summer.

3

Making Mug-Bread

"MUG-BREAD!" THAT WAS WHAT WE USED TO CALL IT at the old home farm—the best flour bread ever made, I still verily believe. When made and baked just right, it is a delicacy. But the making and the baking of it are not easy, and a failure with mug-bread is something awful!

The reader may not know it as mug-bread, for that was a local name, confined largely to our own Maine homestead and vicinity. It has been called milk-yeast bread, patent bread, milk-emptyings bread, and salt-rising bread; and it has also been stigmatized by several opprobrious and offensive epithets bestowed, I am told, by irate housewives who lacked the skill and genius to make it.

We named it mug-bread because Gram always started it in an old porcelain mug: a tall, white, lavender-and-gold banded mug that held more than a quart but was sadly cracked and, for safety's sake, was wound just above the handle with fine white silk cord.

That mug was sixty-eight years old, and that silk cord had been on it since 1842. Its familiar kitchen name was "old Hannah." I suspect that the interstices of this ancient silk string were the lurking places of that delightful yeast microbe that gave the flavor to the bread, for there was rarely a failure when that mug was used.

About once in four days, generally at night, Gram would take two tablespoonfuls of cornmeal, ten of boiled milk, and half a teaspoonful of salt, mix them well in that mug, and set it on the low mantel shelf behind the kitchen stove funnel, where it would keep uniformly warm overnight. She covered the top of the mug with an old tin coffeepot lid, which just fit it.

When we saw old Hannah go up on the shelf, we knew that some mug-bread was incubating and, if all worked well, would be due the following afternoon for supper. You cannot hurry mug-bread.

The next morning, by breakfast time, a peep into the mug would show whether the little "eyes" had begun to open in the mixture or not. Here was where housewifely skill came in. Those eyes must be opened just so wide, and there must be just so many of them, or else it was not safe to proceed. It might be better to throw the setting away and start new, or else to let it stand till noon. Gram knew as soon as she had looked at it. If the omens were favorable, a cup of warm water and a variable quantity of carefully warmed flour were added and a batter made of about the consistency for fritters. This was set up behind the funnel again, to rise till noon.

More flour was then added and the dough carefully worked and set for a third rising. About three o'clock it was put in tins and baked in an even oven.

The favorite loaves with us were "cartwheels," formed by putting the dough in large, round shallow tin plates, about a foot in diameter. When baked, the yellow-brown, crackery loaf was only an inch thick. The rule at Gram's table was a cartwheel to a boy, with all the fresh Jersey butter and canned berries or fruit that he wanted with it.

Sometimes, however, the mug would disappear rather suddenly in the morning, and an odor as of unsulphurated hydrogen would linger about till the kitchen windows were raised and the fresh west wind admitted.

That meant that a failure had occurred, the wrong microbe had obtained possession of the mug.

In such cases Gram acted promptly and said little. She was always reticent concerning mug-bread. It had unspeakable contingencies.

Ellen and Theodora shared the old lady's reticence. Ellen, in fact, could never be persuaded to eat it, good as it was.

"I know too much about it," she would say. "It isn't nice."

Beyond doubt, when mug-bread goes astray at about the second rising, the consequences are depressing.

If its little eyes fail to open and the batter takes on a greasy aspect, with a tendency to crawl and glide about, no time should be lost. Open all the windows at once and send the batter promptly to the swill barrel. It is useless to dally with it. You will be sorry if you do. When it goes wrong, it is utterly depraved.

I remember an embarrassing experience that Theodora and Ellen had with mug-bread on one occasion, when Gram was away from home.

It was the first summer after I had gone to the old farm to live. The Old Squire had a contract to send red oak shooks to Cuba for molasses hogsheads. He himself had four or five men riving and forming the shooks, and he was also buying shooks that others were making. In August he went to Portland for ten days to oversee the shipments by schooner to Matanzas. Grandmother Ruth and Wealthy, who was the youngest, went with him for a little rest from household labors, and they took Halstead, who went most unwillingly, to have his tonsils removed by a Portland doctor. The boy had been having sore throats frequently for a year or more. Theodora, Addison, Ellen, and I were left to keep house and to attend to the farm chores.

The tasks we had been assigned were not too time consuming, and we had made fine plans, which included three evening "gypsy parties," or autumnal feasts, to which the neighboring young folks were to be invited, a hay ride to an adjoining town, and a wilderness trip up to old Hughy Glinds's camp in the great woods. The grandfolks had set off at six o'clock in the morning, for the journey required twelve hours, and no sooner were they off than we began preparations for a festive evening.

At ten o'clock Ellen sallied forth to invite in our young friends, but at the door to the piazza she turned hastily back with a concerned look. "There's somebody coming up the lane," she said. "It's an ox team and the queerest wagon you ever saw! Oh dear! What can it be?" For the prospect of visitors of any sort just then was most unwelcome.

It was indeed a singular turnout. A yoke of sluggish, old, sparked oxen were plodding slowly up the lane between the trees, drawing an old wagon on which was built a little, low windowless hut from the flat roof of which projected a rusted stovepipe. In the open front end of the hut, with a goad in his hand, sat an old man with a bushy gray beard, and as the oxen plodded nearer we caught sight of an old woman's face in a green cotton hood peeping out from the hut.

"Now for mercy's sake, who can that be?" Theodora breathed in an amazed whisper.

None of us had the slightest idea. The strange outfit came creaking alongside the door, and the old man shouted "Whoa-hish!" to the oxen and then stared at us for some moments through his horn-rimmed spectacles. The old woman put out her head and stared also. A large black-and-white dog that had been following the wagon hut now came forward and sat in the road. "Be Joseph and Ruth ter home?" the old man asked at last.

Addison made haste to say that our grandparents were at Portland.

"When be they acomin' back?" asked the old woman.

"Not for a week or more," Addison replied.

The old man sat and chewed steadily; then he looked at the old woman. "What say, Marm, had we better stay, or drive on to Cousin Calista's in Waterford?"

"Wal, sir, I should say as how we'd better stop a spell now we've come so fur to see 'em!" the old woman replied in a determined tone. Whereupon she clambered slowly out of the wagon hut and, reaching back inside, drew forward a good-sized box with leather hinges and holes bored in the lid. Advancing to the side of the piazza, she set the box down and threw back the lid and out stepped a big yellow-and-white cat; while the dog looked on, it stalked to a piazza post and sharpened its claws and stretched. The old woman put the box carefully back into the wagon hut and then mounted the piazza steps.

Perceiving that the old woman's purpose was to enter the house, Theodora and Ellen backed indoors, and Addison and I followed the team to the barn, in the direction of which the old man was now driving it. We opened the great doors, and he drove in.

"Wal, now," he said, "I want you boys to unyoke them oxen o' mine and tie 'em up in the barn and give 'em a good fodderin' o' hay, and bimeby arter they've hed water if ye've got some cornmeal fer 'em it won't hurt 'em a mite."

"All right, sir," Addison replied. "We'll see to it."

The old man looked round the barn while we cared for the oxen and then from the interior of the wagon hut drew forth a crate containing four hens and a rooster, which he asked us to feed with shelled corn. "Now," he charged us, "I want ye to set that 'ere crate up somewheres so that weasels won't get at it."

We carried the crate to the granary, which was a rat-proof room, and satisfied now of the safety and welfare of his livestock, our old visitor went to the house.

Some minutes later as Addison and I were going into the kitchen we met Theodora and Ellen coming out to find us; their faces suggested distress and consternation. "Oh dear! I do believe it is old Elnathan Holeb and his wife!" were Theodora's first words.

We had once or twice heard of the Holebs, an old-fashioned couple and some distant connection of our folks, who usually spent the summer visiting their relatives. They lived up Kittery way, where they had a little farm, which they occupied in winter; but as the weather grew warm and tourists came they were wont to rent out their house, take their dog, cat, and hens and start out with their wagon hut for a grand tour of all their relatives from brother and sister down to the remotest sixteenth cousin—visiting them and remaining anywhere from three days to three weeks at a place. "We git through the summers, and it don't cost us a cent except fer tobarker," old Elnathan used to boast.

It is a fact that in early days, a century ago, many Maine people were accustomed to visit a great deal, but usually in cold weather. There was more leisure then, for that was before lumbering and other winter occupations had begun to engross the attention of so many people. But old "Uncle" Elnathan and "Aunt" Salome were survivors—in a backward way—of earlier times, and it is doing them no injustice to say that they and their outfit had come to be the dread of every family in that part of the state that was unfortunate enough to be related to them by ties of blood. Yet such was the usual hospitality of our people that the old couple never were actually turned away. The last time they had visited at the Old Squire's, shortly before we young folks went home to live, they had stayed twelve days—a circumstance that pretty nearly touched the limit of Grandmother Ruth's forbearance, for they were far from being an interesting pair, and what was worse, they both smoked atrocious old pipes and filled the house morning, noon, and evening with the rankest of tobacco smoke. That habit alone nearly drove Grandmother wild at times!

"Yes, that's just who it is!" Theodora continued. "And, oh, what can we do?"

Ellen was nearly in tears. "Our good time will be spoiled," she lamented. "They'll stay and stay, and we cannot go anywhere or invite anyone here with them round!"

As we passed into the kitchen, we saw our visitors had made themselves comfortable in the sitting room, the old man on one side of it and his wife on the other. They had lighted their pipes, and the room was already smoky. The big yellow tom cat sat composedly between them, and near the outer door lay the large black-and-white dog. The Holebs were in full possession.

The girls made shift to approach the kitchen stove and prepare the midday meal as best they could. When it was on the table and Theodora had announced it, our visitors put up their pipes and, taking their places without a word, began to eat heartily. The large tom cat came and rubbed himself against our legs, and the great dog drew near and looked upon the table with much interest.

"Ezra likes milk," the old woman at last said oracularly and stroked the cat's head.

Ellen took the hint and, going to the tin closet, fetched a basin and fed him.

"Bill likes meat," old Elnathan remarked.

Whereupon Addison called the dog to the wood house and gave him some cold pork. Otherwise the meal passed without incident or conversation.

It was my turn that day to chop wood into kindling for the stove, a somewhat lengthy and toilsome task. I was occupied with it for an hour or so. Meanwhile, as appeared afterward, Addison and the girls took counsel together out in the kitchen and, remembering that Uncle Elnathan was reputed very fussy and particular about his food, decided on a desperate expedient to get rid of the old couple.

When we gathered for our evening meal that night I was not a little astonished at the poverty stricken aspect of the supper table. Everything in the way of food on it consisted of an unsightly tin pan containing very small boiled potatoes in their skins and a platter of badly scorched, and over salted, corn cake. Of butter there was no sign, though there was a salt cellar near the potatoes. I suppose I stared in amazement, for the table at the Old Squire's had always been abundantly served; but Addison pressed my foot with his, and then I understood. I glanced across at Ellen and Theodora, who were sitting with tight-shut lips.

Our visitors took their places and viewed the repast with evident disapproval. Ellen passed the corn cake and then the potatoes. We four young folks made a great show of eating, and the meal proceeded in silence.

"Aren't your folks raising good crops this year?" old Elnathan finally asked.

"Our crops are not what they sometimes have been," replied Addison guardedly, as he passed the little potatoes.

Aunt Salome sniffed and tossed her head. Ezra came round, purring loudly, but Ellen failed to notice him. Bill also drew near to look on and at last barked once as a reminder, and Addison rose and carried three little cold potatoes out to the wood house for him. To the best of my recollection not another word was said at the table or until Theodora showed our visitors to their sleeping room. When they retired we consulted again in the kitchen.

"How long do you think they will stand it?" Ellen asked anxiously.

"I'm afraid they will stand it longer than we can," Addison said, laughing.

"But can't we have something to eat now they've gone to bed?" I asked callously.

"Oh, but that would be too bad!" Theodora said. "We ought not to be playing this game with them, and if we are, then at least we ought to play it fair." And Addison, still laughing, seemed to think so too.

Next morning the girls prepared in a frying pan what was left of the potatoes and warmed over the scorched corn cake. They also made coffee, but it was so weak that you might have seen the bottom of a big pitcher full of it. There were dour looks at the table, but neither of our guests said much. Ezra, after much purring, hopped boldly up beside the girls, but Ellen boxed his ears. Bill barked till Addison gave him three more little cold potatoes.

For our noontime meal the girls boiled the backbone and tail of a salted codfish and made more burnt corn cake. When we sat down to it, Aunt Salome suddenly pushed back her chair and marched with a determined air to the pantry to investigate for herself, but we had provided against that danger the night before by carrying everything eatable to a cupboard upstairs.

That evening there was another pan of little boiled potatoes with salt and more shockingly scorched corn cake. Addison and I partook ravenously—or pretended to. I should have been famished except for the apples that I got between meals from the cellar. The girls, I noticed, looked wan but firm. Aunt Salome did not scruple to free her mind to them. "I used ter think once that Joseph and Ruth sot a good table!" she exclaimed. "But that time 'pears to be gone by. Hain't yer grandmarm never teached ye to cook?"

"I'm afraid I cannot cook very well yet," replied Theodora truthfully.

"Hez Joseph ben a-meetin' with revarses lately?" old Elnathan asked.

"Well, of course he has ill fortune at times," Addison replied soberly. "He has a large family now, you know, and we all feel the need of being economical."

"Yas, I see ye do," the old man rejoined.

Before we were up from the table we heard a noise in the pantry, and the girls espied Ezra on the top shelf, devouring what was left of the codfish's tail.

Later, when the Holebs went to bed, Theodora called another kitchen conference, so shamed was she by that poor cat's desperate action, and declared that we must, from then on, provide them with a better and more abundant fare. Indeed, as a special treat for the next day, she resolved to try her hand at a batch of mug-bread and set old Hannah up for it.

In the morning the girls rose at six and hurriedly brought back to the pantry the foodstuff from the cupboard upstairs. Cereal was soon cooking, and eggs were boiling. Cream, butter, and cheese found their way back to the table. Bread, cookies, pies, and preserves reappeared from their hiding places. And, as they made breakfast, they tried to hurry that mug-bread along, so as to have some of it at noon for dinner.

Theodora peeped into the old mug, saw encouraging eyes in it, and resolved to go on. They mixed it up with the necessary warm water and flour and set it carefully back for the second rising.

Perhaps they had a little hotter fire than usual, perhaps they had hurried it a shade too much, or—well, you can "perhaps" anything you like with milk-yeast bread. At all events, it took the wrong turn and began to perfume the kitchen.

If they had not been hard pressed and a little flurried that morning, the girls would probably have thrown it out. Instead, they took it down, saw that it was rising a little, and hoping that it would yet pull through, worked in more flour and soda and hurried four loaves of it into the oven to bake.

Then it was that the unleavened turpitude of that hostile microbe displayed the full measure of its malignity. A horrible odor presently filled the place. Stale eggs would have been Araby the Blest beside it.

The girls hastily shut the kitchen doors, but doors would not hold it in. It captured the whole house.

In the sitting room, Bill and Ezra perceived it and tore around, yowling and desperate to get out.

Just then the kitchen door leading to the front piazza opened and in stalked Uncle Elnathan with Aunt Salome behind him. They had been out searching the farm for food and had brought back grapes, August Pippins, and some eggs from their chickens.

When that awful odor smote them they stopped short. Uncle Elnathan was a fastidious man. He sniffed and turned up his nose.

"Is it sink spouts?" he gasped. "Are the traps out of order?"

"No, no!" said Ellen, in a low tone, trying to quiet him. "It is only mug- bread."

"Bread!" cried the old man, with a glance of rank suspicion at the two girls. "Bread smelling like that!"

Just then Ellen discovered something white, which appeared to be mysteriously increasing in size, in the shadow on the back side of the kitchen stove. After a glance she caught open the oven door.

It was the mug-bread dough! It had crawled—crawled out of the tins into the oven, crawled down under the oven door to the kitchen floor—to where it made a viscous puddle and was now trying, apparently, to crawl out of sight under the wood box.

At that sight Uncle Elnathan suddenly stopped short and jumped back to the door. He could stand no more. "Marm," he cried, "I guess you and me better be agoin' over to Cousin Calista's."

"That's what I think, Elnathan, and the sooner the better," she said grimly. "Sech victuals I never saw. 'Tain't fit fer a dog to eat! I never was so dis'p'inted in any place in all my born days!" she flung back as she left the room to get Ezra's box and put on her wraps.

I am afraid that neither Addison or I even for courtesy's sake urged them to remain. We rushed to the barn to yoke their oxen and to put the crate of hens aboard the wagon before they changed their minds.

They set off without bidding us good-bye, nor did either of us say "Come again," and I have to record that we were gleefully capering and dancing all about the kitchen, the sitting room, and out through the wood house as soon as they were safely down the lane. Then we flung open windows and doors to free the house of that awful tobacco smoke.

But poor Doad and Nell! As youthful hosts and housekeepers they felt themselves disgraced beyond redemption. For years they did not recover from it and would cringe when anyone mentioned mug-bread.

The Old Squire, Grandmother Ruth, and Wealthy returned during the evening of the tenth day; Halstead was with them, minus his tonsils and looking pale. We had expected them that night. The girls had supper ready, and we all sat down together again.

But on passing through the sitting room, Grandmother had smelled something suspicious. "Who's been smoking in my sitting room?" she exclaimed.

Now to be frank, we had conspired for good reasons not to speak of the Holebs' visit at all, but Grandmother's question took us aback. The girls reddened and looked to Addison for aid, and he rose to the emergency. "Why, when you first went away," he said casually, "an old couple who said their name was Holeb was here awhile, and they both smoked a good deal."

Grandmother Ruth glanced quickly and oddly at the Old Squire. "Why, Joseph," she exclaimed, "that must have been Elnathan and Salome!"

"Yes, I guess it was," Addison said still casually. "They had their dog and their cat and hens with them."

"How long did they stay?" Grandmother asked, evidently much interested.

"Well, now, let me see," Addison replied as if pondering. "They were here two days and two nights."

"That all!" exclaimed Grandmother in astonishment. "I hope you were not impolite to them," she added suspiciously.

"Oh, no," Addison replied. "Not in the least. We were just as polite as could be."

"But how came they to leave so soon?"

"Well, I didn't ask them," Addison replied carelessly. "Perhaps they were disappointed because you and Grandfather were not at home. Possibly we didn't set as high a table as they were accustomed to."

"I don't see why they needed to complain," said Grandmother Ruth, resenting the implied slight to the family table. As if the subject were not worth pursuing, Addison began asking Halstead about Portland and whether it hurt much to lose your tonsils.

Grandmother said no more, though she was plainly puzzled. The Old Squire made no comment; his air was one of quiet thankfulness, as if for having escaped a calamity.

More than fifteen years elapsed before either of the old people learned the explanation of the mystery. By that time all of us except one had left home and had gone our several ways in life. But as often as we could we came back to the old farm at Thanksgiving, and on a certain Thanksgiving Day when we had all come back except Halstead and were sitting round the table after dinner, we fell to talking over old times at the farm—the good times, the adventures, and some of the roguish pranks that we had been guilty of. Theodora glanced thoughtfully at a scrap of mug-bread on her plate; memory was very busy with her. "How about the Holebs, Grandmother?" she asked at last. "Are they still alive and visiting as usual?"

"Oh, yes," Grandmother replied. "I hear of them now and then, but for some reason they gave up coming here ever after that short visit they made while we were away at Portland."

Theodora glanced across at Addison. "Shall I?" she whispered.

Addison laughed and nodded. Whereupon Theodora began, and with numerous promptings from the rest of us, made a clean breast of that sad breach of hospitality on our part many years before. I was afraid that the old folks would feel hurt, but possibly they had suspected something of the sort all along. The Old Squire shook and laughed as if he would split, and Grandmother Ruth listened calmly and with scarcely a word of comment.

"I have always felt a little ashamed of that bread," Theodora continued, "even though we were trying to be nice. And now that we are all at home here and think of it, what do you say to our making up a barrel or a box of good things to eat and sending it to those Holebs— just to ease my conscience a little?" she added, laughing.

"Well, I hardly think I should," Grandmother Ruth said at last placidly. "It will be quite as well to let bygones be bygones."

"Don't you think it would be well received?" Theodora asked.

"Oh, I dare say," Grandmother replied. "No doubt they would like it. But they might feel so grateful that they would come down here to thank us—and stay three weeks!"

4

The Riddle of Halstead

IN LATE AUGUST THERE WERE BRAKES TO CUT AND dry for "bedding" at the barn, bushes and briars to clear up along the fences and walls, and stone heaps to draw off preparatory to "breaking up" several acres more of greensward. The Old Squire's custom was to break up three or four acres so that the turf would rot during the autumn. Potatoes were then usually planted on it the ensuing spring, to be followed the next year by corn and the next by wheat, or some other grain, when it was again seeded down in grass. About this time, too, the beans had to be pulled and stacked, and there were always early apples to be gathered for sale at the village stores. Sometimes, too, the corn would be ripe enough to cut up and shock by the 5th or 6th of September; and immediately after came potato digging, always a heavy, dirty piece of farm work.

Truth to say, farm work is never done, particularly on a New England farm where a little of everything has to be undertaken and all kinds of crops are raised and where pigs, sheep, cattle, calves, colts, horses, and poultry have to be tended and provided with winter food indoors. A thrifty farmer has always a score of small jobs awaiting his hands.

At the Old Squire's it was customary, throughout the fall, when pigs were fattening, to go to the grist mill, which was three miles distant, once a week, and well do I remember the first trip I took there with Addison and Halstead.

After loading some corn, we set off immediately, with all three of us sitting on the seat in front of the bags. Halstead wanted to drive; but Addison had taken possession of the reins and kept them, although Halstead secured the whip and occasionally touched up the horse, contrary to Addison's wishes, for it proved a very hilly road. First we descended from the ridge on which the home farm is located, crossed the meadow, then ascended another long ridge whence a good view was afforded of several ponds and of the White Mountains in the northwest.

Descending from this height of land to the westward for half a mile, we came to the mill in the valley of another large brook. It was a weathered, saddleback old structure, situated at the foot of a huge dam, built of rough stones, like a farm wall across the brook and holding back a considerable pond. A rickety sluiceway led the water down to the waterwheel beneath the mill floor.

When we arrived there was no one stirring about the mill, but we had no more than driven up and hitched old Sol to a post when two boys came out from a small red house, a little way along the road, where lived the miller, whose name was Harland.

"There come Jock and George," said Addison. "Maybe the old man isn't at home today."

"Where's your father?" Addison called out, as the boys drew near.

"Gone to the village," replied the larger of the two, who was apparently thirteen or fourteen years of age.

"We want to get a grist ground," Addison said to them.

"What is it?" they both asked.

"Corn," replied Ad.

"If it's only corn, we can grind it," they said. "Take it in so we can toll it. Pa said we could grind corn, or oats, and peas, but he won't let us grind wheat yet, for that has to be bolted."

We carried the bags into the mill; there were three of them, each containing two bushels of corn, and meantime the two young millers brought along a half-bushel measure and a two-quart measure.

"It's two quarts toll to the bushel, ye know," said Jock, the elder of the two. "So I must have two-quart measurefuls out of every bag." He proceeded to untie the bags and toll them, dipping out a heaped measureful.

"Here, here," said Addison, "you must strict those measures with a square; you're getting a good pint too much on every one."

"All right," they assented, and producing a piece of straight-edged board, stricted them.

"Have to watch these millers a little," Addison remarked. "And I guess, Jock, you had better not toll all the bags till you see whether there's water enough to grind all of it."

"Oh, there's water enough," said they. "There's a whole damful."

They then poured the first bagful into the hopper over the mill-stones and went to hoist the gate. It was a very primitive, worn piece of mechanism, and hoisting it proved a difficult task. Addison and Halstead went to help them. At length they heaved the gate up; the water-wheel began to turn and the other gear to revolve, making a tremendous noise. I climbed down beneath the mill, at the lower end, to see the waterwheel operate. The wheel and big mill post turned ponderously around, wabbling somewhat and creaking ominously. By the time I went back into the mill, above, the first bagful of corn was nearly ground into yellow meal, which came out of the stones into the meal-box quite hot from the molinary process. Addison was dipping the meal out and putting it up in the empty bag.

"Is it fine enough?" Jock called out. "I can drop the stone a little, if ye say so. We will grind it just as ye want it."

"This is fine enough," said Addison. "But thanks for asking."

Another bagful was poured into the hopper and ground out, and then Addison and I brought along the third bagful.

"Hold on there," said Jock, "I haven't tolled that bag."

We thought that he had tolled it.

"No," said both Jock and George. "You said not to toll that last bag till we saw whether there was water enough to grind it."

"But you declared that there was water enough, and tolled it!" cried Halstead.

Addison and I could not say positively whether they had tolled it or not, and they appeared to think that it had not been tolled. The point was argued for some moments; finally it was agreed to compromise on it and let them have one measure of toll out of it. So there were two quarts of loss or gain, whichever party was in error.

When the last bagful was nearly ground and the hopper empty, all save a pint or so, Jock and George ran to shut the gate and stop the mill.

"Hold on!" cried Addison. "That isn't fair. There's two quarts in the stones yet; we shall lose all that on top of toll."

"But we must shut down before the corn is all through the stones!" cried Jock, "or they'll get to running fast and grind themselves. Twon't do to let them get to running fast with no corn in."

"Well, don't be in such haste about it," urged Addison. "Wait a bit till our grist is nearer out."

They waited a few moments but were very uneasy about the stones, and soon after the last kernels of corn had disappeared from the hopper, they pulled the ash pin to let the gate fall. It was then discovered that from some cause the gate would not drop. The boys thumped and rattled it. But the water still poured down on the wheel. By this time the meal had run nearly all out of the millstones, and they revolved more rapidly. The young millers were now a good deal alarmed, and, running out, climbed up the dam and looked into the flume to see what was the matter with their gate.

"It's an old shingle-bolt!" shouted Jock, "that's floated down the pond! It's got sucked in under the gate and holds it up! Fetch the pike-pole, George!"

George ran to get the pike-pole, and for some moments they tried to push, or pull, the block out. But it was wedged fast and the in draught of the water held it firmly in the aperture beneath the gate.

It was impossible to reach it with anything save the pike-pole, for the water in the flume over it was four or five feet deep.

Meantime the old mill was running amuck inside. The waterwheel was turning swiftly, and the millstone was whirling like a buzz saw. After every few seconds we could hear it graze down against the nether stone with an ugly sound, and then there would fly up a powerful odor of ozone.

Jock and George, finding that they could not shut the gate, came rushing into the mill again in still greater excitement.

"The stones'll be spoilt!" Jock exclaimed. "We must get them to grinding something."

He ran to the little bin of about a bushel of corn where the old miller kept his toll and where they had put the toll from our bags. This was hurriedly flung into the hopper and came through into the meal-box at a great rate. It checked the speed in a measure, however, and we took breath a little.

"You had better keep the mill grinding till the pond runs out," Addison advised.

"I would," replied Jock, "but that's all the grain there is here."

It was evident that the mill must be kept grinding at something or other, or it would grind itself. It would not answer to put in pebbles. Ad suggested chips from the wood yard, and George set off on a run to fetch a basketful of chips to grind, but while he was gone, Jock bethought himself of a pile of corncobs in one corner of the mill, and we hastily gathered up a half-bushel measureful. They were old dry cobs and very hard.

"Not too fast with them!" Jock cautioned. "Only a few at a time!"

By throwing in a handful at a time, we reduced the speed of the stones gradually, and then suddenly piling in a peck or more slowed it down till it fairly came to a standstill, glutted with cobs. The water-wheel had stopped, although the water was still pouring down on it; and in that condition we left it, with the miller boys peeping about the flume and the millstones and exclaiming to each other, "What'll Pa say when he gets back?"

But we were not yet home with our guest, by a great deal! Halstead had resented it because he had not been able to drive the horse on the outward trip. While Addison and I were throwing in the last bag, he jumped into the wagon and secured the reins. Not to have trouble, Addison said nothing against his driving, and we two walked up the long hill from the mill, behind the wagon. Reaching the summit, we got in and Halstead started to drive down the hill on the other side. As I was a stranger, he wished me to think that he was a fine driver and told some of his exploits managing horses.

"There's no use," he said, "in letting a horse lag along down hill the way the old mossbacks do around here. They are scared to death if a horse does more than walk. Ad won't let a horse trot a single step on a hill, but mopes and mopes along. I've seen horses driven in places where they know something, and I know how a horse ought to go."

In earnest of this opinion, he touched old Sol up, and we went down the first hill at such a pace that I was glad to hold to the seat.

"You had better be careful," said Addison. "Drive with more sense, if you are going to drive at all—which you are not fit to do," he added.

Out of bravado, I suppose, Halstead again applied the whip and we trundled along down the next hill at a still more rapid rate.

"Now Halse, if you are going to drive like this, just haul up and let me walk," Addison remonstrated, more seriously. But Halstead would not stop, and, touching the horse again, set off down the last hill before reaching the meadow at an equally smart pace.

It is likely, however, that we might have got down without accident; but the road, like most country roads, was rather narrow and as we drew near the foot of the hill, we suddenly espied a horse and wagon emerging from amongst the alder clumps through which the road across the meadow wound its way, and saw, too, that a woman was driving.

"Give us half the road!" Halstead shouted. But the woman seemed confused, as not knowing on which side of the road to turn out; she hesitated and stopped in the middle of the road.

Perceiving that we were in danger of a collision, Addison snatched the reins and turned our horse clean out into the alders; and the off hind wheel coming violently in contact with an old log, the transient bolt of the wagon broke. The forward wheels parted from the wagon body, and we were all pitched out into the brush in a heap together. The bags of meal came on top of us.

Halstead had his nose scratched, I sprained one of my thumbs, and we were all three shaken up smartly. Addison, however, regained his feet in time to capture old Sol, who was making off with the forward wheels.

The woman sat in her wagon and looked quite dazed by the spectacle of boys and bags tumbling over each other.

"Dear hearts," said she, "are you all killed?"

"Why didn't you turn out?" exclaimed Halstead.

"I know I ought to," said the woman, humbly, "but you came down the hill so fast, I thought your horse had run away. I was so scared I didn't know what to do."

"You were not at all to blame, madam," said Ad. "It was we who were at fault. We were driving too fast."

We contrived at length to patch up the wagon by tying the "rocker" of the wagon body to the forward axle with the rope halter and, reloading our mealbags, drove slowly home without further incident. Addison, having captured the reins, retained possession of them, much to my mental relief. Halstead laid the blame alternately to the woman and to Addison's effort to grab the reins. "Now I suppose you will go home and tell the old gent that I did it!" he added bitterly. "If you had let the reins alone, I should have got along all right."

Addison did not reply to this accusation, except to say that he was thankful our necks were not broken. As he drove into the carriage house, Gramp came out and, seeing the rope in so odd a position, asked what was the matter.

"The transient bolt broke, coming down the Sylvester hill," Addison replied. "It was badly worn, I see. If you think it best, sir, I will take it to the blacksmith's shop after work tomorrow."

"Very well," Gramp assented, and that was all there was said about the accident.

Not far from this time, "the threshers" made their annual appearance with "horse-power," "beater," and "separator," which were set up in the west barn floor. These dusty itinerants, I discovered, usually remained with us for two days and threshed the grain on shares: one bushel for every ten of wheat, rye, and barley and one for every twelve of oats. There were always two of them, and for five or six years the same pair came to our barn every fall: a sturdy old man, named Dennett, and his son-in-law, Amos Moss. Dennett himself "tended beater" and Moss measured and "stricted" the grain as it came from the separator, and it was hinted about among the farmers that "Moss would bear watching."

We were kept very busy during those two days; Halse, I remember, was first set to "shake down" the wheat off a high scaffold for Dennett to feed into the beater while Addison and I got away the straw. Halstead complained that it was Addison's turn to shake down this year, but the truth was Halse just didn't like heights. I deemed it great fun at first, to see the horses travel up the lags of the horse-power incline and hear the machine in action, but I soon found that it was suffocatingly dusty work; our nostrils and throats as well as our hair and clothing were much choked and loaded with dust.

We had been at work an hour or two when suddenly an unusual snapping noise issued from the beater; old Dennett abruptly stopped the machine. After examining the teeth, he looked up where Halse stood on the scaffold, shaking down, and said, "Look here, young man, I want you to be more careful what you shake down here; we don't want to thrash clubs!"

"I didn't shake down clubs," said Halse.

"A pretty big stick went through anyway," remarked Dennett. "I haven't said you did it a-purpose. But I asked you to be more careful."

They went on again for half or three-quarters of an hour, when there was another odd noise, and Dennett again stopped and looked up sharply at Halse. "Can't you see clubs as big as that?" he said. "Why, that's an old tooth out of a loafer rake. You must mind what you are about."

Halse pretended that he had seen nothing in the grain, and the machine was started again; but Addison and I could see Halse at times from the place where we were at work and noticed that he looked mischievous. Addison shook his head at him vehemently.

Nothing further happened that forenoon, but we had not been at work for more than an hour after dinner, when a shrill *thrip* resounded from the beater, followed by a jingling noise, and one of the short iron teeth from it flew into the roof of the barn. Again Dennett stopped the machine hastily.

"What kind of a faller do you call yerself?" he exclaimed, looking very hard up at Halse. "You threw that stone into the beater, you know you did."

"I didn't!" protested Halse. "You can't prove I did, either."

"I'd tan your jacket for ye, ef you was my boy," muttered Dennett wrathfully. He and Moss got wrenches from their toolbox and replaced the broken tooth with a new one. The Old Squire, who had been looking to the grain in the granary, came in and asked what the trouble was.

"Squire," said Dennett, "I want another man to shake down here for me. That's a queer Dick you've put up there."

The Old Squire spoke to Addison to get up and shake out the grain and bade Halse come down and assist me with the straw. Halse climbed down, muttering to himself. "I want to get a drink of water," he said, and as he went out past the beater, he made a saucy remark to Dennett; whereupon the latter seized a whipstock and aimed a blow at him. Halse dodged it and ran. Dennett chased him out of the barn and Halse took refuge in the woodshed.

The Old Squire was at first inclined to reprove Dennett for this apparently unwarranted act; he considered that he had no right to chastise Halse. "I will attend to that part of the business myself," he said somewhat sharply.

"All right, Squire," said Dennett. "But I want you to understand you've got a bad boy there. Throwing stones into a beater is rough business. He might kill somebody."

Halse did not come back to help me at once, and at length Gramp went to the house in search of him. Ellen subsequently told me that Halse had at first refused to come out, on the pretext that Dennett would injure him. The Old Squire assured him that he should not be hurt. Still he refused to go. Thereupon, for the first of only two occasions I am aware of, the old gentleman went in search of a horsewhip; and as a net result of the proceedings, Halse made his appearance beside me, sniffing.

"I wish it had stove his old machine all to flinders and him with it," he said to me revengefully.

"Did you throw the stone into the beater?" I asked. The machine made so much noise that I did not distinctly hear what Halse replied, but I thought that he denied doing it; and whether he actually did it, or whether the stone slid down with the grain owing to his carelessness, I never knew.

After supper that evening I saw Theodora in earnest conversation with Addison out in the garden by the bee house.

Later, after we had finished milking and were going into the dairy with our pails, Addison said, "Doad wants me to watch Halse tonight. He is so angry, she thinks he might try sneaking off to Tibbett's store at the Corners. Drinking and gambling are said to take place there. If he gets up to go out anywhere, she wants us to stop him and coax him back to his room.

"It isn't a job I like," continued Addison, "but perhaps we had better try it; Doad thinks so.

"So if you can keep awake till ten or eleven, you had better," Addison went on. "If he gets up to start off, ask him where he is going, and if he really starts, come and call me, and we will go after him. I can dress in a minute."

To this proposal I agreed, and I may add here that at about eleven o'clock we surprised Halse in the act of stealing away to the Corners, but after some parley and a scuffle with him succeeded in locking him up in his room, and I lodged with Addison.

It was but a short night thenceforward till five o'clock in the morning. Before going downstairs we peeped into Halse's room, to see if he were there still. He lay soundly asleep. Addison closed the door softly. "Poor noodle," he said, drumming his milk pail absentmindedly. "Let him snooze awhile. I suppose it isn't really his fault that he has got such a head on his shoulders. He is rather to be pitied, after all. He is his own worst enemy.

"I've heard," Ad continued in a low tone, as we opened the barnyard gate, "that Aunt Ysabel, Halse's mother, was a sort of queer, tempery, flighty person."

When we took in the milk, Theodora was grinding coffee—and how good it smelled! (She had just roasted it in the stove oven.)

"We got him back all right, with no great difficulty," Addison whispered to her, in passing.

"Oh, I'm so glad," she replied.

Halse had not come down, and pretty soon we heard the Old Squire call him, at which Addison laughed a little as he glanced at me.

At breakfast Halstead looked somewhat embarrassed; in fact, he did not look at Addison and me at all, if he could avoid it.

Later that morning Theodora confided her thoughts about Halse to me, when I ducked in for some water. Halse had been first to come to the old farm when Uncle Coville brought him there before enlisting in the navy a few weeks after the outbreak of the Civil War. Theodora arrived next, after Uncle Robert's death at Shiloh.

"You know," she said, "that Halstead has an unsteady temperament and a reckless temper. But, since you arrived here just a few months ago, you may not know that he also has a good heart. Until Addison came after Uncle William's death at Gettysburg, Halstead was a much better boy. He feels and sees, I suppose, that Addison is more talented than he is and that all of us naturally place more confidence in what Addison says and does. That provokes Halstead to do and say what he otherwise wouldn't. Instead of doing his best, he often does his worst. Ad is intelligent and conscientious; he despises anything that is mean or tricky, and he has no patience with anyone who does such things. So they don't get along very well, and I often think that it isn't a good thing for them to be together—not a good thing for Halse, I mean.

"Isn't that a strange thing," continued Theodora thoughtfully, "that because one boy is good and manly and intelligent, another one in the same household may not do nearly as well as he would if the first one were only just stupid?"

Theodora had taken me into moral waters quite beyond my depth, observing which, I presume, she went on to say that she wanted me to see and realize just how it was with Halstead—who, until his father's recent death at the battle of Mobile Bay, had counted on leaving the old farm—and always to try to bring out his best side instead of his worst.

If I could only have seen the matter in as clear a light as she did and labored as hard as she did to bring out that "best side" of my youthful kinsman, his happiness with life at the old farm might have been quite different.

5

The Guest Who Had Been in Jail

FOUR OF US YOUNG PEOPLE AT THE OLD FARM HAD come down with the mumps and were feeling dreadfully "mumpy." We sat in rocking chairs before the fire, wrapped in comforters and drinking chamomile tea. Once in a while Grandmother gave us a spoonful of hoarhound honey to comfort us. To this day I can remember how good that hoarhound honey tasted! But better solace even than the hoarhound honey were the stories that the Old Squire told us to help pass the time. This is one story as we heard it:

It was late in September, on one of the first cold nights of fall when the leaves are beginning to flutter down from the trees and the ripe apples are dropping in the orchards. After clearing the supper table, Grandmother Ruth had kindled a fire in the sitting room fireplace, and she sat by it, knitting, while the Old Squire read the *Independent* aloud to her. Except for a hired man, a woman helper, and Halstead, who was asleep upstairs, they were alone at the old farm for this was in Civil War times, some years before the rest of us young folks went home to live there. Two of their sons had already fallen in battle, and the other three were with the army at the front.

About eight o'clock they heard a knock at the side door. On opening it the Old Squire dimly perceived a stranger—a medium-sized man wearing a cap and jacket and carrying a stout stick in his hand.

"Good evening, sir!" the Old Squire said, peering out at him. "What's wanted?"

The stranger asked whether they could entertain him for the night. "I am taking a long walk," he added, "and I can find no tavern."

"I guess we will try to put you up," the Old Squire replied. "Are you alone?"

"Alone and afoot," the stranger replied dryly. "Perhaps I ought to tell you before I come in that I've been in jail once."

"That so?" the Old Squire said. "Well, step inside here and let me have a look at you."

The stranger entered and stood just within the doorway, perfectly still, with a curious smile on his face, but without speaking, as the Old Squire brought a lamp.

"You don't look like a very bad man, and rogues are not likely to tell of their being in jail," the Old Squire remarked with a smile. "Excuse me for asking, but what's your business in these parts?"

"Stealing apples," the odd visitor replied.

"How do you get them away without a team?" the Old Squire inquired skeptically.

"I don't get them away," the stranger said. "I merely bite them and throw them down. I'm only after the flavor. I bite only natural fruit, mostly apples growing wild by the roadsides or in pastures. Grafts I don't care for. Natural fruit has the fine flavors."

"Just so," the Old Squire rejoined, amused but with some misgivings as to the fellow's sanity. "You can stay here for the night. Do you want supper?"

"I should like some bread and butter, if it is convenient, and a cup of tea," he said.

Grandmother Ruth was not favorably impressed by the stranger's appearance, but she brought a loaf of bread, some butter, and a slice of cake. She spread a little table at one side of the fireplace, and when she had brewed a pot of green tea she bade him help himself. He did so without a word, and for some time did full justice to the simple repast. When he had finished, he extended his feet to the fire.

Wishing to seem sociable, the Old Squire asked the stranger whether he had traveled far and where he was from.

"I have come roundabouts from a town not far from Boston," the man replied. "I came into New Hampshire and walked through the glen of the White Mountains. I've been in Maine three times before this. Yes, four times. I frequently tramp about."

"And how do you like our state?" the Old Squire asked.

"I like it, because much of it is wild country. I like virgin forests and lakes and rivers in the wilderness. Once about eleven years ago, I climbed that hoary, grim mountain the Indians call Katahdin. Twice I have followed the Penobscot in a birch canoe from Chesuncook to Bangor. Once I canoed down the Allagash to the St. John."

"Interested in lumber?"

"Interested in trees. I love trees. I pity them. Men slay them and use their dried flesh for houses and to burn in stoves."

Somewhat impressed by such Delphic utterances, the Old Squire asked his guest whether he thought trees felt the ax when being felled.

"Beyond doubt," said the queer traveler unhesitatingly. "Not as we feel a cut, of course, but they feel it and shrink from death."

"You deem it cruel to cut a tree then?"

"I deem it murder," replied the stranger.

"Yet it can hardly be helped," the Old Squire rejoined.

"No, because man has become man, with his foolish round of artificial wants. That is where cruelty enters—cruelty to all nature round him. Man has become unnatural, hence cruel, and believes now that he cannot be otherwise."

"You think the way we live is a mistake, then?" the Old Squire asked.

"Certainly I do. Human beings ought never to have begun living in artificial ways. The human race should have gone on living naturally, like the birds and beasts. No real happiness can ever come from civilization, because it is unnatural and contrary to terrestrial nature. It will end badly."

"But how can we do otherwise than we do?" the Old Squire asked him. "We live among other people and have to do as they do."

"Not at all. We can live naturally if we have a mind to. It is a duty."

"But, my dear man, have you ever tried that yourself?" the Old Squire exclaimed.

"Yes, sir," the stranger declared emphatically. "I have. I do when at home—and that is the way I got into jail," he added, laughing for the first time, but rather sardonically.

"I can well understand that," the Old Squire remarked dryly. "It is what I should expect for myself, if I started to live wholly according to nature."

Noticing that Grandmother Ruth was knitting faster and faster, he guessed that this talk nettled her, and so he changed the subject. Gram considered being in jail a sign of great moral turpitude.

The Old Squire had at first believed that the wanderer was a border smuggler who had merely invented the tale of stealing apples to cloak some less trivial purpose for his travels. As they conversed, however, the Old Squire perceived that his guest was a man of education, with deep and earnest conviction in his beliefs—not at all the sort of man who would engage in petty smuggling.

"Did you ever go as far as Canada on your tramps?" the Old Squire asked.

"Once only," the stranger replied, "and then I went by train, and not on foot, to Montreal and Quebec."

He described his walk from Quebec to the Falls of Montmorency and thence to the shrine of Ste. Anne de Beaupré. He went on to speak of faith as a means of healing the sick and let fall certain remarks that indicated clearly that he was not a firm believer in miracles.

"What is your belief?" the Old Squire asked.

"I am a pantheist, pure and simple," the stranger said. "So is Ralph Waldo Emerson, though he hedges about avowing it. I do not see how one can be anything else."

Grandmother Ruth did not know what a pantheist was, but she felt sure that it was something not at all proper.

Her needles were fairly flying now.

"Some years ago," the stranger went on, "I traveled the length of Cape Cod. I went to Cohasset and to Providencetown, where the Pilgrims first set foot on the soil of Massachusetts. Magnificently in earnest, those people! But difficult to live with."

"Yes, they would have made it warm for pantheists," the Old Squire remarked. "It is likely, too, that they would strongly have disapproved of stealing apples."

"No doubt they would have jailed me or put me in their stocks," the stranger said. "Yet nature plants wild apples for bird and beast. Why not for me?"

Grandmother Ruth could listen in silence no longer. "You ask why?" she exclaimed. "Because you are not a bird or a squirrel. Because you are a human being and have to stand together with the rest of us to keep order in the world. That's why."

Their guest contemplated her for several moments with disapproval. "Yes, that is the common view of it," he said at last.

"And the right one," Grandmother Ruth insisted. In the interest of hospitality the Old Squire quickly changed the subject.

"I dare say you find now and then a tree of fine-flavored natural fruit," he remarked.

Thereupon the stranger began to describe certain delicious wild apples that he had discovered on his long walks. The Old Squire became much interested in the conversation, for the stranger proved a most entertaining and instructive talker. From apple trees they passed to forest trees, of which, as a lumber man as well as a farmer, the Old Squire possessed an extensive practical knowledge. Even here he found that the stranger had much information to give him.

The clock struck eleven, and after lighting a bedtime candle for their guest, Grandmother Ruth retired. The two tree lovers talked on until past midnight.

"Really, I should like to know your name," the Old Squire said, when at last he showed the stranger his way to a bed in the east room. "I have greatly enjoyed our talk together. You seem to be a philosopher."

"Do names count for much?" the stranger remarked after a moment's silence. "Names always appear to me to befog the personality of my acquaintances. Their names stand for one thing, they themselves for another. Often I think I would know them better if they had no names. Would you not as soon remember me for what I am, as by a name?"

"Certainly, certainly," the Old Squire said, thinking that for some reason the man did not wish to reveal his name—perhaps because of the jail episode.

The stranger sat thoughtfully on the side of the bed. "Of course, as I have entered your house and accepted your hospitality, I ought to give you my name if you wish it," he said.

"No, no, don't mention it," the Old Squire said hastily, and bade him good night.

On going out at sunrise the next morning the Old Squire espied the stranger walking about in the orchard. He came in and took breakfast with Grandmother and Grandfather but seemed rather taciturn; after offering to pay for his entertainment he went his way. That was the last they saw of him.

As time passed, the Old Squire reverted to his surmise that, in spite of the stranger's erudition and love of nature, he was a border smuggler. In the fall of 1862, however, while on a trip to Portland the old gentleman happened to take up a copy of the *Atlantic Monthly* and saw in it an essay entitled "Wild Apples," by Henry D. Thoreau. The title attracted him, and he had not read the article half through before he became convinced that the author was none other than his former guest. The sentiment, the descriptions, and the quotations from classic writers were identical with those that his strange guest had used in that memorable conversation at the old farm.

On returning home he wrote a pleasant letter of reminiscence and sent it to Thoreau, in care of the *Atlantic Monthly*. The letter was returned, with a note from the editor saying that Thoreau had died only a short time before. The Old Squire was not a little shocked by the news, so vividly had the personality of his guest impressed itself on his mind. To the end of his life, the old gentleman never doubted that the sojourner at the farm that night was indeed the celebrated author.

But had Thoreau been in jail? He had, actually. Thoreau at one time lived alone at Concord, Massachusetts, in a little cabin on the shore of Walden Pond. He maintained that because he caused the town no expense, he ought not to be asked to pay taxes.

But the town officials took a different view of the matter. The tax collector called at Thoreau's cabin and demanded payment of the sum assessed. Thoreau refused to pay it.

"I owe you nothing," he said. "I will pay nothing."

The collector departed, but came again the next year only to receive the same answer.

"If people would all live as I live, there would be no need of taxes,"

Thoreau asserted. "Taxes come from living artificially. The town has no proper bill against me, for I live by myself."

He often argued the matter with his friend, Ralph Waldo Emerson, who lived in Concord. Although feeling great affection for Thoreau, Emerson did not agree with him about taxation, and they had many long discussions over it. Thoreau even declared that it was wrong for either of them to pay a tax.

This went on for some time, and at last the town fathers sent the sheriff to arrest Thoreau for repeated and contentious violations of the law. He was brought to Concord jail and locked up, pending trial.

The news flew. Thoreau was in jail! Emerson, greatly distressed, at once bestirred himself. It is said that he appeared at the jail with his surtout unbuttoned and his hat askew. Then, according to report, this bit of dialogue followed between the two philosophers.

Emerson, agitated: "Henry, Henry, why are you here?"

Thoreau, mimicking: "Ralph, Ralph, why are you *not* here?"

Emerson offered the authorities bail to any amount and surety for Thoreau's tax. Thoreau, however, utterly declined bail. He would have none of it, and in the end, the town officials had to put him out of the jail.

When the Old Squire heard of the outcome of this incident, he laughed until the tears came; but Grandmother Ruth said, "Served him right!"

6

Three Days at the County Fair

"CATTLE SHOWS," AS THE AGRICULTURAL FAIRS OF New England are generally called in the country, are the great holidays of autumn for the farm family. Besides the show of neat stock and horses, there are drawing matches, arranged or graded for different classes of horses, steers, and oxen, according to weight, and racing matches such as the slow race, the bona fide horse trots, and the scrub race. Prizes are offered for the best farm products and there are, of course, plenty of "sideshows," where a young man can spend the little money he has carefully saved during the summer and get swindled to the full extent of his verdancy—all of which, however, helps him to "cut his eye teeth" and get the "hayseed out of his hair."

Gram usually sent in one or more firkins of butter, several cheeses, and several types of pickles and jams. The Old Squire exhibited several head of cattle and sometimes his entire herd, also sheep, hogs, and poultry. The girls sewed, embroidered, and baked loaves of bread and cake. Then there were always extensive exhibits of apples, pears, and grapes, arranged on plates, as also seedcorn, wheat, barley, buckwheat, oats, and garden vegetables. We were occupied for fully a fortnight each year, gathering and preparing our various exhibits.

The county fairgrounds were located near Norway Village, about seven miles distant from the Old Squire's, and consisted of a large wooden building and a high fence, enclosing about thirty acres of land. Each year the local cattle show—the admission fee was fifteen cents—

was held there for three days: Tuesday, Wednesday, and Thursday, usually in the first week of October. A great crowd of more than four thousand people poured in each day.

Each year, for those three days, the Old Squire hired "Aunt" Olive Witham, the Elder Witham's spinster sister, who was not at all interested in fairs, to look after the farm, milk the cows, and cook the hearty supper we needed after getting home quite late. But my first fall, just before the fair, Aunt Olive sent word that an emergency would keep her home until Tuesday afternoon, and reluctantly Ellen, Wealthy, and I—the three youngest—agreed to stay home and take care of the necessary chores.

The First Day: Four Stayed Home

EARLY TUESDAY MORNING—on the first day of the fair—Jim and Asa Doane, our two hired men, began driving the cows, oxen, and sheep to the fairgrounds, but old Dan was left behind as too dangerous.

Old Dan was a fearful "butting" ram of extraordinary size, who was as portly as a lord and must have weighed at least two hundred pounds.

What his head could be made of, to be so hard, was in those days a wonder to the whole family. As well as if it were yesterday do I recollect his enormous corkscrew horns, of a dirty gray color, and his eyes, as hard and bleared as a drunkard's.

In his younger days old Dan is said to have been a pleasant fellow, but a long acquaintance with hectoring boys and hired men had made him, like a few old gentlemen I have known, somewhat crusty and short-tempered.

With the singular exception of Ellen, his beloved mistress, whoever went into the barnyard had to look out sharp, for old Dan enjoyed taking people unawares from behind.

In fact, the Doanes had hardly left when the Old Squire rushed in from the barn with his hands and clothes wet and covered with mud, his face red, and his eyes flashing.

"Ellen!" he shouted, as he entered the kitchen. "Where's Ellen?"

"Here I am!" came a cheery voice in reply; and an instant after, she entered the old-fashioned country kitchen from the adjoining woodshed, where she had been cutting potatoes for the evening's supper. "Do you want anything?"

"I want to tell you this," said the Old Squire, as he washed himself at the sink and rubbed his weather-beaten face with the coarse towel until it was even more red than before. "Old Dan must be killed! Just see the state I am in, and all from that worthless old rascal! I won't have him about the house another day. He's good for nothing but to make trouble, and he must be shot before night!" added the old gentleman, wrathfully.

Ellen was about to plead for her pet, when her little sister, Wealthy, came into the room.

"Why Grandpapa, what is the matter?" she cried, running to him in astonishment. "Did you fall into the creek?"

"I might as well," he replied, half laughing. "Old Dan butted me into the watering trough!"

There was a shout of laughter from both children, in which we all joined.

"Well, sir," said Grandma Ruth, coming into the kitchen and still shaking with mirth, "what could you have been thinking about to let an old ram, 'most twenty years old, knock you into the watering trough?"

"But," explained the Old Squire, "he took me unawares. I had just filled one pail to carry to the barn and was stooping to dip the other, when the old rascal came at me like the wind and knocked me completely into the water! He scampered, I tell you, before I could get out. He knew he had done mischief. Anyhow, he's got to be killed today, sure. He's only a nuisance, and I'll shoot him tonight when we come back from the fair, if he's on the farm!"

An hour later, in a loaded double wagon, the old couple, Addison, Halstead, and Theodora left for the fair. As they rattled out of the yard, old Dan suddenly appeared close to the gate, and wagging his tail as if in derision, gave utterance to a hoarse "Baa-a!"

The Old Squire turned, shook his whip at the fellow, and cried, "This is your last day, my boy! Make the most of it!"

Leaving Ellen and Wealthy in the house alone, after we had fruitlessly considered for a while whether there was any way of averting old Dan's sad fate, I shouldered my hoe and marched off to my work, digging up more potatoes in the "back lot."

But the little girls had no thought of being afraid. Ellen had the breakfast dishes to wash, Wealthy some sweeping to do, and both the dinner to get, all before twelve o'clock.

Time fled. The dishes stood in shining rows on the pantry shelves, the broom had performed its work, and Ellen and Wealthy were preparing the vegetables to be boiled, when there came a faint knock at the door. Supposing it to be Aunt Olive, the girls did not rise, but called, "Come in!"

The door was slowly opened, and a man stepped within. He wore a long black coat, buttoned to his chin and very threadbare. His trousers, too, were black and shiny, and much too short for him. On one foot was a boot, while the other was graced by a ragged shoe. He carried a battered silk hat in his hand. His face was long and solemn, but quite red, his eyes bleared, his hands very dirty, and altogether he was a queer looking visitor.

"Where's yer folks, gals?" he said to Ellen in a half whine, as he glanced sharply about the room.

"They've gone to the Norway Fair," replied Ellen, wondering why he asked. "Did you wish to see them?"

"Now that's too bad!" exclaimed the visitor, as he seated himself. "And I've come so far to see them! But perhaps your brothers would do as well."

"We haven't any brothers," said Ellen, laughing, "but one of our cousins is over in the back lot. He'll be in by-and-by, though, if he'll do."

"Well, I don't hardly believe he will, after all," said the man, shaking his head thoughtfully, "and I can't wait today anyway; I haint the time. But I'm terribly hungry. If I could, I'd stay to dinner, miss. However, under the circumstances, perhaps you had better give me a light lunch before I go; a piece of pie and a cup of tea, and a little cold meat, or something of that sort."

"Oh, certainly; only we can't give you the meat for we haven't cooked it yet," said Ellen, rising. "But I will find something." And she brought from the pantry a whole apple pie, which she placed before him, with a knife and fork.

"If you will help yourself, I'll have the tea ready in three minutes."

"All right, my dear!" said the man, seizing the knife and drawing the pie toward him. "I will act upon your advice. The last time I took dinner with General Grant," he continued, as he cut a great piece and began to eat, he said to me, 'Governor, Governor,' he said, 'never disregard a lady's advice,' and I have always remembered what he said." The stranger chuckled merrily and nodded his head at the delicious-looking pastry before him.

The girls wondered a little at the table manners of the man who had dined with Grant, but they steeped his tea, flavored it with rich cream and sugar, and passed it to him.

"I am not much of a hand for tea," said the man, as he drained the cup, "but my doctor says that I must drink it for my digestion. Ruined my digestion while I was in the army, you see," and he winked solemnly. "By the way," he continued, picking up the silver teaspoon from his saucer, "have you any more of these? They are as neat a pattern as I ever saw, and odd, too. I should like to see the rest of the dozen, if you have them."

"Grandmother has only eleven," said Wealthy, in her innocence, "and she is very proud of them, but I will show them to you."

Then she brought the little box with the precious table silver—eleven teaspoons, four tablespoons, and an ancient cream jug, all pure silver and shining brightly—and placed them before her inquisitive visitor to admire.

He had finished his "light lunch." That is, the pie was demolished and the teapot empty. As the little girl handed him the treasures, he arose, took the box to the window, examined its contents with a critical eye for a moment, and then, as if in joyful surprise, cried, "I am right! They are the very spoons! The very same identical spoons that my friend lost when he was a boy! How lucky it is that I have found them at last!"

With these words, and a very low bow, the rascal opened the door and slipped away with the spoons and a silver cream pitcher down the path toward the gate.

For an instant, the girls stood motionless; then, rushing after him, Ellen shrieked, "Give me those spoons! They are my grandmother's spoons, and you are trying to steal them! You are a thief, a thief! Bring them back! Bring them back!"

The man, however, paid no attention to the child's cries, but ran rapidly down the path, carrying the box in his arms; and the spoons and pitcher would have been lost forever if a new party had not appeared on the scene.

Old Dan was quietly nibbling the grass near the gateway. Hearing his little mistress's voice, he looked up at the very instant that the tramp passed. What he saw about the man that disturbed him, I don't know, but erecting his head with a hoarse "Baa-a!" he shot after him like a cannonball.

The man turned to receive him and defend himself, but the ram struck him fairly in front and knocked him, half senseless, flat on his back, scattering the silver in all directions.

For an instant, the fellow remained sprawling in the dust, then he slowly arose, limping and groaning, and without a glance at his enemy, began to gather up his stolen spoils.

He had partly completed his task when old Dan, who all this time had been watching the proceedings from beneath his shaggy eyebrows, shook his long beard and with another tremendous "Baa-a!" dashed at the stranger again, and over he went a second time, his treasures flying from his hands.

And now began a strange battle. With cries of rage and pain, the man recovered his feet and turned on the ram, kicking and striking at him furiously, while Dan, accustomed to such warfare from years of experience with the boys of the countryside, easily eluded him and in return, butted him to the earth again and again.

The spoons and cream pitcher were knocked hither and thither; as the combatants struggled, the road was trampled into something like a racecourse, the air was filled with very bad language, very angry "baas," and a great cloud of dust.

But after some five minutes, victory declared itself on the side of the quadruped, and bruised and bleeding, with clothes in rags, minus hat and shoe, the vanquished man suddenly turned away and ran limping down the road, leaving his antagonist in full possession of the field and the stolen silver.

Old Dan remained motionless, gazing after his enemy, until he disappeared around a distant turn in the road; then, shaking the dust from his coarse wool, he gave utterance to a low grumble of satisfaction and, wagging his tail, returned to his dinner in front of the house.

Half an hour later, as we sat down to dinner and Wealthy washed the coveted spoons and the bright little pitcher and laid them carefully away once more, Ellen told me the story of how the robber was foiled; and I, full of enthusiasm, cried, "The Old Squire will not kill old Dan today, for I do not believe that he would shoot him now for a hundred dollars!"

And I was right. The old ram won more than he knew when he fought the tramp and conquered him. He won the Old Squire's regard, lots of extra food, and a trouble-free life for the remainder of his days.

The Second Day: Sweet Apple Juice

THERE IS A GREAT deal of latent energy in a barrel of sweet apple juice when it is changing to cider. As pressed from the pomace it is a syrupy, saccharine fluid, insipid to the taste and far from clean. In this condition it is quite unfit to drink, but it is a royal garden for bacteria.

In the course of a few days or even, under some circumstances, a few hours, these minute vegetable organisms multiply beyond computation. To say that there are millions of them in every gill inadequately expresses the fact. Were the entire universe one vast barrel of sweet apple juice, bacteria would quickly fill it.

Figures, indeed, are impotent to number the microscopic population of one barrel, which soon becomes a small universe of vegetable life; yet each of the microbes, scarcely one-three-thousandth of an inch long, is an organism that lives its life, maintains itself in the struggle for existence, and reproduces its kind.

The individuals live for a day and leave behind what scientists term ptomaines, that is, the refuse of their life. The ptomaines alter the taste of the sweet juice a little. It is no longer quite so sweet as it was, but tastes flat. It no longer offers a wholesome sustenance for the first race of bacteria, which immediately disappear and are replaced by others, their descendants it may be. Under the microscope they appear larger and more gaunt.

These re-populate the barrel, but not quite so numerously as the first; and in turn they leave their ptomaines behind them, abandoning the struggle for existence in the now slightly acid juice to another larger and gaunter species.

By this time we say of the cider that it has begun to "work," that is, to ferment, and there is a great deal of frothing and fizzing; for the ptomaines consist in part of carbon dioxide, or carbonic acid, a gas that craves room in the world and is a great popper of corks and bung stoppers.

Erelong another and still gaunter species of bacteria appears in the apple juice. Each species has in turn been poisoned out, in a sense, by its own ptomaines, or refuse. Each has consumed all the food particles that were its proper pabulum, and the species that succeeds it is one of hardier type, capable of living on the refuse of the previous species. Thus successive populations of microorganisms follow one another, till the sweet juice has become old, "hard" cider, a ptomaine of many ptomaines. It is no longer a fizzy fluid. The life within it is now very sour, melancholic, and still. Torpor has succeeded; all the fizz and liveliness have gone.

The period of greatest activity in the barrel occurs when the first invaders are rioting in the new juice. All unknown to himself, the boy who then thrusts a straw into the bung hole and takes a "pull" of the agreeably acid cider swallows unnumbered millions of harmless microbes. It is that, indeed, which makes it taste so good; and where ignorance is bliss, it is perhaps only folly to be wise.

Still, it is well to know the "whys and wherefores" of such things; for as I write this, I recall an incident of my boyhood on the old farm, when more knowledge on these subjects than was then current would have prevented a catastrophe that was most dismal to several of us—dismal, although a hundred people or more who were looking on laughed immoderately.

All of us cousins were youthful partners in a "dining shanty" at the county fair. And although this was my first fair, it was not the first experience for the others. Halstead had begun in a humble way to peddle fruit and gingerbread at the fair four years before, and all my cousins had gradually gathered the experience necessary to conduct this eating booth successfully.

There is honest money to be made in such a booth, if it is well managed. We came to rely on what we made every fall at the fair to pay our winter school expenses for the year. And the Old Squire was kind enough to let us ransack the old farm for many of our supplies. We took potatoes, sweet corn, and beans for our shanty, also a pig for pork and a part of our beef. Pastry, in fact, was about the only item that required a cash outlay in advance; and even our pies, cakes, and dough-nuts were cooked at home by Theodora, Ellen, and Wealthy the day before the fair opened.

In this way we were able to set a good table at thirty-five cents a plate and do very well, when rival concerns were obliged to charge fifty cents for no better food. In consequence, my cousins had fed fully eight hundred persons at two annual fairs, in succession, besides doing well from their cider and fruit stands adjoining the booth.

The law in our state then permitted the sale of "sweet cider," and this term was always construed to include cider that had "worked" to some extent but was not palpably sour and alcoholic.

With us who had plenty of apples lying on the ground under the trees at home, there was a handsome profit in sweet cider at five, or even at three, cents a glass. It was not difficult to dispose of three or four barrels at our stand.

In short, as regards the ins and outs of the dining shanty business, there was not much that we did not know. But as to the internal work-ings of a barrel of sweet apple juice, we had still much to learn.

That fall, to accommodate the horse jockeys, rather than the farm-ers, the fair was held a fortnight earlier than was customary. Previously it had been set for the first week in October, when all farm products are ready for exhibition.

Because of the earlier date, all the usual preparations were much hurried—particularly our cider, which we were able to make but a few days before the fair.

All apple juice must work a little to be fit to drink. We knew that warmth promoted fermentation and that keeping the barrels in a cool place retarded it. To hasten the fermentation as much as possible, Hal-stead and I put four barrels of the fresh juice into the beet cellar in the west barn, and a fire was kept in a stove in the cellar night and day.

We took out the bungs and to start it fermenting, poured into each barrel a pint or more of cider that had already begun to work. This and the uniform warmth carried fermentation forward very rapidly.

"It's frothing finely," Halstead told me on the second morning after. "It will be sharp enough by day after tomorrow."

Addison and I had so many things to look after that we did not test the cider, but left that duty to Halstead, who seemed to enjoy it quite a lot. On the morning of the first day of the fair, Addison, Halstead, and Theodora took one barrel of the cider for use on that day.

Now Halstead had driven the bungs into two of the barrels late the evening before, thinking that they might want both. But they took only one and left three for the next, or middle day, which is always the great day at a county fair—since that is the day of the sulky races.

The first day was chiefly spent in preparation, which in this case consisted in laying the tables, setting up a large stove, and unpacking much borrowed crockery and many large boxes and barrels containing food. Not many customers came in. The second day, when we all could go, our harvest was to begin.

Accordingly, the next morning, Addison was ready to start with his load at five o'clock, for we had seven miles to drive. It was a bulky load in a double wagon; especially as we had two extra girls to carry: Kate Edwards and Georgie Wilbur, who had volunteered to act for us as waitresses.

Two of the cider barrels had been hauled to the fair the previous evening; and finding this wagon very much crowded, Halstead came to see whether Addison and I could contrive to take the other one, as our wagon was larger than the one he was driving for the old couple.

Our load had already been put on the wagon, and we had five girls to transport. They were on the two front seats. In addition, we also had a large crate of bread, a huge box of pies, ten pots of baked beans, a firkin of butter, another of applesauce, three immense Indian puddings, three plum puddings, and two large cream cheeses.

In fact, with the five young ladies on the front seats arrayed in all their finery, with Addison standing up in front to drive the span of horses, and myself behind standing guard over the piled-up stock of eatables, we presented an appearance of festive richness that would cause the people on the road to turn and smile unctuously upon us. But by making some changes, Addison and I contrived to put the extra cider barrel on the wagon.

"It's got a big head on!" Halstead said to me, as we heaved it up between us. "Just hear it sizz!"

And once, on our way to the fairgrounds, when we had stopped for a moment to favor a drove of cattle in the road, Wealthy cried out, "What's that sizzing so? I hear it every time we stop!"

"Oh, it's only Halstead's cider barrel," replied Addison. "It's on the sizz this morning."

"He's been putting yeast in it, I guess," said Katherine.

Entering the fairgrounds, we drove to our shanty. Before helping the girls out, Addison partly turned and backed the wagon up to the shanty door so that we could at once unload. I had already jumped to the ground.

In backing the horses, the rear wheels of the wagon went over a bit of joist, causing a slight jolt, upon which the head of that cider went into the air as if fired from a gun. There was a roar like that of a locomotive suddenly blowing off steam. Not only did the barrel head fly, but as much as ten gallons of cider went with it, and possibly twenty. It gushed out as if belched from a geyser.

It flew high in the air, and as what goes up must come down, we were all of us, in an instant, literally drenched and soaked with cider.

The five girls appeared to bear the brunt of the deluge. I never before, nor since, saw five pretty girls so suddenly transformed into yellowed, dripping, pitiful frights. They screamed; they leaped out of the wagon headlong; and then stood dismayed, wringing their hands, and half choked with cider.

Addison, who was in the same condition, managed to hold the horses until I ran and seized them by the bits. The barrel head had fallen exactly in front of them, and they, too, were splashed. We quieted the horses, and then turned to look at the poor dripping wrecks of girls.

"We must get them home, as quick as we can!" said Addison.

"Oh, yes," they all moaned in chorus, "do take us home, for pity's sake, before everybody sees us!"

As speedily as possible we pulled out the load. Then Addison drove the poor girls home and did not return with them, in fresh attire, till past noon.

Halstead and I, meantime, were having plenty of trouble. All those bean pots were soaked with cider, as also much of the bread, pies, and doughnuts. All the dishes that we had aboard the wagon needed to be washed, and about half our napkins and tablecloths were badly stained.

Ah, that was a hard blow at the dining shanty! Putting the best foot forward in the matter, and doing all we could to reorganize, it was past twelve o'clock before we could open our doors to the public. We lost two of the best hours of the day.

Altogether, as nearly as we could estimate it afterward, what we then learned about fermentation cost us at least a hundred dollars, to say nothing of what Theodora, Ellen, Wealthy, Georgie, and Kate suffered, in their feelings, which was something frightful, no doubt.

And the next year, after summer school's rum-induced calamity, Addison had become so rigid a temperance reformer that he would never again deal in cider.

The Third Day: The Madawaska Pig

ON THE THIRD and last day of the fair, the final, and to the boys the most exciting feature of the whole fair, was the scrub race, which came off at four o'clock in the afternoon.

In this race every animal was allowed to take part, except horses. Men, boys, dogs harnessed into carts and carrying their owners, cows, steers, and goats became competitors for the prize; in short, everything or anything, on four legs or two, except, as I have said, the equine race. The prize was ten dollars to the winner, meaning he, she, or it that first reached the judges' stand.

But Tom Edwards and I had no thoughts of entering this competition until there moved into our neighborhood, that July, a Madawaska Frenchman named Corbain. A diminutive horse and cart carried all his goods, together with his little brown wife and three "bambins." The family arrived very early one morning and took possession of an old log house on the outskirts of the neighborhood, which nobody claimed, or cared to live in.

With them, led or driven by some process we could never understand, was a young, gaunt, fearful creature, such as in Madawaska passes for a hog, but in any other part of the world would as soon be taken for a wolf. This one was "calico" color—black and yellow and white. Corbain called it Le Cooshong, from *cochon*, I presume. Sometimes this was changed for Le Poork, from *pork*, I suppose.

Madawaskians are used to letting their hogs run at large in the woods and Poork immediately became well known and infamous. He made himself at home in every farmyard in the vicinity. Not an eatable thing was safe from him. Dogs and boys had their hands full in endeavoring to keep him from mischief.

We soon found out that neither board fence nor stone wall were impediments to him and that he showed most wonderful speed, for neither man, dog, or horse could catch or head him off when once he got his "snoot" up for a race. If he couldn't jump a fence, he would go through it. All he wanted was an open space, big enough to aim his long snout at, and either the hole became larger or the fence gave way.

The brute had fearful teeth, almost tusks. These he would gnash together ominously, and then strike his head sideways with really dangerous force. He was, I think, the nearest approach in aspect, habits, and manners to the wild boar, of any "hog" ever seen in New England.

One morning, after Tom and I engaged in a prodigious scrimmage to get this hog out of his family's squash patch, it came into Tom's head that Poork could outrun Gub, the scrub race's two-time champion, and that if we could secure Poork, there was little doubt that the race's purse would easily drop into our hats. We drove the creature home, and Corbain—tired of being pressed for damages—seized on our overture to buy the animal if it was for sale and the price not too high.

The sale was made for four dollars, and we built a stout log pen for Poork. He jumped out of it before we had fairly shut the gate. He hated being confined in any way, and to secure the animal we literally had to build a pen ten feet high.

Our next endeavor was to put a muzzle of sole leather on his nose. This was a difficult task, but we succeeded in doing it. So lean was the creature's neck that we had no difficulty in buckling the strap round it. Then we fastened a halter to the muzzle and after that were able to have our "property" somewhat under control. At length we hitched

him into the dog cart we had manufactured. He was sulky, of course. That we expected. No amount of coaxing, or tempting with foods, or pushing, would make him budge an inch. But we found that a green switch used lightly about his ears would put his legs in motion at any time and call forth shrill expostulations that moved our hearts.

In our leisure hours through the next two months, we trained Poork for the cattle show, more or less successfully. In September we took him in a cart to the fairgrounds and entered him for the scrub race.

Among the competitors were three men and about a dozen boys. The interest of the spectators, however, centered on the four-footed "racers."

There were several dogs. Jimmy Stirks drove two-time champion Gub, a small, stocky, reddish-yellow dog of surly expression of countenance and no particular breed. Then there was a boy with a stub-tailed, brindled bulldog. The dog was harnessed into a little four-wheeled wagon, just big enough for the driver to sit in. Another lad, in a two-wheeled cart, drove a great, curly, shaggy Newfoundland dog.

There was a little black-and-white Canadian cow with fawn-colored legs and slim, black-tipped horns. This creature was the property of a Frenchman, who could speak scarcely a word of English. She was harnessed like a horse and dragged an old pair of wheels. Jinnay, as her owner called her, galloped over the track at an astonishing speed.

Then there was an old man with a large, mouse-colored jackass and another man with a mule. The mule, however, was ruled out by the judges, on the grounds that he had "horse blood in him." There was an excited argument about the matter, however, and the point remained in some doubt.

But Poork was the favorite with the crowd of spectators, from their very first sight of him. Such a shout as was raised when Tom and I led him upon the course harnessed in the cart and muttering to himself, "Reh-reh!" and "Rah-rah!" This was a novelty indeed. Never before had a hog been seen—on that racecourse, at least. Nobody dared bet on his success, for which I am glad; but every eye was on the ungainly animal, to a chorus of "Wheh-wheh!" "Whee!" "Whee, there!" "Where's yer swill pail?" and the like.

Tom got in the cart with his switch. We pushed the obstinate brute well up into the front line. Every dog was growling at the smell of him.

When the word "Go" came from the judges, Tom laid on the switch. With a trumpet-like squeal, Poork sprang into that old-time gallop we both of us knew so well. Tom used the switch pretty actively, and with shrill, angry squeals, Poork dashed past men and boys, actually going between the legs of one fellow and upsetting him, greatly to his disgust and indignation. The dogs resented his company and turned on him fiercely. Poork was more than even the well-disciplined Gub could tolerate. In spite of Jimmy Stirk's desperate efforts, Gub rushed at the hog, throwing Jimmy sprawling out of the cart, knocking over other contestants, and producing an unbelievable confusion. The race ended with men, boys, dogs, cow, donkey, and pig tumbling over one another amid an uproar of howls, barks, yelps, and piercing squeals from Poork as he struggled to be free from grabbing hands and snapping jaws. Dirt and gravel flew. The cow's rig was upset, pinning two or three contestants beneath it. But Poork had broken clean away and started to run again—minus Tom, the cart, and all but a stub of his beautiful curling tail.

In the height of the confusion, the jackass brayed. That was the final touch of fun for the crowd. They yelled with delight and shouted, "Good pig!" "Good pig!" "Bully for the pig!"

Off along the track his angry pursuers followed at speed in a thick cloud of dust. But at length Poork espied a chink in the fence about the track, where a board was off near the ground, and dived for it. Under full headway with his hundred and eighty pounds, he carried away two more of the boards and issued among the wagons parked outside amidst such applause as had never before been called forth by any event at that cattle show.

Distanced for the moment, his two-footed pursuers had to scale the fence; and before they could again close in on him, Poork, going like a streak amidst or under the obstructing vehicles, gained that quarter of the grounds occupied by the sideshows and fakir booths called the "Midway," a popular feature of our county fairs.

Then active pursuers, coming up, nearly captured him there—had him by one leg for several struggling, squealing instants. But Poork pulled away from them and, seeing the open flap of the Fat Lady's tent, rushed in—without paying admission. Sad things are alleged to have happened therein. The Fat Lady screamed repeatedly. The tent yawed, shook perilously, and nearly collapsed. In fact, the Fat Lady subsequently sued the Agricultural Society and eventually, I believe, recovered damages for several tears in her yellow satin gown and the loss of a whole stack of her printed descriptive pamphlets.

Here Poork escaped by the back side of the tent and, being set upon by indignant fakirs with beer bottles and tent poles, butted headlong into the booth of Madame Homer, the Blind Fortune Teller, who also sued the society later, her complaint stating that a mad hog, followed by a motley mob of crazy, dirty fellows and dogs had pushed through her place, upsetting her table and causing the loss of her precious crystal ball from which she read the future.

Poork somehow got out of there and blundered directly into the Anaconda Charmer's tent, which abutted on that of Madame Homer, at the back. But perhaps he smelled the big serpent, for he rushed forth shrieking and with a wild burst of speed took refuge behind the crates of turkeys, geese, and other poultry ranged against the high fence of the fairgrounds. Here his panting followers believed they had him cornered and closed round him *en masse*. The wildest mix-up of all then followed. Every crate was overturned, for Poork dived behind the entire row of them. Twice he was caught by the legs, his defiant squeals rising above the cackle of the disturbed fowls. Here, too, he lost nearly all of his right ear to the bloody-minded bulldog. Yet once again that embattled pig slipped through them all and, emerging unexpectedly from the melee, dashed clean across the grounds.

So far everything had gone against the freedom-loving Poork. As he now neared the front of the fairgrounds, however, his luck turned; the entrance gate opened to admit a gala party arriving in a barge drawn by six horses. Past prancing animals and rattling barge wheels scooted Poork to liberty outside the gate before it could be closed against him.

Accounts vary as to where he went next, but apparently he crossed the lawn of a dwelling on the opposite side of the highway and his muzzle and tracks were found in a vegetable garden in the rear. Beyond was a pine woodland, and a straggling squad of pursuers trailed him there. But among the pines all trace of him was lost; neither boys nor dogs were able to find him. That was the last seen of Poork in this part of the country.

We thought that he might return home to Corbain or us after his first fright wore away, since it is well known that every pig carries a little compass in his head—or what answers for one—that will unerringly direct him to the place of his abode, even when transported to a distance of miles in a sack or basket.

But Poork did not come back. Evidently his hate and disgust for mankind ran deeper than the homing instinct. He seems to have taken to the depths of the forest and as time passed fled farther and farther away.

A railway extends from Montreal through the northern portions of Vermont and New Hampshire and down through Maine to Portland. It was on this line, nearly a year previously, that a stock train transporting eight or nine carloads of live hogs was derailed in a woody region near the Maine boundary. Several of the cars were overturned, and the frightened hogs strayed off into the woods. Exasperated trainmen and others were said to have chased hogs there for days afterwards, but numbers escaped to long distances and were never retaken.

There is pretty good evidence that Poork found and joined himself to certain of these fugitives, of which he became leader. From being occasionally shot at, they grew so terrified at the report of firearms—and perchance from having been wounded—that as time passed they ranged farther and farther north into that then unbroken wilderness along the Canadian border.

Eventually they appear to have found sanctuary in the never fully explored tract known to lumber men and timber cruisers as the Great Bog: a district as large as two or three townships, situated at the headwaters of the West Branch of the Penobscot and the Upper St. John River, to the northwest of Moosehead Lake.

Although conversant with the northern portions of Maine, I never visited the Great Bog, and my knowledge of it is derived wholly from what has been told me by my boyhood friend Willis Murch.

One winter Willis had made his camp on the eastern border of the bog to trap beaver, and so far as he knew there was then no settler's clearing within a hundred miles. He was therefore much astonished one morning—the 21st of November—to hear hogs squealing at no great distance. He had traps to look after that day, for a snowstorm was evidently pending; but later on he became so curious about those hogs that he took his gun and set off in the direction of the sounds he had heard. Soon he stumbled on something queer: nothing less than an immense heap of dry swamp grass. There was, Willis affirmed, enough of this to make a big load of hay. It lay in a circular pile on the ground, higher than his head and thirty or forty feet in diameter. At first he supposed it to be a stack of hay cut by some person; but while he stood viewing it, wondering who could have done it, he heard rustling noises within. He drew back a little and remained, watching for some moments. He now fancied that he could perceive movements inside the heap and thought he heard the heavy breathing of some animal concealed there. He cocked his gun, then, glancing about, found a clod, threw it into the pile, and gave a yell.

The effect was magical. The entire mass stirred at once and an instant later disgorged a drove of hogs that streamed away into the swamp, giving vent to wild "woofs" of surprise and terror while close in their rear scurried a shrieking mob of little pigs.

There were ten or twelve of the old hogs, one, apparently their leader, being of greater size than the others. This one faced about several times, as if guarding the rear, grunting savagely and casting foam clots from its tusks. Willis noted that it had but one ear and a mere stump of tail, not more than two inches long, that stood straight up from its rump. Could this wild boar be Poork?

Willis's account of that big heap of dry marsh grass in which the hogs were lying up in shelter from the storm at first appeared to border too much on the marvelous. That the hogs had collected it themselves seemed unlikely; but an acquaintance who made a business of raising hogs in western Kansas informs me that just before a blizzard he has seen a whole drove of hogs working busily for two or three hours, fetching mouthfuls of dry grass, corn butts, and Jimson weed and making a pile of sufficient size for forty hogs to nestle in, completely out of sight!

It was no part of Willis's plan to remain there after deep snows came. He left a week later without seeing anything further of the hogs, and probably we never would have heard more of them but for a French Canadian who subsequently worked at one of the Old Squire's logging camps. This woodsman, whom his mates called Glam Mercier, hailed from the parish of Grandes Coudées on the Chaudière River in the province of Quebec. Two winters previously he had been—so he told us—of a party of six hunters who had gone from his parish on a hog hunt over its boundary into Maine. They had heard of a band of wild hogs in the Great Bog and went there during the month of December, taking six long, narrow handsleds for drawing the pork from the woods to a point where they had teams waiting to smuggle it.

They finally surprised the hogs rooting beaver lily from the bed of one of the muddy ponds. Ice nearly a foot thick had already formed there; but owing to the water beneath having been drawn away by beaver hunters, there were wide open spaces where the ice had not settled down. The hogs had worked their way beneath the ice sheet and were evidently subsisting on the succulent tubers, wrenched up from the now shoal water and mud.

Where the ice had broken down there were cracks and crevasses, and through these the hog hunters were able to fire upon the terrified animals as they attempted to escape, still farther under the ice. But the ice erelong broke up about them, and the beleaguered hogs were at last brought to bay; they defended themselves valiantly.

The fiercest battle of all, Glam said, was waged with the leader of the band, a very large hog with only one ear and a bobbed tail—the last to succumb. This hog had tusks at least two inches long on each side of its jaws and would have weighed, he thought, five hundred pounds.

We had little doubt that this was our lost Poork. He had perished like a porcine hero, defending his clan, but not till he had enjoyed six years of complete freedom from the ruthless enslavers of his species.

The pork hunters reported that they had caught glimpses of a number of little pigs that escaped too far beneath the sheltering roof of ice to be captured. I have always cherished the hope—whimsical perhaps—that this was so and that somewhere in the far depths of that northern wilderness, a drove of gallant free descendants of old Poork still survives.

7

A Boyish Odyssey

WHEN I WAS A BOY AT OUR OLD FARM IN MAINE ONE of my daily tasks every fall—generally from the first of September to the last of October—was to boil a kettle of food for the pigs. That was not so small a chore as it might seem, for there were a good many pigs, never fewer than a dozen and sometimes as many as eighteen, and the kettle was huge. It held more than twenty bucketfuls. I believe the Old Squire had got it from a "potash," once situated at the Corners, where "sale-ratus" had been leeched from wood ashes. It was set in a brick arch out of doors at the far side of the farmyard.

My business with it was first to put in three bucketfuls of water from the farm pump, then to fetch wood and kindle a fire under it in the arch. While the kettle was heating and the water coming to a boil, I trundled a wheelbarrow to the field and dug a bushel of potatoes, which I washed off at the pump and put into the kettle. Next came ten or twelve large pumpkins, which I broke up with a maul before stowing them in the kettle on top of the potatoes. The pumpkins too had to be wheeled either from the field or from a rick of them piled at the far end of the west barn. In seasons when the pumpkins ripened well there would frequently be thirty cartloads of them in that long yellow rick. Then, when the heavy round cover of planks was pressed down on the broken pumpkins in the kettle, I had to tend the fire and keep the mess boiling smartly till it was well cooked and ready to be mashed with a small amount of cornmeal. For no Western corn came to us in those days, domestic animals were fattened largely on potatoes and pumpkins or squashes. In Maine we never raised corn enough so that we could feed liberally with it, and sometimes we lost our corn crop altogether owing to early frosts.

I was busy at the kettle one morning about the middle of September 1864, when a boy came running across the fields, "coo-ee-ing" eagerly. He was Edson Wilbur from the Wilbur farm, next beyond the Murch place, and his first words were, "My Aunt Emma Sweetzir wants me to go over to Sweden"—Maine—"and stay at her house while she goes to Franconia"—New Hampshire—"to find out about Uncle Ruel. She wrote to Mother last night and wanted me to be sure to come over today. But I've got to go afoot, and I don't want to go alone and stay there alone. She's going to be gone four or five days, and my folks said I might ask you to go with me."

Ned's Aunt Emma and his Uncle Ruel, it should be said, had had domestic difficulties; Uncle Ruel, who appears to have been a handsome but flighty sort of man too much concerned with his own good looks, had abandoned his family in quite an improper manner, and his wife, feeling greatly aggrieved at his behavior, was determined to find him. Matters indeed had gone so far between them that they had disputed over the ownership of their domestic goods and furniture, each claiming a part—all of which was rather scandalous, though at the time neither Ned nor I (we were each only about thirteen years old) knew much about the affair.

Boylike I wanted to go; it would be a fine change from steady chores at home. I hope I wasn't influenced by a desire to escape my daily job at the pig's kettle, but I am afraid I was—at least in part. I did not believe that my folks would let me go; but after I had replenished the fire under the kettle, Ned and I ran off to ask the Old Squire, who was at work with Addison and Halstead in the farther field.

He shook his head at first, as I had expected him to do, but Ned pleaded with him and, getting hold of his hand, hung on so long that finally the old gentleman said to me, "You go ask your grandmother. If she says you may go, I am willing."

Thereupon we ran to the house to coax Grandmother Ruth—a harder task. "Humph!" she said at first. "I guess not."

But Ned pleaded in turn with her, and at last he got hold of her hand too while I looked on imploringly. Ned was a great boy for coaxing; he hung on to her hand and teased so long that at last the old lady yielded and went to fetch my Sunday suit, cap, and shoes. But before letting me go, she took me aside by the arm and, leading me into the dairy, said, "Now you know that Edson is a very hasty, impulsive boy. When you are off with him you must always be cautious and not get drawn into trouble." And I promised with exuberant gratitude!

She put up a lunch for me to eat on the way, and we two boys set off as happy and frolicsome as a couple of young dogs. We did not leave the Wilbur farm, however, till afternoon, for Ned had preparations to make. Since the distance to his Aunt Emma's place in Sweden was nineteen miles, his father hitched up and drove us for the first ten. Ned had never before visited Sweden, in fact he had never seen his Uncle Ruel; and after Mr. Wilbur set us down, we hurried on foot, stopping only to study guide boards and inquire our way at farmhouses, for we were anxious not to get lost in that strange new country.

Much of the way was through forest, and once we thought we saw a bear in the underbrush; but finally, just at sunset, rather tired and footsore, we reached the farm where Ned's aunt lived. I was astonished to find his Aunt Emma so young; she looked scarcely older than my cousin Theodora at the Old Squire's, who was only fourteen years old. Aunt Emma's eyes looked as if she had been crying a great deal, and there was a baby boy, whom she called Ruley, not more than a year old.

The house, a two-story structure that Ned said had once been a tavern, was a poor old place with neglected buildings. I recollect feeling a little homesick as night came on. We had only cornmeal mush for our supper, of which we partook by the dim light of a tallow candle. While we were eating, Ned's aunt told us what to do and what to care for during her absence. There were two cows to be milked night and morning, a pig to be fed on boiled potatoes, nine hens to watch, and eleven turkeys to be driven in at night from the fields where they were searching grasshoppers for a livelihood. Foxes and owls were a menace there and had already taken much of the poultry. There was a patch of potatoes that Ned's aunt asked us to dig if we had time and also a little field of corn, the ears of which she wanted us to gather, husk, and spread to dry on the floor of one of the empty rooms upstairs. She also mentioned other chores, cares, and cautions, the most of which I forgot, I was so sleepy.

Finally Ned and I asked whether we could go to bed, and his aunt showed us up the bare, steep stairs to a front room with two windows overlooking the yard and the road past the house. I remember only that the bed seemed much harder than mine at home, and that just as we were going to sleep we heard Ned's aunt crying in the next room. Why she was crying puzzled us; we couldn't imagine what ailed her. That is about all I remembered till I heard her out in the yard early the next morning, hitching up her little black horse to an old wagon, both shafts of which were repaired with bits of rope. Little Ruley was lying wrapped up on the wagon seat. Evidently Ned's aunt was about to set off; she wore a hat with roses on it and had donned a worn old velvet cloak, for the morning was frosty and cold.

We dressed in great haste and ran downstairs, and by the looks of her eyes we knew that she had been crying again. She told us what we were to eat while she was away. There was salt pork, she said, in a barrel down in the cellar, and cornmeal in a chest in the pantry. The hens would lay eggs, which we could fry with the pork. We could make cornmeal mush and bake "bannocks," and she told us how to do it. There were potatoes out in the field that we could roast in the oven or boil. Then there were milk and cream; after we had milked the cows, we were to set the milk in pans down cellar for the cream to rise. We should have to boil potatoes to mix with the skim milk for the pig, and she showed us the skimmer and the cream pot. We could churn, she said, and get butter, but she guessed we had better not try that. Her last words to us as she drove away were not on any account to leave and go home till she had returned. "And don't let the foxes get my turkeys!" she called back to us from the road.

Left to ourselves, we got pails from the pantry and went off to the old barn, which stood some way from the house, to milk the two cows. What we didn't know was that one of them milked easily and that the other milked painfully hard and also kicked. We took our choice at a venture, and by good luck I got the easy, gentle one—much to Ned's disgust; he had a dreadful time milking that kicking cow, and I just sat at mine and laughed. Afterward we cooked breakfast of a sort and then went to our job of harvesting corn at the little field near the woods. But we discovered that it was fast being harvested ahead of us; field and fence were swarming with squirrels—gray ones, red ones, and striped ones—all busy gathering their winter stores. The whole place was chittering with them.

"By jiminy! This will never do!" Ned exclaimed. "They'll carry off all of Aunt Emma's corn."

I remembered seeing a gun standing behind the door leading to the stairway; a boy generally has a quick eye for a gun. We ran to look at it. Apparently it was a good, single-barreled piece and probably belonged to Ned's vagrant Uncle Ruel.

"I think we ought to shoot those squirrels," Ned said.

I was doubtful and remembered my promise to Grandmother Ruth. But Ned began searching for ammunition, and we finally found some in an old coffeepot set far back on the top shelf in the pantry— about a pound of coarse black powder, a box containing fine bird shot no larger than turnip seed, and a box of little brass percussion caps. Finding that bonanza quite dispelled all my thoughts of caution.

We sallied forth with the gun, and, oh, didn't we have a great time that day blazing away at the squirrels, taking turns firing! If we stood within ten yards of them, the bird shot was very effective.

It would have been as well perhaps if we had fallen to work harvesting instead of shooting, for the next morning there were nearly as many squirrels there as ever. Next day too was Sunday, but after some earnest consideration Ned said that saving Aunt Emma's corn was plainly a "work of necessity." Accordingly we set about it with a bushel basket and a wheelbarrow, and before night we had most of what the squirrels had left safe inside the old barn, ready to husk.

Monday it rained for a part of the day, but we husked the corn and spread the ears in an empty room upstairs adjoining the room in which we slept. That night loud outcries from the poultry at the barn wakened us. We imagined that foxes had got in or else that a thief had come. Not quite daring to go out, we fired the gun from one of the back windows to frighten off the marauder. The moon shone bright, but we saw no one.

In the morning, however, two of the turkeys were missing—a loss that afflicted us deeply, particularly Ned. "What will Aunt Emma say?" he exclaimed at intervals all day.

I burned my wrist in an effort to make mush that morning; the hot stuff flew up suddenly from the kettle. Ned too had his face spattered with hot fat while he was trying to fry eggs. But we were learning a good deal every meal we prepared.

That day we began to harvest the potatoes and dug out two bushels, but if there is any kind of farm work a boy of twelve dislikes more than another, it is to dig potatoes from a tough, grassy field. After an hour or two Ned said he felt it was our duty to watch those nine remaining turkeys more closely. I agreed with him at once, and leaving our hoes in the field, we got the gun and spent most of the day rounding up those turkeys when they wandered too near the edge of the woods. There was a great deal of forest thereabouts, and no neighbors lived within half a mile or more.

Next day was wet again, much too wet to dig potatoes! We did the chores at the barn, boiled a squash for the pig, skimmed milk, cooked, and watched the turkeys. But despite our vigils another turkey disappeared during the afternoon. Ned's grief was now quite poignant. "Oh, what will Aunt Emma think of us?" he cried. The woe of the unfaithful steward was as nothing compared with that of poor Ned! After much anxious thought we shut the turkeys up in the barn and decided to feed them on boiled potatoes and skimmed milk.

All the next day we were looking for Ned's aunt to return, for this was the fifth day since she had left us. It seemed to me that she had been gone a month! We tidied up and rehearsed what we should say to her about the turkeys, but we couldn't make our conduct look like much except neglect, word the matter as we would. She did not come during the day, but we thought she might arrive late in the evening. Ned said we would not fasten the outside door as usual, and we finally fell asleep upstairs with it unfastened.

Late in the night a great noise below waked us. "She's come!" Ned exclaimed and, jumping up, began to dress in haste so as to go downstairs.

But I went to the window to look out, for I had heard sounds in the yard. The moon had risen and was shining bright. There was a span of white horses harnessed to a long wagon or cart backed up near the door, and as I looked down someone hauled a bureau that had stood in the sitting room out over the doorsteps and with difficulty lifted it into the wagon. I could see chairs and rolls of bedding in the cart.

"Ned," I whispered excitedly, "come here! That isn't your Aunt Emma! It's a man, and he's stealing things from the house!"

Ned was astonished. "It's a burglar!" he whispered. "What shall we do?"

For a few moments we kept very still and watched. Plainly a robber was at work. A terrible noise began below; the rascal was tearing down the stovepipe and dragging the stove to the door. Ned grew wildly excited. "Oh, he's getting all Aunt Emma's things! We mustn't let him!" he whispered.

I was alarmed for our own safety. "Suppose he will come upstairs?" I asked.

"Of course he will!" said Ned, who was so excited that he shook. "We must shoot him! We must shoot him!" he cried and grabbed the gun, which we had taken up to bed with us every night.

"But that bird shot would only make him mad!" I remonstrated. "Don't, Ned, don't!"

"But he's getting all poor Aunt Emma's things!" exclaimed Ned, nearly beside himself. "He thinks nobody's here! Let's shoot at him!"

Ned raised the window, and I tiptoed to the door to make sure it was bolted.

"Here, you scamp! What are you doing there? You clear out!" Ned cried down, but he was so frightened that his voice was a mere childish squeak.

The man, who was lifting the stove into the cart, stopped short and stared up at the window; then he laughed. "How did you get up there, sonny?" he exclaimed.

"None of your business!" Ned retorted. "You clear out or I'll shoot ye!"

The fellow laughed again. "Oh, I guess you wouldn't hurt anybody," he replied and began heaving at the stove again.

Ned cocked the gun and whispered, "I'll scare him! It'll drive him off."

"Don't fire right at him," I urged, remembering Grandmother Ruth's cautions about Ned. "Fire over his head or into the ground."

Ned shoved out the gun and let drive. The report was followed instantly by a yell below, then another and another!

The horses started violently. Stove and man tumbled out at the rear end of the cart onto the doorstep, and then we heard the fellow groaning, "Oh, I'm shot! Oh, I'm killed! My head's all shot to pieces!"

Where Ned thought he had pointed the gun isn't clear. I imagine he didn't know. If we were frightened before, we were terrified now. "You've killed him!" I whispered.

"He'd no business to be robbing then!" cried Ned stoutly.

"He will kill us if he's got strength enough left," I said quaveringly.

"Let's load the gun again," muttered Ned, and then by the faint moonlight in the room we put in another charge, a big one, listening all the while.

The wounded intruder had not gone away. He was now in the house. We could still hear him groaning. At length we mustered courage to unbolt the door and go softly downstairs, holding the gun ready for emergencies. Apparently the scamp was on the bed in a back room next to the kitchen. He was moaning distressfully.

We peeped in. Hearing us moving, the fellow suddenly cried out to us to get a doctor. "Whoever you be, go get a doctor!" he entreated. "Go to Lovell Village and get Dr. French! Tell him to come to Ruel Sweetzir's place and come quick. Tell him Ruel Sweetzir's been shot!"

We drew back, horror struck. "Ned, that's your uncle! You've shot your Uncle Ruel!" I cried in a whisper.

Ned stood speechless.

"Oh, do hurry and get Dr. French!" the distressed voice moaned again from the bedroom.

We stole out limply into the yard. The horses with the cart were now across the road, browsing among the bushes. Without stopping to unload the chairs and bedding, we mounted the driver's seat and drove off along the road at a venture, for we had not the slightest idea where Lovell Village was; we were so upset we did not half know what we were about.

Day broke, and it soon grew light. The horses were slow old beasts; it was nearly impossible to make them trot. As it chanced, we went two or three miles astray before coming to a guide board with "Lovell Village" on it and an index finger pointing the way. We turned about, made three turns more, and afterward were as good as lost for fully an hour, since at the two farmhouses where we called to inquire everyone appeared to be either asleep or gone away. At last we overtook a girl who told us she was going to Lovell Village. Ned coaxed her to ride with us, and finally we reached Dr. French's house, but not until nearly nine o'clock.

The doctor was busy with a patient who had broken her arm, but he said he would come in an hour. We then started to drive our tired team back to Uncle Ruel's, but we did not arrive till almost noon. On entering the yard the first thing we saw was the little black horse and wagon that Ned's aunt had driven away. She had just returned.

Ned rushed in, and I followed. The scene in the little back bedroom may have been one to bring joy to the angels, but hardly to us! Ned's aunt was embracing and kissing Uncle Ruel and sobbing over him, calling him her "dear" and her "poor darling," trying to wipe the dried blood from his face and imploring him to get well and never leave her again! "Oh my darling Ruley!" she cried. "I forgive you all! Only say you will never run away again!"

Hearing us at the door, Ned's aunt turned like a tigress and screamed, "Oh you wicked, wicked boys! See what you've done! See what you've done! Look at my poor Ruley's face! You've shot him! You've shot him. Oh, I hate you! I never want to set eyes on you again!"

Ned caught his breath and looked at me, and I looked at Ned. Instinctively we backed off and out into the yard, then we beat a retreat to the barn. Just then the doctor drove up and went in, and after a dreadful, silent while we stole back to the door.

At last the doctor came out with his little trunk and went to his buggy. Ned rushed to him. "Oh doctor, will he die?"

Dr. French laughed. "Oh, no, not yet awhile," he said.

Ned tried to seize his hand to ask more.

"Oh, no," the doctor continued, seeing our agitation. "Don't worry. I've picked out about twenty of those little shot from the skin of his face and his scalp. But he will soon be all right. He could get up and be

out now if he had a mind to," he added with no great amount of sympathy. "I guess you have spoiled his good looks for the present," he said as he drove off.

It is probable that the doctor knew something of his patient's antecedents.

We left the cart and the furniture in the door yard, but put the tired horses into the barn and gave them hay. We also let out the turkeys to eat grasshoppers, fed the pig, and turned out the cows. Afterward we watched the house awhile rather anxiously; we were hungry, for we had eaten nothing since the afternoon before. Within much tearful affection was still outpouring, and the prospect for food was bad.

We did not quite dare to go in, and after hanging round awhile longer Ned suddenly threw up his head and cried, "Let's go home!"

That proposal was most welcome to me. We set off at a run, but stopped whenever we saw blackberries by the roadside to partake of them. A man in a wagon overtook us and gave us a lift as far as Waterford. I had twenty-five cents, and at the grocery there we invested largely in crackers and cheese. We hastened on, stopping only for an occasional drink at wayside brooks, and we finally reached our home neighborhood by half past six that evening.

I went in at the Wilburs' with Ned to help him tell the story of our Odyssey. His parents were much concerned at first, but after hearing what Dr. French had said, Mr. Wilbur suddenly rose with a snort and went out to do his chores. "I hope this will be a lesson to that good-for-nothing loafer to stay at home and behave himself!" he muttered. I supposed he meant Ned's Uncle Ruel.

Then I hastened home to tell the story there, where it created quite as much of a sensation. The Old Squire questioned me rather closely about the shooting and also about the shot. Indeed, he was so solicitous lest I might be involved with Ned in a homicide that he and Addison drove over to Sweden the next forenoon to investigate the matter.

During the afternoon they returned, smiling. As nearly as they had been able to learn, Ned's recreant uncle, hearing that his young wife was out looking for him at Franconia, had seized the opportunity to come home between days and capture the household furniture! But all was now condoned, forgiven, made up. The dove of affection had flown back, and that bare old house was joyful with the flutter of its happy wings. The truant husband was up and about, but Addison said that his face looked as if he had had smallpox.

We heard a year afterward that he was considerably pitted—little blue pits—and that Ned's aunt felt very bad about it! Still it's an "ill wind which blows no man good," and the reduction of his handsomeness may have been for the best. At least, we never heard of any further infelicity at the Sweetzir farm.

8

The Downfall of Master Lurvey

The New Schoolmaster

THE WINTER SCHOOL AT THE OLD SQUIRE'S WAS TO begin on Monday following Thanksgiving, and for several weeks our interest and attention had centered about the old red schoolhouse down at the forks of the road leading to the Corners.

They have built a new schoolhouse there now in place of the large old red one—a neat, modern structure, painted white, with new patent desks and chairs, also adjustable blackboards and globe; and there are portraits of Washington, Lincoln, Lafayette, and Ben Franklin on the walls. It is a great improvement; everyone says so. Yet I cannot help missing the old red one where I went to school that first winter after coming to Maine.

The day they tore the old house down I really felt quite sad. It does not seem like the same place there now, and memory runs back somewhat regretfully, as I pass to those old eventful winter terms under Master Joel Pierson, Master Cummings, Master French, and Ellen's fiancé, young Thomas Jefferson Cobb, who was drowned in the Kennebec. Excellent teachers they were; possibly there are as good instructors now, but I cannot help doubting it.

We set great store by our winter school then, and so would boys and girls at present, if they had but ten weeks a year—for only girls and little boys attended the summer school. Throughout the entire year we doted on that coming winter term of school.

Really, we made remarkable progress; those old masters pushed us lovingly on. In one winter, when thirteen, my cousin Addison mastered Greenleaf's *National Arithmetic* and could perform every example in it, but to do this he had worked morning and evening as well as during school hours. Those teachers possessed the gift of firing our hearts with an ambition to learn. How did they do it? Their own hearts were in it. To this day I feel the thrill of Master Pierson's enthusiasm and his faith in us, as he laid out long lessons and somehow made us feel sure that we could learn them. What a true friend he was! I take off my hat reverently to his memory.

They were all good teachers, everyone—but no, there was an exception. We did have one poor teacher; yes, he was a bad teacher. It came about in a singular way. It was "the year rum reigned in Number Eleven"—for that was the way we always referred to it. That winter— the winter of 1864–65—there was a strange state of things at the old schoolhouse. I shall have to explain it a little.

In Maine at that time, each and every country school district governed itself and managed its own affairs. A school meeting of the legal residents of the district was held every spring to elect a school agent, bid off teachers' board, fuel, and such. The agent chosen hired the teachers and was in charge of the school property. The day of centralism and supervisors was not yet. In the matter of its school business every district was a small republic, largely independent of the town or county in which it was situated.

The system had its advantages, also a few disadvantages. It kept the people keenly alive to the interests of their school. An abuse of it was the tendency on the part of agents, sometimes, to hire teachers in whom they were personally interested from kinship or otherwise. But as a rule, there was an honest intent on the part of the agent to get the best teachers he could for the money.

In Number Eleven harmony had prevailed for years. There had been few dissensions until the spring of 1864. Then an element of discord and disorder entered, and I must admit that the cause of it was the state liquor law.

Now the "Maine Law," so called, of 1851 has done an untold amount of good. It would be indeed strange, however, if some abuses had not attended its enforcement. The law sometimes fomented animosity and set not only school districts but whole towns by the ears. Yet there are many who hold that intemperance is an evil so terrible that it is better to set people by the ears than to ignore it—but we need not go into that here.

Three-fourths of the families, or heads of families, in Number Eleven were temperate, law-abiding citizens, but we had one bad man among us.

For some reason nature, in fashioning men, does not always produce a good citizen. It must needs be owned that there are many bad jobs, and one of the worst of these was our neighbor, Tibbetts, out at the Corners. Tibbetts was one of those men who their lives long drag the community downhill. He sold rum in defiance of the state law, and he manufactured the rum himself; that is to say, he made four barrels from one by the addition of substances deleterious to the human organism. In a small and mean way he was a gambler and his "store" a resort for such as could be drawn into card games, hustling, and dicing.

Personally he was a heavyset, wheezy man, much bloated from intemperance, red-faced, repulsive, yet possessed of strong vitality and not a little energy, abetted by great craftiness.

At first thought one might say that such a person would have very little influence in any average community and that it ought not to be difficult to suppress him. But in a state with a strict liquor law such a man is often able to enlist strong support.

During the winter of 1863–64, Tibbetts's place was the scene of a brawl, ending in a manslaughter and altogether became so scandalous that the Old Squire felt it incumbent on him to enforce the law, with the result that Tibbetts was fined one hundred dollars and costs.

It followed, of course, that such a man would seek to be revenged, and the way Tibbetts took to spite us was to get control of the school district. Not that he cared the least for the welfare of the school. It was purely for revenge, and he went about this with a cunning worthy of a better object.

Near his grocery at the Corners, he owned two ramshackle old houses, and in these he contrived to domicile, as tenants, two shiftless families that would do his bidding. He had also a son, Jerry Tibbetts, recently arrived at the age of twenty-one, who though absent from home still retained a residence there as a voter. That winter, too, he hired a man of his own stamp to tend store for him and had the fellow fetch his trunk and make his legal residence at the Corners.

Thus, before we were aware, he secured a majority in the school meeting of March 1864 and elected a man of his own choosing, named Simeon Glinds, as school agent. There were but eighteen legal voters in the district, and as six of them were opponents of the Maine Law— two of them very intemperate—Tibbetts was able to get his man elected. Glinds was one of his rum debtors.

When we young folks at the Old Squire's learned what had happened at the school meeting, we were both angry and alarmed. Particularly Addison, Theodora, and Ellen, and our two young neighbors, Katherine and Thomas Edwards. These five were the best scholars in the district and had now but a few years more to attend school.

Before this, for two winters, the school had been taught by Master Pierson, a talented young man who was working his way through college. He excelled in algebra and English grammar. He hung the walls of the old schoolhouse with maps and charts of his own and brought with him a cabinet organ, also his own property.

To secure the services of such a teacher, twenty-seven dollars per month—large wages then—were paid, with board. But never before had the school made such progress; in two winters Number Eleven came to rank first in the town.

Hence we were all very desirous of having Master Pierson returned the following winter, and when it was learned that Glinds had been elected agent, a petition to this effect (bearing the names of forty out of forty-nine of the scholars in the district) was presented to Glinds.

On reading it Glinds seemed confused but made no reply, nor could we learn anything as to his intentions if he had any; but Tibbetts gave out that no more high-priced teachers would be hired. The excuse was "economy," so often the pretext of those who wish to do wrong.

We knew from this that Master Pierson was lost to us and felt bad over it. Theodora, Ellen, and Kate Edwards actually shed tears of regret and resentment.

Being greatly interested, we made frequent inquiries, but during that whole season, till near Thanksgiving, we could learn nothing as to whom that old sot at the Corners meant to hire as our teacher. Tibbetts was gratifying his malice. Well he knew how he could best do so.

Proper care was not given the schoolhouse for the next two seasons. Agent Glinds and Tibbetts did not deem such matters worthy of attention. In consequence there was diphtheria among the small pupils during the summer term of 1865, which the physician who attended them pronounced due to the bad sanitary conditions there.

Shortly before Thanksgiving a rumor reached us that the new schoolmaster's name was Samuel Lurvey and that he hailed from Lurvey's Mills, ten or eleven miles from us. Some of the young folks had seen him. He was about twenty-one, they said, a large, strong young man, the son of "old Zack Lurvey," the owner of the lumber mills. Those who knew him did not speak very highly of him, but they said that he had attended the village academy for two years and that his father wished him to teach.

Everyone in that county knew old Zack Lurvey, an illiterate man of violent temper who had become wealthy in the lumber business. It was said of him that, being unable to read or write, he kept his accounts with kernels of corn and beans of different colors on the attic floor of his house, but that no one ever got the better of him in business matters.

To those who are interested in heredity, I may add here that this Lurvey's second wife, our new master's mother, had been a coarse servant girl, whom old Zack met in a Portland tavern. While this ought not to be mentioned against the son, it may even show an apology for him, since his boyhood at home was amidst rude, rough associations—where violent outbursts of temper and bad language were of daily occurrence.

But old Zack had sent his son to the academy and was now determined that he should "keep school." It transpired afterward that he had a private understanding with Tibbetts to hire Samuel; Lurvey senior was not adverse to a glass of rum at times himself.

Young Master Lurvey was to be paid seventeen dollars per month; he would have been dear at less. At Lurvey's Mills municipal affairs went on as old Zack dictated; in a small way he was an adroit politician and knew how to manage people. Even before our school began a curious instance of his craftiness showed itself.

Saturday afternoon after Thanksgiving, Addison and I, with my cousin Halstead, were cutting up turnips and beets for the young cattle at the west barn when we heard bells, and, looking out, saw that an elderly man driving a spirited chestnut horse with a new sleigh and bearskin robes had come up the lane. The man got out and hitched his horse to a post, and we noticed that he tested the ring in the post carefully.

"That looks like old Zack Lurvey, our new master's father," whispered Addison. "I wonder what he's come for?"

Lurvey Senior glanced at the house, then came to the open barn door, nodded, and inquired for the Old Squire, who was away from home that day. He did not seem greatly disappointed, looked at our livestock, asked how we fed them, and talked for some time, addressing himself mostly to Addison.

"What think o' that colt o' mine, young man?" he at length said to him.

"He's a handsome one," replied Addison.

"Yes, he is a good colt, and he's a pretty stepper, too," continued our visitor. "Never drawed rein over a hoss I liked better. Hop in and let me show ye how he handles a sleigh."

Addison was a little surprised, but he buttoned up his coat and got in the sleigh beside the owner of the colt, who turned and drove down the lane and out onto the road at a fine pace.

As much as half an hour passed before they came back to the foot of the lane, where our caller put Addison down and drove away. The latter came back to the barn, but seemed preoccupied; he was smiling covertly.

"How did you like the 'stepper?'" I asked him.

"Oh very well," he said absently. But later in the winter he told us what had passed.

It would appear that Lurvey Senior had learned that Addison was the most advanced scholar in the school district and the boy who had most influence. After "talking horse" awhile, he turned the conversation to school matters and the subject of his son, soon to be our teacher. Very adroitly he sounded Addison as to his goodwill toward him.

"Now, my Sam's all right on book-larnin', I guess," he remarked, "but he's young and never teached before and he may have some ways that some of ye, over here, may not quite take to at fust." (It would seem that old Zack was not blind to certain of his son's traits and deficiencies.)

"Now I'm anxious to have him git through all right," Lurvey Senior continued. "I can see that you know 'bout how a school oughter be run, and I can see that ef a boy like you went in fer the master and stood up fer him, stiff and strong, 'twould make a big difference with the other scholars. An' you can see, yerself, that 'twill be better to stand by him and all pull together fer a good school than to pull apart. So I ax ye, as a favor, to go in for my Sam, good and solid and," lowering his voice, "I never axes anybuddy to help me for nothing. Here's a nice new five-dollar bill ter slip into yer vest pocket."

Addison had already begun to mistrust what was coming. He was a good deal taken aback, nonetheless, but gathered his wits to extricate himself from a position so equivocal and delicate; and he got out of it pretty well.

"Oh, I want a good school, Mr. Lurvey," he said. "I'll help the master in every way I can to make the school a success. I like money, too, Mr. Lurvey. I would be glad of that five dollars. Still, as I do not yet know how much I may be able to help him, I would not like to take this beforehand. If I find that I have been of any real service to your son, at the close of the school, I will remind you of this."

Old Zack was not wholly satisfied. It was not what he wanted. He said no more, however; but he was much too keen a man not to form a favorable opinion of Addison's sagacity, and he always kept him in mind. Several years later, quite unexpectedly, he made him a proposition to take charge of a wood pulp manufacturing business in which he had embarked.

Peradventure, old Zack's influence had assisted his son in passing his examination before a member of the town school committee. There was much wonder as to this later in the winter. Then, however, we knew very little of our new master save by hearsay, and hoped to have a good school. Theodora, I remember, was feverishly anxious as to this. On Saturday evening before school began on Monday, there was a general muster of our school books from the "book cupboard." Theodora even tried some of the hardest examples in the *National Arithmetic*, which she had been able to perform at the close of school the winter before.

"Oh dear, it seems as if I had forgotten everything I ever knew!" she lamented. "I cannot get these right!"

"It will all come back to you, Doad, after a day or two at school," said Addison to comfort her. But she was far from reassured.

"If I have forgotten how to do this sum in equation of payments, when I worked it so many times last winter, it's of no use for me to study at all!" she declared disconsolately. "I cannot do it now to save my life!"

"Doad, you've fed chickens too long this summer. Your head has weakened!" cried Halstead to hector her; but he had himself forgotten how far he had advanced in his own arithmetic and even did not know his own book, by sight!

In order to lengthen the winter school, the Old Squire had, long before, made a standing offer to the district to board the master at the nominal sum of one dollar per week, if no one else wished to board him at that rate. Master Pierson had been so popular that, expecting he would return, the Batchelder family in the district had bid off the board at ninety-five cents to have him with them evenings. But now, on Saturday, Mrs. Batchelder, hearing who was to teach, called and asked us to board the master. Not wholly pleased, the Old Squire and Gram assented, and the "east chamber" was put in order. He was expected Sunday evening but did not arrive.

How well I recall that Monday morning and our setting off for school!

According to former law and custom, the old schoolhouse stood at the geographical center of the school district, at a place where three roads diverged, one to the Corners half a mile away, one to the Old Squire's farm and our neighbors beyond us, and the third to the Darnley neighborhood.

It was a cloudy morning; snow had fallen during the night, but by eight o'clock a blithe smoke was rising from the schoolhouse chimney, and from that time on till nine, groups of the scholars could be seen approaching along all three roads. Some had even gone before eight, Newman Darnley and Alfred Batchelder among the number, in order to secure the best seats. There were benches and desks for about fifty pupils, placed in four rows opposite the teacher's higher desk, with one much longer seat on each side, flanking the floor and stove. On either hand of the teacher's desk was an enclosed "cuddy," one for the girls' wraps, the other for the boys' caps, and the water pail and dipper. The outer door was also at the right of the teacher's desk, between it and the boys' cuddy.

The boys occupied two rows of seats and one of the long seats on the north side of the schoolhouse, and the girls an equal number on the south side. The back seat was the place of honor and seniority, and the next seat, most preferred, was the long seat flanking the floor and stove.

There were five of us from the Old Squire's that morning. Halstead, however, had gone on in advance. As the distance was considerable and the road snowy, we carried a lunch basket that was generally in charge of Theodora. Katherine and Thomas Edwards had come to go with us, also Edwin and Elsie Wilbur and the two Murch boys, Willis and Ben, who lived farther along our road. Octavia Sylvester and Adriana Darnley, Newman's sister, joined us near the schoolhouse door.

A tremendous hubbub of voices was heard inside. Disputes concerning seats were running high. Our Halstead, Alfred Batchelder, and Billy Glinds had got possession of the long seat on the boys' side and were holding it against all comers. Newman Darnley and Absum Glinds were threatening to eject them. A scuffle appeared certain. Several other disputes were passing the argument stage.

Altogether forty-seven scholars had arrived. Thomas and I pushed for a bench next to the back seat, got into it, and put our books on the desk in sign of possession. We dared not leave it, however, and sat there for some time holding the fort.

It was past nine o'clock, and thus far no one of us had seen or heard anything of the new teacher; but now suddenly above the din of contention a jingle of bells was heard outside, and Ned Wilbur cried, "The master's coming! Here he is!"

A lively scramble followed, and those who had not secured seats took what was left, grumbling angrily; but the most of us had our eyes fixed on the door.

It opened and the new master walked in.

"The Important Man"

EVERY EYE was on him. Truth to say, he was a handsome fellow, nearly six feet tall, of fine form and strong. His face was fresh and ruddy, his hair abundant, curly, and black. On his upper lip a faint black mustache was beginning to show and gave him a youthful appearance, despite his size and height.

Handsome was the word for him, externally at least, and shy looks of admiration showed on the faces of Adriana, Octavia, and other large girls in the back seat. Hitherto our schoolmasters had not been remarkable for good looks, but this was a handsome one. He wore a stylish dark suit and was of the type of young men who set off their clothes well.

First impressions are sometimes quite erroneous, but it seemed to us boys that his glance around was hard and morose. He appeared sullen and disdainful, as if displeased at the start; and his first words were, as he laid his books and a very large ruler on the desk, "I don't want to hear another such a noise when I come into this house. If I do, there'll be trouble for somebody."

It was not a gracious remark to open school with, but there was justice in it; the most of us felt it so. The noise had been outrageous, but it was still enough now. He began to take off his overcoat, and thereupon Addison went down to the desk, bade him good morning, and showed him the two pegs always reserved for the master's hat and coat. "We do not often have such a noise," Addison then said apologetically, as he took his seat.

It was but common courtesy to a stranger in our schoolhouse, but the new master stared at Addison in a suspicious way, without even saying "good morning" in response. But no doubt he was somewhat uncertain, or embarrassed, and too much on his guard. He had just come from an interview with Tibbetts and Glinds, and it is likely that the rum seller had not given many of us a good character.

After removing his coat, Master Lurvey advanced to the stove and, holding his hands to the warmth, ran his eyes slowly around the room again.

"Well, you all mean to know me the next time you see me, I guess," he said at length. "You seem to like the looks of me, by the way you stare."

No doubt we were all watching him rather more attentively than true politeness warrants. With this hint most of the scholars took up their books.

"Oh, you needn't begin to study just yet," he said. "I've got something to say to ye before we begin lessons."

Thereupon we laid our books down and tried to sit without looking at our new master, since he resented our regards. He stepped up behind his desk, took up his ruler, and began in a set tone of voice to make us an address, which, evidently, he had thought over in advance.

"I don't doubt," he went on after a little pause, "that you all want to have a good school. I want you to have a good school, too. The first thing to have is good order. I shall make such rules as I think you ought to have, and when I make a rule I expect you all to obey it prompt—promptly," he added.

"If any boy here thinks he can get around a rule I make, he will find out his mistake quick. Order is the first thing, and order I'll have if I have to ferule ten boys a day."

"When I give out a lesson, too, I expect that it will be learned, right off, that day. I shall give only such lessons as I think suitable.

"I shall not expect that you will all be running to me to do sums for you in school hours, or here in the schoolroom. I've seen enough of that sort of thing. It isn't the teacher's business to do hard sums in school hours. If you have hard sums that you cannot do, after you have tried them for two or three days, fetch them to me at night, when school is dismissed. If I have time, I'll take them home with me and do them for you, and will hand them to you done on paper. Then I shall expect you to look them over and explain them to the others. But don't you think that I have come here to do hard sums for you all the time, for I haven't. I'm here to give you your lessons and hear them."

It would be difficult to describe the harsh and defiant tone in which these remarks were delivered to us. It was evident that the new master was resolved to govern us strictly and also that he had a distaste for hard sums.

"Generally," he continued, after pausing for a while to give his words time to take effect in our minds, "generally I shall have you read in the Testament, mornings, and I want you to read up loud and plain. But this morning I will read part of a chapter myself, so you can see how I want you to read."

He then took a Testament from his books and read to us a portion of the fifth chapter of John, wherein is described the miracle of healing the impotent man. He read loud and slow, with long pauses. We noticed that he pronounced the word *impotent* as *important*. Many of the forty or more pupils probably did not know the difference. I recall being in doubt myself, yet it occurred to me that I had never heard of an "important man" in the Gospels.

The mistake would probably have passed as a slip of the tongue, but our young instructor saw fit to comment on what he had read, after he closed the book. "You all see," he said, "that this was an *important* man. That's why so much is said about him. That's why he was healed. He was a very *important* man."

I knew now that something was wrong and glanced at Theodora. She blushed and sat looking very uncomfortable. I saw her steal a look toward Addison, but that pledged ally of the schoolmaster was gazing steadfastly at his hands. A curious kind of hush pervaded the room.

The master put away his Testament and looked around on us again. "You heard me read," he remarked. "That's the way I want you to read. Readin' is the most important thing in school. So first of all this morning, I'm going to call out the class with the *Fifth Reader*. All who read in the *Fifth Reader* come to the front seats. I want to see what kind of readers you are, and whether you know the rules of reading or not."

As many as twenty of us found our readers and arranged ourselves on the front seats, facing the floor and the master's desk.

"I want to hear one of you read," he said. "This young lady right in front of me—she looks as if she thought she could read. I'll hear her."

He opened the reader to a selection, called "A Plea for Blennerhassett," and named the page. "Read the first section," he said.

The young lady whom he had selected chanced to be Katherine Edwards, one of the best readers in the school. She flushed a little at being addressed in a manner so pointed but immediately complied with the request, reading fluently and well, as any good reader would.

"There! That's about what I thought. Just about what I expected," commented the master in a tone far from flattering to Katherine. "That's the way you've been reading here, I suppose. Runnin' on like that, no regard for yer stops, no regard for the rules of readin'. Young lady, do you know what the rules of readin' are?"

Katherine was much embarrassed. "Why, yes," said she. "I think I do, but I'm afraid I do not quite understand what you mean, Mr. Lurvey."

"Oh, yes, yes, I thought so. I thought you didn't know," said the master. "I knew ye didn't. Now listen to me. I'll teach ye something. After a comma, stop long enough to count one. After a semicolon, stop long enough to count two. After a colon, stop long enough to count three. After a period let yer voice fall and stop long enough to count four. The whole class now, repeat the rules of readin' after me."

We all repeated the above "rules" after our teacher, sentence by sentence.

"Now, young lady, read that section again and read it according to rule," said the new master.

"But is that really necessary, Mr. Lurvey?" Katherine ventured to ask. "If the voice is allowed to fall at a period and a new sentence is properly begun, isn't that enough?"

"What do you suppose rules are for?" exclaimed the master in a loud, harsh tone. "Let the voice fall and stop long enough to count four—every time."

Katherine was a spirited girl and resented the tone in which she was answered. "Certainly, Mr. Lurvey," she replied. "The only reason why I asked was that our teacher last winter instructed us differently."

The master slapped his book down on the desk. "Now look here!" he exclaimed, "I don't care what the teacher last winter did! Maybe he didn't know his business. I don't know and I don't care. I teach by rule, and I want you to go by rule. Next may read."

The next chanced to be Theodora, who sat with Katherine. She also was a good reader. But she now attempted to make pauses, according to "rule," and her section consequently seemed to pause and hop along so oddly that we all laughed. No one could help laughing.

The master flushed. "Silence!" he shouted in a tremendous voice. "What are you laughing at? That's the way to read," he asserted stoutly. "Slowly and distinctly and accordin' to rule; only of course you needn't be quite so slow counting four as that last young lady was. Count four right off smart, as if you had some life in you."

He went on lecturing us and spent fully an hour that morning drilling a class of good readers in the practice of pausing long enough to count four after every sentence!

After the *Fifth Reader*, the *Fourth*, *Third*, and *Second* were called out and put through the same drill.

The class in the *National Arithmetic* was next called. It consisted of Addison, Theodora, Katherine, Myra Batchelder, and two others. They had been through the book the previous winter and wished merely to review it. The new master did not even inquire as to their progress, but opening the book hastily, assigned as their next day's lessons, the two rules for reduction ascending and reduction descending.

"Learn those two rules by heart," he said and shut the book.

Addison now ventured to say to him pleasantly that they knew these rules in principle and could give them in substance, if called for, at any time.

"Now, I don't want to hear any such excuses as that," replied the master. "That is just an excuse to shirk studyin'. We are going to do thorough work here this term. You've got to learn every rule by heart, or I will keep you at it till you do. There's nothing like having rules by heart. At the end of the term I shall call for all these rules and every one of you must be able to give any rule that I call for by heart. I am going to beat the rules of this arithmetic into you so that you'll never forget 'em if you live to be as old as Methuselah."

"But Mr. Lurvey," said Katherine, who had not yet recovered her equanimity, "they could perhaps have a different kind of arithmetic by that time."

"Now look here, young lady!" exclaimed the master, "I don't want any more nonsense from you. When I am speakin', I don't expect to be broke in on by anybody. When I want scholars to speak to me, I will let them know it. The next time anyone interrupts me like that, they'll be sorry for it."

He looked around upon us in a very determined, not to say savage, manner, and it was plain to see that he fully meant what he said. Katherine sat regarding him with mingled indignation and fear. It was not an auspicious opening for a pleasant term. Our new master appeared to regard us as his enemies. Katherine and Theodora were good scholars who wished to be on the best of terms with the teacher and aid him in all respects; they rarely, or never, needed even to be cautioned as to their deportment and naturally were aggrieved to be treated so rudely.

When the lower class in the *Practical Arithmetic*—my own class—was called, the master gave us the same two rules in reduction that had been assigned to the higher class. "They are important rules," he said. "Learn them by heart for tomorrow."

When school was dismissed for the noon intermission of one hour, Addison again approached the new master and, mentioning to him that his boarding place was to be with us, offered to escort him thither, and they went away together. Certain of the others also went home.

We who remained then opened our lunch baskets and while refreshing ourselves compared notes, so to speak, in a quiet way. At length I ventured to ask Katherine how she liked the new master. She did not reply for some time but merely glanced at me. "If you want to know what I think," she said at last in a low tone, "I think he is a great rude fellow. I don't think he knows much, either." My cousin Ellen agreed with her. Theodora would not express an opinion. She said there were some advantages in learning rules "by heart"; it strengthened the memory. But Katherine made sport of such rules. Between them, she and cousin Ellen had quietly christened the new master "the important man." Theodora was so much disappointed that she took but a small share of the lunch. She had hoped to make fine progress during this term. Addison and she expected to go on with algebra, in which they had made a beginning under Master Pierson.

On the other hand, Adriana Darnley and Octavia Sylvester were much impressed by our new master's appearance. "Oh, but isn't he fine lookin'!" Adriana went about saying to all of us. "We never had such a handsome schoolmaster before. He's real stylish lookin'," Octavia agreed with her. "I wish he boarded at our house," said Adriana, overhearing which Katherine and Ellen exchanged wondrous-wise glances.

At one o'clock Addison and the new master returned, and in the afternoon we were again drilled in reading by "rule." Afterward the class in English grammar was called to the recitation seats.

"Now I suppose," said Master Lurvey, "that you've been in the habit here of spending an hour a day, parsin' and construin'."

"Yes, Mr. Lurvey," replied Ellen.

"I thought you'd say so," he said with a sneer. "I expect that some young lady" (glancing toward Katherine) "will tell me that the master last winter had you do that. I've been hearing a good deal about that tremendous master, last winter, the tremendous great Mr. Pierson! But let me tell you all right here that he don't scare me a bit.

"Now see here, parsin' and construin' is a waste of time, and I shall not waste time on it. So you can carry those parsin' books home with you. It's a miserable waste of time. What you want in life is the rules of grammar, and that's what I'm going to give ye. Take nouns and pronouns for tomorrow, and see that you have every word of it. Take your seats."

As we did so, I recollect glancing at Addison. His face was a study. Katherine and Theodora looked bewildered. Adriana was trying to have Mr. Lurvey notice that she approved of him.

"I suppose there are geography classes," the new master remarked presently. "Will anyone tell me how many?"

"There were three last winter, Mr. Lurvey," said Addison.

"Oh, yes, yes, yes, last winter!" exclaimed the new master with a laugh. "There 'tis again. This school seems to be all 'last winter.' Nothin' but 'last winter.' But you're going to have something different this winter. I shall teach geography on a new plan. This book you use here takes ye flying all over creation and when you get back, you don't know where you are.

"Now, listen; you are going to begin geography with this town you're living in, and then this county, and then this state."

That seemed a rather good idea to me; it sounded practical.

"How many of you know anything about your own state of Maine?" the new master demanded reproachfully.

The question was so general that no one replied.

"How many of ye know what the largest river in yer own state of Maine is?"

"The Penobscot," said Addison, smiling, and not to have us all seem too ignorant. "It is said, however, that as much or more water flows in the Kennebec in a year," he added.

"I didn't suppose you knew," said the master in an overbearing tone. "And no matter about that last part. You're not supposed to know more than your books.

"What is the largest lake in Maine? Perhaps this very bright young lady who knew so much about arithmetic this morning can tell me," he continued with sarcasm, looking at Katherine.

"Moosehead Lake," replied Katherine indifferently, as one grown weary.

"Oh, you did happen to know that," commented the master. "Do you say it is a large or a small lake?"

"Large," replied Katherine, then she cast a sudden keen look at the new master and to our astonishment, added, "It is the largest body of fresh water in the world!"

We looked for another outburst of sarcasm. But to our still greater astonishment the new master said nothing.

"The lesson tomorrow will be the map of Maine," he announced, after making a note with a pencil. "That's for all three classes."

I stole a glance at Katherine, as we went to our seats. Her eyebrows were arched in a peculiar way. Addison's face wore a curious smile. In my own mind, an odd query was turning itself over: did he know?

Exercises in spelling followed, the master then said, "Lay aside your books." But Addison raised his hand.

"Well, young man, what is it?" said Master Lurvey rather gruffly.

"There is one class, sir, that has not yet been called today," Addison replied.

"What's that?"

"The class in algebra."

"Did you have a class in algebra last winter, under the great Mr. Pierson?" asked the master ironically.

"We had algebra last winter and the winter before," replied Addison.

"Didn't you know that was contrary to law?" demanded Master Lurvey. "It's against the law to teach algebra in a common school like this."

"I have heard that a teacher is not obliged to teach algebra unless he is willing," said Addison. "I did not know there was any law forbidding it."

"There are lots of things you don't know," retorted the master. He laughed condescendingly. "Not but that I would be willing enough to teach algebra," he said, offhandly. "Fact, I'd like to. But I've been warned not to teach it. The agent warned me not to. I'd like to, but I can't lay myself liable to the law, you know! So we won't have it. Lay aside your books.

"Now, remember what I said about noise here, mornings. When I come into this house tomorrow morning every boy is to be in his seat, every girl, too, with their Testaments out, ready to read.

"Another thing: I've seen some of you whispering in school today. No more whispering. You hear that? School is dismissed."

The Sudden Departure of Master Lurvey

IF THE FIRST day of school, under Master Lurvey, had been tumultuous, the second proved even more so. We soon had earnest that his rule against whisperers would be enforced. Reading from the Testament had scarcely concluded that morning when he made a sudden rush up one of the aisles to the long back seat and collaring Newman Darnley (who was certainly whispering to his seat mate), dragged him down the aisle to the open door of the room. Newman made some feeble efforts at resistance but was whirled around in a circle, his heels nearly knocking down the stove, then trounced smartly on the floor, shaken nearly out of his jacket, and finally shoved back up the aisle and fairly flung into his seat—a much rumpled Newman!

Clearly Master Lurvey was a powerful youth, physically. Moreover, he appeared to enjoy the fracas; his face grew very red but took on an aspect of glee. As he marched back to his desk, he faced around to the school and said, "I'll serve the next one I catch whispering in the same way!"

This menace was probably directed to the boys, but he was facing the entire room and said, "the next one!" The thought that he might pull out a young lady of sixteen onto the floor and shake her as he had shaken Newman astounded us for a time. Addison appeared greatly amused, although he was looking into a book. At the forenoon recess, too, three of the boys delayed a little in returning indoors after the bell was rung; Master Lurvey expedited their movements by seizing them, one after another as they appeared in the doorway, and throwing them headlong to their seats. The room was very quiet during all the remainder of the day. In fact, we sat in a kind of breathless expectancy waiting some fresh manifestation of the master's rigor in discipline. Although we had our books well in hand, we were not studying exactly but watching out.

At recess that afternoon Newman, who was much incensed by the trouncing he had received, declared that he would be one of three to put the master out of the house. William Tibbetts and Edgar Merrill said the same, but Addison dissuaded them.

Alfred Batchelder, generally a bad boy at school himself, perfidiously reported this to the master as he went home from school that night. In consequence of this bit of tale bearing we witnessed a fresh evidence of the master's prowess the following morning. After reading in the Testament (stopping long enough to count four after every sentence), Master Lurvey remarked that there was a little business to be transacted before beginning lessons. "I understand that three of you talk of carrying me out of school," he said. "If that's so, now is a good time to begin. I'm all ready. Come on now and carry me." He squared himself in the floor and clenched his fist.

No one cared to accept the challenge. I do not think that there were four boys in school who could have put him out of the room. "Well," he said at length, "if you are not going to tackle *me*, I've got a little bone to pick with *you*. Newman Darnley, come out onto the floor."

Newman hesitated.

"Start!" shouted the master, "or I'll come after you again."

Newman came out, reluctantly enough, and the master feruled him on both hands, very severely; in fact, he applied the ruler with all his strength. William Tibbetts and Edgar Merrill were then called out in turn and punished in the same manner; both cried out from pain. Their hands after a few moments puffed up white and became much swollen. It was cruel punishment.

"Does anybody else want to carry me out of school?" demanded the master exultantly, striding forward past the stove, ruler in hand. Several of the little fellows began to whimper. Then, to our amazement, Katherine Edwards exclaimed, "Yes, I do. I think you are a hateful tyrant!"

The master rushed toward her, his eyes blazing with rage. We all thought he was about to strike her. If he had done so, there would have been a general *émeute*. I think that we would all have fought him, tooth and nail. Kate was as white as paper. She was woefully frightened. Afterward she said that she hardly knew how she came to say what she did. She faced the master, however, with a species of desperation in her eyes, and he evidently thought it better not to attempt her chastisement.

"You sassy piece!" he growled and, turning, went back to his desk, where he made a number of marks in his record, saying, "I'll give you the lowest rank in school."

During the last two days of the week our rigorous instructor developed a very unpleasant habit of using his foot on the floor to enforce his orders. If any pupil did not start, or reply, instantly when spoken to, he would stamp with his foot so heavily as to jar the whole house. He heard lessons quickly, spending very little time on them, and rarely asking a question concerning them. During most of the time he sat watching us, evidently, to surprise someone in the act of breaking a rule. No one dared ask him a question, much less carry a hard sum to him. He had terrorized us.

Joel Pierson, while boarding at the Old Squire's the previous winter, had been very genial with the young folks and assisted them with their studies in the sitting room during the long evenings. Master Lurvey held himself aloof and scarcely spoke to us at home, nor we to him.

I overheard Theodora talking of the school to Addison Friday evening; she was lamenting that we bade fair to make no progress.

"Yes, he is a pill," Addison replied, "but I guess we shall have to make the best of him."

The fact was that many of the parents in the district had gained an idea that Master Lurvey must be a pretty good teacher, because he had feruled the boys who talked of putting him out of the house. He was no doubt aware that he was incompetent to teach scholars like Theodora, Katherine, or Addison; but he knew that he possessed the brute strength to repress anything like rebellion, and he resolved to rule by the strong arm and keep us in fear of him. He was sufficiently coarse in disposition to enjoy the exercise of his absolute power. I never saw so quiet a schoolroom as ours during Friday and Saturday that week—for we had a holiday in our district school only on every second Saturday of the term.

On Saturday our new master began to display another odd trait. When anyone of us in the classes recited or made even a simple state-ment of a rule, or a fact, he now called out, "Sure of that, sir?" or "Do you know that is so?"

He was, in truth, far more ignorant of dates, the names of capital cities, the location of countries, and of historical events than we sus-pected, but he was crafty about committing himself to any statement of his own until he had looked in the book.

One of the town's school committee usually visited the schools twice each term, once during the opening week and once near the end of the term. We looked for the "committee man" on Thursday and on Friday. It then transpired that Glinds, the school agent, had neglected to notify the committee that the term had begun.

The second week opened with little change for the better. It was Master Lurvey's first taste of the sweets of absolute power, and he was of the stuff that Neroes and Caligulas are fashioned from; he enjoyed witnessing the fear that he inspired. Very likely it was his idea of a well-governed school where every pupil jumped at the master's nod and lis-tened, when he spoke, in awed expectancy.

Addison alone had preserved his ordinary easy demeanor, attending to his studies without much reference to the master but addressing him whenever he desired. Addison, indeed, was never disorderly in school; he was much too busy with his books. He alone of us all would now raise his hand to attract the master's attention and then address him in ordinary tones during school hours. Although Master Lurvey must have been aware that Addison was the most friendly to him of anyone in the room, it soon began to be apparent that he did not like to see even Addison unterrified. Perhaps he deemed him a bad example to the others. Be that as it may, he determined to humble him and watched for a pretext to do so. In the utter quiet of the room he could hear the least whisper in any part of it, and while sitting in his desk Tuesday afternoon, the sound of communicating lips reached his ear from the direction of the long seat where Alfred, Halstead, and Addison now sat. Picking up his ruler, he strode along in front of that seat and looking at Addison, said, "Were you whispering?"

"No, sir," replied Addison.

"I think I heard you!" exclaimed the master.

"I repeat that I was not whispering," replied Addison firmly.

The fact was that Halstead had whispered to Addison but the latter had not replied.

"Somebody whispered here!" shouted the master. "Was it you?" pointing his ruler at Halse.

I regret to say that my kinsman could not always, under pressure, be relied on to tell the truth.

"No, sir," replied Halse.

"Was it you, then?" demanded the master, pointing at Alfred.

"No, it was not," said Alfred. "I haven't whispered this week."

"Who was it then?" asked the master.

"I don't know," said Alfred. "I did not hear anybody."

This may have been falsehood number two.

"One of you three has lied to me!" cried the master in a loud tone, "and I think it is you!" pointing at Addison.

"You are entirely mistaken, Mr. Lurvey. I have not broken a rule of your school thus far," rejoined Addison with great distinctness.

"Then which of those two boys did whisper?" exclaimed the master, pointing at Halse and Alf.

"It is not my business to spy on, or report, other scholars," replied Addison with great spirit. "I do not think you have any right to ask me to do it. I will be spy and informer to no teacher."

This resolute attitude nonplused the inexperienced master some-what; he was staggered by the firm stand that Addison took on the question and did not press that point.

"I'll find out someday who whispered here," he exclaimed wrathily and, turning, walked to his desk and for a long time sat there staring hard at Addison again. Theodora and I—all the scholars, in fact—were also looking furtively at Addison. He was a little flushed, but I did not see that he smiled. Mr. Lurvey appeared to think differently, however, for he suddenly strode toward him again and shook his fist at him. "Don't you grin at me!" he exclaimed at shouting pitch. "I still think you are the one who whispered. If I find out you did, I'll ferule you till you can't get your hands to your head! I'll take that grin off your face!"

Addison did not change countenance; he looked the master in the eye as he uttered his threat, and said, "Very well, Mr. Lurvey."

We expected that the master would collar him for that, but for some reason he did not. Addison resumed his algebra (which he was taking without assistance, at odd hours) and kept very busy during the rest of the afternoon.

After school that night Newman Darnley again sounded Addison as to whether he would join a party to put the master out of the house by force, but Addison strongly advised them to mind the rules of school and give up that project. He would not let them know that he resented the master's language, but Theodora and I knew Addison well enough to feel pretty sure that Mr. Lurvey would live to regret his threat.

The master did not speak to any of us that night, and the Old Squire noticed that something had gone wrong, although none of us had said anything concerning the school. Next morning as I was pumping water at the barn, the old gentleman asked me privately if the master had taken offense at anything.

"He is pretty savage with us all," I replied, but did not like to tell him of Addison's trouble.

"Savage, is he?" said the Old Squire with a chuckle; he still held old-time ideas about order in the schoolroom.

About twelve o'clock the following night, Master Lurvey was taken very ill. Gram heard him crying out dolorously and set herself to care for his ailment. At length, she judged it necessary to administer an emetic of mustard and water, the result of which gave evidence that her patient had been partaking very freely from a sack of dried apples that hung in the passage leading to his room. In consequence of this imprudent refreshment, he not only came near expiring *intra dies*, from congestion of the stomach but was unable to appear at breakfast, or go to the schoolroom till near eleven o'clock.

Not knowing when our tyrant might appear on the scene, however, we all repaired to the schoolhouse at the usual hour, and after waiting awhile, Katherine proposed that Addison should keep school till the master came. To this all agreed. Addison, however, declined; but the others insisting, he at length called the school to order and laid himself out to do his best. For a while he kept a bright eye out at the window for Mr. Lurvey's approach, intending to take his seat before the master should come in. But there were numbers of hard examples to be worked in arithmetic, and Addison solved several, one after the other on the blackboard. Presently he became absorbed in his task and was ciphering away at the board on a tough example in cube root, explaining it as he did so in a loud, clear voice, when the door opened softly and in walked Master Lurvey, looking far from well and decidedly sour. How long he had been listening outside no one could say. Instead of enjoying Addison's confusion and thanking him for the pains he was taking, he seemed far from pleased and his first words were, "So you think you can take my place, do you?"

Addison brushed the chalk off his fingers. "No, Mr. Lurvey," he said. "I should never try to take your place.

"I was only doing a few examples for some of the scholars, while we waited," he added, seeing that the master's face was growing very black. He started to go to his seat, but Mr. Lurvey suddenly stepped in front of him.

"You seem to think that you can do just as you've a mind to here!" he cried in an angry tone. "You think you can set yourself up for a pattern for me to keep school by! A big schoolmaster you would make! Let's see now how you would look. Take a seat at the desk. I want them all to look at ye!"

For an instant Addison flushed and looked rebellious. I think that he was half minded to resist. If he had done so every boy in the room would have sprung to assist him. Whether we could have overcome the master is uncertain. He was a powerful youth. Muscle was his one strong point. "Take your seat at my desk," he shouted, advancing on Addison while the rest of us sat breathless.

It had taken Addison but that one moment to think twice and rise above his first rash impulse.

"Why, certainly, Mr. Lurvey," he replied in a cordial tone. "If you think we need two teachers here. But you are so well able to govern a school that I never thought of our needing another." He went to the desk and took the master's seat there, and then looked around at us all with a queer smile.

"That is the great schoolmaster!" exclaimed Mr. Lurvey, pointing at him in derision. "Isn't he a big one?"

We laughed, but rather at the master than at Addison, who laughed, too; the master himself had put on a grin, for Ad's ambiguous compliment to him on his ability to govern the school had pleased him and disarmed his temper somewhat.

"Do you want me to hear classes?" Addison asked after a few moments. "If I am going to be the master's assistant, I should like to make myself useful."

"If I want you to do anything, I'll tell you," replied Mr. Lurvey gruffly; he then called out a class in arithmetic and began to drill us on the verbatim recitation of rules again. Addison took up a book and read. After every few minutes the master would turn around and point at him, saying, "He thinks he's the schoolmaster." The joke was rather weak.

At the noon intermission, Addison quietly withdrew from the desk and nothing more was said, but this affair had wounded his feelings even more than the previous threat to ferule him, and I think that from that moment he began to plot the master's downfall. Addison, however, was naturally a strategist and possessed the strategist's instinct to work quietly and to attack an enemy at his weak point. For that reason he would have nothing to do with any plan for carrying the master out of the school-room. He said nothing to the others and gave no hint of his intention.

School proceeded far from pleasantly all day, perhaps because the master was not yet feeling very well. He was more than usually fractious and overbearing with us. "Is that so?" he would exclaim after nearly every answer we gave in the classes. "How do you know that is so?" or "Give your reasons for that!" He even asked this latter question when Ellen said that Peking was the capital of China! She replied that she did not know any reason, and he bade her be prepared to give a reason at next recitation.

When in the history class Newman Darnley replied that John Adams was the second president of the United States the master cried, "Are you sure of that?"

"Pretty sure," said Newman.

"Why?" said the master.

"Because George Washington was the first, and John Adams came next," replied Newman.

The master looked in the book. "You are not half as bright as you think you are," he said. "George Washington was the second president and the first president, too; he was president twice."

This was so fine a point that Addison, as well as the rest of us, laughed, and the master shouted, "Silence!" in an awful voice and stamped on the floor.

Next afternoon, about half an hour after school began, one of the school committee appeared to visit the school. In our town there was then a School Committee consisting of three members to any one of whom an applicant for the position of teacher might apply to be examined and obtain a certificate as to fitness. As is often the case in country towns, men were occasionally elected to the office who were not wholly competent to properly examine proposing teachers and who did so in a very superficial manner. One such person was on the board that year, and it was from him that Master Lurvey had obtained his certificate to teach. But the member of the committee who came to visit the school that day was the Congregationalist clergyman at the village, Mr. Lowell Furness, a young gentleman not more than twenty-four years of age, of good education and talent.

Mr. Furness had been in town but two years; he was elected on the committee the previous spring and made chairman of the board, it being understood that he was better qualified than his fellow members. His personal appearance was unusually attractive; he was gentlemanly and had an animated, cheery way of speaking.

Having hitched his horse outside, he came in without rapping; and as he was a stranger to us all and to the teacher, he introduced himself and stated his business there, in a very genial happy manner. "I would like to hear most of the classes," he said, "in order that at my second visit, near the end of the term, I may be able to judge the progress made."

He conversed pleasantly with Master Lurvey for some moments; the latter then called the arithmetic classes, in order, one after another. When we of the more advanced class took our places, Mr. Furness inquired of each what progress we had made the previous winter and asked a few questions. "Why, this ought to be a pretty good class," he said to the master. "All they need is a review of the arithmetic. I should have them advance rapidly over the principal rules, dwelling on the more difficult ones only."

The master said something about learning the rules and showed him where he had given lessons in reduction and common fractions.

"Well, that may be of some advantage," replied Mr. Furness doubtfully. "But I would not keep them back there long. This is a class that can go ahead. This class can master everything in the book this term."

It was plain that Master Lurvey did not like this advice very well; he did not reply to it.

The *Fifth Reader* class was presently called for a brief exercise. Katherine sat at the head of the class, and at a nod from Mr. Furness, she rose and read a section from the reading lesson for that day; and she took particular pains to stop *long enough to count four* at every period. As she read Mr. Furness at first appeared amused, then perplexed.

"Why, you read correctly," he said, when she had finished. "But why do you stop so long at every sentence?"

"So as to count four," replied Kate in a demure and melancholy tone.

Mr. Furness burst into a hearty laugh. "When did you take that up?" he exclaimed, still laughing.

"On the first day of this term," replied Kate with sadness.

Mr. Furness rose hastily from his seat and walked to the window. We could see that he was still shaking as he looked out. After a time he came back and clapping his hand kindly on the master's shoulder, said in a low voice, "My dear young fellow, rules are good things, no doubt, but many of them are somewhat antiquated. It isn't best to insist on them too closely."

But the master had grown very glum and morose by this time. He muttered something about teaching as he thought best, then abruptly dismissed the class. Mr. Furness regarded him with an inquiring eye for some moments, then begged his pardon if he had said anything to injure his feelings.

The master did not reply but turned to call a geography class, and there was no more laughter on the part of anyone after this; matters had already taken a serious turn, and Addison—the strategist—perceived that his opportunity had come.

The more advanced class in geography had the map of North America for a lesson that day, and Mr. Furness, perceiving that the master was offended, refrained from asking questions. Mr. Lurvey therefore heard the lesson himself.

"Where is Great Bear Lake situated?" he asked Addison at length.

The latter purposely hesitated an instant, then replied in a rather uncertain manner that it was situated in British America.

"Sure of that?" exclaimed the master, brusquely.

"Perhaps I was wrong," replied Addison with seeming candor. "I remember that it is situated in the southern part of Mexico. Its outlet is the Snake River, which flows into the Gulf of Georgia."

This astonishing answer struck amazement to all our minds. We glanced quickly at the master and saw his eyes wandering vaguely over the map in the book, which he held in his hand. He did not find it and did not speak for several moments. We perceived instantly that he was all at sea himself. Addison watched him, his lip curling in a scornful smile; and Mr. Furness glanced first at Addison, then at the master, who to extricate himself from his dilemma at once put another question to the next member of the class. Presently he came around to Addison again, and being, I think, a little suspicious that his former answer was not quite what it should have been, he took care this time to ask him a question that he was himself sure of, or thought that he was.

"Where does the St. Lawrence River rise?" he demanded, and we saw that he had put his forefinger on the Great Lakes.

"In the Great Lakes," replied Addison, "according to this book. But," he added with assured confidence, "it really rises in the Rocky Mountains! The waters find their way by a subterranean passage into Lake Superior. This passage is over a thousand miles long," he continued in a lower, matter-of-fact tone. "It was only recently discovered." Under his breath, he added, so that some of us sitting near him heard, "I discovered it myself."

The master looked at him hard but helplessly. He did not like to acknowledge his ignorance of something that Addison and Mr. Furness might know to be a fact, and he was so ill informed that he did not know that Addison's burlesque answer was absurd and impossible. Determined at least not to commit himself, he hurried on to the next question. By this time Katherine had divined what the game was to be; when her turn came next, she replied with a serene countenance that the Colorado River emptied into Great Salt Lake! And we all saw the master looking in British America for it. He did not find it and, abruptly assigning a lesson for the next day, dismissed the class.

By this time Mr. Furness's face wore an aspect of intense dissatisfaction, but he leaned back and made no comment; he knit his brows occasionally, but a smile appeared to be hiding at the corners of his mouth.

The last class called was the class in United States history. We had begun the term with the chapter treating the causes of the Revolutionary War, and that afternoon had for our lesson the one describing the campaign in the Carolinas and Georgia, also the chapter following it. One of the textbooks was handed to Mr. Furness by either Theodora or Katherine. But the master put the questions as set down at the margin of each page.

Presently the question, "What American officer took command in the Southern States?" came to Addison.

"General Lincoln," he replied.

"Sure of that?" demanded the master, for he had his eye on the paragraph and was therefore sure himself.

"Very sure," Ad replied, smiling; then bethinking himself that the given name of this officer was not set down in our school history, he added boldly, "It was Abraham Lincoln, the same who was afterward president of the United States!" Mr. Lurvey looked hard at him but did not dare to dispute it. He was ignorant to this gross extent.

"Seems to me that he must have become a very old man by 1860," remarked Mr. Furness, regarding Addison with a strange smile.

"Yes, sir," replied Addison with a smile equally strange. "That is why his face always looks so deeply wrinkled—on account of his great age."

Mr. Furness cast a glance of pity at the master who stood regarding them both in angry perplexity. He was out of his depth and really did not know what to make of it.

"Name some of the advantages of the French alliance!" was the next question. Theodora answered at considerable length, speaking of Lafayette, and of the French fleet and the French army, which were dispatched to assist the Americans.

"Who can name any other advantage?" the master asked.

Addison raised his hand and said with a semblance of gravity, "One other great advantage was that the cavalier French officers taught the American ladies how to waltz and thus kept up their spirits through a gloomy period of the War. Another advantage was that in battle they could give orders in French, which the British could not understand."

These manifest advantages pleased Mr. Furness so much that he again made excursion to the window, ostensibly to see if his team was standing quietly, but Master Lurvey appeared to be considerably struck by the cogency of these suggestions.

The last question of the lesson was to name the principal battles of the Revolution. Thomas Edwards did so, and Mr. Furness, rising to take his coat and hat, remarked that *Brandywine* was an odd name for a battlefield. "Can anyone tell why it was thus called?" he asked.

"Because," said Thomas, who also wanted to distinguish himself in the farce, "because on that occasion the British drank wine and the Americans brandy. That was before the Maine Law. The Americans took so much brandy that they were defeated in that battle. Washington paced his room all the following night. 'Oh, my bleeding country!' he cried, 'but don't let it happen again!'"

This was too broad even for Master Lurvey; he stamped his foot and bade Tom behave himself, intimating that he would settle with him after school. Mr. Furness made no comment, further than to remark that he saw that it was already past four o'clock and that he hoped that we would excuse him for keeping us after school hours.

"I wish to see the school agent to make a few inquiries as to the length of the term," he added, "and as I am a stranger in your district, will one of you boys kindly point out the way to his house?"

"I will do so," said Addison, and taking his hat and coat went out with him, while the rest of us lingered to lay aside our books and be dismissed in the regular order.

Mr. Furness and Addison were driving away from the schoolhouse as we came out, and as soon as they were fairly on the road and out of ear-shot (so Ad told us that evening) the young clergyman turned to him and asked, "What sort of master have you got here?"

"Well, I am only a scholar," replied Addison, "but if you desire my opinion of Master Lurvey, I will give it."

"I would like your opinion of him," said Mr. Furness.

"Well, then, he is as ignorant as a horse and even more of a brute," replied Addison.

"That is a strong opinion," observed Mr. Furness with a smile, "but from what I have seen this afternoon, I am much inclined to accept it. At least I am quite sure that he is unfit for the position."

Shortly after we had arrived home from school, Mr. Furness and school agent Glinds drove up and went into the house. Addison, Halse, and I were busy with our night chores, but Theodora came out to inform us that they were holding a conversation with Master Lurvey in the sitting room, behind closed doors.

"His goose is cooked," Ad exclaimed.

After some time Mr. Furness came out and drove away. Mr. Glinds also went away after a talk with the Old Squire.

Nothing was said that evening, but next morning, Saturday, Master Sam Lurvey set out for home on foot, without saying anything to anyone. During the day we learned that the committee and the agent had advised him to withdraw quietly from the school and that he had probably gone home to consult his father.

We saw no more of him till Monday morning, when Mr. Lurvey Senior appeared with his promising son. We had repaired to the schoolhouse before nine o'clock as usual and were all in our seats, when at a quarter past they drove up to the door. Master Sam then entered (while his father sat outside in the sleigh) and called the school to order. Instead of proceeding with the classes, however, he made us a pompous speech in which he asserted that he had just received an offer to go into business, so much more lucrative than school teaching that he had accepted it at once. Consequently, we would be obliged to get a new teacher. "My time is worth too much to me to spend it in a school like this at seventeen dollars a month," he added.

Without further farewell he took his books, walked out to his father's sleigh, and they drove off.

Something that sounded very much like three groans followed him as soon as he was fairly outside the door. From the windows we saw that he heard them and that he shot a malignant look back at us, and that was the last we saw of Master Sam Lurvey.

Theodora said that she pitied his father, but the most of us young folks wasted very little pity on father or son.

9

The Old Rantum-Scooter

THE NUMBER ELEVEN SCHOOLHOUSE STOOD AT THE fork of the county road with the cross-town road, which led down Downing Hill on one side and Mill Hill on the other. The county road extended north and south along the crest of a fine, broad ridge of land divided into ten fertile farms, owned by as many well-to-do farmers whose families made up our school district.

We young people of Number Eleven had always been a little inclined to look down on the boys and girls of Number Ten at the Corners, near the foot of Downing Hill, for the denizens of Number Ten were a somewhat poor and shiftless lot, and Number Ten was the most backward school in town. The larger boys were pugnacious and ill-disposed, and unless a schoolmaster were strong enough to thrash four or five of them, he must suffer the humiliation of being carried out of the schoolhouse.

At Number Eleven, on the contrary, the pupils were well-advanced, self-respecting, and orderly. An able teacher was required, but less to govern than to instruct. Still, I now think that the contempt in which we held the Number Ten boys was rather pharisaic, and I do not wonder they resented it. We nicknamed them "Bagdaders" because of their low, flat valley land, and they retorted by calling us "Hill Dogs." The two districts also belonged to two rival political parties, a fact that sharpened the animosity between them.

Downing Hill was the best coasting place in the county. It was on the eastward side of one of those long, high ridges, which, like great sea waves, rise rank on rank far out to the east of the White Mountain group. It was not quite a mile in length from top to bottom.

The descent, however, was not a regular incline but consisted of five steep "pitches," as we used to call them—with nearly level "flats" between them, each leading to the pitch below—which made altogether a run of more than a mile, continuing across a broad meadow and over the Little Androscoggin River Bridge to the foot of the hill beyond. It had always been, and is to this day, the favorite coast of the Number Eleven boys. Indeed, we boasted that few save Number Eleven boys dared steer a sled down that hill.

When the road was smooth and icy, terrific speed was attained on the lowest pitch, and any error in steering might easily cost the coaster his life. Strangers coming into the neighborhood were always astonished at the reckless manner in which we slid down this long declivity. Looking back to those times, I do not now wonder at it.

To launch boldly on this long ridgeside and shoot pitch after pitch with ever-increasing velocity was really a grand feat and a very reckless one. It is a marvel that there were no fatal accidents. But sliding down this familiar hillside seemed the most natural thing in the world to do. If a Number Eleven boy had not made the run at thirteen or fourteen years of age, we deemed him a backward lad.

The coasting sleds most in favor with us were small and narrow. They were shod with half-round steel shoes, which were slightly bowed to make a "spring" space of an inch at the middle of the runner. Our favorite posture for coasting on this hill was face downward, with toes extended behind to aid in steering. Usually in starting at the top of the hill we ran forward, one after another, flung ourselves down on our sleds, and thus set off at speed.

On moonlit evenings, when there were girls in the party, trains were often made up of ten or twelve sleds—some of them large hand sleds on which four or five could sit at ease. The forward or leading sled was called the "engine" and was steered by one of the oldest, strongest boys. Such a train, humming down that long hill by moonlight, gaining speed at every pitch till it shot past the Corners at Number Ten going sixty miles an hour, afforded an exhilarating spectacle. There was an almost uninterrupted view from top to bottom of the long descent; and besides the steerer on the engine, there was a "horn-man," whose business it was to blow a tin horn if he saw a team or pedestrian coming up. All the others, too, joined in a tremendous shout of "Road! Road! Road!"

A hired man from one of the farms, with a span of horses and long pung sleigh, saved us the drudgery of pulling our sleds up the hill.

The hill was so long that not more than four or five coasts could be made in an evening and generally not more than two during the hour's nooning each day when school was in session. What troubled us most during the day was to get time to eat our dinners, which, of course, as country boys, we always took to school with us. We could any of us eat what we had brought in five minutes; but that five minutes used to make us late on the second "heat."

At length one of the boys suggested that we could save the time by eating our dinners in school. So about ten minutes before school was dismissed at noon, we would lay our heads on our arms on the desks and commence to feed from beneath. You could have seen a dozen heads bobbing up and down on their arms at once as their dinners were in process of mastication.

"Little Foster," as the boys called him, was the replacement for our ousted schoolmater, Mr. Lurvey, that winter. He was one of those easy teachers who prefer, if possible, never to see any mischief. He did ask a boy one day what he was doing with his head down.

"I'm getting my spelling lesson," was the reply.

The master said he was afraid he would make his head ache if he studied so hard as that!

The plan of disposing of dinner worked well till one day a boy named Freem Milliken ate the string with which his dinner had been tied up. About two yards of white twine had been used to tie the package. As Freem was hurriedly cramming down a lot of soft pie, he took in the string with it and swallowed about a yard of the twine before he knew it.

Then he began to gasp and dragged it out hand over hand, but it scared him so that he jumped up onto his seat, with his eyes starting out of his head like walnuts. He was a tall, thin, loose-jointed boy, and the scholars were so amused that they burst into laughter and made a great uproar. The master himself laughed, and order was not secured again that forenoon.

But the story was told at home, and the next day but one who should ride up to the schoolhouse but all three of the committee men. They talked to us so severely and threatened us so grievously that not a scholar dared to eat dinner in school again. We still continued sledding, but our noontime trips were cut back to one.

Laws relative to coasting were not then very strict in Maine, and we supposed we had a right to coast down the road at sixty miles an hour. Nobody had ever made any objection. The only drawback to the sport was that we had to run past the schoolhouse in Number Ten, and the Bagdaders were accustomed to rush out and pelt us with snowballs. Their schoolhouse stood on the north side of the road. Directly opposite was a grocery store, which was commonly haunted by a number of loafers. A few steps below were the post office and another grocery. The place was locally known as Downing Corners.

There had been good coasting for three or four weeks; the entire hill was smooth as glass. Nearly every morning, noon, and night some of us Number Eleven boys were coasting, and often there were parties of twenty or thirty.

The loafers and Bagdaders had jeered at us as we flew past, and snowballed us as in former years, but before long the Number Ten boys actually undertook to stop all Number Eleven coasters. They rolled great snowballs into the road in front of the schoolhouse and built a high fort clear across the road. Four of our boys who started to coast down were obliged to take to the ditch. The Bagdaders then rushed from their fort and by pelting the boys in the ditch with snowballs forced them to run back up the hill. They shouted that no Hill Dog should pass that schoolhouse.

But as their fort stopped teams as well as coasters, one of the selectmen of the town ordered them to remove it at once, and during the following evening a train of ten sleds from Number Eleven coasted defiantly by.

But the next noon they played a new and worse trick on us. Eight or ten of us set off to go down singly, one sled a few yards behind another. When as we drew near the Number Ten schoolhouse, Addison, who was ahead, noticed that Tim Jackson, one of the larger boys at the Corners, was standing on one side of the road and his crony Merrick Robbins on the other.

"Look out for snowballs!" Addison shouted back to us. Neither he nor any of the rest of us saw that a new rope lay across the road on the snow till the two boys raised it and caught us. Addison's sled was capsized, and all the rest of us were piled up in a heap. Some of us were scraped off our sleds, some had our sleds upset; the Number Ten crowd had three or four boys at each end of the rope, and as fast as a sled came along, it was caught by the rope and jerked over. Meantime a dozen other Number Ten boys were raining snowballs on us. We had to pick ourselves up, recover our sleds, and get away as best we could.

"Try it again!" they shouted after us. "If you think you can run by Number Ten, try it again!"

For a day or two we had little disposition to try it again. They were too big and too many for us to thrash, as we would perhaps have been justified in doing; and we did not dare to try the coast, but we chafed under the restraint and beat our brains for a device to break it effectually.

We hit on the solution a few days later at one of those auction sales (or "vendues," as old folks call them) so characteristic of a Yankee neighborhood. "Housing stuff" and "farming tools" were for sale. Everybody within four or five miles—men, women, and boys—was always ready for big bargains.

An old red pung was put up, and the auctioneer cried out lustily, "How much am I offered?"

But nobody seemed to want it. Though remarkably stout, it was not stylish. Somebody derisively remarked that it would do for sliding down hills. On that hint several of us boys, at Addison's urging, put our scrip together and bid two dollars. As nobody could be induced to bid more, it was knocked off to us.

We at once dragged it away, stored it under one of the meeting house sheds, and started drawing up our plans.

Tom Edwards, who, after Willis Murch, was probably the bravest of our boys, proposed taking one of the thills under each arm as he lay face down on his narrow coasting sled between them. Tom's idea was that the pung, loaded with ten or a dozen boys, would break the rope

or jerk it away from those who tried to hold it. It was evident, however, that if the rope were so held as to upset his sled the pung thills would drop and the pung come to grief, to say nothing of the danger to Tom himself from being run over by it.

It was then that Willis proposed to take the thills off the pung and steer it down himself, by lying directly beneath it on his own low sled and grasping one pung runner at the forward upward turn in each hand and planting a foot against one of the iron braces of the runners on each side. He declared he could steer the pung in that way and be completely covered by it.

The most of us were afraid, however, that the Bagdaders would scrape us off of the pung with their rope. At this stage of the argument, Addison proposed making the pung into a wooden armor-clad.

Tom, Willis, and Addison worked nearly all the following night. They took off the low pung-box and replaced it with one far larger and stronger, made of joist and pine boards. It covered the pung-runners entirely, being over eight feet long by four feet wide, and the sides rose to a height of over three feet, quite sufficient to shield all who sat within them. The box was made fast to the runners and had a kind of prow in front, projecting three or four feet in a wedge-shaped triangle.

When they hauled it to the schoolhouse the next day, everyone who saw it, including our teacher, agreed that it was the most singular coaster ever seen in those parts. Willis, when lying under it on his little sled to steer, was almost completely hidden from view; a short trial trip down the first pitch of the hill showed it to be necessary that he should be strapped to the little sled.

Willis, Tom, and Addison were ready to start at once, but the courage of many of us was not quite equal to taking passage in so novel a contrivance. Indeed, some little bravery was required, for if Willis failed to steer it, broken necks might be the result. Then, too, no one knew how strong the Bagdaders' rope would prove to be or what would happen when we ran foul of it.

But the next day after we had eaten our noon lunch, Willis, having sent his father's hired man with a span of their horses down the hill in advance, placed himself under the pung in position for steering.

"Come on, boys!" he called. "Who's afraid?" Tom and Addison were the first to climb in, and eight of us followed them.

"Shove off!" exclaimed Willis, and in a moment more we were gliding down the first pitch. Altogether the pung, the heavy box, and its load of boys must have weighed a ton. It rapidly gathered speed. Down the second pitch it swept, hummed across the level stretch, and took the third pitch, faster and faster.

It was amazing that Willis steered so well, but he seemed to know how at once. My own sensations swung between terror and wild elation. Down the long fourth pitch we shot, gaining tremendous headway. The pung was now going so fast that the jar and jolting motion had entirely ceased. It seemed as if the road had been oiled. The keen rush of cold air cut our faces and brought to my eyes, I remember, a haze of tears, through which I saw dimly a wild procession of hurrying trees and roadside fences!

The Number Ten boys had seen us coming. As we headed down the fifth and last pitch we heard them shouting, and seven or eight of them ran across the road.

"They're stretching their rope!" Tom exclaimed. Jumping to his feet, he pulled off his red woolen muffler and waved it defiantly, where we all yelled like wild Indians. The Bagdaders yelled back defiance and raised their rope. In their ignorance they probably thought that, with five or six boys at each end of the rope, they would be able to upset us.

But the next moment they received an impressive object lesson. The momentum of the heavy pung was something prodigious! We scarcely felt the rope when we struck it, and the next instant a dozen Number Ten boys were taking most extravagant leaps as they were jerked into the road behind us! All of them had been gripping the rope hard, and some of them were carried fifty feet before they could let go! They were about the most astonished looking boys I ever saw!

As for the pung, it did not stop till it reached the foot of the hill beyond the bridge over the Little Androscoggin River, where we found the man and horses waiting to haul it back up to Number Eleven.

The Bagdad boys had not wholly recovered from their discomfiture when we went by; their school bell was ringing, and when Addison politely asked them what they thought of our blockade runner, they had little to say.

"Ho!" Tim said feebly. "What do we care for your old rantum-scooter?" And the name stuck. We soon came to call it the rantum-scooter ourselves.

The Number Ten boys knew better than to attempt to hold a rope in front of the blockade runner again, but they still imagined that the rope would stop us if only the ends could be made fast. Next day at noon when we coasted down, we found that they had drawn it tight across the road and tied one end to a tree near the schoolhouse and the other to a horse post in front of the grocery opposite. The rope snapped like twine when we struck it.

A day or two later as we coasted down, we found that they had collected eight or ten ox chains, but they did not dare to use them, perhaps because they feared to kill some of us or possibly because the selectman had threatened to have them punished if they seriously molested us more.

After this they no longer tried to stop us, but they pelted us hard with frozen snowballs. For ordinary snowballs we cared little, since we could draw our heads down into the box as we passed; but soon Tim, Merrick, and some of the others began hurling heavy lumps of ice into the pung.

To set such missiles at defiance, Addison, Tom, and Willis rebuilt the box of the pung, making the sides higher and putting a top on it.

That winter, as it chanced, the people in Number Eleven had repaired the meeting house, which stood near the schoolhouse, and replaced the stove with a furnace. A quantity of old stovepipe of little value was left.

The boys procured seven or eight lengths of this old stovepipe and, opening the joints, straightening out the sheet iron, and nailing it along the sides of the rantum-scooter, converted it into a homely iron-clad—probably the only armor-clad coasting sled ever devised in this or any other country.

During the following week we made the coast not less than twenty times with this curious contrivance. Lumps of ice and even stones were launched at it, but no violence that the disgruntled Bagdaders could inflict prevented our running their blockade as long as the good coasting weather lasted.

Willis was the only one who ever attempted to steer the rantum-scooter, however, and as I look back to those days it is now a wonder to me that he or some of us who took that wild run with him were not killed. Indeed, an accident that might well have proved fatal occurred in February, soon after the close of winter school. It was in the evening, but there was a moon. We had just started from the top of the hill and had run thirty or forty rods, far enough to get under rapid headway, when a sudden jolt shook the pung runners from Willis's grasp.

The pung swerved off the road and plowed nose first into a bank of hard snow. Willis bit his tongue completely through when his head struck the snow bank and wrenched one of his legs so badly against the pung's undercarriage that he was lame for more than a week. The back of the pung rose over the prow, pitching off the top and hurling the rest of us resistlessly forward! We were thrown out and tumbled headlong into the surrounding snow. Addison received such a shock that he lay gasping on the ground for some seconds. Tom Edwards escaped with a torn jacket. Halstead had his face scratched, and I was somewhat injured.

Had the accident happened farther down or at the bottom of the hill, we should hardly have escaped without more serious injury still. The great Newtonian law is not to be thus rashly trifled with!

Of course, that was the last of our rantum-scooter. Our folks and the "public generally" raised an outcry against this manner of coasting, and this together with the commands of another selectman of the town who lived in our district put the old pung under permanent embargo. It was never used again.

10

A Strange Discovery of Moose Eggs

A VERY POOR, PRIMITIVE HABITATION WAS THE HOVEL or cabin in which "old Hughy" lived, half a mile up the lumber trail on the southern border of the Great Woods; but to all the boys of the vicinity it was a little paradise.

The old woodsman seemed to occupy an intermediate place between the Indian and the settler. He trapped at certain seasons of the fall and winter, hunted a little, fished, braided baskets, and sometimes during the snowy season made snowshoes. He never planted nor sowed, nor kept a cow for milk or a pig for pork. Apparently he subsisted chiefly on tobacco; for when he was not smoking it in his brown old "T. D.," he was chewing it. It was currently reported that he could chew tobacco in his sleep.

He was accustomed to go to the grocery with a backload of baskets to sell, and say, "Gass yer may gimme pound tea today 'n' pound pork 'n' three pounds terbarker!" The last part of the order was uttered very emphatically, as if it were by far the most important.

This was his regular purchase, except that sometimes he omitted the tea or the pork.

Two or three times every summer for many years he came to my grandfather's farm, always with two bushel baskets, one of which he wished to exchange for a bushel of potatoes to be carried home in the other. It did not matter what was the current price of a bushel of potatoes, whether thirty cents or a dollar; old Hughy expected to give a basket for a bushel of "pertates," as he called them. His baskets were well made and would always sell for seventy-five or eighty cents apiece at the village.

In the spring, when he was preparing ash strips for baskets, we heard his "maul" in the woods two days or more at a time. The blows were more slowly delivered and more resonant than the ax strokes of wood choppers, and woke hollow echoes in the woodland.

"Old Hughy's pounding basket stuff," the people said, and then all the boys were seized with a longing to go up to his cabin and hear the old man tell stories of moose hunting, of bears, of panthers, and of Indians.

My grandfather did not altogether approve of our going to visit old Hughy, for he filled our heads with notions of hunting and trapping; and "Such notions," my grandfather said, "make boys unsteady."

The cabin had once been a "shook shop," where country coopers made red oak staves for molasses hogsheads for export to the West Indies.

The hut was built of spruce logs, partly hewn, was roofed with riven pine shingles, each four feet long, and stood in the woods close beside a former lumber road now much overgrown.

In a corner of the cabin was the cooper's wide fireplace. It was a spot to delight a boy's heart for the old gun stood in the corner; the peeled ash fishing pole for pickerel was outside the door; the row of traps hung up by their chains on pegs inside; and sorted bundles of basket stuff, with always a basket or two on the "stock" in process of being woven, were piled about.

Moreover, there were mink, muskrat, and marten skins on stretchers up in the loft and perhaps a bear's hide nailed to the wall outside, or the head and antlers of a moose, recently shot, set on a high stump near the door. We listened breathlessly while Hughy told how he had shot the moose, or trapped the bear, and sometimes went with him to visit his bear trap, set on the mountain or beside a pond in the forest. The old man never failed to welcome visiting boys. He seemed to like to teach us his craft—the setting of traps and snares for rabbits and partridges; the tracks, traces, and cries of animals and birds; and even the principles and art of basket weaving.

His remarkable stories, magnified to suit our tastes but accepted as truth by us, were the greatest attraction; and the picture of his squat, gray-clothed figure and brown, kindly old visage crowned with a coonskin cap, as he sat filling in the ash-strip for baskets and narrating his hunting experiences, is very vivid among my boyish memories.

Sometimes, when in a humorous mood, he would pass his thumb critically over our youthful chins and say, "Sorter poor show fer whiskers here. Soil's poor, I gass. Wants latherin' with my kind o' shavin' soap, made o' cedar ashes and rabbit's taller."

The rabbits or large northern hares were very numerous there. Often on summer evenings we heard them "stamping" about the cabin and occasionally squealing pitifully in the thickets when beset by wild rats or foxes.

One winter the old man shot three moose. One of them had attacked him and chased him to the cover of bushes. This episode greatly roused the enthusiasm of all the young amateur hunters.

On one of the last afternoons in March I visited Hughy's cabin with my particular friend Ed Wilbur. We besought the old man to take us with him on a moose hunt.

"Too fur!" he said. "Too fur fer them little sparrer legs o' yourn. They'd get purty tired trav'lin' on snowshoes all day."

"But the snow's most gone now, Hughy," Ed urged. "We wouldn't have to go on snowshoes now."

"Wal, but moose all off rangin' now, 'cept cow-moose nestin' round in the swamp and leetle moose jost hatched."

The chance ambiguity of that word "hatched" took root in our ignorance. We pondered it for some moments.

"Why, I didn't know—" said Ed doubtfully.

"Why, I thought—" I began in some mental bewilderment.

"Did you ever find a moose's nest?" Ed asked.

The old woodsman did not at once reply to this question. For several moments he appeared to be busy arranging the ribs of a nose-basket.

"Did you ever, Hughy?" I prompted him.

He did not answer directly but said at last, "Shouldn't much wonder if there was an old cow-moose up round Squaw Pond this spring."

"Would she take after anybody if they got near her nest?" asked Ed.

"Wal, she mout," replied Hughy. "I've hearn tell on their doin' it. I've ben thinkin' o' takin' a tramp up thar 'fore very long," he continued after a pause, looking up at us from his basket. "But I'll go orful kinder still, I promise ye."

"Oh, couldn't we go with you?" I asked imploringly.

"'Fraid ye'd make too much racket," remarked old Hughy.

"Oh, we wouldn't!" said Ed. "We'd creep along after you just as still as mice."

Hughy did not assent. He seemed inclined to change the subject. But before we went home Ed again besought the old man to take us with him.

"Wal, wal, I'll see 'bout it," he said.

"When are you going?" I asked eagerly.

"Oh, 'long 'bout day arter termorrer in the arternoon, I gass, ef 'taint tu wet," he replied.

We accepted this declaration as an implied permission to accompany him, if by any means we could get away from home.

The season's stock of firewood was at that time being sawed and split in Grandfather's door-yard, and I was expected to work for several hours every day with the others. But I obtained consent to go to old Hughy in order to get my boot mended; I had accidentally cut it with an ax. Ed obtained his liberty by getting up very early and finishing his stint at the woodpile by noon.

When we reached Hughy's cabin, the old basket maker was about finishing his noonday meal of fried pork, potatoes, and tea.

"Are we going, Hughy?" Ed asked.

"Did I say as how ye mont go?" asked Hughy with an air of depressing coldness.

"We thought you was going to let us," I urged.

Old Hughy did not respond but lighted his pipe and smoked awhile. At last he took down his powder and shot and loaded his gun. After bidding us very strictly to keep a certain distance behind him and to take care not to break twigs under our feet, he set out for Squaw Pond, a rather dark and somber sheet of water, surrounded by a growth of evergreens.

"Now, yonkers," he said impressively, as we came out on the shore of the pond, "I want ye ter jost mind yer eyes, an' du jost 'zactly as I tell ye. It won't du ter be foolin' round. Ef that ar moose has got her nast anywheres round this pond, 'tis most likely not fur away from the water. We'll s'arch a leetle, but we must du it mighty easy and move as slick and still as ef we's all greased with goose ile."

Old Hughy moved slowly along in the bushes up the cast shore of the pond. There were still little banks of hard, dirty snow among the cedar and fir thickets. At every thick patch of evergreens the old hunter paused and listened intently. Then, in a whisper or with a motion of his hand, he bade us creep forward and search there.

We scared out several hares and partridges, and once a deer, but found nothing resembling a moose's nest. At the upper end of the pond there was a dense growth of low hemlock at the foot of a broken line of rocks and ledges. Near the shore here in the damp, leafy loam, old Hughy pointed to some holes that looked like large hoof prints; and after listening again very attentively, he motioned to us to search the thicket. We did so and at first discovered nothing; but upon Hughy's again motioning us to creep in while he watched, we began a more thorough search.

As we were crawling about, parting the boughs with our hands, our eyes suddenly fell on a strange spectacle.

Back under the evergreen, partly beneath the overhang of a great rock and lying half buried in old leaves and dry twigs, were two of the queerest objects that ever met the eye of a hunter. They were reddish-brown, and egg-shaped and covered with hair. They were about a foot and a half long and perhaps a foot thick.

Half frightened, we crept out and hurried to old Hughy. "We've found it—two eggs!" was all I could say for the moment.

After glancing cautiously all around and listening again, the old trapper laid down his gun and entered the thicket with us.

"By halibut, you've found it!" he exclaimed in great apparent excitement.

Then he crawled up to the nest, lifted the egg-shaped objects one by one in both hands, shook them gently, and held them to his ear.

"Most ready ter hatch!" he muttered. "I kin hear the leetle fellers stampin' round inside. 'Baout by day arter termorrer, I gass, the ole moose's be along and give the shell a rip with one of her stub horns. Then out'll pop that ar leetle moose! Never'd git out ef she didn't—the shell is so ha'ry and tough. But she knows jost when to come. 'Spect she's a-harkin' round not fur off," he added, again listening. "Gass we'd better be gittin' away."

Scarcely daring to draw breath, Ed and I crept out of the hemlock. We hurried away, and the only question that I remember asking on our way to the cabin was if moose eggs were always covered with hair.

"All 't ever I see was," replied old Hughy.

While we were at the pond, fear had kept any such project from our minds, but on our way home we began to think of robbing the nest. How well old Hughy understood boys! That was the very thing he knew we should want to do.

"Jingo!" cried Ed. "Wouldn't it be fun to get those moose eggs and carry them down to the barn and raise the little mooses just like calves?"

"Oh, wouldn't it!" I exclaimed. It seemed to me that a more attractive idea had never entered my head before.

"Old Hughy didn't say we shouldn't," said Ed. "We found it, too. It's as much our nest as anybody's."

From that moment we were quite agog with this project. I had quite forgotten my cut boot already, and when questioned concerning it at home, I could only reply weakly that I didn't think to speak to Hughy about it.

We were much too eager and excited to run the risk of not being permitted to go to Squaw Pond the next day. Without obtaining consent, and without the knowledge of our families, we "cut" directly after dinner.

I found Ed impatiently awaiting me behind his father's barn. Then an anxious question arose. We had nothing to arm ourselves with except a small hay fork. We could not make an attack on a moose's nest without some sort of gun.

Willis Murch, a boy of about our age who lived at the next farm beyond the Wilburs', owned a little shotgun. With some reluctance we agreed to take him into our confidence, in order to get him to go with his gun.

We called him out into the field and told him our business. He was densely incredulous at first, but consented to go and got his gun.

When we reached the spot, the Murch boy stood with his gun cocked, ready for a sudden attack. Ed and I crept through the evergreen to the foot of the great rock.

There lay the eggs among the dried leaves. Trembling in our haste and excitement, we rolled them out and each seized one. They were quite heavy; but, clasping them with both arms, we dashed out of the thicket without stopping to give Willis a chance to look at them.

The consequences of being pursued and overtaken by an enraged mother moose whose eggs had been stolen were fearful to think of. We did not halt till we had gained the foot of the pond.

There we rested for a few minutes and let Willis Murch see our prizes. The tough, hairy skins of the eggs could be dented by bearing hard on them with our fingers, and it was manifest that they would soon hatch, for we could feel and at times could see a movement inside the shell.

Ed and I agreed that each of us should keep his own egg and allow it to hatch in his own barn.

On a rising swell of land near the barn I came suddenly on the Old Squire. He had a cane in his hand and was attentively examining certain tracks on a still lingering snowdrift in the lee of a stone wall, which I had crossed in my hurried flight from the house to join Ed.

"Well, well, young sir," he said. "Where have you been, and what have you got there?"

"A moose egg, sir," I replied with both anxiety and pride.

"A *what*?" he exclaimed loudly, looking hard at my burden.

"A moose egg, Grandpa," I repeated in a conciliatory tone. "There were two of them. We found a nest. Ed Wilbur, he's got the other one."

"Let me see that thing!" he cried. Taking it out of my arms, he looked it over with a grin that kept broadening till it ended in a snort of ironical laughter. Yet it was evident that he could not make much out of it.

I hurriedly and eagerly narrated the particulars of the discovery.

"You went with Hughy Gerrish to find it, did ye?"

"Yes, sir, but Ed and I were the ones that found it."

"Humph!" he ejaculated, and then strode away toward the house, with the egg under his arm. I followed on behind him.

When we reached the kitchen door, the family was assembling for supper. Elder Witham, a Methodist minister, had arrived during the afternoon to attend a quarterly meeting that began the next day. The good clergyman was walking up and down in the yard with his hands crossed behind his back and a hymn book in one of them.

"Elder Witham!" the Old Squire called out with ill-concealed merriment. "Did you ever see a moose egg? Our boy here has got one."

The elder came forward without speaking and Grandfather deposited the egg on the doorstep. Grandmother and several of my cousins had come out, and the two hired men drew near from the woodpile.

The elder stooped down and turned it over and started back a little when he saw a movement inside it.

"A moose egg! A moose egg!" he cried, his face relaxing into a broad smile. "Why, Squire, that's against nature, ain't it?"

"According to my lights it is," said Grandfather, joining in the smile.

Meantime my older cousin, Addison, had come near and was examining the egg, slowly parting the hair on it in places. There were several small holes in it. "Here seems to be a kind of hard ridge," he said, carefully opening the hair in another place. "It looks to me like a seam. Yes, here are stitches." He took out his knife and with a few slashes opened up the stitches. Then with his fingers he pulled the edges wide apart; and there jumped out, almost in his face, and went hopping across the yard a big, blinking rabbit!

Shouts of laughter followed. The hired men rolled over on the ground and smote their knees, convulsed. My younger cousins gave chase after the rabbit. I alone was not amused.

Tears of mortification were in my eyes. Sudden disappointment and great shame fell upon me. My grief-stricken looks attested my innocence but only added to the general mirth.

At last the Old Squire gave me a half-contemptuous pat on the head.

"Never mind, my son, never mind it," he said.

"'Tis pretty near the fust of April, ye know. Never mind it; you'll larn something yet, if ye live long enough!"

But the elder regarded me doubtfully. Grandmother also made a diversion in my favor by saying briskly, "Supper's all ready and waiting."

It was a very shamefaced meal for me. For weeks and months afterward the words "moose egg" were sufficient to bring a hot flush to my face. Old Hughy had converted two baskets and two pieces of moose skin over a framework of basket stuff into the worst Fool's-day joke that ever befell me.

After dark that night I contrived to slip out of sight for a few minutes and, running all the way to the Wilburs', beckoned Ed out into the yard.

"Get that moose egg o' yours out o' sight, Ed, just as quick as you can!" I whispered. "And if you haven't told anybody about it, never lisp a word!"

"What's up?" he exclaimed.

"Cut it open and you'll find out," said I, and ran back home.

Owing to this warning, Ed was spared the ridicule that had overwhelmed me.

11

Addison's War with Tibbetts

MAY DAY CAME AND PASSED, AND ACCORDING TO custom thereabouts the boys were now hanging May baskets to the girls, evenings. On the night of May 4, Addison, Thomas, Halstead, Ned Wilbur, and I set off with two May baskets apiece, ten in all, for the Corners where we intended to hang several to the girls living there, and also to visit three farmhouses near the grist mill two miles beyond.

There was no moon, but the night was still and warm, with the spring brooks roaring and the frogs peeping in the swamps. Theodora and Ellen wanted to go, and at length it was agreed that they and Katherine Edwards with Thomas should set off together, taking neighbor Edwards's horse and wagon, and drive over past the Corners, about a mile and a half, to what was locally known as "the picnic grove." There was a cart trail leading off the highway into this grove, and here they agreed to turn in quietly, hitch up the horse, and wait for us boys to come on afoot after we had hung a number of baskets at the Corners. They were to take no part in the frolic at the Corners but wait there for us to join them later.

As it chanced they were obliged to wait much longer than they or we expected. For we were hotly chased by a party of the Corners girls and boys and only saved ourselves from capture by taking refuge in the woods half a mile to the northward, where we lay hidden for an hour or more before our pursuers retired and gave up the search.

In consequence, it was past ten o'clock before we were able to reach the picnic grove. Thomas and the girls, in fact, had come to the conclusion that we had been taken captive and shut up for the night. We explained our absence and recounted our adventures; then, leaving the horse and wagon concealed in the grove, we proceeded along the road to Miller Harland's house, half a mile distant, to hang a basket for Alice Harland.

I do not know how late it had grown, for none of us carried a watch, but presume that it must have been past eleven o'clock.

"It will be too bad to knock on their door and rouse them all at this time of night," Theodora said. "Let's pin the basket to the front door and go away without knocking, this time. Alice will find it in the morning."

This less boisterous plan was adopted, and after pinning up a basket for Alice we went on toward the house of a farmer, named Merrill, to leave a basket there for his daughter Lizzie.

There was a long hill to climb and we had reached the summit when we heard a horse and wagon, toiling slowly up from the other side.

"Wonder who is out at this time o' night?" exclaimed Thomas in a low voice, for in that sparsely settled community it was somewhat unusual to find persons abroad at that hour.

"Maybe the Merrills, themselves," said Katherine. "Let's get out of sight." Thereupon we all covertly left the road and hid in a clump of hemlock shrubs on the south side of it, till the wagon should pass us.

It came slowly up the hill. "Guess they've got a heavy load," whispered Ned. He and Addison peeped out as the team went by. "It's one man alone," whispered Addison, for it was starlight and not uncommonly dark. "What's that he's got on the hind part of the wagon?"

"Looks like a barrel," said Ned. "'Tis a barrel." The wagon had passed by this time, and we all stepped forth.

"That looks like Tibbetts's old express wagon," said Tom. "I believe it is, and I shouldn't wonder if that was Tibbetts, himself, driving."

We had started to go on down the hill, when Addison suddenly said, "You go ahead and hang the baskets. I'm going back along."

"What for?" said Tom.

"Oh, I've got a reason," replied Addison.

"Don't, Ad," said Theodora. "I wouldn't go chasing after that man."

Addison laughed. "Needn't wait for me at the grove. I shall be at home by the time you are," he said and hurried back along the road, in the wake of the team that had passed.

We went on and hung a May basket for Lizzie Merrill, then retraced our steps to the grove and all rode homeward. There was little fun in it; it was too late at night.

On the orchard hill, just below the Old Squire's, we overtook Addison.

"Well, what did you find out?" Tom asked him.

"Oh, not much," he replied evasively, but we noticed that he seemed jolly and a good deal amused about something. He would not answer any questions that night.

Next forenoon, however, while he and I were plowing in the south field, I asked him if that was really Tibbetts whom we had seen the previous night.

"No," said Addison. "That was Simeon Glinds, our new school agent. But 'twas Tibbetts's horse and wagon," he continued after a moment, "and I think I've got that old sinner in a tight place."

"Do you think it was a barrel of rum?" I asked.

"I'm sure it was," said Addison. "I followed along after the wagon as close as I dared and once or twice got quite near. When at last he stopped at Tibbetts's store, I went around through a field and came up close behind the place. Tibbetts was there waiting for him and came out but did not have a lantern. They scarcely spoke, and as soon as they could get the barrel out of the wagon, they took the horse and wagon into Tibbetts's stable. I slipped round the corner while they were unharnessing and smelled of the barrel. It smelled rummy. I rolled it just a little easy, too, and heard it swash. Then Tibbetts and Glinds came back to the platform of the store and opened the bulkhead door there, leading into the cellar. They made scarcely a bit of noise and worked pretty fast, too. In half a minute they had that barrel down the stairs and rolled it away in the cellar. I couldn't tell what part of the cellar they had put it, for as soon as they got the barrel down the stairs, Tibbetts came back and, sticking his head out, glanced around and listened, then eased the bulkhead door down.

"After that they were down cellar there for fifteen or twenty minutes, and I guess they sampled the liquor, for when they came out Glinds was sort of smacking his lips and I heard him say, 'Pooty good stuff, Mr. Tibbetts,' and Tibbetts said, ''Twill do.'

"And now," continued Addison with great satisfaction, "I think I know how that old fox has managed to get his liquor so long and beat the law. We have all wondered how he did it and have had the officers watching for him at the village and at the railroad station where his other goods and groceries come. But his liquor does not come that way at all. It comes over this hilly country road to the west, from over New Hampshire way somewheres. No one ever has thought of watching that road, for it doesn't seem to lead anywhere, you know. But that's the route the rum comes by; and Glinds—the man he put in for school agent—does the hauling, between days."

"But do you suppose you have got evidence enough to convict him in court?" I asked, for I had heard a great deal about liquor cases since I came to the Old Squire's.

"I don't know," replied Addison a little doubtfully. "It takes strong evidence, for half the jurymen nearly always favor the rum seller; and if we were to summon Simeon Glinds as a witness, he would most likely swear it was a barrel of kerosene, or vinegar. These old topers always side with the rum seller and will commit perjury, without turning a hair, in a liquor case.

"But I've got another plan," Addison continued, in a lower tone. "I think I can use this to trap Tibbetts another way. Perhaps it will not work, for he is as cunning as old Nick himself; but if it does work, I'll make him dance like a rat on a hot stove, see if I don't!"

My curiosity was much excited, but Addison would not say anything more that day.

Two evenings after, while he and I were on the way to the post office together to get the papers, he told me he was going to say a word to Tibbetts that night. "You watch and see how he takes it," he added.

We went into the store and after standing about a few moments, till nobody else chanced to be near, Addison called for our mail and as Tibbetts handed it to him, asked, "How does that barrel o' rum sell—

the one you got in last Tuesday night at about twelve o'clock?"

Tibbetts started perceptibly and looked very hard at Addison but did not reply.

"Oh, you are wasting time being so sly about it," Addison went on coolly. "I know all about it, who hauled it, where it came from, and where you've been getting all your other liquor for a year past. And the county attorney will soon know, too."

Tibbetts, who had been visibly alarmed, now began to grin a little at the injudicious manner in which Addison threw out his information, from mere bravado.

As soon as we were outside the store and on our way home, I asked Addison if it was not foolish to tell Tibbetts anything about it beforehand. "He thought you were a greenhorn," said I. "You've been and warned him now, and he will have time to get things all fixed before you can do anything."

"That was just what I wanted him to think," replied Addison. "But you wait and see. You know he has had the name of stopping letters at the post office. Two or three times folks have suspected him. Maybe he did, maybe he didn't; I don't know. I am sure he has no more principle than to do it. A man who will break the law constantly in one thing is likely to in another, if he takes the notion. But it is a saucy business, breaking open another person's letter, you know, a state prison offense. A liquor trial he would get out of, somehow; but if we could catch him stopping letters, we could make it hot for him. But I am not going to say anything more of this just now, and don't you," Addison continued.

Saturday Addison asked the Old Squire if he and I could drive to the village to get us each a pair of summer shoes and some calico shirts, by way of a summer outfit. Permission being obtained, Gram, who knew nothing of Addison's schemes, suggested that Halstead should go with us to purchase similar articles. Addison looked slightly nonplused at this proposition, and at first opposed it, offering to buy the articles for Halse and fetch them home to be tried on. Gram insisted that Halstead should go, however, and go he did; but after we had reached the village, and Halstead was at the shoe store, Addison made a signal to me to come away and leave Halstead there. Addison and I then drove off together. At first I was much in the dark as to what was afoot. Addison explained it, however, as we went along.

"I want to see the county attorney," he said. "I am going to notify him in advance that I shall mail a letter for him at our post office Monday morning. I shall tell him that folks have suspected Tibbetts of opening other persons' letters, and that if he is that sort of postmaster, we want to find him out, and that this letter is to be a test—a decoy letter.

"I am going to explain about the liquor barrel," Addison continued. "Also some other facts, and ask Attorney Foster to be on the lookout Monday evening for a letter from me, mailed at our office. For I think that Tibbetts, when he sees a letter from me to the county attorney in the office, will stop it and break it open to find out what is going on. I am pretty sure he will, for he is just that kind of man. So I am setting a trap for him—a regular bear trap—and if once I get his old paw into it, he has got to do as I tell him, or I'll have his skin nailed up to dry on my barn door!"

This project on Addison's part excited me not a little. I do not think that the spirit that animated him was a wholly amiable one, but perhaps it was justifiable as such matters go.

"To make it all the surer," Ad went on, "I am going to call at the village post office, as we go back, and have a little talk with the postmaster there, who knows me pretty well. The mail bag from our small office at the Corners, you know, is taken to the village office first and is there opened and the letters put in the village bag. I am going to have a little talk with the postmaster there, give him a hint of what is afoot, and ask him to take particular notice of the letters that come from our office, Monday forenoon, to see whether there is one for the county attorney. I want him to take such careful notice that he can testify if he should be called as a witness. You see," Ad continued, "if we can show that a letter mailed at our office never reached the village office we shall have a tight squeeze on Tibbetts's fingers, particularly as it is a letter about him and his illegal traffic."

When we reached Attorney Foster's office, I sat and held the horse while Addison made his call. He had to wait some time, and when he at length got an audience the matter came near miscarrying altogether, for Attorney Foster said it was an irregular affair that he did not care to have any connection with. But when Ad had made the whole matter plain and told what we had seen the night we hung the May baskets, the lawyer finally laughed and bade him go ahead, adding that if Tibbetts was innocent no harm would be done him or anybody else.

We drove back to the village, where Addison saw the postmaster as he had planned. We then looked up Halse and drove home.

Addison and I had been so much engrossed in his project that we hurriedly bought calico shirts two or three sizes too large for us, much to Gram's disgust. Halse had bought an excellent fit, and he blurted out at the supper table that we had run off and left him at the village and that he believed we had driven a good ways, for old Sol was in a sweat when we came back. No questions were asked, however, and the topic of conversation was changed.

Next day Addison wrote his letter to the county attorney, stating what we had seen a few nights previously, but it was largely a repetition of what he had already told him. Monday morning we went to the office and mailed it. Before starting, however, Addison showed the envelope to the Old Squire and asked him to bear in mind that on that day we went to the post office to mail such a letter. The old gentleman wished to know why he was writing such a letter and what it contained. Ad explained briefly, not entirely to the Old Squire's satisfaction, although he did not say much.

On our way to the Corners Mr. Wilbur overtook and gave us a ride. Addison bethought himself to show the letter to him and asked him to take notice, after we got to the office, that he mailed it that morning, and to remember the day and the date. Mr. Wilbur said he would do so, but he looked a little curious, and to satisfy him Addison gave him a hint as to what was afoot.

When we reached the post office, Ad went in alone at first so that Tibbetts would see him. Afterwards, when Mr. Wilbur came in, Addison stepped up and dropped the letter into the letter box. I was standing near and saw Tibbetts glance at us when the cover of the slip rattled. We then came away.

The next day, in the afternoon, the Old Squire drove to the village, and Gram sent us down with him to change our calico shirts for smaller ones. Addison seized this opportunity to see the postmaster and learned from him that no letter to the county attorney had passed through the mail that day. "He may be holding it," the postmaster suggested. "I will keep watch for a week."

Saturday, following, Addison found excuse for going to the village again and learned that his letter had not appeared at the post office there. We had now no doubt whatever that Tibbetts had stopped the letter and destroyed it after reading the contents. It would have been necessary now merely to obtain the affidavits of the county attorney and the village postmaster, along with those of Mr. Wilbur and the Old Squire, to put Postmaster Tibbetts in an exceedingly unpleasant situation. I suppose it may have been our duty to enforce the law. Crime ought not to be covered up, nor shielded from its proper penalty. But Addison was a boy who, when he had an object in view, never lost sight of it; he would turn any and every circumstance to account to forward that object. All that winter and spring he had worked to beat Tibbetts and get a school agent appointed who would hire Joel Pierson the following winter. It seemed as if he cared little for anything else.

A few nights afterward we went to the post office, and on the way there Addison gloated over his victory. "We've got his old paw in the trap," he exclaimed, "and now he shall do as I say, or we'll roast him."

"Well, we are going to have a new postmaster, aren't we?" said I.

"Oh, I don't know," replied Addison indifferently. "If Tibbetts will do as I say about the school, I don't much care for turning him out."

"But he isn't fit for postmaster," said I. "A man who will break open letters ought not to be kept in as postmaster."

"Of course he hadn't," replied Ad. "But if he will give in and help hire Joel Pierson, I'll let him go on awhile."

I was not clear in my mind as to this.

"I guess we will stir him up a little tonight," Ad continued. "He doesn't realize that he is caught yet, you know. So I'm going to rattle the trap chain a little, just to let the old bear see the fix he is in, and then punch him a few times with a pole. I shouldn't wonder if he showed his old teeth and growled, at first. But we have got him hard and fast. You keep your ears open for all he says. He may say or do something that there ought to be a witness for."

We went into the store and Addison asked for the Old Squire's mail. Tibbetts was putting up kerosene for little Mamie Davis, who had come in with a can. After she had gone out, he came around to the enclosed space where the post office desk and box frame stood and handed Addison our mail, without speaking.

Addison took it and said, "Well, Mr. Tibbetts, how does the new barrel hold out? Most time to haul home another one, isn't it?"

The grocer was a heavy, red-faced man; he looked at Addison with an expression of hatred actually venomous.

"Look-a-here, young imppidence. You take your mail and get out of this store," he said in a low but savage tone.

"Oh certainly, Mr. Postmaster," Ad replied, going to the door.

"I shouldn't have come into the post office if I had not had business here. I am within my rights."

In the door he stopped, and turning toward Tibbetts, who had taken a step after us, said, "By the way, Postmaster, there is something a little queer about a letter that was mailed here last Monday morning at eight o'clock. You probably remember the letter I refer to. It was addressed to the county attorney at the village. Now you thought, the other day, Postmaster, that I was a greenhorn to say anything about that liquor barrel to you, and to go and write a letter in that way to the county attorney. But it wasn't so green as it looked. That letter you stopped and broke open was a decoy letter, mailed here on purpose to trap you."

Tibbetts's angry face changed color a little. "Yes, Postmaster," Addison continued, "we know about your tricks with letters here; that letter was to catch you, and we've caught you. The county attorney was notified the Saturday before that this letter was to be mailed Monday morning, and the postmaster at the village was also notified to be on the lookout for it. He is ready to make oath that it was not in the bag, neither on that day nor any day this week."

"No such letter was ever mailed here!" shouted Tibbetts.

"Not too fast, Postmaster," said Addison coolly. "I looked out for that part. I have three witnesses of the fact that I brought the letter here, two of whom can make oath that they saw me put it in the letter box, under your very nose."

Tibbetts was not lacking in intelligence. He perceived at once that he was in a fix. His face had turned quite white, either from rage or sudden apprehension. The effects of his bad habits suddenly showed in him. We noticed that the hand he thrust out against the case of letter boxes shook and that his coarse, hard nerve suddenly failed him. Ad and I, thus far, had stood ready to run if he attacked us; but now our fear of him abated. We felt instinctively that he would not be able to harm us much.

"Oh, we've got you, Tibbetts. Don't you think we haven't!" exclaimed Ad. "You walked right into the trap. It isn't a liquor case at all, this time, though we can make a pretty case out of that if we choose. But it is something, this time, that you cannot get out of by paying a fine. It isn't the Maine Law but Uncle Sam's postal laws that you're foul of. We've got you now where we can handle you. I have been getting this thing ready for you for some time, and now I've got you where I can break you. I can close your rum hole here, take this post office away from you, and put you in the state prison. You cannot stop a letter to the county attorney for nothing, you know!"

Tibbetts's visage was a study for me as I stood in a species of juvenile fascination, watching him. To this day I can see the purple and white spots that showed on his face. He did not speak but stood staring at Addison.

"I want you to understand," Addison continued, walking up closer to him now, looking him full in the face with cool scrutiny, speaking, too, with an intensity of suppressed feeling that made me glance at him curiously, "I want you to understand that I have beaten you at last. There's been trouble in this school district for two years; but it was you and I who have really been doing the fighting, and now I've beaten you and got you in a corner, and I'll put the screws on you, too—unless," Addison continued after a little pause, still looking him in the eye, but changing his tone, "unless you want to knuckle down and do as I say about the school. Joel Pierson is a good teacher. Everybody admits that. We want him here next winter. Now, Postmaster, if you give Simeon Glinds the word to hire him, right off, pretty quick now, before he is otherwise engaged, why, I may not press this matter, just yet. Understand?"

Still Tibbetts stood looking at Addison, measuring him, so to speak, and pondering the situation without speaking. I could see that he was somewhat broken up.

"Joel Pierson is going to teach this school next winter anyhow, you see if he doesn't," Addison said confidently. "If you stand out, I'll put you behind bars. When you are gone, we will choose another agent who will hire Master Pierson."

"Wal, I never said anything agin Pierson, or agin hirin' him," Tibbetts said at length in a changed, conciliatory tone. "Did you ever hear me say that I didn't want him?"

"Oh that's all right, Postmaster," Ad exclaimed with a grim laugh. "You and I understand each other pretty well. I don't trust you at all, in anything. But if Simeon Glinds writes to Joel Pierson Monday morning, offering him the school, I shall know what that means. If he doesn't, the United States marshal will be around here by Wednesday." And with that we came away.

I was, I remember, much staggered in mind by the compact Ad had made. I asked him as we went home if he thought such a bargain was the right thing. He laughed and said it was the way to get a good school the next winter.

"But what suppose the Old Squire would say?" I asked him.

"Well, I don't mean to say much about this at home for a while," Addison replied. "I'm pretty sure that the county attorney will not take it up, because, as he said, it is irregular procedure; and I do not think that the postmaster at the village will move in the matter, unless complaint is made. I calculated that I held the game in my own hands, and I've played it in the way I wanted to. I've got Tibbetts where I can chuck his old head under water if he doesn't do as I bid him."

Addison wrote, himself, to Master Pierson on Monday and received a reply from him saying that agent Glinds had written that day offering him the school! When Addison read this letter at the supper table Wednesday evening, there was a general exclamation of surprise as well as pleasure. The Old Squire himself appeared to be astonished and puzzled, then recalling the matter of the letter to the county attorney, the outside of which he had seen, he remarked that it looked as if Tibbetts was trying to curry favor with us.

"That's what I think, sir," said Ad, giving me a nudge to keep quiet.

"Well, well," said Gram. "I can hardly believe it, but Tibbetts may not be so bad after all as we have thought he was. I suppose we ought to have charity."

This ingenuous remark made me feel rather queer, and it amused Addison so much that for some moments he sat fairly shaken with suppressed laughter. "Grandma," he said at length, "don't you waste any charity on Tibbetts. He didn't do this out of any kindness to us, you may be sure."

"I don't believe he did either!" exclaimed the old lady, promptly rejecting her charity theory. "But I don't see what has got into him."

Theodora and the Old Squire looked more puzzled than ever.

"What has Ad been doing?" the former asked me after supper, but I would not reveal anything, further than to wink knowingly and exasperatingly. The Old Squire did not learn the particulars of the compact with Tibbetts for a year or more. When he did, he quite disapproved of it, and even declared that Addison, to some extent, rendered himself answerable for compounding an offense against the postal laws. But the old gentleman did nothing else since, by then, poor Wealthy had died of diphtheria as a result of Tibbetts's failure to clean out the schoolhouse well.

12

Learning to Shear Sheep

IT IS NOT OFTEN THAT A BOY BROUGHT UP IN THE city makes a successful farmer, but I remember one who did, and the story of his first appearance in our part of the country is an amusing one—and points a moral.

There was a prospect of a game of ball at the Corners that Saturday, I remember, and my cousin Addison and I had planned to take part in it. But things had not been going on just right at the old farm. Grandma Ruth, Theodora, Ellen, and Wealthy were away on a much-needed shopping trip to Portland, and Halstead had had to accompany them. The firewood was not yet all worked up, there was a newly cleared lot to pile and burn off, and five hundred bushels of potatoes to get out of the cellar. To our disappointment, that morning the Old Squire said, "Boys, you mustn't go away today. Work is in too bad a shape. I can't let you go. You must shear forty sheep today. I want to get the whole flock off to pasture next week."

Unlike most of his neighbors, the Old Squire always sheared his sheep before sending them out to pasture in the spring and kept them in the warm barn cellar for five or six nights afterward, so that they need not take cold from parting with their fleeces.

We had not had a play day since the winter school closed. I have to own that there was grumbling. But we ground four pairs of sheepshears, swept the barn floor, then penned the sheep at the farther end of it and began work. Twenty sheep apiece is a fair stint.

"Be careful about cutting them," the Old Squire cautioned us, and he brought out the tarpot, to touch the spots where the skin got snipped off, for even an expert shearer will sometimes clip a bit off the sheep's hide with the wool.

We sheared away from nine till twelve and got no more than ten apiece done; they were large sheep, carrying seven or eight pounds of wool each. There was no prospect of going to the ball game, and after seeing us at work in the afternoon, the Old Squire harnessed and drove away to a farmer's place, four miles distant, to look at a yoke of working oxen he had thoughts of buying.

We had been at work about an hour, feeling pretty glum, for we could hear the shouts of the ball players out at the Corners, and I think that Addison was saying that whatever he did in life he would not be a farmer—at least that was what he almost always did say at such times. Suddenly we heard a step on the barn floor, and there stood a stranger.

He was very much of a stranger, indeed. We saw at a glance that he did not belong in that part of the country. His clothes fitted better than did ours. He was tall and rather good looking; there was very little spring tan on his face, and his hands were white and delicate. Yet there was something about him that led us both to think the same thing; namely, that ill fortune had overtaken him and that he had recently seen hard times. We supposed that he was a book agent, or had something to sell.

"Good afternoon!" he said. "Pleasant day."

"Oh, the day's all right," said Addison shortly. "What's wanted? Because if you are an agent for anything, you will only waste your time on us."

The young man laughed. "No," he said. "I'm looking for work. They told me at the house below that you wanted to hire a man on the farm here."

"Well, that's so," replied Addison with a glance at me. "The Old Squire's going to hire a man, but—do you know what farm work is? Did you ever work on a farm?"

"No," replied the stranger. "I never did. But I am going to be a farmer, and I want a place to work."

We laughed.

"Oh, I will work," he said. "I'll take hold of anything."

"The Old Squire's away this afternoon," replied Addison evasively.

"Do you think that he would hire me if I were to wait till he came home?" the stranger asked.

Addison glanced at me. "No," he said. "I don't think he would."

"We want a man who is used to farm work," I added, to smooth matters over.

"But I could learn very quickly," urged the stranger. "And I'm not afraid of work. I'm strong and well. I can do as much as anyone—in a day or two.

"You see," he continued, "I need to get a place. I was hoping you would hire me and let me begin now, so that I could have a place to stay tonight. I should like to begin work this afternoon."

His urgency disturbed us. We were thinking how we could get rid of him, for it was plain to see that he was not the sort of man to hire on a farm.

"What do you call what you are doing to that sheep?" he asked suddenly.

"Shearing," replied Addison.

"I can do that!" the stranger exclaimed. "Let me try. I'm sure I can do it."

"A knack goes with shearing sheep," replied Addison. "It takes practice not to cut them. Round here they don't let a beginner begin on sheep."

"What does he begin on?" asked our persistent caller.

Addison did not reply at once. He turned his sheep over, made a few clips, then glanced at me. "Generally on a hog," he said.

I held my face straight.

"A hog is tougher," Addison went on. "No matter if you do cut a hog a little. A hog's skin is thick, you know. When a beginner has sheared three hogs, they let him go on to sheep."

The stranger looked thoughtful. "What do they do with the shearings of the hogs?" he asked.

"The bristles?" said Addison. "They make paintbrushes of them."

"Oh, yes," said the stranger. "I know that now. I've noticed them in paintbrushes."

We went on shearing. The stranger watched us for some moments. "Well, I'll do it!" he suddenly exclaimed. "I will begin on a hog, if you say so."

Not a word was said for some time. We were in a mood that afternoon for almost any kind of hard joking.

"You're bound to begin, then?" said Addison, while he rolled up the fleece he had just finished shearing.

"Yes, siree, I am!" exclaimed the stranger.

"All right, then," said Addison. "Here's a pair of sheepshears, just ground sharp. The hogs are down in the barn cellar. Come on."

We went round and down into the cellar, where away back on the dark side of it there were four large shoats in a pen. "Keep still," Addison whispered to me, as we went along. "Let's see what he will do."

We shut the outer door of the cellar, and then let the biggest and ugliest of the four shoats out of the pen into the open space.

"There you are!" cried Addison. "Down with him now and shear him! Mind he doesn't bite you. It's against the rules for anybody to help. He will squeal some, but that's nothing."

And with that, by way of introduction, we left him there with the hog.

All remained quiet for as much as ten minutes. We had resumed our shearing.

"I guess he has left," said Addison, laughing.

But he had not. He was only studying the situation. Suddenly a terrific outburst of squealing began, and it continued! We cautiously pulled aside a scuttle in the floor and peeped down. The stranger and the hog were having a pitched battle!

The hog squealed, roared, and snapped at its assailant, but the newcomer steered it into a corner and, seizing hold of its legs on one side, overthrew the beast and held it down. He had trouble reaching his shears, and the hog got up; but after another tussle he threw the irate animal down again, and then began shearing it. The bristles cut hard, but he sheared them off and kept at work.

"Ad, he's going to shear those hogs!" said I. "And what will the Old Squire say?"

"I don't know," replied Addison. "But let him work."

We went back to our sheepshearing, and for an hour or two bedlam reigned in that barn cellar. It was one continuous squeal and roar. The other shoats began hoarsely barking, in sympathy at first; but growing excited by the wild outcries of their comrade that was being sheared, they soon squealed as loudly as he did, and by and by broke out of the pen and rushed to the rescue. There was trouble then! That poor fellow had them all on his hands at once!

"I'm really afraid they will hurt him, Ad!" I exclaimed.

"I guess not," said Addison. "But if we hear him yell, we will go down."

We heard nothing from him, however, except whacks from a piece of board with which he was belaboring the hogs. At last he drove the three back into their sty. Then the steady squealing began again.

Peeping down after a time, we discovered that he had taken a piece of wire from a bunch of shingles in the cellar and wired up the hog's snout with it, to keep it from biting him.

"He is going to shear them, sure," said I.

"I guess he will," said Addison, looking a little foolish.

We knew when he had finished the first one by the outbreak of squealing that ensued as he put the sheared hog back in the pen and got out another. And while the noise was still at its height, the Old Squire came driving into the yard. He heard the uproar and without stopping even to hitch came hastily into the barn floor. "What's the matter with the hogs?" he cried.

"Well, sir," replied Addison, looking up slowly from his sheep, "there's a fellow down there shearing them."

"Shearing the hogs!" exclaimed the Old Squire. "What d'ye mean? Who is it?"

"Don't know, sir. Never saw him before. He's bound to shear them," replied Addison, his voice nearly drowned in the squealing below.

The Old Squire stared at us, then rushed out and down to the cellar. Addison and I tiptoed to the scuttle.

"Here you, sir! What in the world d'ye think you are doing?" the old gentleman shouted.

The stranger looked up. He had the second hog's mouth wired and was working away on him, but he had been bitten in three or four places, and he looked a good deal disheveled.

"Do you know what you are about?" demanded the Old Squire.

"I am learning to shear sheep, sir," replied the stranger. "I have the second pig almost done, and here are all the bristles. I will get the other one sheared in an hour more."

The Old Squire thought he was crazy and told him so. "But who set you at this?" he suddenly exclaimed.

The stranger hesitated; evidently he was no telltale. "I was informed, sir," he replied, "that this is the way to learn to shear sheep. I want to learn. I want a job working on a farm. So I took hold of it."

"Oh, those boys, those boys!" muttered the Old Squire. Then he began to laugh. "You let that hog get up," he said, "and come away.

Young man, those boys up there have been fooling you. What's your name?"

"Edward H. Lowe, sir," the stranger replied. "I do really want a place to work. I am going to be a farmer."

The Old Squire laughed heartily. "I will say this much for you," he exclaimed, "you've got grit! I wouldn't have undertaken to shear those hogs for twenty dollars!"

Addison and I heard them coming round to the barn floor and made haste to take the horse to the stable, and so keep out of sight. We had begun to feel ashamed of the prank—as one always does afterward.

It proved a good opening for young Lowe, however. The Old Squire had taken a liking to him and ended by hiring him for the season.

He was with us three years in succession and proved to be the best farmhand we ever had. Moreover, he saved his wages, and at the end of the third year he had enough to buy a farm of his own. Mr. Lowe is now one of the four most prosperous farmers in the county.

13

An Embarrassing Fourth of July

SPRING COMES SO TARDILY IN MAINE THAT LAKES AND streams are rarely warm enough to bathe in before the first of July. Even then the water is often too cold for comfort, but the boys at our place generally planned to go in swimming on the fourth.

In my home neighborhood we had a swimming hole down on the Robbins brook where there was a pool that we had enlarged by building a dam; and it was said that the girls also had one, in the woods half a mile farther up the brook.

But when all was done, our swimming hole was nothing to boast of since it was scarcely fifty feet long and had a poor bottom, besides being badly infested by mosquitoes. It was not to be compared with the one in the Lurvey's Mills district on Lurvey's Stream; nor yet with the one in the Bagdad school district, three miles to the east of our place, for that was on the Little Androscoggin River where, below rapids, there was a great lovely pool that had a sandy bottom soft to the feet and was enclosed along both banks by white birches. On the bare ledges above it, screened round by alder clumps and hung with festoons of clematis, there was a nice place to undress and leave one's clothes.

The only drawback about it was that the boys of the Bagdad district claimed ownership there and tried to keep it wholly to themselves. At one time they posted notices, warning outsiders to keep away. The only response to that was that certain mischievous fellows threw old stumps and a number of broken bottles into the swimming hole.

For several years or more, there had been ill will between the Bagdad boys and those of our district, and last winter it had been capped off by a dispute about whether we could coast past the front of their schoolhouse. An ironclad sleigh had helped us enforce our rights, but the boys over there resented it and were, no doubt, on the lookout for a chance to square the account. The trick they played on us the Fourth of July afternoon of my story was almost too mean for words.

There was a celebration that day at the village six miles from the Old Squire's place; "fantastics," tub race, sack race, and other attractions were advertised, and eleven of us boys—Willis and Ben Murch, my cousins Addison and Halstead, Tom Edwards, Ned Wilbur, myself, and four others—hitched up a span of our workhorses to the farm wagon, provided with temporary seats across the body, and set off at five in the morning so as to be sure of reaching the scene of festivities by six when the fantastics were scheduled to parade.

But of this it is enough to say that we arrived in good time, enjoyed the celebration, spent what money we had to spend on the usual lemonade, peanuts, and gingerbread, patronized a number of fakirs, and by three in the afternoon concluded that we had seen about all that was worth seeing and were ready to go home. The day had been unusually hot and dusty. We had perspired uncomfortably, and just as we were about to leave, Tom Edwards proposed that we drive around by the Bagdad road and have a swim in that fine hole. Ned Wilbur, I remember, thought there might be some danger of the Bagdad fellows surprising us there, but Tom said he had seen the most of them at the village and didn't believe they had yet come home.

In fact, the whole outlying country appeared quiet and deserted. On our drive up the river road to Bagdad, we met no teams nor saw a solitary pedestrian. All was propitious for a dip in the forbidden hole; no one was there, or was likely to come, and after hitching our horses to the fence by the roadside, we proceeded through the alder clumps for thirty or forty yards to the bare ledges where the little river was purling gently down to the pool. Here we leisurely undressed. It was a fine, secluded spot, sheltered from view by the thick bushes and vines—this being a prime requisite of a good swimming hole in those days when as yet bathing suits were an undreamed of encumbrance among country boys.

Willis Murch was, I believe, the first to skip down the sloping, water-worn ledges and jump in; but the rest of us soon followed, leaving little piles of our discarded wearing apparel—first the shoes and socks, then the Sunday suit, topped by shirt and new straw hat. Eleven of those little unguarded piles were lying there on the ledge, each apart by itself. And by all the unwritten laws and ethics of country life, a boy's clothes while in swimming were sacred from molestation. To "play hanky" with another boy's clothes while he was in the water was nearly the unpardonable sin.

Well, we had a good swim and were there for an hour or more, trying out various feats and stunts in the water. Midway, the pool was eight feet deep, and at one point directly off the farther bank there were five feet of water where those who dared could dive. Near the foot of the pool, too, were numbers of smooth flat stones of fifteen or twenty pounds weight, which could be laid on one's back as an aid to "crawling" on the bright sandy bottom. Willis, Addison, and Ben essayed this exploit with some success. Ned, Tom, and Halstead failed to accomplish it; for my own part, it was about all I could do to swim the length of the pool, plain frog fashion. The other boys said my bones were too heavy for my bulk, and it was true that I could not float on my back and keep to the surface without much effort in aid of buoyancy. Willis was constantly advising me to "swallow air," but I was never able to do it properly.

While standing on the bank, watching the others dive, I heard a team come along the road from the direction of the village, and I thought it stopped but after listening awhile, I concluded that it had passed on. Sometime later, however, when we left the water and went up past the alder clumps where we had left our clothes, every pile was missing! Not so much as a necktie was visible. For some dreadful moments we stared at the bare ledges, then at each other. Who could have committed such an outrage? Who had been there? Then I told of hearing a team pass. "It's those Bagdad fellows!" Addison shouted. "But I guess they've only hidden our things somewhere round here," he added.

Thereupon we searched the thickets and roadside, keeping a sharp eye out for approaching teams, then warily crossed the road to look in our wagon and about it, for we were still slow to believe that all that clothing including pocketknives, three watches, *portemonnaies*, and other trinkets had actually been stolen.

But look as we might and did, not a stitch of our garments could be found. Our best Sunday suits, too! Someone had taken everything and made a clean sweep. In nautical language, we were left under bare poles. With tropical tribes, in equatorial countries, I suppose this would have been no great matter. But in New England to be wholly unclad, three long miles from home, and in a hostile district was an alarming situation. Never till that day had I realized how terribly helpless and forlorn a fellow feels without his clothes.

After the first flurry and outburst of indignation, we retired into the alders to take counsel. "Let's all get into the wagon and curl down just as low as we can, then drive like split-and-oak for home!" was Ned's suggestion.

"Oh, but that would never do!" Addison said. "To get home we have to go around through the Crockett district, and we would be sure to meet all the folks coming back from the celebration."

"Besides," said Tom, "all of us couldn't curl down out of sight in the wagon. And what would we do when we got home, with the folks rushing out, girls and all, to see what had happened?"

"We had better hide in the bushes till dark," said Ben. "Then drive home and slip in at the back door when nobody is looking." But that, in July, meant lying up for four hours or more, and when evening did come, the mosquitoes in the woods would nearly devour us.

Willis then suggested making white-birch bark jackets; and something in that line might possibly have been done, since there were numbers of white birches growing along the river bank, if a jackknife had been left us with which to peel the bark.

Nothing else could be thought of, and Addison at length declared we would have to hook it across country in the direction of the home neighborhood, keeping to cover of wood lots, scudding from one to another, wherever forest or bushes offered cover from the public eye.

But there was our team, still hitched up by the roadside. "Never mind, we can come back for that when once we are home in our old clothes," Addison said. But as this might not be brought about till late that evening, the horses would manifestly need fodder. So while Ned watched the road for approaching vehicles, the rest of us pulled and fetched handfuls of grass, enough at least for their immediate wants.

Following Addison's lead, we then set off, first across a thistly pasture, then through a brushy swamp, and afterward crossed another pasture and picked our way through a newly cleared lot north of the Bagdad schoolhouse. Thorny blackberry canes abounded here, and oh, didn't bare feet and legs suffer!

Next beyond came the old Thomas farm, where a large dairy herd was kept. Here a broad expanse of open land confronted us, and what was worse we saw at a distance the sunbonnets of not less than six women, or girls, out strawberrying in the fields of yellow buttercups.

"Oh, dear! It's miles around this farm to get to the woods on the Eastman place," groaned Ned, nursing first one scratched ankle, then the other. "By the old Horn Spoon, if I had hold of the fellow who stole my shoes," he cried, "I honestly believe I would murder him— and take the consequences!"

Indeed, it was well for the criminal record of the county that the miscreants who had robbed us were not in our power that day. The bitterness of gall was in our hearts.

Then again we took counsel together, crouching among the blackberry bushes, and again Addison rose to the occasion. An idea had occurred to him. In a crisis he usually took the lead. "You stay right here and keep out of sight, all of you, till I come back," he said. "I'm going to creep through that orchard yonder to the back door of the Thomases' barn. There doesn't seem to be anyone about it, and I've a notion I may find something there."

He left us, examining our scratches and picking the thorns and thistles out of our feet; and after a time we espied him stealing back to us, bringing a huge bundle of some brown stuff, which proved to be meal sacks such as stock feed comes in.

"Here we are, boys!" he cried in great glee, flinging down the bags. "I've got one for each of us. There was a big pile of them in the granary." He had also brought an old ax that he had picked up in the barn.

By laying the bags on a log, we cut a hole large enough to get our head through in the bottom end of each one; and we cut another hole on the right side so as to be able to thrust out a hand.

The bags were very mealy inside and when we pulled them on over our heads, our hair was filled with the dust and our faces streaked with it, but we were much too desperate to stand for a trifle like that. I am sure a queerer looking party of boys was never before seen in those parts. It would have been hard to say who or what we were for our tousled, mealy heads added to the strangeness of the spectacle we presented. Appearances were of little consequence just then, however; home was the goal we were seeking. "Come on now!" cried Ad, and struck off across the fields of the Thomas farm, the rest of us limping on in the rear as fast as the painful condition of our feet permitted. We kept at distance from the strawberry pickers, but they espied us. First one sunbonnet, then another rose from amidst the buttercups to stare at the strange apparition. Evidently the women were alarmed, for a few moments later we saw all six bonnets streaming away at top speed in the direction of the Thomas farmhouse. We heard later that they took us for some new tribe of savages on the warpath!

From the cover of the friendly forest that we soon gained, we emerged erelong into the cleared lands of the home neighborhood. Here our distressed party broke up, each one making for his own place of abode. Addison, Halstead, and I stole in through the plum orchard in the hope of reaching the back door at the Old Squire's and tiptoeing upstairs to our rooms, unseen by the family. We had no such good luck. The girls had returned from the celebration, the folks had had supper, and Ellen was washing dishes at the kitchen sink by a back window. She saw us making for the door and uttered a cry of astonishment, then actually screamed! She, too, took us for savages attacking the house! Before the family could be roused, however, we had got in and upstairs to shelter.

Later, in the evening, when all had been explained, Addison and I hitched up old Nance and, driving over to Bagdad, recovered our abandoned team.

We contemplated energetic steps to discover and bring to punishment the rascals who had stolen our clothes. On the following morning however, the affair was largely cleared up. The summer school in the Old Squire's district was in session, and when the teacher, Miss Emmons, unlocked the house to begin school after the holiday, she discovered a vast heap of boys' clothes, shoes, hats, and socks lying higglety-pigglety just inside one of the back windows, which had manifestly been pried up. Nothing was really missing, although considerable difficulty was experienced in sorting the heap. Everything was there, including jackknives, watches, *portemonnaies*, and other trinkets, but had been handled roughly.

We were pretty sure now that we had been victims of a prank by the Bagdad boys and awhile later learned with considerable certainty the outrage had been perpetrated by two of them—Tim Jackson and Merrick Robbins—who had come driving home from the celebration and, while passing the swimming hole, heard us in the water.

Indignation burned so hot with us that many rancorous vows were made to square the account with them. No good opportunity offered that summer, however, and during the ensuing winter Tim and Merrick both left home on account of trouble with the schoolmaster and at length enlisted in the regular army. A year or two later we learned that the regiment they were in had been ordered to the far Northwest, to fight the Sioux Indians. I remember that when we heard this, Halstead said he hoped the redskins would scalp both of them!

The Indians, I am glad to say, failed to avenge us, however, and subsequently, when the term of enlistment expired, Tim and Merrick became prosperous prune farmers in the Willamette Valley of Oregon. Years afterward—not long ago, in fact—while on a visit to the Pacific Coast, Addison and I went to see them and they greatly enjoyed talking over our boyhood days in Maine and particularly the experience at the swimming hole.

As I now recall it, we were so loath to have the girls at the Thomas place know who it was they saw crossing their fields so ridiculously arrayed that for a long time nothing was said or done about settling for those meal bags. Two years later, however, Addison found opportunity to mention the matter to farmer Thomas and offered payment. The old man laughed heartily and said that those bags had long since been set down to profit and loss.

14

The Stranger and the Fried Pies

DURING THE WEEK FOLLOWING HAYING TIME THAT summer, Grandfather and Grandmother went to a "conference-meeting" in the town of Bridgton twenty miles away. They were gone four days, leaving us young folks with many instructions to keep house and look after things at the farm; that is to say, Theodora and Ellen kept house, while Addison, Halstead, and I looked after the farm chores and harvested an acre of buckwheat. A great deal of interest had centered in that acre of buckwheat, for with it had grown up large anticipations of buckwheat cakes and maple syrup.

We had a pretty lively time that week. Tom and Kate Edwards, two youthful neighbors, and the Wilbur boys, who lived on the farm next beyond the Edwardses', came over to see us every evening. Sweet corn was in the "milk" at that time, and early apples, pears, and plums were ripe. We roasted corn ears and played hide-and-seek by moonlight all over the house, wagon house, wood shed, granary, and both barns.

I am inclined to believe that Grandfather did not leave work enough to keep us properly out of that idleness that leads to mischief, for on the afternoon of the third day we broke one wheel of the ox cart and hayrack while coasting. There was a long slope in the east field down which we coasted; we would all get into the cart and let it run down backward, dragging the tongue on the ground behind. It was certainly not a proper and farmer-like manner of using a heavy cart.

After coasting down, we would haul the cart back with the oxen, which we kept yoked for the purpose. On our last coast one evening, the cart ran off diagonally and struck a large stone, breaking the wheel.

We owned up to the whole matter on Grandfather's return. He did not scold us, but after considering the affair overnight, he held court in the sitting room, heard all the evidence, and then good-humoredly sentenced Addison, Halstead, and me to work out on the highway that fall till we had earned enough to repair the wheel—six dollars. It was the most salutary bit of correction that I ever received. It led me to feel my personal responsibility for damage done foolishly.

But it is not of the broken cart wheel, or hide-and-seek by moonlight, that I wish to speak here but of another diversion the next day and of a mysterious stranger who arrived in the nick of time to participate in it.

Generally speaking, my cousin Theodora did not excel as a cook. She was much more fond of reading than of housework and domestic duties, although, at the farm she always did her share conscientiously. Ellen had a greater natural bent toward cookery.

But there was one article of food that Theodora could prepare to perfection, and that was fried pies. We boys thought that if she had known how to do nothing else in the world but fry pies, she would still have been a shining success in life. We esteemed her gift all the more highly for the reason that it was extra hazardous. Making fried pies is nearly as dangerous as working in a powder mill; those who have made them will understand what this means. I know a housewife who lost the sight of one of her eyes from a fried pie explosion. In another instance fully half the kitchen ceiling was coated with smoking hot fat, thrown up from the frying pan by the bursting of a pie.

Let not a novice like myself, however, presume to descant on the subject of fried pies to the thousands who doubtless know all the details of their manufacture. Theodora first prepared her dough, sweetened and mixed like ordinary doughnut dough, rolled it like a thick pie crust, and then enclosed the filling, consisting of mincemeat, or stewed apple, or gooseberry, or plum, or blackberry, or perhaps peach, raspberry, or preserved cherries. Only such fruits must be cooked and the pits or stones carefully removed. The edges of the dough were wet and dexterously crimped together, so that the pie would not open in frying.

Then when the big pan of fat on the stove was just beginning to get smoking hot, the pies were launched gently in at one side and allowed to sink and rise. And about that time it was well to be watchful, for there was no telling just when a swelling, hot pie might take a fancy to enact the role of a bombshell and blow the blistering hot fat on all sides.

After suffering from a bad burn on one wrist the previous winter, Theodora had learned not to take chances with fried pies. She had a face mask that Addison had made for her from pink pasteboard and a pair of blue goggles for the eyes, which some member of the family had once worn for snow blindness. The mask wore an irresistible grin.

When ready to begin frying our two dozen pies, Theodora donned the mask and goggles and put on a pair of old kid gloves. Then if spatters of hot fat flew, she was none the worse; but it was quite a sight to see her rigged for the occasion. The goggles were of portentous size, and we boys used to clap and cheer when she made her appearance.

As an article of diet, perhaps, fried pies could hardly be commended for invalids; but to a boy who had been working hard, or racing about for hours in the fresh air out of doors, they were simply delicious and went exactly to the right spot. Few articles of food are more appetizing to the eye than the rich doughnut brown of a fine fried pie.

That forenoon we coaxed Theodora and Ellen to fry a batch of three dozen pies and two "Jonahs"; and the girls, with some misgivings as to what Grandmother would say to them for making such inroads on "pie timber," set about it by ten o'clock. Be it said, however, that "closeness" in the matter of daily food was not one of Grandmother's faults.

They filled half a dozen with mincemeat, half a dozen with stewed gooseberry, and then half a dozen each with crabapple, plum, peach, and blackberry. They would not let us see what they filled the Jonahs with, but we knew that it must be a fearful mixture. Generally it was something shockingly sour. The Jonahs looked precisely like the other pies and were put on the same platter with the others. And the rule was that whoever got the Jonah must eat it or crawl under the table to serve as a footstool during the rest of the meal.

What the girls actually put in the two Jonahs this time was wheat bran mixed with cayenne pepper—an awful dose such as no mortal mouth could possibly endure. It is needless to say that the girls usually kept an eye on the Jonah or placed some slight private mark on it, in order not to get it themselves.

When we had something particularly good on the table, Addison and Theodora had a habit of making up rhymes about it. Kate Edwards had come in that day and was contributing her wit to the rhyming contest when, chancing to glance out of the window, Ellen espied a gray horse and a buggy with the top turned back standing in the yard. In the buggy was a large elderly gentleman, a stranger to all of us, who sat regarding the premises with a smile of shrewd and pleasant contemplation.

"Now who in the world do you suppose that can be?" exclaimed Ellen in low tones. "I do believe he has overheard some of those awful verses you have been making up."

"But someone must go to the door," Theodora whispered. "Ad, you go out and see what he has come for."

"He doesn't look just like a minister," said Halstead.

"Nor just like a doctor," Kate whispered. "But he is somebody of consequence, I know; he looks so dignified and experienced."

"And what a good, old, distinguished face!" said Ellen. Thus their sharp young eyes took an inventory of our caller, who, I may as well say here, was Hannibal Hamlin, former vice-president during Abraham Lincoln's first term and one of the most famous antislavery leaders of the Republican party before the Civil War.

The old Hamlin homestead, where Hannibal Hamlin passed his boyhood, was at Paris Hill, Maine, six or seven miles to the eastward of Grandfather's farm; and he and Grandfather had been young men together and close friends and classmates at Hebron Academy.

At this time Mr. Hamlin had not yet entered on his long tenure of the senatorship from Maine. During Lincoln's second term he had been collector of customs for the port of Boston, and the following year he would resign this office because he could no longer endorse the administrative policy of Andrew Johnson, the new president.

But now, however, he was on vacation. He was making a brief visit to the scenes of his boyhood home and had taken a fancy to drive over to call on Grandfather. We did not even know "Uncle" Hannibal by sight and had not the slightest idea who he was. Addison went out, however, and asked if he should take his horse.

"Why, Joseph Stephens still lives here, does he not?" queried Mr. Hamlin.

"Yes, sir," replied Addison. "I am his grandson."

"Ah, I thought you were rather young for one of his sons," Mr. Hamlin remarked. "I heard too that he had lost all his sons in the war."

"Yes, sir," Addison replied, soberly.

Mr. Hamlin regarded him thoughtfully for a moment. "I used to know your grandfather," he said. "Is he at home?"

Addison explained the absence of Grandfather and Grandmother. "I am very sorry they are away," he added.

"I am sorry, too," said Mr. Hamlin. "I wished to see them very much." He began to turn his horse as if to drive away; but Theodora, who was always exceedingly hospitable, had gone out and now addressed our caller with greater cordiality than Addison.

"Will you not come in, sir?" she asked. "Grandfather will be so sorry! Do please stop a little while and let the boys feed your horse!"

Mr. Hamlin regarded her with a paternal smile. "I will get out and walk round a bit to rest my legs," he replied.

Addison and I took his horse to the stable, and Theodora, having first shown him the garden and the long row of beehives, led the way to the cool sitting room and settled him in an easy chair. We heard her relating recent events of our family history to him and answering his questions.

Meanwhile the fried pies were waiting and getting cold, and when Addison and I returned from the stable, we all began to feel a little impatient. Ellen and Kate set the pies in the oven to keep them warm. We did not like to begin eating them with company in the sitting room and so lingered hungrily about, awaiting developments.

"How long do you suppose he will stay?" Halstead exclaimed crossly.

"He is a pretty fine old fellow," Addison remarked to Kate. "Have you any idea who he is?"

But Kate, although born in the county, had never seen him. Just then the sitting room door opened, and we heard Theodora saying, "We haven't much for luncheon today but fried pies, but we shall be glad to have you sit down with us."

"What an awful fib!" whispered Ellen behind her hand to Kate. But Mr. Hamlin had taken a great fancy to Theodora and was accepting her invitation with vast good nature. What a great, dark man he looked as he followed Theodora out to the table!

"These are my cousins whom I have told you of," she was saying, and then she mentioned all our names to him, and afterward Kate's, although Mr. Hamlin had not seen fit to tell us his own. We supposed that he was merely some pleasant acquaintance from Grandfather's early years.

He was seated in Grandfather's place at the table, and after a brief flurry in the kitchen the big platter of fried pies was brought in. What Ellen and Theodora had done was carefully to pick out the two Jonahs and lay them aside. Addison and Theodora exchanged glances, and there was a little pause of interrogation in case our caller might possibly be a clergyman, after all, and might wish to say a grace.

He evinced no disposition to do so, however, and Theodora raised the platter and passed it to our guest.

"And are these the fried pies?" he asked with the broadest of smiles. "I now remember that my mother used to fry something like this when I was a boy at home, over at Paris Hill, and my recollection is that they were very good."

"Yes, most of them are very good," said Addison, by way of making conversation, "unless you happen to get the Jonah."

"And what's the Jonah?" asked our visitor.

Amidst much laughter this was explained to him—also the penalty. Mr. Hamlin burst into a great shout of laughter.

"But we have taken the Jonahs out of these," Theodora made haste to assure him.

"What for?" he exclaimed.

"Why, why—because we have company," stammered Theodora, much confused.

"And spoil the sport?" cried our visitor. "Young lady, I want those Jonahs put back."

"Oh, but they are dreadful Jonahs!" pleaded Theodora.

"I want the Jonahs put back," insisted Mr. Hamlin. "I shall have to decline to lunch here unless the Jonahs are in their proper places."

Very shamefaced, Ellen brought them in.

"No hocus pocus now!" cried our visitor, and we all had to turn our backs and shut our eyes while Kate put the Jonahs among the others in the platter.

Then we each chose a pie. "Each take a good, deep mouthful!" cried Mr. Hamlin, entering into the spirit of the game. "All together now!"

Eight long bites were taken at once; but as it chanced no one got a Jonah, and the eight fried pies quickly disappeared.

"But these are good!" cried our visitor. "Mine was gooseberry." Then, turning to Theodora, "How many times may a fellow try for a Jonah here?"

"Five times," replied Theodora, laughing and pleased by the praise.

The platter was passed again, and again no one got bran and cayenne.

But at the third passing I saw Ellen start visibly when our visitor chose his pie. "All ready! Bite!" he cried, and we bit; but at the first taste he stopped short, rolled his eyes round, and shook his head with his mouth full.

"Oh, but you need not eat it, sir!" cried Theodora, rushing round to him. "You need not do anything!"

But without a word our bulky visitor had sunk slowly out of his chair and, pushing it back, disappeared under the long table.

For a moment we all sat scandalized, then shouted in spite of ourselves. In the midst of our confused hilarity the table began to oscillate; it rose slowly several inches, then moved off toward the sitting room door. Our jolly visitor had it on his back and was crawling ponderously away with it, and the rest of us were getting ourselves and our chairs out of the way! In fact, the remainder of that luncheon was a perfect gale of laughter. The table walked quite round the room and came back to its original position.

After the hilarity had subsided and the luncheon had come to an end, our visitor told us of his boyhood at Paris Hill; of his fishing for trout in the brooks thereabouts; of the time he broke his arm and of the doctor who set it so unskillfully that it had to be broken again and reset; of the beautiful tourmaline crystals that he and his brother found at Mount Mica; and of his school days at Hebron Academy.

When at last he declared that he positively must be going on his way, we begged him to remain overnight and brought out his horse with great reluctance.

Before getting into the buggy he took us each by the hand and saluted the girls, particularly Theodora, in a truly fatherly manner.

"I've had a good time!" he said. "I am glad to see you all here at this old farm in my dear native state; but"—and we saw the tears start in his great black eyes—"it touches my heart more than I can tell you to know of the sad reason for your coming here. You have my heartiest sympathy.

"Tell your grandparents that I should have been very glad to see them," he added, and he took the reins from Addison.

"But sir," said Theodora earnestly, for we were all crowding up to the buggy, "Grandpa will ask who it was that called."

"Oh, well, you can describe me to him," cried Mr. Hamlin, laughing, "and if he cannot make me out, you may tell him that it was an old fellow he once knew named Hamlin! Good-bye!" and he drove away.

"Well, whoever he is, he's an old brick!" said Halstead, as the buggy passed between the high gateposts at the foot of the lane.

"I think he is just splendid!" exclaimed Kate enthusiastically.

"And he has such a great, kind heart!" said Theodora.

When Grandfather and Grandmother came home late that evening, we were not slow in telling that a most remarkable elderly man named Hamlin had called to see them, and stopped to lunch with us.

"Hamlin, Hamlin," repeated Grandfather, absently. "What sort of looking man?"

Theodora and Ellen described him with zeal.

"Why, Father, it must have been Hannibal Hamlin!" cried Grandmother.

"So it was!" exclaimed Grandfather. "Too bad we were not at home!"

"What! Not Hannibal Hamlin that was vice-president of the United States!" Addison almost shouted.

"Yes, Vice-President Hamlin," said Grandfather.

And about that time it would have required nothing much heavier than a turkey's feather to knock us all over. Addison looked at Theodora, and she looked at Ellen and me. Halstead whistled.

"Why, what did you say or do that makes you look so queer?" cried Grandmother with uneasiness. "I hope you behaved well to him. Did anything happen?"

"Oh, no, nothing much," said Ellen, laughing nervously, "only he got the Jonah pie and—and—we've had the former vice-president of the United States under the table to put our feet on!" Grandmother turned very red and was much disturbed. She wanted Grandfather to write that night and try to apologize for us. But Grandfather only laughed. "I have known Mr. Hamlin ever since he was a boy," he said. "He enjoyed that pie as well as any of them, and no apology is needed."

15

The Old Minister's Girl

AS NIGHT WAS FALLING ONE BLEAK, WINDY AFTER-noon in November, when the last leaves from the maples and birches were whirling across the fields and roads under a gray and dreary sky, and when everybody instinctively wished to get indoors and remain there, little crippled Muncy Willhope came hopping along in the dusk and thumped with his crutch at my grandfather's farmhouse door. We were just comfortably seated at the supper table: Grandfather, Grandmother, and half a dozen of us grandchildren who were living there at the close of the Civil War, and we all turned and waited in some surprise while my cousin Halstead arose and opened the door.

"Pony's lost in Quog-Hoggar!" cried Muncy, in shrill frightened tones.

"Dear me, what next at that house!" Grandmother exclaimed. "When did your folks see her last, Muncy?"

But Muncy had already gone hopping down the lane to carry the alarm to the other neighbors.

"I saw Pony, myself, about ten o'clock this forenoon when I came home from the mill," said Halse. "I heard a rumpus just as I was passing the house there. Pony was up to something or other, and the old woman was threatening awful things! Her bedroom door was open, and she was shouting to Eliza and Cynthia and Lois to catch Pony and bring her in there. The old woman's rheumatism is so bad that she can't get off the bed; but I heard her bawl out, 'Bring Pony here and let me knock her down!'"

"Oh dear, oh dear, what talk and what goings on!" sighed Grandmother. "Poor Parson Willhope's girls, too!"

"I looked back, after I got by," Halse continued, "and I saw Pony hop out the back window and run to the woodshed. She climbed up by the old gatepost to the roof and from that onto the roof of the ell. I stopped the horse to see what she was going to do. She peered down, then climbed up the house roof and walked along the ridge pole to the chimney. She stood there when Lois and Muncy came out. 'Mother says you come down,' Lois cried. 'Mother!' mimicked Pony. 'What do you call her Mother for? She isn't our mother, she's only Father's second wife—more's the pity!'"

"Oh, what a child!" sighed Grandmother.

"I suppose," continued Halse, "that Mrs. Willhope was still threatening her. Anyway, Pony called out, 'Oh, I hear you, madam!' and then she put her head over the top of the chimney and cried down it, 'Peek-a-boo! You would like to whack me with that big cane of yours, wouldn't you? I hear you, and I once heard you tell poor old Father that you would like to put me in a bag and drown me!'

"I didn't stop to see whether she came down or not," Halse went on. "But she probably did and ran away to hide. I don't believe she's lost, and I shan't start out to search for her—yet. Pony knows Quog-Hoggar like a book."

"But it is a bitter night for the child to be out," murmured Grandmother. "Our old minister's daughter, too—why did he ever go and marry that woman?"

That was a mystery none of the late Rev. Mr. Willhope's former parishioners had ever been able to solve. How this spare, pale, tall, Puritanic minister had come to take as his second wife and stepmother to his four daughters a coarse, uneducated, bad-tempered woman, widow of a dissolute and fit only for life in a dissolute's shanty, was beyond comprehension.

"Is it three or four years that the old parson's been dead?" asked Grandfather.

"Three years last February," replied Grandmother, whose accuracy in remembering dates of births and deaths was never questioned. "Pony was nine years old that month, the third day; she was a winter baby. She didn't cry at the funeral, but she looked a long time at her father's face in the coffin, after they tried to have her go past, and she wouldn't sit in the mourners' room with her stepmother and sisters. They couldn't make her sit there. She came into the sitting room and crouched down beside my chair. When I tried to have her go in with her sisters, she hid her face in my lap. I hadn't the heart to lead her back in there, for I couldn't help seeing the look that woman shot at her. But there!" concluded Grandmother self-reproachfully, "I oughtn't to say that perhaps; the poor woman has rheumatism."

"All the same I shouldn't like to come within reach of that old cane of hers," said Halse.

"You may be sure that she doesn't get Pony to come within reach of it!" exclaimed Addison, laughing as he drew back from the table and moved up to the fireplace, for Ad had been plowing in the cold wind all the afternoon. "What distresses me about that woman is her voice," he went on. "Worst voice I ever heard!"

"The poor creature cannot help that," remarked Grandmother placidly. "But don't you think, boys, that you ought to try and see where Pony is? I feel disturbed about the child. Who knows but she's slipped into some of those soft sloughs or has fallen into Bog Brook?"

"Now, Grandma, don't you go to worrying about Pony," said Halse. "Pony knows more about Quog-Hoggar than all of us put together. If she's there at all, she's safe in some snug place that she knows of, where nobody could find her in a week."

The truth is that we boys who had been out in the cold all day and were tired and sleepy did not relish the thought of sallying forth to scour Quog-Hoggar on a dark, bleak night. We soon went to bed, but I think that Grandmother passed an uneasy night. Before we were astir next morning, she had dressed and gone on foot to the Willhopes' house. It was a dim, cheerless morning; snow in fine icy pellets was driving against the windowpanes, and two or three inches had already fallen. Grandmother came back with her cheeks red inside her hood.

"Now, boys," she said at once, "you must all start off just as soon as you eat your breakfast and try to find Ada." (Ada is Pony's real name.) "She's been gone all night. They've no idea what has become of her, and in this snowstorm, too!"

"But what sent her off?" Addison asked.

"Oh, the old troubles there!" replied Grandmother sadly. "I am worried about that poor child. Nobody in the neighborhood has paid the least attention to her being lost."

Somewhat conscience-stricken, we ate a hurried breakfast and, going around to the neighbors, raised a party of sixteen men and boys with two dogs and a foxhound to search Quog-Hoggar; but first we all proceeded to the forlorn little Willhope cottage to learn, if possible, what direction Pony had taken and where she had last been seen. The snow was still falling fast and thick, and there was no hope now of tracking her, even with a hound.

Lois Willhope told us that Pony had come down off the house roof and, approaching Mrs. Willhope's window, had said "Peek-a-boo" to her again and then pirouetted away along a little path into the bushes bordering the Quog-Hoggar woods; that was the last seen of her. But Lois had heard her whistle through her fingers—as boys sometimes do—to Aesop, and Aesop was not in his pasture or in any of the neighbors' fields, from which he often helped himself to grass and sometimes to corn.

In fact there was not much we could learn, except that Pony had been missing since noon the previous day and had probably taken her horse; and we set off much as such searchers are wont to do to beat through the woods, shouting "Pony, Pony!" and looking for traces of the lost one.

Several of the boys had brought guns, for bears and deer were sometimes seen in Quog-Hoggar. The party soon separated into little groups to search different portions of the woody tract, and throughout the forenoon Halse and I heard distant shouting and occasionally the report of a gun. We had undertaken to follow Bog Brook in its devious windings, from Mud Pond to where it emerged from the meadows and bogs at a sawmill five miles below in another township.

The snow ceased falling at about ten o'clock and the sun came out, but not a track or trace could we discover, save of minks and squirrels. The dog with us had been allowed at the Willhopes' to smell one of Pony's old shoes, but his canine sagacity failed to find the trail of the lost girl.

Now and again we would hear some other group of searchers approaching. We could hear them talking together as they beat up and down, and their voices sounded strangely through the snowy waste.

"No wonder they named it Quog-Hoggar," one exclaimed. "Such a muddy, rocky, craggy, tangled hole I never was in before! Any idea how much there is of it?" Then we heard the speaker's comrade reply, "Well, I've heard my father say there's twenty-seven square miles of it. I don't believe anybody knows exactly."

"Who pays taxes on it?"

"Oh, the Burdeen heirs—New York folks."

"Lots of wood and timber on it."

"Yes, but nobody can get to it."

Before long some other men crossed the brook at a distance in front of us, and we heard them talk as they pushed their way through the alder bushes. "Awful place!" one exclaimed.

"Right you are!" agreed the other. They climbed a craggy hillock and then one of them shouted, "Pony! Pony! Answer if you hear!"

"Queer name that, to call a girl," the other remarked, and although we were now a quarter of a mile away we could still hear every word they said. "What is her right name anyhow?"

"I believe 'tis Addie, or Ida or Ada—something like that; but they call her 'Pony,' on account of that little gray crook of a Shetland pony she's always riding. One of her New York aunts sent her that pony years ago. She was named after that aunt, I heard say. Her mother, the old minister's first wife, was a Burdeen, you know. Nice folks."

"But that second wife's a terror!"

"Right you are!"

Going on down the brook, Halse and I at length came to Garland's Meadow, a partly open tract where there was a weather-beaten old hay barn. A man named Garland had once cleared ten or twelve acres of the low land with the idea of raising hay; but the grass proved of bad quality, and he soon stopped cutting it. The meadow was now brown with the uncut grass, and bushes had sprung up about the barn. Probably not one person in a year, except perhaps a few mink trappers or other hunters, visited this dreary opening.

When we had passed down the hither side of the brook, we had seen by tracks in the snow that two of the searchers had been to the barn already, and we therefore thought it useless to enter it; but coming up the other bank on our return, we made a discovery. About a quarter of a mile below Garland's Meadow at a deep end of the brook, where there were a cedar thicket and several dense fir trees, our dog suddenly barked, and when we tried to push our way through, we came upon a fence of little poles. It was completely screened from view and extended quite across the neck of the bend.

On passing it we found little Aesop snugly ensconced beneath the drooping branches of a fir, quite sheltered and protected by the cedar. Scarcely a flake of snow had reached him, and he had a nest of dry leaves a foot deep. On one side, in a rude crib of sticks, there was a generous wad of hay, and for water he had only to push through the cedar to the still unfrozen brook.

"Well, well, here's Aesop, all snug! And I guess Pony herself isn't far off!" Halse exclaimed.

We searched in the cedar and called "Pony!" softly, but received no response, and made sure she was not there.

"She may be in that old hay barn, after all," Halse remarked. "Let's look!"

Crossing the brook, with some difficulty, we pulled open the large old swing door, which creaked dismally on its long-rusted hinges, and entered the barn. Two other searchers had been in before us; the caked snow from their boots littered the barn floor.

The old hay bays were empty. Apparently, there was no place to hide in. The building was a hollow old shell with bare beams and wide cracks between the wall boards—the dreariest interior imaginable.

"She cannot be here," Halse muttered, "unless," he added, peering up into the bare, cobwebbed roof, "she's on that little old scaffold of loose poles in the far end there, way in the gable corner of the roof. Pony!" he called out. "Are you up there, Pony? Hi, Pony!"

There was no answer, but as we stood looking up, the wind, which had begun to blow a little and toss up the light snow outside, made the big open door close with a bang that jarred the whole building, and there rattled down to the floor from the scaffold aloft a hazelnut shell, which bounced at our feet.

"There's a fresh shell, just cracked," said Halse, picking it up. "I believe Pony's up there!"

"Most likely squirrels," I said.

"Maybe," replied Halse. "But I'm going to see."

He picked up an old alder fish pole that someone had flung into the empty hay bay and, climbing to one of the cross-girths of the barn where he could barely reach the underside of the scaffold, began prodding through the hay with the little end.

Standing on the barn floor below, I saw at the very first thrust a shaggy, flaxen head and small white face appear and heard a wrathful voice cry down to us. "You let me alone. What are you plaguing me for?"

We both burst out laughing in spite of ourselves. To see her away up there in the roof of that old barn, with all that hair round her face, was so comical!

"Pony, how did you ever get up there?" I exclaimed.

"None of your business, and I would just like to know why you're all shouting and hallooing all over the woods!"

"Why, they think you're lost. The whole town's looking for you."

"Lost!" cried Pony contemptuously. "You had better all go home and mind your own business. I can take care of myself—I'd have you know!"

"But Pony, you had better come down and go home," Halse expostulated.

"I shan't go home! And I guess you wouldn't, either, if you had such a home as I've got!"

"Well, then, come home with us," Halse urged. "Grandmother will be glad to have you come to our house. The old lady worried all night about you."

"Sorry, but I've no money to spend for board at anybody's house," retorted Pony. "I can live here and board myself cheaper."

"What have you to eat?" Halse asked.

"No matter."

"Oh, but you can't live so!" I argued.

"Yes, I can, too," cried Pony angrily.

"You will freeze to death some cold night," said Halse.

"Oh, don't you worry! I'll look out for myself, and don't you tell any-body that I'm here, either!" replied Pony with tremendous earnestness.

"But we shall have to tell them, and about Aesop, too," replied Halse.

"If you have found Aesop, you just let him alone!" cried Pony in fresh wrath. "Sopsy's all right. I'm looking out for him. Don't you dare disturb him."

She was so exasperated with us for discovering her retreat, and that of Aesop, that she flung a handful of nutshells down at our upturned faces.

"Spitfire!" said Halse. "I'm going to climb up there and see what sort of a place you've got." (Considering Halse's dislike for heights, this was an amazing statement.)

"If you do, I'll poke you down!"

But Halse clambered up by means of two braces at the back side of the barn, and gaining footing on one of the great crossbeams on a level with the scaffold, walked along opposite where Pony was perched.

"Oho, old lady!" he said. "Quite a heap of hay and old duds there! What have you got in that box and that bucket?"

"I'll let you know what I've got, if you dare to come across here, you sneaking, prying thing!" cried Pony in great indignation. "This is my house, and you keep out of it."

We told her that we should be obliged to let the others know that we had found her.

"But don't tell where!" she implored. "I can't go back home, and I won't. You tell them I'm all right—and so's Aesop."

"But aren't you afraid to stay here in the dark, at night?" Halse asked.

"No, I'm not. Nothing can get up here. And who said I'm in the dark? I've got a kerosene lamp, if I've a mind to light it." She held up a little old lamp with the top broken off the chimney.

"Well, you think you're fixed fine, don't you?" said Halse teasingly. But all we could say wholly failed to induce her to come down and go home. And after poking fun at her awhile, we went away saying, to plague her, that we should send the selectmen of the town to get her and carry her to the "poor farm." Her last words to us as we went out were that if we dared to tell anybody where she was, she would never speak to us again as long as she lived! And to this day I recollect just how she snapped that out and how black her eyes were in the midst of that tangle of flaxen hair as she looked down on us from high up under the old brown barn roof.

Both Halse and I knew that we really ought to tell where Pony was hidden; but darkness had fallen when we emerged into the cleared land; the other searchers had given up the quest and gone home, so we merely looked in at the Willhopes' door and said hastily, "Pony's found. She's all right," and then ran home.

Aesop, Pony, and the Wild Gray Gander

AT THE SUPPER table that night, Halse and I freely confessed having found Pony, and very early the next morning Grandmother sent us with a special message, telling Pony she was welcome to stay at our house for the winter or until some better arrangement could be made for her.

So again we tramped in the crisp snow through Quog-Hoggar, and politely knocked at the old barn door. There was no response, but as we listened we heard a noise of scrambling within, and pushed the door open. No one was in sight, but our eyes lighted upon a knotted pole about fifteen feet long, which extended from the high scaffold down to one of the middle girths of the barn.

It looked to us as if it had been used as a ladder, and we guessed that Pony had scrambled hastily up it when she had heard us coming and that she had not had time to draw it up after her.

"Oh, we heard you!" shouted Halse derisively. "You needn't hide."

"What are you back here for?" cried Pony, peeping down. "I wouldn't come uninvited, if I were you. I don't want callers!"

Nor did Grandmother's message much soften her tone.

"I can't be living on other folks," replied Pony. "What could I do to pay my board? I shall stay here."

And this was all the answer we could get from her—this and another invitation to be off.

But Grandmother, when we reported to her, would not hear of Pony remaining there another night. "Why, she will get her death of cold!" cried the old lady, and naught was to do but we must harness our steadiest horse immediately after the noonday meal and carry her in the market-pung along an old winter road in the borders of Quog-Hoggar to where it came nearest to Garland's Meadow. Thence, escorted by Halse, Grandmother walked through the woods, over ledges, and across bogs to the hay barn.

Her kind old heart prevailed where our boyish banter had been repulsed. Pony came down, released Aesop from his cedar pen by the brook, and accompanied Grandmother home; but first the child exacted a promise that she should be allowed to sew and knit enough to pay for her board and for Aesop's keep. "Sopsy will eat anything," she confided to Grandmother. "He will live off the oats the cows leave in their cribs, but he must be put in a pen by himself for he will bite the cattle."

Grandmother told us this privately and laughed over it, after they came home. "But remember, boys," she charged us expressly, "don't let Ada hear a word from you about my going after her or her staying in the old barn; she is the proudest child I ever saw."

And so, indeed, she was. Throughout the long winter evenings, as we gathered about the round table studying our school lessons for the next day, Pony sat with us, conning her own lesson but knitting fast with her book propped open before her. The rest of us were taking life easily, eating apples and snapping the seeds at each other; yet if Halse or I sent a seed in her direction, Pony never noticed it, even if it hit her, and only knit the faster.

She seemed never for a moment to forget that she was "eating the bread of dependence in the house of strangers," and it was always, "Yes, madam" and "Yes, sir" to the old couple. I have seen Grandmother's eyes fill with tears as she watched her knit evenings, for Pony seemed to remind the old lady of Wealthy. As it drew toward nine o'clock, Gram would whisper, "Don't work so like a little slave, dear child. There's no need." Pony would sometimes smile back to her but rarely answered, and never ceased plying the needles till she thought that a proper evening's work was accomplished.

At Christmas we boys made up three dollars and bought a woolen frock to be hung on the Christmas tree as a present to Pony. But when it was given her she handed it back to Grandmother, saying that she could not accept gifts of clothes from anybody. Halse was indignant, but his indignation seemed to make no difference to Pony.

Afterward, however, she told Grandmother she would shell corn at five cents a bushel to pay for the frock, if we wished. We had a great deal of corn in those days for shelling, which Grandfather was accustomed to pay us boys at that rate, and it was agreed that Pony should shell corn on Saturday afternoons. She shelled five bushels the first Saturday and wore the skin nearly all off the palms of her hands. We knew from experience that they must be horribly sore, but Pony made no complaint. She was eleven weeks earning that frock and would not wear it till she had paid for it in full.

Although Pony was as tall as most girls of thirteen, she was very slender and could not have weighed more than seventy pounds; but no boy in the place excelled her in climbing, whether in trees or in the barn, and for her size she was remarkably strong. She could easily take up a bushel of shelled corn and pour it into a barrel. She was quick and agile; some of her sudden movements were like a flash of light.

Such a mass of crinkly, flaxen hair no one had ever seen in that county; it made her look all head! Once Grandmother coaxed her into having it braided, but usually she wore it in a great "bush" all about her neck and shoulders in the middle of which her little pale, white face, looking no larger than the palm of one's hand, showed two great dark brown eyes and a row of little white teeth.

There was never the slightest color in her face. According to the prevalent rural standard of beauty, which insists on red cheeks and plumpness, she was anything but pretty, yet in after years certain critics deemed her beautiful.

She did not go home during the winter and could not be induced to speak of her stepmother. Her three elder sisters, Cynthia, Eliza, and Lois, and her stepbrother, little crippled Muncy, called occasionally at our house. The older sisters were rather meek, submissive girls, very devout and careful in speech and deportment.

All winter long she was manifestly revolving plans for self-support, and she often asked odd questions about various farm crops, particularly poultry. At one time she had a fancy for taking all of Grandfather's corn to shell and asked him about it, and she also talked about husking it in the fall and about drying apples on shares.

Then she became greatly interested in Grandmother's flock of fourteen geese, which were wintering in the barn cellar. She would boldly catch old Tim, the gander, when he ran forward hissing at her. When the big bird tried to beat her with his wings, she seized him by one leg and lifted him off the ground so quickly and deftly that he was soon taught who was master of the situation. The geese soon came to know her and would break forth in loud, joyous cries whenever Pony appeared with their food. Grandfather detested the geese and always opposed keeping them, and indeed they are a nuisance on a farm, far worse than turkeys or other fowls. "Nasty things! I wish they were all dead!" Grandfather often exclaimed.

"Now, Joseph," Grandmother would reply, placidly, "you like a warm feather bed and a soft down pillow just as well as anyone, and as long as I have granddaughters to 'set out' I shall keep my geese."

Keep them she did, and she generally took care of them herself. In the winter this was hard for her to do. We boys ought to have been ashamed of ourselves for not helping her. That Pony should like the geese, and be willing to chop up turnips to feed to them along with their barley and corn and to fill the old half-barrel in the barn cellar once a week with tepid water for them to splash in, was an added bond of goodwill between her and Grandmother.

In return for Pony's care of the geese, Grandmother lovingly instructed her in those mysteries of goose lore of which forty years' experience had made Gram complete mistress. As winter advanced, they often spent hours together in the back sitting room or the kitchen "talking goose," and all this led in April to some sort of a woman's compact, by virtue of which Pony was to take Grandmother's geese on shares.

Not to have them annoy Grandfather and do damage to crops—for Pony was more conscientious about that than Grandmother—she planned to take them away to a small pond in what we called "the calf pasture," where a little brook flowed through the farm. She and

Grandmother were somewhat secretive about it, and as we boys were busy at this season of the year with our farm work, we did not concern ourselves much about their business.

Pony assisted Grandmother about her domestic work for an hour or so in the morning, and then both of them would set off together for the pond in the calf pasture, where they were making goose houses and gosling pens. For this purpose they gathered up all the bits of board upon which they could lay their hands, and carried off every nail and screw on our carpenter bench. They built a fence, too, about the little pond, and in May we learned that they had eleven old geese sitting on eggs.

Pony, scudding like a swallow on the wing across the fields to the goose preserve, was a picture of happy enthusiasm. Half a dozen times in a forenoon we would see her fleeting thither, often singing like a bobolink. Grandmother herself, too, looked as happy as a girl. Frequently we would see her ambling along in Pony's wake.

Such was their interest in their enterprise that on the night five of the geese were expected to hatch broods, both were up until four in the morning; and they were in untold anxiety about a thunder-squall that occurred that day, lest the thunder should kill the unhatched goslings, but it did no harm. Twenty-seven of the eggs hatched, and some time later twenty-eight other goslings were brought off.

To us boys all those straw-colored, downy goslings looked exactly alike, but Pony knew them apart. She had named all the old geese; there were Juno and Hebe, Venus and Hermia, and a whole pantheon of other web-footed, pink-beaked divinities, and what was more remarkable, she had actually contrived to teach some of them to answer to their names.

With the goslings came worries concerning foxes and prowling dogs, but Pony turned Aesop loose in the calf pasture, and by some art of her own taught the queer, pugnacious little brute to charge after dogs and even to chase away foxes by night—at least they said so, but I myself never saw him chase a fox. Later the old geese had to be "picked." If all the flying steps that Pony took that summer in caring for those geese were numbered, their number would no doubt exceed a million! She appeared to be afoot night and day in their service, to say nothing of the work she did at the farmhouse.

The net result of it all was that in October Grandmother and she had fifty-one young geese, and as Pony wished to keep them all, save two, our barn cellar was fairly aswarm with geese and uproarious from their squallings. Pony took all the care of them, and consequently we managed to endure their presence, although of course we grumbled a little.

But poor Grandmother! In August, despite Pony's best efforts, a yellow fox had borne off Hosannah, the old feathered matriarch of the flock. Queen, ruler, and chief shouter for more than forty years, old Hosannah had been a part of Grandmother Ruth's "setting out" when she first came from Connecticut to Maine in her eighteenth year. And after that, Grandmother never again seemed interested in keeping her geese.

"You shan't be troubled with them anymore, Joseph," she said to Grandfather at the table one night. "I have given them all to Ada, and she is going to take them away."

"But I don't see what you can do with them, Pony," Grandfather said. "There isn't a place in this neighborhood where you can keep sixty geese without trespassing on somebody."

"I know they are a great bother," replied Pony, "and I have written to my Aunt Ada and my cousins in New York for permission to keep them in Quog-Hoggar."

"In Quog-Hoggar!" we all exclaimed at once. "Why, the foxes and lynxes and stoats would get the whole of them in a fortnight!"

"Oh, but I think that Sopsy and I can guard them," said Pony quietly.

At that, we all assured her that she was welcome to keep them in the calf pasture as long as she desired.

"There wouldn't be room," she replied, "for by fall I mean to have two hundred!" We then perceived that she was really cherishing an ambitious plan to keep great numbers of geese for profit, that Grandmother had known all about it from the start, and that even at her age she had intended to be a partner with Pony!

Our attempts to dissuade Pony from her Quog-Hoggar scheme were without avail. "It's the only place where I could possibly keep them and not disturb people," she said, and that was true.

She obtained the permission she needed, and on April 15, Halse, Ad, and I assisted her to drive the geese slowly through the woods to the old hay barn at Garland's Meadow. Pony's two sisters, Cynthia and Lois, also helped us. The distance was fully three miles, and we were the best part of the day guiding the slow-waddling, hissing, stubborn creatures through the woods and bogs.

To keep them safe for the night, we shut them up in the old hay barn; but the next forenoon Pony turned them loose to eat watercress and catch frogs and otherwise disport themselves in their new pasture.

It was really ideal—this new pasture. There was nearly a mile of partially cleared land about the barn, and through this ample meadow flows Bog Brook—a deep, sluggish, crooked stream, always thirty or forty feet wide and still broader at the great pools formed at its crooks and elbows. Here by day Pony, with her bush of yellow hair, and shaggy Aesop, stood vigilant guard over the geese. By night, for a time, she kept them in the old barn.

But trouble of a kind that neither Pony nor anyone else had even thought of was close at hand. She had but just arrived at the meadow on the third morning and turned the geese out, when suddenly they all raised their wings and squalled in a manner in which she had never heard them squall before. For a little they ran to and fro with flapping wings, and then, suddenly standing still, each turned one eye skyward.

Pony now heard the cry of wild geese high in the air over the meadow and, looking up, saw a flock of five winging its way northward over Quog-Hoggar. Although the wild geese were very high in the sky, they had apparently heard or seen the domesticated geese below for, swerving from their line of flight and describing a semicircle, their gander changed his quiet "honk-honk" to loud cries, which sounded strangely so far aloft.

In response, Pony's flock again broke into vociferous "quark-quarks," and immediately the wild geese, wheeling in three great circles, descended to the bank of the brook, where their gander—a tremendous gray bird—made the whole meadow resound with his triumphant squawks! The domesticated geese gathered about the new-comers, and Pony, standing by the barn, looked on with much interest.

But the "king" gander of the tame flock resented the intrusion of the wild gander. Before Pony could approach, a battle royal had begun and, indeed, ended—for almost in no time the big gray stranger beat the tame gander senseless and knocked him into the brook.

Seizing a large stick, Pony rushed forward to drive off the intruder and avenge her own bird. The gray gander, flushed with victory, flew at her furiously and tried to bite and to strike her with his powerful wings; but this time he had met his match. Pony showered such swift hard blows on his anserine majesty that the warlike bird, suddenly taking to flight and squawking loudly to his charges to follow him, rose into the air.

A curious thing then happened. Although neither these white domestic geese nor their ancestors for many generations had been used to other than very short flights, the power to fly appeared suddenly to return to Pony's flock, along with the old wild spirit and the desire for liberty. One after another, squalling as if demented, they took flight. Pandemonium seemed to break loose there! Every goose squalled at once, and the roar of their flapping wings was like thunder.

In vain, Pony, running among them, called, "Choog! Choog!" and invoked each goose by name. The summons of that gray gander aloft seemed to set them all crazy. Around and around the great bird circled over the meadow, while he uttered wild cries of incitation. Within thirty seconds every goose—except two that were very old and fat and the disabled gander—had taken wing. All the younger white geese appeared to fly now without the least difficulty, yet thus far in their lives they had never really flown fifty feet!

In dismay and despair Pony ran along the bank of the brook and kept calling to the truants to come back—quite in vain! Once and yet again, led by the gray gander, the now magnificent flock aloft circled around the meadow, still squalling, perhaps derisively, to the laggards to rise and join them and then, heading northward, flew away and disappeared from sight over the fir woods up the brook.

To Pony, helplessly watching her truant geese, it was as if all her hopes and plans had suddenly taken wing and vanished in the azure vault.

"Oh, they're gone! They've all gone!" she cried, and for a moment her brave heart sank within her.

"But they can't fly far!" she exclaimed after a moment or two. "They're not used to flying. Their wings will ache. They'll have to light!"

And so, being a girl of indomitable pluck, she started to run after them through the woods along the brook in the direction of Mud Pond. "Indomitable pluck" is a strong expression, but I use the words purposely, and I am quite willing to let the reader say, when he learns what followed, if they are justified.

This all happened as early as seven o'clock of that raw April morning, but at the farm we did not know until evening that anything had gone wrong. At about six o'clock Aesop came home. The little, worn old sidesaddle was turned under him, and it looked as if he had been rolling, or rubbing hard, to get it off.

Pony's Wild-Goose Chase

THAT NIGHT when Aesop came home without Pony and with the saddle turned under him, we boys felt sure that a serious accident had happened. We put Aesop in the barn, and then, without saying anything to alarm our elders—especially Grandmother, who had been having one of her despondent days—we lighted a lantern and hastily set off for Quog-Hoggar.

We found no clue to the nature of the accident along the path that Pony usually followed, and half an hour brought us to Garland's Meadow where Halse ran ahead, swinging his lantern, to the barn.

"The door's open!" he shouted back to us, "and the geese are gone!" And then, as we came hurrying up, he added, "That proves she didn't start for home."

"Then let's find the geese," Addison said.

Running along the bank of the brook, we held the lantern out over the water and presently we saw two geese, and close to the bank near them the gander, with neck and wings awry, dead and partly submerged. We shouted but heard nothing save hollow echoes from the woody crags and hills.

"Now what do you think?" said Halse.

"Something, or somebody, has attacked her here and stolen most of the geese," replied Addison.

We did what we could to unravel the mystery; we searched the banks of the brook carefully for half a mile through the woods both above and below the meadow. The weather had been raw and chilly all day; the light was very dark and cloudy, and about eleven o'clock mingled snow and rain began to fall. Shortly after, we gave up the search and set off for home with very gloomy forebodings.

"It is something serious this time," Halse said.

"Yes," said Addison. "I think Pony's dead."

Our people were in bed and asleep when we reached home. We did not waken them but slept ourselves until daylight, when we went out and, raising a party, searched Quog-Hoggar to its uttermost nooks and borders. As many as twenty men and boys took part in the quest, which lasted all that day and the next; but save for a single, small footprint in a bog two miles above the meadow, no one was able to find any trace of the lost girl—and little wonder, for Pony was twenty miles away even before Aesop came home!

Her first surmise, that the geese, unused to flying, would tire and alight in Mud Pond, proved correct. When, after following the brook for nearly four miles through the woods, she emerged on that dreary expanse, she espied the entire flock sitting on the water near its upper end.

After an hour's stealthy creeping through the bushes and dead reeds, she reached a covert near the geese and began calling, "Choog! Choog! Come, Juno! Come, Hebe!" The truants craned their necks and several came, swimming toward the shore, and Pony's heart grew hopeful. But the wild gander promptly discovered her and, squalling loudly, rose into the air.

His cries and the roar of his wings quite drowned Pony's softer entreaties; the other wild geese, rising instantly, added their own clamor to the din of the gander, and again, to Pony's unspeakable chagrin, the white domestic geese rose after them—and away they all flew northward.

"Oh, that gray gander—the thief!" cried the baffled girl, but she did not allow herself to be daunted. She had heard of a certain Otter Pond several miles to the north and, reasoning that in time her tame geese must certainly grow tired and hungry and would probably alight there, she ran on in the wake of the flock.

Again her conjecture proved correct. When she emerged about noon from the thickets of Quog-Hoggar and came into the cleared land about Greenridge and in plain sight of Otter Pond about a mile away, she saw her geese resting on the water. Once more she began a stealthy approach.

But while she was still a good way from the birds, the report of a gun rang out suddenly. She darted forward in time to see the flock rise in great alarm and fly away. One white goose struggled feebly in the water. A boy had shot it and was now poling out with a raft to secure it.

"That's my goose!" cried Pony.

"Why, I thought they were wild geese!" exclaimed the youngster, as much astonished at the appearance of this strange white-faced girl from the woods as at the statement she made. Her little white face and her hands were crisscrossed with scratches; her abundant hair was in snarls that beggar description! Her dress skirt was frayed to fringes, and her shoes and stockings hardly held to her feet.

"No, they are my tame geese!" said Pony.

"Wal, I swow!" exclaimed the boy, gazing doubtfully at her. "You don't look very tame yourself."

"All the white ones are mine," said Pony. "That wild gray gander led them away."

"By gum!" cried the boy. "I set out to pick him instead of the goose."

"Oh, if you only had!" sighed Pony. "I shall never get my geese back till he's shot!"

"Wish I had," said the boy. "But they're gone now, and they won't stop short of Pratt's Pond, and that's five or six miles from here."

Pony, feeling now only too certain she must kill the wild gander if she was to regain her geese, tried to bargain for the boy's gun. "You may have my goose that you've shot," she proposed, "if you will load your gun and let me take it to shoot that gander."

"I don't believe you could shoot him, anyhow," replied the boy evasively. "It takes practice to shoot on water. Girls can't shoot!"

"But I must shoot that gander!" urged Pony.

"I've got to have my gun to shoot a hen hawk," he said, by way of further excuse.

"But I will fetch it right back," Pony pleaded.

Forced to be explicit, the boy refused bluntly. "'Taint likely," he said, "that I'd let a witch-cat like you carry off my gun!"

"Then come and shoot the gander yourself—and you can have it and the goose, too," Pony still urged.

"I'd like to," said the boy. "But, jingo! Father'd whip me if I went away off to Pratt's Pond. But I'll tell you what you do," the boy called after her as she started on. "If you find those geese in Pratt's Pond, you go get Jim Berry. Jim lives right there by the sawmill, next house. He's got a gun, and he's the best shot there is in this town. You get Jim; he'll shoot the gander fur you.

"But, my!" he added, "I never saw such a head of hair as you've got! Guess you're a smart one, though!"

Pony hastened on through the woods, and then followed a road over hills for a mile or two. A long pond was now in sight in the north-west, and by the middle of the afternoon, by dint of running more than half of the way, she reached the sawmill at the outlet. An old man and two girls, who were peeling poplar bolts for paper pulp, said that a large flock of wild geese, flying low, had passed over shortly after noon.

Pony climbed a hill above the mill stream, which afforded a view of the pond; and again she took heart a little, for far up the pond, in a bay partially surrounded by fir woods, her sharp eyes discovered a glimmer of white on the water. The tired runaways had again descended to rest their unused pinions.

Running back to the house at the sawmill, she eagerly inquired for James Berry, but was told by a pale sick-looking woman who came to the door that Jim was away that day carting poplar bolts to the railroad.

"Would you let me take Mr. Berry's gun?" Pony asked. "And is it loaded?"

The woman regarded the strange girl with the "head of hair" in weak amazement: "What do you want of it?" she at length asked.

"To shoot a gander—a wild gander that's stolen my geese," Pony replied.

"Did you ever fire a gun?" the woman asked.

"I did once—at a rat," said Pony.

"I—I don't believe—I would dare lend Jim's gun," said the woman, seeming suddenly to grow faint, and leaning heavily against the door. "I guess I shall have to go in and lie down."

Disappointed in her attempt to get the gun, Pony set off along the shore to approach the flock again. "They may be so tired and hungry by this time that I can call them to me," she said to herself. Then it occurred to her that she might get corn at the mill with which to feed them, and hastening back, she asked the old man for some. He had no corn, vegetables, or oats but finally gave her a quart of his seed wheat in a paper bag.

With this scanty provision she again set forth, and after making her way along the shore of the pond, mostly through woods and bushes, for fully three miles, came just at dusk to the bay, where the geese were sitting at rest on the water more than a hundred yards from the shore. As the northern shores of the pond were covered with forest, no rustic sportsman had as yet discovered the geese.

Approaching in the dusk, Pony began calling gently, "Choog! Choog! Come, Hebe! Come, Juno!" Before long there was a responsive "Quark-quark!" and several hungry and repentant geese came swimming toward the shore. But the masterful gray gander squalled menacingly and, sailing imposingly around the strays, gathered them together on the open water.

Two geese, however, escaped, and came and ate from her hand. These she caught and carried to an empty "shook" shanty, which she had passed half a mile down the east shore of the pond, and shut them in. Her plan now was to catch the geese one after another and shut them up there until she could find means to take them home.

But by the time she had reached the shanty, night had fallen cloudy and quite too dark to permit of traveling through the woods. She was thus obliged to give up returning to her geese until morning, and remained in the shanty all night. She made the door fast with props, took off her soaked shoes, and sat down in the old bunk of the shanty with her feet under her to keep them warm, and a goose on each side.

Since early in the morning she had not eaten a morsel, except a few handfuls of red checker berries, snatched up as she ran; and she now chewed mouthfuls of the wheat kernels, but they made unsatisfactory food. She said afterward that she was not hungry and did not think of eating and—what seems well-nigh incredible—that she did not feel much fatigued. She intended to go back up the shore and call her geese again at earliest dawn, but she fell sound asleep and did not waken until long after daylight. In great haste she put on her shoes and, opening the door, looked out. Sleet was falling, and there was a trace of snow on the evergreens.

At that moment she heard a noise in the underwood as of some large animal approaching. Shutting the door tight and peeping through a chink, she saw a man with a gun on his shoulder coming through the woods. She scanned him anxiously. Although roughly dressed, he was on the whole prepossessing in appearance, and Pony determined to speak to him.

"Good morning, sir," she said, opening the door.

"Good morning," replied the man, regarding her curiously. "Are you the girl they say lost some geese?"

"Yes," said Pony. "And who are you, sir?"

"Well, my name's Berry. My wife said you called at my place and wanted a gun and that you'd gone up the pond here after some geese. Thought I'd start out this morning and see what the matter was."

Pony thanked him and explained briefly why she wanted so much to shoot the wild gander.

"That's just what you'll have to do!" exclaimed Berry. "I'll shoot him for you, if I can."

Going cautiously through the bushes up the shore, they soon discovered that the geese were still there; but the wary gander was keeping the flock well out on the pond—too far, Berry said, for his shotgun to carry. Evidently the gander suspected the presence of enemies, for it made several attempts to lead the flock aloft; but the tame geese would not fly.

For two hours or more Berry, with Pony close behind him, crept around the woody shores, trying to get within range; but always the gander would veer away. "He's a cunning old feller!" the woodsman whispered. "My gun's a shotgun and don't carry ball well, but I'll have to try ball on him and risk it."

He replaced the charge of goose shot with ball and tried but missed. At the report the gander rose with tremendous squalls. This time the geese all followed him, and away they flew again.

"Confound it!" cried the vexed marksman. "I ought to have known better. And now they'll go clean to Lotte Pond over in Durgin's Grant."

"How far is that?" Pony asked soberly.

"Four or five miles, and all woods," replied Berry. "You couldn't go there."

"I'm going," said Pony. "Can you go?"

"I'd go," replied Berry ruefully, "but my wife's sick abed. She's worse today. I ought not to have come up here this morning, but I heard about you and wanted to see what had become of you. But I don't dare leave my wife alone all day."

"Then please load your gun again and let me take it," said Pony.

"Well," exclaimed the lumber man, "you beat all the gals I ever saw! But I know I hadn't ought to let you go off alone like this with a gun!"

"I'll have to go without it then," said Pony.

"Well, you're a plucky one," cried Berry, "and I'm going to let you take the gun—though I oughtn't! Had any breakfast?" he asked.

"Oh, I was eating all night," said Pony with an odd smile.

Berry loaded the gun with coarse shot. "There's a pretty good charge in it," he said. "But you needn't be afraid of its hurting you." He showed her how to rest the gun and sight it.

Pony laid hold of the gun and set off as fast as she could go, but Berry strode along beside her, giving directions for reaching Lotte Pond. "And if you don't find them there, come back same's you went," he added. "And if you do find them there, stay by them. I'll come up there this afternoon myself, if you don't come back—and Lucindy ain't too sick."

Pony darted away though the fir woods, but for some moments the good-hearted lumber man stood looking after her. Then he smote his thigh with his open palm.

"Never saw anything like that for grit!" muttered he. "I oughtn't to let her go—but I don't believe I could have stopped her if I'd tried! And I wonder to Great Gideon whose girl she is and where she came from!"

In two hours Pony, coming out through a wide alder bog, caught sight of Lotte Pond.

Berry had been a true prophet; the geese were there, near the lower end. Plainly the gander had difficulty in making his domesticated new recruits fly far, but perhaps his keen ear had caught the sound of her approach for immediately he began leading the flock up the pond, swimming as fast as a man could walk. Growing wise in the gander's ways, Pony made a wide detour through the bogs and came around to the upper end of the pond, which was at least two miles long, to head them off. She was in time, although the flock had approached within three or four hundred yards of a narrow arm of slack water connecting Lotte Pond with another smaller expanse that could be seen north of it. The gander plainly intended to lead his swimming flock through this arm into the other pond.

By the aid of the green cedar thickets that grew here, Pony was able to steal to the very water's edge, unseen by the geese. There she hid behind a stranded old tree and found herself commanding the channel as the gander led the way into it. With her heart beating fast, as much from excitement as from the exertion of running, Pony rested the gun across the log and aimed it at the flock, which was now less than a hundred yards away and swimming almost directly toward her.

"Now or never," she thought, "and I must aim straight, or I'll never see my geese again!" She brought the pinhead sight on the gray gander's breast. On he sailed, glancing warily to right and left as he entered the narrow arm. Gripping the gun as if her life depended on the shot, Pony pulled long and hard at the trigger, but the gun did not go off. Again sighting, she pulled harder still, but still the hammer did not fall! Glancing at it in sudden despair, she saw that she had not cocked the gun!

Reaching her fingers carefully forward so as not to derange the position of the gun on the log, she pulled the hammer back very cautiously, for by this time the gander and its foremost mates were within thirty yards, and coming on fast. But unused to firearms, she did not know that the ratchet of the gunlock must catch audibly in the notch. When it clicked, she let go in alarm; the hammer fell, and the gun, discharging, hopped quite over her small shoulder, and its heavy report boomed over the water.

With a cry of despair, Pony sprang up, for she heard a tremendous squalling and splashing, but as the smoke cleared away, she saw the gray gander flopping over on the water, his long neck outstretched and only one wing moving. Another gray goose that had been close behind lay helpless, and one of the white ones also was red with its own blood. Although the gun had gone off prematurely, it had done execution.

The three other gray geese had risen in the air, and with them two of the tame ones; but being without a leader, they circled about twice and again alighted on the pond. "Ah, you thief! At last you are done for!" cried the exultant girl.

Then she began calling her geese: "Choog! Choog! Come, doodies! Come back to Missy!"

But the geese, alienated by their taste of wild freedom and frightened by the gun, were slow to come to her. They turned back on the pond, and it was not till mid-afternoon that she succeeded in enticing them to her on the east shore. There she finally drew fifty-three of them together about her. The three wild geese fled to the other side of the pond.

There good James Berry found her, shepherding her recovered flock. The geese made no further effort to fly, but to be quite safe, Berry helped her clip the right wing of each.

The wild gander and the disabled white goose drifted ashore in the arm—dead; the gray one either sank or made shift to escape. Berry carried the gander home. Its wings had a spread of nine feet, and it weighed twenty pounds and five ounces.

I have described Pony's wild-goose chase at length for the details are authentic, and no exploit that I ever heard of a girl performing showed such unfaltering resolution.

Berry and Pony drove the geese out of the woods along an old lumber road to a point where Berry was able to approach with his horses and a rack cart. They also recovered the two geese left shut up in the old "shook" camp. Just at sunset on the third day—when we had searched all Quog-Hoggar and when the entire community had concluded that Pony was lost and probably dead—she came driving into our yard, sitting high beside James Berry with all those geese in the long rack cart behind them!

Berry remained with us overnight, but flatly refused to accept remuneration for his services. "I'm a poor man," he said, "with doctor's bills to pay, but I wouldn't have missed seeing that girl do what she's done for a hundred dollars!"

Success Takes Wing

IN ORDER that Pony should not again be alone in Quog-Hoggar, Grandmother persuaded Mrs. Willhope to let Pony's sister Lois stay at the meadow. And that the two girls might live the more comfortably there, we boys took saw, hammer, and nails, and gathering up all the boards we could find, partitioned off a small room on the sunny side of the old barn. We cut two windows and set up a stove. When a table and chairs were brought, the room had a comfortable, homelike look.

Fortune smiled on Pony for a time. Her aunt in New York sent her fifty dollars in money and a fine shepherd dog, who soon became invaluable in guarding the geese.

Pony bargained with a neighbor to plant a crop of rutabaga turnips, which Pony agreed to take at ten cents a bushel to chop up and feed to the geese in winter. She and Lois, with Dandy, the shepherd dog, and Aesop, the pony, guarded and cared for the flock. If I remember right, they had at one time a hundred and fifty goslings, and by autumn the entire flock must have numbered nearly two hundred. She sent the live-geese feathers from the summer and autumn picking to her relatives in New York, who procured for her what seemed to us the large price of a dollar and fifty cents a pound.

During the following winter thirteen geese died of disease. The old hay barn was not fit for so large a flock; Pony planned to build a very long shed with a glass front, which could be heated, and so provide a bathing place free of ice for the geese. She had received ninety-two dollars for feathers, and if she had marketed the young geese in November, she would doubtless have received as much more; but she preferred to enlarge her flock, and in spite of all losses, she began her second year with about a hundred and sixty birds.

Pony's plans were ambitious. She intended to go on increasing her flock and forming new flocks until the entire length of Bog Brook from

Mud Pond to the lower border of Quog-Hoggar was one immense goose farm, five or six miles in length. She and Grandmother estimated that there was ample room there for twenty thousand geese; they calculated that with ordinary good fortune the receipts from each goose, in feathers and goslings, would be eighty cents more than the cost of keeping them. At that rate, they would make a profit of $16,000 a year.

Whether such returns are probable, or even possible, I cannot say from experience. A goose farmer in Minnesota, whom I questioned, said that with proper management a profit of eighty cents a bird should ordinarily be realized from a flock of geese or of Peking ducks. He believed that in a favorable locality, like Quog-Hoggar along the brook, "a bright young woman might get rich if she would stick to it and learn from experience."

The fact is, however, that Pony did not become a rich and successful goose farmer. In this world of change, events rarely turn out as we plan them. Pony's aunt, Miss Ada Burdeen, a wealthy spinster, visited her niece the following summer and became much interested in Pony. Miss Burdeen persuaded Pony to sell her geese and go to a school for young ladies near New York City.

Two years later Pony entered Bryn Mawr College and remained there for four years. Her three elder sisters also went to New York for an education.

Only the rheumatic stepmother and Muncy remained in the cottage by the edge of Quog-Hoggar, and their wants were amply provided for.

When Pony—or rather Miss Ada Burdeen Willhope—graduated, she "came out" in society in New York. As her aunt's heiress, Pony did not need to earn a living. Ultimately she married a well-known lawyer, who has since been the minister of the United States at one of the capitals of Europe. To these scenes we need not follow her, but I think that her success with her flock of geese contains a hint to many young people. For there are many places, like Quog-Hoggar, where large flocks of geese may be kept without disturbing other people.

16

When Old Zack Went to School

IN THE WINTER OF 1866 THERE WAS A COMMOTION throughout the town on account of exciting incidents in what was known as the Mills school district, four miles from the Old Squire's, where a "pupil" nearly sixty years old was bent on attending school—contrary to law!

For ten or fifteen years Zachary Lurvey had been the Old Squire's rival in the lumber business. We had had more than one distracting contention with him and his brute of a son, Sam, our former schoolmaster. Yet we could not but feel a certain sympathy for him when, at the age of fifty-eight, he set out to get an education.

Old Zack would never tell anyone where he came from, though there was a rumor that he hailed originally from Petitcodiac, New Brunswick. When, as a boy of about twenty, he had first appeared in our vicinity, he could neither read nor write; apparently he had never seen a schoolhouse. He did not even know there was such a place as Boston or New York and had never heard of George Washington!

But he had settled and gone to work at the place that was afterward known as Lurvey's Mills; and he soon began to prosper, for he was possessed of keen mother wit and had energy and resolution enough for half a dozen ordinary men.

For years and years in all his many business transactions he had to make a mark for his signature, and he kept all his accounts on the attic floor of his house with beans and kernels of corn even after they represented thousands of dollars. Then at last a disaster befell him; his house burned while he was away, and from the confusion that resulted the disadvantages of bookkeeping in cereals was so forcibly borne in on him that he suddenly resolved to learn to read, write, and reckon.

On the first day of the following winter term he appeared at the district schoolhouse with a primer, a spelling book, a Greenleaf's *Arithmetic*, a copy book, a pen, and an ink bottle.

The schoolmaster was a young sophomore from Colby College named Marcus Cobb. He was the older brother of Ellen's future love, Thomas Jefferson Cobb. When Master Cobb entered the schoolhouse that morning he was visibly astonished to see a large, bony, formidable-looking old man sitting there among the children.

"Don't ye be scairt of me, young feller," old Zack said to him. "I guess ye can teach me, for I don't know my letters yit!"

Master Cobb called the school to order and proceeded to ask the names and ages of his pupils. When Zack's turn came, the old fellow replied promptly: "Zack Lurvey, fifty-eight years, five months, and eighteen days."

"Zack?" the master queried in some perplexity. "Does that stand for Zachary? How do you spell it?"

"I never spelled it," old Zack replied with a grin. "I'm here to larn how. Fact is, I'm jest a leetle backward."

The young master began to realize that he was in for something extraordinary. In truth, he had the time of his life there that winter. Not that old Zack misbehaved; on the contrary, he was a model of studiousness and was very anxious to learn. But education went hard with him at first; he was more than a week in learning his letters and sat by the hour, making them on a slate, muttering them aloud, sometimes vehemently, with painful groans. "M" and "W" gave him constant trouble, as did "B" and "R." He grew so wrathful over his mistakes at times that he thumped the desk with his fist, and once he hurled his primer at the stove.

"Why did they make the measly little things look so much alike?" he cried.

He wished to skip the letters altogether and to learn to read by the looks of the words; but the master assured him that he must learn the alphabet first if he wished to learn to write later, and finally he prevailed with the stubborn old man.

"Well, I do want to larn," old Zack replied. "I'm goin' the whole hog ef it kills me!"

And apparently it did pretty near kill him; at any rate, he perspired over his work and at times was near shedding tears.

Certain of the letters he drew on paper with a lead pencil and pasted on the back of his hands, so as to keep them in sight. One day he tore the alphabet out of his primer and put it into the crown of his cap—"to see ef it wouldn't soak in," he said. When, after a hard struggle, he was able to get three letters together and spell cat, "c-a-t," he was so much pleased that he clapped his hands and shouted "Scat!" at the top of his voice.

The effect of such performances on a roomful of small boys and girls was not conducive to good order. It was only with difficulty that the young master could hear lessons or induce his pupils to study. Old Zack was the center of attraction for every juvenile eye.

It was when the old fellow first began to write his name, or try to, in his copy book that he caused the greatest commotion. Only with the most painful efforts did his wholly untrained fingers trace the copy that the master had set. His mouth, too, followed the struggles of his fingers, and the facial grimaces that resulted set the school into a gale of laughter. In fact, the master—a good deal amused himself—was wholly unable to calm the room so long as old Zack continued his exercise in writing.

The children, of course, carried home accounts of what went on at school, and certain of the parents complained to the school agent that their children were not learning properly. The complaints continued, and finally the agent—his name was Moss—visited the schoolroom and informed old Zack that he must leave.

"I don't think you have any right to be here," Moss said to him. "And you're giving trouble; you raise such a disturbance that the children can't attend to their studies."

Old Zack appealed to Master Cobb. "Have I broken any of your rules?" he asked. The master could not say that he had, intentionally.

"Haven't I studied?" old Zack asked.

"You certainly have," the master admitted, laughing.

But the school agent was firm. "You'll have to leave!" he exclaimed. "You're too old and too big to come here!"

"All the same, I'm comin' here," said old Zack.

"We'll see about that!" cried Moss angrily. "The law is on my side!"

That was the beginning of what is still remembered as "the war at the Mills schoolhouse." The agent appealed to the school board of the town, which consisted of three members—two clergymen and a lawyer—and the following day the board appeared at the schoolhouse. After conferring with the master, they proceeded formally to expel old Zack Lurvey from school.

Old Zack, however, hotly defended his right to get an education, and a wordy combat ensued.

"You're too old to draw school money," the lawyer informed him. "No money comes to you for schooling after you are twenty-one, and you look to be three times as old as that!"

Thereupon old Zack drew out his pocketbook and laid down twenty dollars. "There is your money," he said. "I can pay my way."

"But you are too old to attend a district school," the lawyer insisted. "You can't go after you are twenty-one."

"But I have never been," old Zack argued. "I never used up my right to go. I oughter have it now!"

"That isn't the point," declared the lawyer. "You're too old to go. Besides, we are informed that you are keeping the lawful pupils from properly attending to their studies. You must pick up your books and leave the schoolhouse."

Old Zack eyed him in silence. "I'm goin' to school, and I'm goin' here," he said at last.

That was defiance of the board's authority, and the lawyer—a young man—threw off his coat and tried to eject the unruly pupil from the room; but to his chagrin he was himself ejected, with considerable damage to his legal raiment. Returning from the door, old Zack offered opportunity for battle to the reverend gentlemen—which they prudently declined. The lawyer re-entered, covered with snow, for old Zack had dropped him into a drift outside.

Summoning his two colleagues and the schoolmaster to assist him in sustaining the constituted authority, the lawyer once more advanced on old Zack, who retreated to the far corner of the room and bade them come on.

Many of the smaller pupils were now crying from fright; the two clergymen, probably feeling that the proceedings had become scandalous, persuaded their colleague to cease hostilities, and in the end the board contented itself with putting a formal order of expulsion into writing. School was then dismissed for that afternoon, and they all went away, leaving old Zack backed into the corner of the room. But regardless of his "expulsion," the next morning he came to school again and resumed his arduous studies.

The story had gone abroad, and the whole community was waiting to see what would follow. The school board appealed to the sheriff, who offered to arrest old Zack if the board would provide him with a warrant. It seemed simple enough, at first, to draw a warrant for old Zack's arrest, but legal difficulties arose. He could not well be taken for assault, for it was the lawyer that had attacked him; or for wanton mischief, for his intent in going to school was not mischievous; or yet for trespass, for he had offered to pay for his schooling.

There was no doubt that on account of his age he had no business in the school and that the board had the right to refuse him schooling, yet it was not easy to word his offense in such a way that it constituted a misdemeanor that could properly be stated in a warrant for his arrest. Several warrants were drawn, all of which—on the ground that they were legally dubious—the resident justice of the peace refused to sign.

"I am not going to get the town mixed up in a lawsuit for damages," said the justice. "Lurvey is a doughty fighter at law, as well as physically, and he has got the money to fight with."

The proceedings hung fire for a week or more. The school board sent an order to the master not to hear old Zack's lessons or to give him any instructions whatever. But the old fellow came to school just the same, and poor Cobb had to get along with him as best he could. The school board was not eager again to try putting him out by force, and it seemed that nothing less than the state militia could oust him from the schoolhouse, and that would need an order from the governor of the state! On the whole, public opinion rather favored old Zack's being allowed to pay his tuition and to go to school if he felt the need of it.

At any rate, he went to school there all winter and made remarkable progress. In the course of ten weeks he could read slowly, and he knew most of the short words in his primer and second reader by sight. Longer words he would not try to pronounce but called them, each and all, "jackass" as fast as he came to them. In consequence his reading aloud was highly entertaining but somewhat ambiguous. He could write his name slowly and with many grimaces.

Figures, for some reason, came much easier to him than the alphabet. He learned the numerals in a few days, and by the fifth or sixth week of school he could add and subtract on his slate. But the multiplication table gave him serious trouble. The only way he succeeded in learning it at all was by singing it. After he began to do sums in multiplication on his slate, he was likely to burst forth singing in school hours: "Seven times eight are fifty-six—and carry five. Seven times nine are sixty-three—and carry seven. No, no, no, no—carry six!"

"But Mr. Lurvey, you must keep quiet in school!" the afflicted master remonstrated for the hundredth time. "No one else can study."

"But I can't!" old Zack would reply. "'Twouldn't come to me 'less I sung it!"

Toward the last weeks of the term he was able to multiply with considerable accuracy and to divide in short division. Long division he did not attempt, but he rapidly learned to cast interest at six percent. He had had a way of arriving at that with beans before he came to school, and no one had ever succeeded in cheating him. He knew about interest money, he said, by "sense of feeling."

Grammar he saw no use for and did not bother himself with it, but curiously enough he was delighted with geography and toward the end of the term bought a copy of Cornell's textbook, which was then used in Maine schools.

What most interested him was to trace rivers on the maps and to learn their names. Cities he cared nothing for, but he loved to learn about the mountain ranges where pine and spruce grew.

"What places them would be for sawmills!" he exclaimed.

Much as he liked his new geography, however, he had grown violently angry over the first lesson and declared with strong language that it was all a lie! The master had read aloud to him the first lesson, which describes the earth as one of the planets that revolve round the sun and which says that it is a globe or sphere, turning on its axis once in twenty-four hours and so causing day and night.

Old Zack listened incredulously. "I don't believe a word of that!" he declared flatly.

The master labored with him for some time, trying to convince him that the earth is round and moves, but it was quite in vain.

"No such thing!" old Zack exclaimed. "I know better! That's the biggest lie that ever was told!"

He quite took it to heart and continued talking about it after school. He really seemed to believe that a great and dangerous delusion had gone abroad.

"It's wrong," he said, "puttin' sich stuff as that into young ones' heads. It didn't oughter be 'lowed!"

What old Zack was saying about the earth spread abroad and caused a great deal of amusement. Certain waggish persons began to "josh" him and others tried to argue with him, but all such attempts merely roused his native obstinacy. One Sunday evening he gave a somewhat wrong direction to the weekly prayer meeting by rising to warn the people that their children were being taught a pack of lies, and such was his vehemence that the regular Sabbath service resolved itself into a heated debate on the contour of the earth.

Perhaps old Zack believed that, as a recently educated man, it had become his duty to set things right in the public mind.

The day before school closed he went to his late antagonist, the lawyer on the school board, and again offered to pay the twenty dollars for his tuition. After formally expelling him from school, however, the board did not dare to accept the money, and old Zack gave it to the long-suffering Master Cobb.

17

Peddling Christmas Trees

I USED TO GO TO SCHOOL AT A SCHOOLHOUSE THAT I fear city boys of my acquaintance would make sport of.

For many years it was unplastered, and the big fireplace on one side had to roar and fight hard against the airy draughts that came through the great cracks in the walls between the boards.

In the winter of 1863, tired of this style of ventilation, Thomas Edwards and Willis Murch sold their pet bear for twenty-five dollars. With this money they had the schoolhouse lathed and plastered.

From this act, done by the scholars themselves, I date the beginning of the extraordinary progress in scholarship that marked the school for a number of years.

The very fact that the scholars did this lathing and plastering with their own money caused them to take a personal interest in the schoolhouse. They determined to have the best schoolhouse and the best school in that town.

The second winter after I had arrived, we raised money to buy four large maps—each five feet square—a globe, and a large blackboard. The cost of these was thirty-one dollars.

Now thirty-one dollars was a large sum for country boys to raise and not easily obtained. To earn it we went into a "great speculation," at least for school boys. It was one I have always been a little proud of.

The previous year a gentleman from the city of Portland, visiting our neighborhood on business a few days before Christmas, had cut a little fir tree—for a "Christmas tree," he said—to take home with him.

At that time Christmas trees had not come in vogue with us; we had scarcely heard of them. At most farms the only rite or festivity at Christmas consisted of hanging one's stocking in the chimney corner. Sometimes a few cents or a stick of candy or a roll of lozenges had been known to be found in stockings on Christmas mornings. But the visitor explained that Christmas trees were beginning to come into use in cities, where people put wax tapers and presents on them.

He made the remark that such a fir as his would be worth a dollar or two in Portland at Christmas time. This was remembered. When we were planning to get money to buy maps, someone spoke of it.

"Well, why can't we take a lot of trees to Portland and sell them?" exclaimed Willis Murch. Willis, sometimes known as Wilts, was then in his fifteenth year.

"But it's seventy miles to Portland!" one of the girls cried out.

"What's seventy miles?" said Wilts. "Any good horse can go seventy miles in a day."

"But how are you going to carry the firs?" asked Tom Edwards. "One fir will fill a sleigh."

"Then take a big hayrack!" cried the sanguine Wilts.

That settled the matter.

Mr. Wilbur, Ned's father, owned a large hayrack, nearly twenty feet long, on which a ton and a half of hay had sometimes been loaded. He consented to let us take the rack. This rack we set on two "traverse sleds," such as are used for winter teaming, and harnessed to the pole two farm horses.

Some three miles up the lake, along which the farms lay, there was a swamp full of young firs.

On the morning of December 22, a merry party of us set off up the lake on the ice for the fir swamp with our rack and axes. About a foot of snow had fallen. There were ten or eleven of the boys and girls of the school, and we made the shores echo with our happy shouts that clear, bright morning.

Reaching the swamp, the boys searched for the handsomest firs. It was an entirely new business, and there were a great many diverse opinions and much earnest discussion as to how it should be conducted. Wilts had the clearest idea as to what was wanted and took the lead in selecting the trees to be cut. Most of the evergreens chosen were from eight to ten feet in height, and we took great care not to mar the graceful boughs and "balsam buds" of the firs.

The girls dragged them out to the rack and soon had the snow around it covered with green heaps.

I recollect that we cut three large trees, for we argued that in some of the churches the Sunday school children might be holding a festival and would want a "big one." One of these larger firs was fully twenty feet in height and not less than thirty-five feet in circumference—a "monster," the girls said.

We were puzzled how to pack them in the rack so as not to crush the delicate boughs. At last we tried standing them up, beginning at the forward end, and crowding them as closely as possible, and succeeded in packing more in the rough vehicle than one would suppose possible. I think there were fifty-seven or fifty-nine trees. The three large ones were set in the rear and allowed to lean back over the rail.

It was a prodigiously bulky, green load, though by no means a heavy one. We were tired and hungry enough before we reached home with it.

Four of us boys arranged to start for Portland at four o'clock the next morning. Tom's sister, Kate Edwards, suggested that Wilts should dress up as St. Nicholas, with Tom, Ned, and me as his assistant sprites. Such a device, she fancied, would help the sales.

She and the other girls worked two signs, the words CHRISTMAS TREES, 50 CENTS EACH! on them. The letters were in red yarn a foot high on a broad strip of white cloth. These were to be stretched on each side of the rack on entering the city. For something to sit on in our drive to Portland, we rigged a board across the top of the rack at the forward end.

On the next morning we were astir at three o'clock, but it was between four and five before we got our horses fed and harnessed, ready to start.

Day had but just broken. The morning star shone cold and bright. The wind blew sharply, making the snow fly at times.

But our seat was pretty well sheltered by the green boughs, and we sat as snugly as we could to keep warm, though we had to get down at times and run smartly to stir our blood.

It was a tedious day's drive, yet we had some sport out of it. Almost everyone we met would cry out, "What are you going to do with all that green stuff?" or "Where are ye taking all those firs to?"

Wilts's answer was always, "Christmas trees, for Portland!"

We ran against a load of hay in the road, but got clear without any great damage. At a place where the road ran near the railroad, our horses, unused to the steam cars, tried to run away, and it was hard holding them from that high board without any fender to brace our feet against.

In the afternoon we passed a schoolhouse just as the boys came out at recess. Full of fun, they began to snowball us. We jumped down and retaliated. The snowballs flew! There was a regular battle, but we routed them and drove them into their entry.

Several snowballs flew in at the door. The master came out, and we fell back, leaving one fellow rubbing his ear.

That night we put up at a farmer's in the town of Westbrook, a few miles out of Portland. He charged us nine shillings for our night's lodging.

Getting an early start the next morning, we drove into town. It was the first time any of us had been in Portland or any other city. Near the bridge from Westbrook into the city, we put out our signs, but we could not muster the courage to don the old hats, coats, and belts that we had brought to represent St. Nicholas in.

Following this street, which had a track laid for horse cars, we came out into another long, broad street—Congress Street.

It was early, much too early, in fact. The great street looked gray, cold, and deserted. There were dusty patches of ice on each side of the horse car track. Just then an almost empty car came grinding past. The driver did not so much as notice us with a cast of his eyes.

Here and there a muffled-up passer's boot heels struck loudly on the sidewalk. A policeman from the other side of the street gave us a surly glance. It seemed as if nobody would or could possibly want any-thing of us or our load.

"Well, what are we going to do, Wilts?" Tom asked at last.

"Say something. Sing out 'Christmas trees!'" Wilts suggested.

But for one, I felt as if I couldn't open my mouth.

"You call out, Wilts," said Tom.

"No, you," said Wilts. "I'm driving."

At length Ned mustered his voice and cried, "Christmas trees!"

But it was in such a timid tone, with such a shamefaced accent (for all the world as if he were afraid somebody would hear him), that the rest of us laughed.

A little fellow inside a doorway took in the situation and reviled us.

"You keep quiet!" Tom shouted at him, and having thus got his mouth open, he cried, "Christmas trees!" and did a little better.

At that we all shouted, "Christmas trees! Christmas trees!" making the lonesome street echo.

No sort of notice, however, was taken of this appeal, a circumstance that confounded us not a little.

We journeyed on, up and down different streets, and at intervals "cried our wares," but a great and ever-darkening cloud of discourage-ment had fallen on us. The streets filled. Carts and hacks rumbled past us. There were more people passing in the streets, but they seemed to ignore us as if from a settled purpose.

Never in my life had I felt so out of place, so utterly and depressingly ignored, as if I was at disreputable business. If I could only have got home and fairly out of our boyish enterprise, I felt as if nothing would ever tempt me to another such an undertaking. I saw my own feeling expressed in the faces of my partners, though we scarcely dared to look at each other.

Martin, the visitor who introduced us to Christmas trees, had told us to go along with our load and ring the doorbells as we passed, and tell the people what we had to sell. After a time we bethought ourselves of this advice.

As Willis drove on, Ned, Tom, and myself began to ring at the doors. We were on a street where there were handsome, brick dwelling houses. But our calls, however, were mostly answered by frowzy-headed servant girls who cried, "Be off with ye!" and slammed the doors in our faces.

We conceived a bad impression of the manners of Portland people, and after a time gave up ringing doorbells.

Ten o'clock! Not a tree had been sold!

We had frequently stopped beside the curbstones and made halts of keen disgust. During one of these "stagnant spells," a door opened close beside us, and an old gentleman, gray-haired and much wrinkled but of whom we somehow got the idea that he was or had been a doctor, came out, picking his way with his gold-headed cane.

"Ah," he said, stopping short. "Who are these balsams for, boys?"

"For Christmas, if anybody wants 'em," said Wilts.

The old gentleman was critically examining the buds.

"They are very good for the lungs," he remarked. "It's a pity folks do not plant them round their houses."

"But these are for Christmas trees," Tom interposed. "Ah!" said the old gentleman absently. "They are nature's sovereign remedy for the terrible disease of the climate in which they grow."

"These are Christmas trees—Christmas trees—Christmas trees!" we all told him as gently, yet insinuatingly, as possible.

"Blind, blind! How blind! Our children die of consumption month by month, score by score," the old gentleman ran on, "when a little grove of these round every house would be as sure a preventive as food is of hunger."

Tom pulled one out of the load.

"Have one?" he said. "Have one of these good balsams? Only fifty cents."

"Yes, this is the cure nature has planted all round us in the North," the old gentleman went on, fumbling in his pocket. He drew out two quarters, which we took at once and drove quickly on, fearing, as Ned said, that our customer might "wake up." We left his balsam leaning against a shade tree with the old gentleman contemplating it, rapt and oblivious.

But our luck had turned.

We had not gone a hundred yards before we met on the sidewalk a very nicely dressed lady of middle-age who looked wide awake enough, too. We saw her eyes brighten.

"How do you sell your Christmas trees, my good boys?" she asked.

"A beauty for fifty cents!" cried Willis.

Seeing her unloose the little chain of her purse, we picked out a nice one, and Ned went with her to carry it to her door two or three blocks away. He said she gave him ten cents more for that.

Before he had got back, however, we had sold another to a gentleman in a coupé, who took it carefully into the carriage with him. Not ten minutes after, a butcher in a long white frock bought another.

In a word, the tide had turned. We sold one every five or ten minutes after that. So wrought up were we by this happy change in our fortunes that not one of us thought of dinner, either for ourselves or our horses, that day. We grew bold in our cries.

"Christmas trees! Christmas balsams! Good for the lungs! Sure cure for consumption! And only fifty cents!"

But the greatest rush came at about four o'clock in the afternoon, when the children came out of school. We drew a crowd then, and such a running for Papa's and Mamma's consent, and for scrip to buy a "tree!"

Our stock became small in a very few minutes, and our customers themselves forced us to put up our price. They began to offer a dollar and a dollar and a half for the remaining trees.

A party of them ran off to the superintendent of the Sunday school at their church and coaxed him to come and buy one of the three big trees for their vestry. We received two dollars for it.

The other two large firs we did not sell. But I think we might easily have sold fifty more of the small ones if we had had them.

We were happy boys, you may be assured. Never with us had a day begun with such discouragement and ended in such triumph.

Determined to be magnanimous now, we drove past two churches in the gathering dusk and left a big fir on the steps of each. It was in the *Argus* next morning, that "some unknown Santa Claus" had left a "beautiful Christmas tree" on the steps of both churches.

We drove back to the same house in the evening where we had spent the previous night, and I'm sure the good lady there thought we did justice to her supper and were bound to have our nine shillings' worth.

Next morning we set off for home. It so happened that we passed the schoolhouse where we had had the battle, just as the boys came out at their forenoon recess. We felt so good-humored over our successful venture that we were now for having a jollification with them. But they pitched into us like hornets! Their snowballs were all made up and frozen overnight. We received an awful pelting. The ice balls whistled about our ears most vindictively, and we were glad to put our horses to their speed and get away as fast as we could.

That night we reached home. The net proceeds of the sale after taking out all expenses were thirty-three dollars and fifty cents, with which we bought the maps, blackboard, and globe. So much for enterprise and pluck! And I do not doubt that this endeavor to make our school attractive—and the energy and invention and self-denial it called forth—had a most important and beneficial influence on the characters of every boy and girl who took part in it.

18

How to Thaw a Frozen Pipe

IT WAS SEVEN DEGREES BELOW ZERO THAT JANUARY morning, with a bitter wind blowing, as is often the case in Maine at this time of year. And to me, at least, the world looked black as well as cold, for I was in disgrace! I had let the barn pump freeze up that night, and there were sixteen cows, eight yearling heifers, four work horses, two colts, and a flock of fifty sheep to water before school time—and nothing but ice in the trough!

What was harder even than ice, Cousin Addison had no sympathy for me. "I told you last night to run that pump down," he said. "Why didn't you? Now you may lug water, for all of me—and serve you right!"

He and I were doing the farm chores together that week. The Old Squire was away, up at a logging camp in the Great Woods. Halstead was laid up in the house with a severe cold and had not been out of doors for several days; he generally had two or three of those colds every winter, caught imprudently, nearly always. Addison did all the feeding and the milking, and I the pumping and watering, night and morning.

It was quite true, too, that he had reminded me to run the pump down, but I had been in a kind of haze all day over two hard examples in complex fractions at school. One of them I still remember distinctly:

$$\tfrac{7}{8} \text{ of } \frac{60\tfrac{5}{10}}{10\tfrac{3}{8}} \text{ of } \frac{8}{5} \div 8\frac{68}{415} = \text{What?}$$

The answer, of course, is one, but I could not get it, and it was still worrying me when I reached home that night; so much so, that after "fetching" the pump and watering the cattle, I had somehow forgotten to run the pump down, as was the rule every night in winter.

Addison was so righteously indignant with me that at a quarter to nine he went off to school, without speaking, and left me there with that whole stock of cattle to water as best I could.

I could not complain. It was my job, and after he and the girls had gone to school, I set to work to carry water for all those cattle in two buckets from the pump in the farmhouse kitchen—all the way out through the long wood house, wagon house, and stable to the west barn, and then down a flight of stairs to the watering trough in the barn cellar!

I am wondering, too, whether many of those who read this realize how much water thirty head of cattle will drink. I let them out to the trough one by one, as I hastened back and forth from the house well, and it did seem to me that never would they stop drinking or get enough. The less water there was in the trough, the thirstier they seemed to be. Some of them actually drank four bucketfuls.

As I hurried to and fro, water slopped from the buckets, which instantly turned to ice as it fell on the floor and stairs; and the monotony of the trips was enlivened for me by tumbling down occasionally, with two buckets of water.

It was eleven o'clock, and I had made forty-five or fifty trips before all those thirsty cows and horses were satisfied; and then I set to work to thaw out the pump with hot water.

For in the house Grandmother and Aunt Olive were making complaint against me for slopping water about; they feared, too, lest I might pump the well dry, since wells everywhere were low that winter.

Did you ever try to thaw out an iron or a copper pump with the mercury below zero—and fetch your hot water in a bucket from a kitchen stove three hundred yards away?

The pump itself I thawed with no great difficulty, down past the "boxes" to the point where it was screwed to the inch-and-a-half lead pipe that led off aslant to the barn well forty feet distant. But that inch-and-a-half pipe was also frozen up hard and fast. I was afraid it had burst, and that added to my troubles, since the ground over the pipe was hard frozen and now buried under six feet of snowdrifts. It would be near to impossible in such weather to dig it up and put in new pipe. That was what Addison said—for my comfort!

But the pipe, as I may add here, was very thick and of good stock. The Old Squire always made use of the best material he could purchase for all such work. The ice in the pipe, as we afterward learned, had bulged it in places, but did not actually burst it.

As soon as I had cleared the pump, I unscrewed the coupling to the pipe with a wrench, and then tried to thaw the pipe by pouring hot water into it. This one can do for five or six feet downward without great difficulty, but soon a point is reached where the hot water no longer operates, for the reason that as it cools it is not much displaced by what is poured in at the top; and still deeper it is not displaced at all, the hot which you pour in merely running over at the top.

Eight or nine feet down, where the pipe turned off underground, I came to a standstill. I persevered and fussed with it two or three hours, but quite in vain. Meanwhile I had scalded one hand rather painfully through my mitten.

Boys who read this may laugh at my troubles that day, but at fourteen they were very real troubles to me. I knew not what to do and was not a little terrified at the prospect ahead. For by three o'clock that afternoon I had to begin carrying water for the cattle again, to get them watered before dark.

I knew Addison would not help me. He was properly indignant at my carelessness, and he was not a particularly softhearted boy.

Moreover, he had his own large share of the chores to do. In short, I was in a hard spot.

And it got harder; for by the time I had carried fifteen or sixteen turns of water from the house well that afternoon, the kitchen pump sucked and gurgled. I had pumped the well out, and now Grandmother and Aunt Olive came down on me again. "Don't you take another drop of water from here!" Aunt Olive exclaimed. "Do you think I want to melt snow for water?"

"But the cattle must have water. What can I do?" I cried, nursing my scalded hand and nearly in tears but for shame of shedding them.

"Kindle a fire under the arch-kettle in the wagon house and melt snow yourself," said Aunt Olive austerely. "Why in the world, too, don't you put rock salt or saltpeter in that pump pipe? Rock salt in it overnight will thaw it out."

Thus adjured, I kindled a fire in the "arch," filled the big kettle with ice and snow, then got rock salt, such as we gave to the herd. But by this time the hot water that I had poured into the pump pipe earlier in the afternoon had cooled and frozen. I thawed it down for two feet again with more boiling hot water, then filled it up with salt grains.

Soon after, Addison came home from school and began doing his share of the chores. His face was still hard set against me. "You will have to stay at home and melt snow the rest of this winter, I guess," he said grimly.

"Snow water isn't good for cattle either," he added. "And I don't believe you can melt enough for them, anyway."

I was afraid I could not myself, for it melted slowly in spite of the good fire I kept. All that evening I tended the kettle, carrying the water in a bucket to the cattle and horses in their stalls. It was nine o'clock before I could give them even one bucketful apiece. But it had to suffice; and I crept away to bed, with my smarting hand, completely tired out and discouraged by the day's struggle with cold and adversity.

My hand, I remember, kept me from sleeping much till past midnight. Then it got easier, and I was comfortably dreaming when Addison roused me at six. "Come, come!" he said. "You had better be up melting more snow, instead of snoozing there. Those cattle need water."

It was, in good truth, a hard, cold world to wake into! I had cherished faint hopes that the rock salt grains would thaw out the pump pipe, and dressing in haste, I rushed out to ascertain. The water, strongly impregnated with salt, had not frozen at the top end of the pipe; and on thrusting in a long stick, I found that the salt had actually eaten its way downward in the ice for about five feet. But it had gone no farther, and the prospect of its working its way underground to the well outside the barn was poor indeed. It might do so in a week or two, perhaps, but even that was uncertain.

My teacher, Master Pierson, who had now learned of the trouble at the barn, came out with the kind purpose of aiding me but shook his head after trying the pump.

"That pipe is frozen, probably clean down to the water in the well," he said.

"It is hard on you, and I am very sorry to have you lose time at school," he added with genuine sympathy.

But even sympathy does not greatly help a case like that. In still gloomier mood, I rekindled the fire in the arch and later saw Addison depart for school, while I put in another day melting snow for those ever-thirsty cattle. Theodora and Ellen pitied me, but there was not much that they could do to help matters. So far as I could see, there was not a ray of hope ahead anywhere. I should probably have to melt snow day and night all the rest of that winter, or at least till the Old Squire came home. That, too, was a bitter thought. I was ashamed to have the old gentleman learn how thoughtless I had been.

By afternoon I had grown desperate, as well as tired and disheartened. Doing my best with the arch-kettle, I could not melt snow enough to water so numerous a herd. I had been able to give them no more than a bucketful apiece that day. Some of the cows were lowing plaintively whenever they saw me enter the barn with the bucket, and as for the sheep, they were eating snow. What to do I knew not.

But relief was at hand. My good genius was about to appear. I had now been absent from school two days, and by this time my arithmetic class had begun to ask after me. Addison, I suppose, told them where I was and what I was doing; and that night six or seven of my schoolmates called on their way home, to see me at my task and sympathize or have a little fun at my predicament, according to their dispositions.

Among them were Thomas and Katherine Edwards, who lived next beyond the Old Squire's, and were always our fast friends. As I was emerging from the barn, bucket in hand, they all met me, laughing, and then must needs go to see the pump and ask all sorts of questions, which I was in no mood to answer.

But Katherine lingered, with Theodora and Ellen, after the others had gone.

"Couldn't you pour hot water into the pipe here?" she asked me.

"Oh, I have" I said, impatiently. "But it will only thaw the ice about so far down the pipe. It gets cold down there. The hot water from the top will not work down much deeper than eight feet."

"Isn't there any way you could get the real hot, boiling water down there where the ice is?" Katherine persisted in asking.

"I don't know any way," said I, not very graciously, for I was cross and had no very exalted idea of girls' wisdom.

But Katherine's eyes were still thoughtfully bent on that pipe. "If only you had a little pipe, smaller than that, to run down into it, where the ice is, and then poured the boiling water into the little pipe with a funnel. Wouldn't it go right down hot against that ice and thaw it?" she persisted.

"Maybe, but I haven't any such little pipe," said I, and hastened away to the arch to get another bucket of water.

Katherine lingered there, studying on it for some moments longer, then started off hastily.

I had no idea that she could help me, and renewed my fire; but a little later, in the twilight, Katherine and Thomas came back. They had Tom's handsled, and on it was a coil of old, half-inch lead pipe, the pipe of an aqueduct at the Edwardses' farm, which had become clogged the summer before and had to be dug up and replaced by larger pipe.

Tom was laughing, but Katherine was much in earnest. "Let's try this!" she exclaimed. "It will go into your pump pipe, and it will bend easy. Get hot water and a funnel."

There were forty or fifty feet of this little, thin, old lead pipe. We poked one end of it down the pump pipe till it touched the ice in it; and then, elevating the other end six or eight feet, we began pouring in hot water through a tin funnel.

The effect was immediately apparent. Within five minutes we were able to thrust the small pipe down two feet deeper in the pump pipe, and we now elevated the upper end of the little pipe still higher, so as to give the hot water in it greater pressure. The longer we worked, too, the faster was the ice in the large pipe melted, since the pipe was now getting hot. The water, boiling hot, came directly in contact with the ice, and as it cooled, it came bubbling up about the little pipe and flowed out at the top of the large one.

Dusk had fallen, but a lantern was lighted; we went on as fast as Aunt Olive, Addison, and the girls could fetch hot water from the kitchen stove, for now they all turned out to help me. Within an hour that pump pipe was free of ice clear down to the well.

I was not long screwing on the pump again and within another hour had my thirsty herd comfortably watered once more.

Master Pierson deemed Katherine's idea such a bright one that he wrote a brief account of it for the county newspaper, under the heading "How to Thaw Out a Frozen Pump," and a plumber in Portland has since told me that he saw that item in the paper and, recognizing its practical value, had a small, flexible pipe made of Britannia metal for his own use in just such cases of frozen water pipes. Other plumbers, he said, copied it from him, till it came into quite general use through-out the northern United States. So far as he knew, plumbers in this country had not thought of that plan previously.

I hope I was really grateful for my rescue from disgrace, and I think I was, but my recollection is that I had little opportunity to express my gratitude that night—for the moment that Katherine found that the plan was about to succeed, she and Thomas scampered away home to supper.

19

Cutting Ice at Fourteen Degrees Below Zero

GENERALLY SPEAKING, YOUNG FOLKS ARE GLAD when school is done. But it wasn't so with us that winter in the Old Squire's district, when Master Joel Pierson was teacher. We were really sad, in fact quite melancholy, and some of the girls shed tears when the last day of school came and "old Joel" tied up the melodeon, took down the wall maps, packed up his books, and went back to his class in college.

He was sad himself—for he had taken such interest in our progress.

"Now don't forget what you have learned!" he exclaimed. "Hang on to it. Knowledge is your best friend. You must go on with your Latin, evenings."

"You will surely come back next winter!" we shouted after him as he drove away.

"Maybe," he said, and would not trust himself to look back.

The old sitting room seemed wholly deserted that Friday night after he went away, for he had boarded with us that winter. "We are like sheep without a shepherd," Theodora said. Katherine and Tom Edwards, our neighbors, came over. We opened our Latin books and tried to study awhile, but 'twas dreary without old Joel.

Other things, however, other duties and other work at the farm immediately occupied our attention. It was now mid-January, and there was ice to be cut on the lake for our new creamery.

For three years the Old Squire had been breeding a herd of Jerseys. There were sixteen of them; Jersey First, Canary, Jersey Second, Little Queen, Beauty, Buttercup, and all the rest. Each one had her own little book that hung from its nail on a beam of the tie-up behind her stall. In it were recorded her pedigree, dates, and the number of pounds of milk she gave at each milking. The scales for weighing the milk hung from the same beam. We weighed each milking and jotted down the weight with the pencil tied to each little book. All this was to show which of the herd was most profitable and which calves had better be kept for increase.

This was a new departure in Maine farming. Cream separators were as yet undreamed of. A water creamery with long cans and ice was then used for raising the cream, and that meant an icehouse and the cutting and hauling home of a year's stock of ice from the lake, nearly two miles distant.

We built a new icehouse near the east barn in November, and in December the Old Squire drove to Portland and brought home a complete kit of tools: three ice saws, an ice plow or groover, ice tongs, hooks, chisels, tackle, and block.

Everything had to be bought new, but the Old Squire had visions of great profits ahead from his growing herd of Jerseys. Grandmother, however, was less sanguine.

It was unusually cold in December that year, frequently ten degrees below zero, and there were many high winds. Consequently, the ice on the lake thickened early to twelve inches and bade fair to go to two feet. For use in a water creamery, ice is most conveniently cut and handled when not more than fifteen or sixteen inches thick. That thickness, too, when the cakes are cut twenty-six inches square, as usual, makes them quite heavy enough for hoisting and packing in an icehouse.

Half a mile from the head of the lake, over deep, clear water, we had been scraping and sweeping a large surface after every snow, in order to have clear ice. Two or three times a week Addison ran down and tested the thickness, and when it reached fifteen inches, we bestirred ourselves at our new work.

None of us knew much about cutting ice, but we laid off a straight baseline of a hundred feet, hitched old Sol to the new groover, and marked off five hundred cakes. Addison and I then set to work with two of our new ice saws and hauled out the cakes with the ice tongs, while Halstead and the Old Squire loaded them on the long horse sled (sixteen cakes to the load), drew the ice home, and packed it away in the new icehouse.

Although at first the sawing seemed easy, we soon found it tiresome, and learned that two hundred cakes a day meant a hard day's work, particularly after the saws lost their keen edge—for even ice will dull a saw in a day or two. We had also to be pretty careful, for it was over deep, black water, and a cake when nearly sawed across is likely to break off suddenly underfoot.

Hauling out the cakes with tongs, too, is somewhat hazardous on a slippery ice margin. We beveled off a kind of inclined "slip" at one end of the open water, and cut heel holes in the ice beside it, so that we might stand more securely as we pulled the cakes out of the water.

For those first few days we had bright, calm weather, not very cold; we got out five hundred cakes and drew them home to the icehouse without accident.

The hardship came the next week, when several of our neighbors—who always kept an eye on the Old Squire's farming, and liked to follow his lead—were beset by an ambition to start icehouses. None of them had either experience or tools. They wanted us to cut the ice for them.

We thought that was asking rather too much. Thereupon, fourteen or fifteen of them offered us two cents a cake to cut a year's supply for each of them.

Now no one will ever get very rich cutting ice, sixteen inches thick, at two cents a cake. But Addison and I thought it over and asked the Old Squire's opinion. He said that we might take the new tool kit and have all we could make.

On that, we notified them all to come and begin drawing home their cakes the following Monday morning, for the ice was growing thicker all the while; and the thicker it got, the harder our work would be.

They wanted about four thousand cakes, and as we would need help, we took in Thomas Edwards and Willis Murch as partners. Both were good workers, and we anticipated having a rather fine time at the lake.

In the woods on the west shore, nearly opposite where the ice was to be cut, there was an old "shook" camp, where we kept our food and slept at night, in order to avoid the long walk home to meals.

On Sunday it snowed and cleared off cold and windy again. It was eight degrees below zero on Monday morning when we took our outfit and went to work. Everything was frozen hard as a rock. The wind, sweeping down the lake, drove the fine, loose snow before it like smoke from a forest fire. There was no shelter. We had to stand out and saw ice in the bitter wind, which seemed to pierce to the very marrow of our bones. It was impossible to keep a fire, and it always seems colder when you are standing on ice.

It makes me shiver now to think of that week, for it grew colder instead of warmer. A veritable cold snap set in, and never for an hour, night or day, did that bitter wind let up.

We would have quit work and waited for calmer weather—the Old Squire advised us to do so—but the ice was getting thicker every day. Every inch added to the thickness made the work of sawing harder—at two cents a cake. So we stuck to it and worked away in that cruel wind.

On Thursday it got so cold that if we stopped the saws even for two seconds, they froze in hard and fast, and had to be cut out with an ax; thus two cakes would be spoiled. It was not easy to keep the saws going fast enough not to catch and freeze in, and the cakes had to be hauled out the moment they were sawed, or they would freeze on again. Moreover, the patch of open water that we uncovered froze over in a few minutes and had to be cleared a dozen times a day. During those nights it froze five inches thick and filled with snowdrift, all of which had to be cleared out every morning.

Although we had our caps pulled down over our ears and heavy mittens on, and wore all the clothes we could possibly work in, it yet seemed at times that freeze we must—especially toward night, when we grew tired from the hard work of sawing so long and so fast. We became so chilled that we could hardly speak, and at sunset, when we stopped work, we could hardly get across to the camp. The farmers, who were coming twice a day with their teams for ice, complained constantly of the cold; several of them stopped drawing altogether for the time. Willis also stopped work on Thursday at noon.

The people at home knew that we were having a hard time. Grandmother and the girls did all they could for us, and every day at noon and again at night the Old Squire, bundled up in his buffalo-skin coat, drove down to the lake with horse and pung and brought us a warm meal, packed in a large box with half a dozen hot bricks.

Only one who has been chilled through all day can imagine how glad we were to reach that warm camp at night. Indeed, except for the camp, we could never have worked there as we did. It was a log camp, or rather two camps, placed end to end, and you went through the first in order to get into the second, which had no outside door. The second camp had been built especially for cold weather. It was low, and the chinks between the logs were tamped with moss. At this time, too, snow lay on it and had banked up against the walls. Inside the camp, across one end, there was a long bunk; at the opposite end stood an old cooking stove, which seemed much too large for so small a camp.

At dusk we dropped work, made for the camp, shut all the doors, built the hottest fire we could make, and thawed ourselves out. It seemed as though we could never get warmed through. For an hour or more we hovered about the stove. The camp was as hot as an oven; I have no doubt that we kept the temperature at 110 degrees, and yet we were not warm.

"Put in more wood!" Halstead or Thomas would exclaim. "Cram that stove full again! Let's get warm!"

We thought so little of ventilation that we shut the camp door tight and stopped every aperture that we could find. We needed heat to counteract the effect of those long hours of cold and wind.

By the time we had eaten our supper and thawed out, we grew sleepy, and under all our bed clothing, curled up in the bunk. So fearful were we lest the fire should go out in the night that we gathered a huge heap of fuel, and we all agreed to get up and stuff the stove whenever we waked and found the fire abating.

Among the neighbors for whom we were cutting ice was Rufus Sylvester. He was not a very careful or prosperous farmer, and not likely to be successful at dairying. But because the Old Squire and others were embarking in that business, Rufus wished to do so, too. He had no icehouse, but thought he could keep ice buried in sawdust, in the shade of a large apple tree near his barn; and I may add here that he tried it with indifferent success for three years and that it killed the apple tree.

On Saturday of that cold week he came to the lake with his lame old horse and a rickety sled and wanted us to cut a hundred cakes of ice for him. The prospect of our getting our pay was poor. Saturday, moreover, was the coldest, windiest day of the whole week; the temperature was down to fourteen degrees below. Halse and Thomas said no; but Rufus hung round and teased us, while his half-starved old horse shivered in the wind, and we finally decided to oblige him, if he would take the tongs and haul out the cakes himself, as we sawed them. It would not do to stop the saws that day, even for a moment.

Rufus had on an old blue army overcoat, the cape of which was turned up over his head and ears, and a red woolen "comforter" round his neck. He wore long-legged, stiff cowhide boots, with his trousers tucked into the tops.

Addison, Thomas, and I were sawing, with our backs turned to Rufus and to the wind, and Rufus was trying to haul out a cake of ice, when we heard a clatter and a muffled shout. Rufus had slipped in! We looked round just in time to see him go down into that black, icy water.

Addison let go the saw and sprang for one of the icehooks. I did the same. The hook I grabbed was frozen down, but Addison got his free, and stuck it into Rufus's blue overcoat. It tore out, and down Rufus went again, head and ears under. His head, in fact, slid beneath the edge of the ice, but his back popped up.

Addison struck again with the hook—struck harder. He hooked it through all Rufus's clothes, and took a piece of his skin. It held that time, and we hauled him out.

He lay quite inert on the ice, choking and coughing.

"Get up! Get up!" we shouted to him. "Get up and run, or you'll freeze!"

He tried to rise, but failed to regain his feet, and collapsed. Thereupon Addison and Thomas laid hold of him and lifted him to his feet by main strength.

"Now run!" they cried. "Run before your clothes freeze stiff!" The man seemed lethargic—I suppose from the deadly chill. He made an effort to move his feet, as they bade him, but fell flat again, and by that time his clothes were stiffening.

"He will freeze to death!" Addison cried. "We must put him on his sled and get him home!"

Thereupon we picked him up like a log of wood, and laid him on his horse sled.

"But he will freeze before we can get this old lame horse home with him!" exclaimed Thomas. "Better take him to our camp over there."

Addison thought so, too, and seizing the reins and whip, started for the shore. The old horse was so chilled that we could hardly get him to hobble, but we did not spare the whip.

From the shore we had still fifteen or twenty rods to go, in order to reach the camp back in the woods. Rufus's clothes were frozen as stiff as boards; apparently he could not move. We feared that the man would die on our hands.

We snatched off one of the side boards of his sled, laid him on it, and, taking it up like a stretcher, started to carry him up through the woods to the camp.

By that time his long overcoat and all the rest of his clothes were frozen so stiff and hard that he rolled round more like a log than a human body.

The path was rough and snowy. In our haste we stumbled and dropped him several times, but we rolled him on the board again, rushed on, and at last got him inside the camp. Our morning fire had gone out. Halse kindled it again, while Addison, Thomas, and I tried to get off the frozen overcoat and long cowhide boots.

The coat was simply a sheet of ice; we could do nothing with it. At last we took our knives and cut it down the back and after cutting open both sleeves, managed to peel it off. We had to cut open his boots in the same way. His undercoat and all his clothes were frozen. There appeared to be little warmth left in him; he was speechless.

But just then we heard someone coming in through the outside camp. It was the Old Squire.

Our farmhouse on the higher ground to the northwest afforded a view of the lake, and the old gentleman had been keeping an eye on what went on down there, for he was quite farsighted. He saw Rufus arrive with his team and a few minutes later saw us start for the shore, lashing the horse. He knew that something had gone wrong, and hitching up old Sol, he had driven down in haste.

"Hot water, quick!" he said. "Make some hot coffee!" And seizing a towel, he gave Rufus such a rubbing as it is safe to say he had never undergone before.

Gradually signs of life and color appeared. The man began to speak, although rather thickly.

By this time the little camp was like an oven, but the Old Squire kept up the friction. We gave Rufus two or three cups of hot coffee, and in the course of an hour he was quite himself again.

We kept him at the camp until the afternoon, however, and then started him home, wrapped in a horse blanket instead of his army overcoat. He was none the worse for his misadventure, although he declared we tore off two inches of his skin!

On Sunday the weather began to moderate, and the last four days of our ice cutting were much more comfortable. It had been a severe ordeal, however; the eighty-one dollars that we collected for it were but scanty recompense for the misery we had endured.

20

Lost in the Encyclopedia

THERE WERE NO MORE THAN THIRTY OR FORTY
books in the farmhouse at the Old Squire's place when we young
folks first went home to live: books of all sorts, including two family
Bibles, half a dozen Testaments, *Pilgrim's Progress*, a hymn book,
Murray's *Grammar*, Welch's *Arithmetic*, Colton's *Geography*, Town's
Fourth Reader, and a spelling book. There was also a Walker's dictionary and a surveyor's guide, for the Old Squire was the possessor of a
compass and chain and had been accustomed to run lines for his fellow pioneers.

He and Grandmother Ruth had been too busy farming, summers,
lumbering, winters, and raising a family to accumulate a library; they
would hardly have found time to read one. Except for a single worn
copy of Scott's *Waverley*, there wasn't a novel in the house.

When my cousin Addison came, however, he brought a number of
books that had been his father's—his father was preceptor of an academy—among them a copy of Audubon's *Ornithological Biography*, Wil-
son's *American Ornithology*, Dana's *Geology*, and Parker's *Natural Philosophy*, all of which he treasured highly, even jealously.

Cousin Theodora's heirlooms were less of the scientific order; they
included two of Fenimore Cooper's novels, *The Prairie* and *The Last of
the Mohicans*, and quite a ponderous Bible dictionary.

Cousin Ellen, too, enriched the sitting room bookcase with three of
Mary J. Holmes's stories and a *Scottish Chiefs*, which had been her
mother's; and even Halstead had what he called his "pirate book,"

which he kept in the depths of his trunk and never let the old folks see him reading, though I feel sure Grandmother Ruth knew all about it!

I was the only one of the group who contributed nothing to the literary treasures of the old homestead, and I remember feeling shamefully insignificant on that account; to this day I have never quite got over that sense of inferiority.

It was my second winter at the farm, when we began taking up certain new studies at the district school and at home, that the schoolmaster, Joel Pierson, who boarded at the Old Squire's, insisted that we needed a reference work for looking up facts and general information in history, biography, and the sciences.

"What you need here in this family is a good encyclopedia," he said to the Old Squire. "You have at least four young folks who I know are going ahead to the academy to get an education. An encyclopedia will be a great help to them. Better have one."

The Old Squire assented at once, but even he was a little staggered when we learned that the cost of a proper encyclopedia in a durable binding would be a hundred and twenty-five dollars, and Grandmother Ruth at once cried out against such an outlay. "A hundred and twenty-five dollars for a book!" she exclaimed. "That is extravagant. We can't afford it, Joel; you mustn't put us up to it!"

"It does seem a good deal of money, Mother," Master Pierson replied. (He always called Grandmother Ruth "Mother.") "But these young folks must all help pay for it. They must work for it, same as I do to get books, clothes, and college expenses. That's the way to prize things, work for them. I'm sure these five boys and girls can raise half of that money if they will try hard."

We declared we could and would. "Then what say, Squire, could you put in half of that hundred and twenty-five dollars if these young folks will raise the other half?"

The Old Squire laughed and said he could.

"Good enough. Go ahead then!" Master Pierson exclaimed jovially. "And when I come to teach school here next winter, I shall expect to see that encyclopedia right here in this sitting room, all ready to refer to."

Grandmother Ruth, I recollect, was not quite as sanguine as the rest of us. "It sounds to me extravagant," she said more than once.

We found that actually earning sixty-two dollars and fifty cents was not easy. Theodora and Ellen said that they would raise twenty dollars, somehow, if we boys would find the balance; and the method Addison and I adopted during February was to cut and draw ten cords of white birch to the "spool mill," six miles from the farm. We thought we had done a fine thing, and I doubt if we properly realized at the time that the Old Squire was obliged to furnish team, feed, and board, beside the birch, while we were thus occupied. He did not complain, however, and did not even mention it, though once while we were boasting of our exploit to the girls, Grandmother Ruth quietly reminded us of it, for poor Ellen and Theodora were finding their share much more difficult to raise. At first, during the latter part of the winter and spring, they attempted to "draw" two rugs, with hooks, from colored woolen stuff, for which a lady in Portland had offered ten dollars apiece. But they at length gave that up as impracticable; they had not been able to shear them properly and spoiled both rugs.

Later, in May, they hit on the expedient of raising a flock of turkeys over at the Aunt Hannah Lot, half a mile from home—so as not to mix up with the home poultry. Fifty-two turkey chicks were at length hatched; and for the care and feeding of those wretched little bipeds, I suppose those two worried girls made more than a thousand trips over there, generally on the run. Care and troubles multiplied daily. Nearly twenty of the chicks died during the first two or three weeks of summer; and in September foxes got eight of the half-grown turkeys. There were several other casualties, so that when Thanksgiving week arrived there were only seventeen marketable birds. But meantime Ellen had been industriously drying apples to make up a threatened deficit, and they came proudly forward with their twenty dollars (and two dollars to spare) the week before Master Pierson arrived and the winter school began. It had been a really heroic effort on their part— yet, as in our case, I suppose the Old Squire had to furnish food, board, and shoe leather for it.

The encyclopedia was sent for and came during the first week of the winter school. It was in sixteen large volumes, handsomely bound in leather. Addison meantime had made a special bookcase for it, fashioned from oak boards and set alongside the other, larger book-case in the sitting room. It was a proud evening in the family annals when we unpacked the work from the large box in which it had come and, after arranging it in alphabetical order, stood back to observe the effect, while Master Pierson shouted, "Bravo! Well done! I'm proud of you!"

But something smaller and more simple in the way of a reference work would have answered quite as well for me at least, during several years thereafter. I did not use those fine volumes much. They were too learned; I had not yet grown up to them, nor do I think that Theodora and Ellen often had recourse to them of their own accord, although while school was keeping that winter, Master Pierson made a point of sending us to look up things daily.

Oddly enough as it seemed to us then, the Old Squire, with all his cares of farming and lumbering was the one who really studied the encyclopedia! The work came to him as a means of gratifying a long-felt want for information on a thousand subjects concerning which he had felt curiosity all his life. The fact was that the Old Squire belonged to a generation of men—the Hamlins, the Fessendens, the Morrills, the Washburns—who did honor to their native state and rose to eminence in political life. With better opportunities for edu-cation in his youth, I feel sure he would have taken his place among the best of them.

That encyclopedia opened an avenue to a wealth of information and culture that he had the kind of mind to appreciate. He fell upon it greedily, like a hungry man at a feast. Throughout those winter evenings, I recall that while we young folks conned our lessons or played and clattered about the farmhouse, the Old Squire sat by a little lightstand in a corner of the sitting room, with spectacles astride his nose, wholly absorbed in first one, then another volume of that new encyclopedia. He must have been about sixty-eight at the time, but a school girl in possession of a new romance could hardly have been more keenly interested. He read so late at night and became so absorbed at times that Grandmother Ruth grew concerned lest he was neglecting his Bible and "the means of grace"; the old lady had all along been a little suspicious of that encyclopedia.

The first week in May was always housecleaning week at the old farm—dreadful days of soap and water and a general upset of everything in the way of furniture. Sweeping, rug beating, and tidying up of course came every week; but housecleaning was the dire event of the year. "Aunt Olive Witham" then appeared on the scene. Certain other neighboring women often came in. Grandmother Ruth and the girls put on old dresses and a look of determination. The kitchen steamed with hot water kettles. Tables and chairs went out on the piazza and were joined there by three or four "airtight" stoves from the chambers. Gaunt bedsteads migrated to the yard; mattresses balanced themselves on the yard fence, and inside, the rites were performed!

Generally there were two or three days during which it was highly unsafe for a boy or man to come poking indoors for anything save the most urgent business. Nights we slept wherever we could find a place, and meals came at all sorts of hours, with anything that was handy for food. Then followed two or three days of fresh paint, shellac, or whitewash, hazardous because we had to walk the floors on narrow boards, laid down on cleats, and woe be to him who made a misstep. In short it was a week of domestic tribulation.

Wise from past experience, the Old Squire was wont to betake himself to work in some remote field or pasture of the farm, and take us boys with him. When hungry, we approached the house warily and made covert reconnaissances at the kitchen door but not till long after the usual hour for meals. If food had been laid out on the table, we stole in, captured what was in sight without noise or questioning, and stole out again. It was no time to be putting forward masculine pretensions.

On the second morning of housecleaning in the spring of 1867, the Old Squire posted us boys off to repair the fence about the back pasture—nearly a mile distant from the house—and remarked that we had better not return for luncheon until we had gone completely around the pasture. He would have accompanied us, but it chanced that he was looking for a lumber dealer from Portland on that day—a certain Charles Farnum—to arrive on the morning train to bargain for our next winter's cut of pine. He therefore busied himself trimming apple trees in the orchard beyond the garden, in sight of the road. Mr. Farnum came, as was observed by someone in the house; they were seen talking together as late as eleven o'clock that forenoon. The Portland man then drove away, and after that the Old Squire wholly disappeared.

Addison and I did not return from the pasture till past two in the afternoon and then, perceiving that a table was set in the kitchen with food, we went in and proceeded to regale ourselves. While doing so Grandmother Ruth passed through the kitchen and asked where the Old Squire was and why he had not come in with us. Addison replied that he had not been with us that day. The old lady seemed a little surprised, and half an hour later, when we were out in the garden planting a few rows of sweet corn, she came out to inquire again about him. No one, it appeared, had seen him since his visitor left at about eleven o'clock, but Ellen was sure that the Old Squire had not gone with him; she had glanced out and seen the lumber man go away alone.

"But he may have hitched up and driven to the village later," Addison suggested. That conjecture was disproved when we looked in the stable. All four horses and the driving wagon were there.

Thereupon Grandmother Ruth went to have look at the Old Squire's wearing apparel. "He hasn't gone far away," she said. "He wore his working clothes; his better suit is in the closet."

"Oh, he is out at work somewhere on the farm," Aunt Olive remarked. "Blow the horn for him."

Sounding the dinner horn was generally Theodora's task, one for which she had come to pride herself, since it had taken her some months at first to set up the requisite "lip" for it. Going out past the east barn she now blew the horn loud and long. But there was no response, even after a second blowing.

That he had gone to some of the neighbors, and for some reason remained awhile, was the next supposition. Ellen ran up to the Murch farm to inquire, Theodora also hastened across lots to the Edwards farm, and Addison went out along the highway toward the Corners to make inquiries at the Sylvesters' and other places, while I scuttled off by the cart road to the Aunt Hannah Lot. In the course of half an hour, however, we were all back with much the same report: none of the neighbors had seen him, and I had discerned no sign of him about the old buildings of the Aunt Hannah Lot. We feared then that he might have met with some accident in the barns, and both these capacious old structures, also the barn cellars and the apple house, were thoroughly searched. It was even thought that he might have fallen down the barn well while repairing a leak in the log pump, and the well was sounded—all quite without result.

In short the Old Squire had vanished utterly, leaving no trace, not even a working clue, and when another hour passed we were in a state of much anxiety. Grandmother Ruth in particular was badly worried. As it drew toward night we gathered in the kitchen, taking council together and trying to decide what had best be done. Addison favored starting a general search of the surrounding country. "We had better notify the neighbors, send out inquiries, and begin looking everywhere," he said, and Ellen and I were setting off to do so when a door was heard to shut far upstairs, seemingly in the attic. "Was that the wind?" Theodora queried, but there was no wind. "Can't be Aunt Olive," Ellen decided. "She went home at four o'clock."

Just then steps were heard descending the stairs in the front hall and another door closed—the door into the sitting room, accompanied by sounds as of someone stumbling over a displaced chair.

Addison rushed into the sitting room, the rest of us following, and there was the Old Squire stooping in the act of replacing a volume of the encyclopedia in the bookcase. He looked up, as one quite innocent of wrongdoing.

"Well, well, Joseph, where in the world have you been all day?" Grandmother Ruth cried, her alarm suddenly changing to indignation. "I should like to know! Will you tell us where you've kept yourself?"

"Why Ruth," the Old Squire explained, surprised by her vehemence, "I've only been up in the little 'clock room' at the end of the attic. I thought I would be out of your way up there," he went on. "There were several interesting articles in the encyclopedia I had been wanting to read for some time, and after Farnum left I got the book and slipped up the back stairs. I kept as still as I could. I guess you didn't hear me."

"I guess not, too!" Grandmother Ruth exclaimed with growing reprehension. "I should rather think we didn't! We have been worried nearly to death about you!"

"But didn't you hear me blow the horn, Gramp?" cried Theodora in wonder.

"Why, it seems to me I did hear it," the Old Squire replied, reflecting. "I suppose I thought you were blowing it for the boys to come home from the pasture."

"And it never occurred to you to come down!" commented Grandmother Ruth with sarcasm. "I wonder you didn't stay up there all night!"

"I did stay longer than I meant to," the Old Squire went on to explain. "It was very interesting reading—and it came on dusk before I was aware it was so late." His mind appeared still absorbed with the subject that had so lately engrossed him. "I was reading of the great fires there have been in the world," he began to tell us. "That terrible fire at Portland last year was not really the worst that history records, though people called it so. The one at Rome when Nero is said to have burned the city was as great or greater, and that one at Moscow in 1812, when Napoleon invaded Russia, was much more terrible. Only think of it! Seventeen thousand houses were burned there, and over fifty churches and cathedrals. Two hundred and fifty thousand people were rendered homeless and not less than two thousand were thought to have perished. And it was the Russians themselves who burned their city, to prevent it from giving shelter to the French invaders. Wonderful resolution!"

Grandmother Ruth sniffed, not wholly entertained. But the Old Squire, still rapt in what he had read, went on: "London, Lisbon, Alexandria, Tokyo, and even New York have all had their great fires, but the city of all others that has suffered most from fires is Constantinople. French cities seem to be those that have had fewest of them. It is probably due to their better system of building. Paris—" But Grandmother Ruth interrupted the inopportune recital.

"Joseph, you had better come back home and let me get you something to eat," she said austerely. "It's most night and there are things to do.

"The next time we lose you, I guess the place to look first will be in that encyclopedia!" she added sententiously.

Afterward whenever the Old Squire was missed, Grandmother Ruth and the girls were wont to look in the sitting room bookcase. If a volume of the encyclopedia was gone from its place there, they concluded that the old gentleman was safe somewhere, though he might not come back until it became too dark for him to see to read.

21

Addison's Pocketful of Auger Chips

FEBRUARY OF 1867 HAD NOW PASSED, AND WE WERE not much nearer realizing our plans for getting an education than when Master Pierson left us the month before.

Owing to the bad times and a close money market, lumbering scarcely more than paid expenses that winter. This and the loss of five workhorses the previous November put such stress on the family purse that we felt it would be unkind to ask the Old Squire to send four of us to the village academy that spring, as had been planned.

"We shall have to wait another year," Theodora said soberly.

"It will always be 'another year' with us, I guess!" Ellen exclaimed sadly.

But during March, a shrewd stroke of mother wit, on the part of Addison, greatly relieved the situation and, in fact, quite set us on our feet in the matter of funds. This, however, requires a bit of explanation.

For fifty years grandsir Cranston had lavished his love and care on the old Cranston farm, situated three miles from our place. He had been born there, and he had lived and worked there all his life. Year by year he had cleared the fields of stone and fenced them with walls. The farm buildings looked neat and well cared for. The sixty-acre wood lot that stretched from the fields up to the foot of Hedgehog Ledge had been cleaned and cleared of undergrowth until you could drive a team from end to end of it, among the three hundred or more immense old sugar maples and yellow birches.

That wood lot, indeed, had been the old farmer's special pride. He loved those big old-growth maples, loved them so well that he would not tap them in the spring for maple sugar. It shortened the lives of trees, he said, to tap them, particularly large old trees.

It was therefore distressing to see how, after grandsir Cranston died, the farm was allowed to run down and go to ruin. His wife had died years before; they had no children, and the only relatives were a brother and a nephew in Portland and a niece in Bangor. Cranston had left no will. The three heirs could not agree about dividing the property. The case had gone to court and stayed there for four years.

Meanwhile the farm was rented first to one and then to another tenant, who cropped the fields; let weeds, briars, and bushes grow; neglected the buildings; and opened unsightly gaps in the hitherto tidy stone walls. The taxes went unpaid; none of the heirs would pay a cent toward them, and the fifth year after the old farmer's death the place was advertised for sale at auction for delinquent taxes.

In March of the fifth year after grandsir Cranston died, Willis and Ben Murch wrote to one of the Cranston heirs and got permission to tap the maples in the wood lot at the foot of the ledge and to make sugar there.

They tapped two hundred trees, three spiles to the tree, and had a great run of sap. Addison and I went over one afternoon to see them "boil down." They had built an "arch" of stones for their kettles up near the foot of the great ledge and had a cozy little shed there. Sap was running well that day, and toward sunset, since they had no team, we helped them to gather the day's run in pails by hand. It was no easy task, for there were two feet or more of soft snow on the ground and there were as many as three hundred brimming bucketfuls that had to be carried to the sap holders at the shed.

Several times I thought that Addison was shirking. I noticed that at nearly every tree he stopped, put down his sap pails, picked up a hand-ful of the auger chips that lay in the snow at the foot of the tree, and stood there turning them over with his fingers. The boys had used an inch-and-a-half auger, for in those days people thought that the bigger the auger hole and the deeper they bored, the more sap would flow.

"Don't hurry, Ad," I said, smiling, as we passed each other. "The snow's soft! Pails of sap are heavy!"

He grinned but said nothing. Afterward I saw him slyly slipping handfuls of those chips into his pocket. What he wanted them for I could not imagine; and later, after sunset, as we were going home, I asked him why he had carried away a pocketful of auger chips.

He looked at me shrewdly, but would not reply. Then, after a minute, he asked me whether I thought that Ben or Willis had seen him pick them up.

"What if they did?" I asked. But I could get nothing further from him.

It was that very evening I think, after we got home, that we saw the notice the tax collector had put in the county paper announcing the sale at public auction of the Cranston farm on the following Thursday, for delinquent taxes. The paper had come that night, and Theodora read the notice aloud at supper. The announcement briefly described the farm property, and among other values mentioned five hundred cords of rock-maple wood ready to cut and go to market.

"That's that old sugar lot up by the big ledge, where Willis and Ben were making syrup," said I. "Ad, whatever did you do with that pocketful of auger chips?"

Addison glanced at me queerly. He seemed disturbed but said nothing. The following forenoon, when he and I were making a hot-bed for early garden vegetables, he remarked that he meant to go to that auction.

It was not the kind of auction sale that draws a crowd of people; there was only one piece of property to be sold, and that was an expensive one. Not more than twenty persons came to it—mostly prosperous farmers or lumber men, who intended to buy the place as a speculation if it should go at a low price. The Old Squire was not there; he had gone to Portland the day before, but Addison went over, as he had planned, and Willis Murch and I went with him.

Hilburn, the tax collector, was there, and two of the selectmen of the town, besides Cole, the auctioneer. At four o'clock Hilburn stood on the house steps and read the published notice of the sale and the court warrant for it. The town, he said, would deduct $114—the amount of unpaid taxes—from the sum received for the farm. Otherwise the place would be sold intact to the highest bidder.

The auctioneer then mounted the steps and read the Cranston warranty deed of the farm, as copied from the county records, describing the premises, lines, and corners. "A fine piece of property, which can soon be put into good shape," he added. "How much am I offered for it?"

After a pause, Zachary Lurvey, the owner of Lurvey's Lumber Mills, started the bidding by offering $1,000.

"One thousand dollars," repeated the auctioneer. "I am offered one thousand dollars. Of course that isn't what this farm is really worth. Only one thousand! Who offers more?"

"Fifteen hundred," said a man named Haines, who had arrived from the southern part of the township while the deed was being read.

"Sixteen," said another, and presently another said, "Seventeen!"

I noticed that Addison was edging up nearer the steps, but I was amazed to hear him call out, "Seventeen fifty!"

"Ad!" I whispered. "What if Cole knocks it off to you? You have only $100 in the savings bank. You couldn't pay for it."

I thought he had made a bid just for fun, or to show off. Addison paid no attention to me, but watched the auctioneer closely. The others, too, seemed surprised at Addison's bid. Lurvey turned and looked at him sharply. I suppose he thought that Addison was bidding for the Old Squire, but I knew that the Old Squire had no thought of buying the farm.

After a few moments Lurvey called, "Eighteen hundred!"

"Eighteen fifty," said Addison, and now I grew uneasy for him in good earnest.

"You had better stop that," I whispered. "They'll get it off on to you if you don't take care." And I pulled his sleeve impatiently.

Willis was grinning broadly; he also thought that Addison was bluffing the other bidders.

Haines then said, "Nineteen hundred," and Lurvey at once cried, "Nineteen twenty-five!"

It was now apparent that Lurvey meant to get the farm if he could, and that Haines also wanted it. The auctioneer glanced toward us. Much to my relief, Addison now backed off a little, as if he had made his best bid and was going away, but to my consternation he turned when near the gate and cried, "Nineteen fifty!"

"Are you crazy?" I whispered, and tried to get him to leave. He backed up against the gatepost, however, and stood there, watching the auctioneer. Lurvey looked suspicious and disgruntled, but after a pause, said in a low voice, "Nineteen seventy-five." Haines then raised the bid to $2,000, and the auctioneer repeated that offer several times. We thought Haines would get it; but Lurvey finally cried, "Two thousand twenty-five!" and the auctioneer began calling, "Going-going-going for two thousand twenty-five!" when Addison shouted, "Two thousand fifty!"

Lurvey cast an angry look at him. Haines turned away; and Cole, after waiting for further bids, cried, "Going-going-gone at two thousand fifty to that young man by the gate, if he has got the money to pay for it!"

"You've done it now, Ad!" I exclaimed in distress. "How are you going to get out of this?"

I was frightened for him; I did not know what the consequences of his prank would be. To my surprise and relief, Addison went to Hilburn and handed him $100.

"I'll pay a hundred down," he said, "to bind my bid and the balance tomorrow."

The two selectmen and Hilburn smiled, but accepted it. I remembered then that Addison had gone to the village the day before, and guessed that he had drawn his savings from the bank. But I did not see how he could raise $1,950 by the next day. All the way home I wanted to ask him what he planned to do. However, I did not like to question him before Willis and two other boys who were with us. All the way home Addison seemed rather excited.

The family was at supper when we went in. The Old Squire was back from Portland; Grandmother and the girls had told him that we had gone to the auction. The first thing he did was to ask us whether the farm had been sold and how much it had brought.

"Two thousand and fifty," said I with a glance at Addison.

"That's all it's worth," the Old Squire said. "Who bought it?"

Addison looked embarrassed, and to help him out I said jocosely, "Oh, it was bid off by a young fellow we saw there."

"What was his name?" the Old Squire asked in surprise.

"He spells it A-d-d-i-s-o-n," said I.

There was a sudden pause round the table.

"Yes," I continued, laughing, for I thought the best thing for Ad was to have the Old Squire know the facts at once. "He paid $100 of it down, and he has to get round with nineteen hundred and fifty more by tomorrow noon."

Food was quite forgotten by this time. The Old Squire, Grandmother, and the girls were looking at Addison in much concern.

"Haven't you been rather rash?" the Old Squire said gravely.

"Maybe I have," Addison admitted. "But the bank has promised to lend me the money tomorrow at seven percent. If—if—" he hesitated and reddened visibly, "if you will put your name on the note with me, sir."

The Old Squire's face was a study. He looked surprised, grave, and stern; but his kind old heart stood the test.

"My son," he said after a short pause, "what led you into this? You must tell me before we go farther."

"It was something I noticed over there in that wood lot. I haven't said anything about it so far, but I think I am right."

He went upstairs to his trunk and brought down a handful of those auger chips and also a letter that he had received recently. He spread the chips on the table by the Old Squire's plate, and the latter, after a glance at them, put on his reading glasses. Dry as the chips had become, we could still see what looked like tiny bubbles and pits in the wood.

"Bird's-eye, isn't it?" the Old Squire said, taking up a chip in his fingers. "Bird's-eye maple. Was there more than one tree of this?"

"More than forty, sir, that I saw myself, and I've no doubt there are others," Addison replied.

"Ah!" the Old Squire exclaimed with a look of understanding kindling in his face. "I see! I see!"

During our three or four winters at the Old Squire's we boys had naturally picked up considerable knowledge about lumber and lumber values.

"Yes," Addison said. "That's why I planned to get hold of that wood lot. I wrote to Jones & Adams to see what they would give for clear, kiln-dried bird's-eye maple lumber, for furniture and room finish, and in this letter they offer $90 per thousand. I haven't a doubt we can get a hundred thousand feet of bird's-eye out of that lot."

"If Lurvey had known that," said I, "he wouldn't have stopped bidding at two thousand!"

"You may be sure he wouldn't," the Old Squire remarked with a smile.

"As for the quarreling heirs," said Addison, "they'll be well satisfied to get that much for the farm."

The next day the Old Squire accompanied Addison to the savings bank and endorsed his note. The bank at once lent Addison the money necessary to pay for the farm.

No one learned what Addison's real motive in bidding for the farm had been until the following winter, when we cut the larger part of the maple trees in the wood lot and sawed them into three-inch plank at our own mill. Afterward we kiln-dried the plank and shipped it to the furniture company.

Out of the three hundred or more sugar maples that we cut in that lot, eighty-nine proved to be bird's-eye, from which we realized well over $7,000. We also got $600 for the firewood; and two years later we sold the old farm for $1,500, making in all a handsome profit. It seemed no more than right that $3,000 of it should go to Addison.

At the time, the rest of us more than half-expected that Addison would retain his anticipated profits and use them wholly for his own education, since they would be due entirely to his own sagacity.

But no, he said at once that we were all to share it with him; and after thinking the matter over, the Old Squire saw his way clear to advance two thousand from his future share of the profits.

We therefore entered on our course at the academy the following fall, with what was deemed a safe fund for future expenses.

22

Criminal Types

OF ALL THE MANY MEMORIES OF MY BOYHOOD AT THE
Old Squire's farm in Maine, few are more vivid than those associated
with the bees in the farmhouse garden—perhaps because such recol-
lections were now and then impressed on me by the sharp stings of
the bees themselves.

The bee house was a long, open shed that stood on the south side
of the garden wall, shaded a little by two very large blue pearmain
trees. There were thirteen colonies, two of which were unusually large.
About half of these were black "native" bees, the others "Italians."
Grandfather was gradually changing all his native bees for Italians, and
he was to experiment with several other kinds. One colony, a sort of
bees called "Egyptian," would prove unpleasantly irritable.

Our old native bees were of a quiet sort, and on the whole gave us
little trouble. True, they were given to absconding to the woods, but
we could always hive them easily if we discovered them in time. As a
rule they wintered pretty well, and were not so free with the use of
their stings as some of the foreign stocks were.

After we began to seed our hayfields with red, or Southern clover,
we found that the native bees could not gather honey from the clover
heads; their "honey suckers" were not long enough to reach to the
depth of the blossoms. A great deal of red clover was sown in the
neighborhood, and as Italian bees were reported to have longer
tongues, one farmer after another began to replace his native colonies
with pure Italians, or to Italianize his native colonies by taking out the

native black queen and replacing her with an Italian queen. By so doing he had a purely Italian stock in the hive within ten weeks, for all the eggs that the new queen laid would hatch Italians, and as the worker bees were short-lived and the male drones soon killed, the original swarm soon died out.

But as a matter of fact, however, there is no difference in tongues. Neither blacks nor Italians can reach the nectar of red clover, but there are times when, either because the tubes are shorter or because they are very full of nectar, either kind of bee can work on the flowers. And Italians did store more honey than the blacks—they were hardier, better workers, and gathered honey from many flowers that native bees neglected.

During my first year at the old farm, we took one hundred pounds of box honey per hive. We had two hundred and seventy boxes on hand on the first day of September, each of four and one-half pounds' gross weight, the box itself weighing about a pound. Necessities tempted us to make sale of our product as soon as possible, and we made an agreement with the purchaser of the previous year's "crop," Mrs. Strong, an old family friend and a robust, forceful, keen-eyed Boston merchant.

The transportation of twelve hundred pounds of honey and boxes from our place to Norway station, over a road that was hilly and far from good, was a troublesome undertaking. The Old Squire hired from Norway the staunch old passenger barge, "Yankee Doodle," to haul our precious sweets to a freight car. However, the old gentleman was one of the county commissioners that year, and just prior to our shipping, he received notice to lay out a new road in the town of Sumner, eighteen miles distant. He set off on a two-day trip with Addison and Halstead, leaving Jim Doane—the less trustworthy of our hired-man brothers—to do our driving. Thereby hangs a tale, as the storybooks say, of what seemed to us for a time, a crushing disaster.

At eight o'clock of a brisk, cool morning, Doane and the barge, with a span of strong horses, arrived to find Theodora, Ellen, Wealthy, and myself waiting, with our straw ticks—to break the force of the jolts on country roads—and honey.

The straw beds were laid on the floor of the barge between the two long, cushioned sideseats; then the two hundred and seventy honey boxes were placed on the ticks very carefully in tiers.

At nine o'clock we were ready to set off, Theodora and I having been told to help with the packing of our honey on the car at Norway. Room was left at the rear end of the barge for us, and when the little door was closed we had the interior quite to ourselves, as Doane had a high seat outside in front.

Now that we were fairly off, I felt unusually cheery, but Theodora seemed uneasy. "I'm afraid, Nicholas," she confided to me, "that Jim has been drinking again. Don't you notice how flushed his face is?"

"He works so much in the open air," I said.

"But it isn't that kind of a red," Theodora insisted, "and his eyes look suffused."

"He spoke correctly," I replied. "I rather think he is all right. And you know he is a good driver."

We had bidden him drive gently, and all went safely for the first mile, when we overtook a girl named Jenny Moody, from Lurvey's Mills, who was going into Norway Village on foot, to work as table girl in the hotel there.

Doane was acquainted with her, and pulling up, he invited her to ride. So she took a seat beside him in front, and it was well for us that she did.

About a half-mile farther on at the Corners was the Wayside General Store where Tibbetts, the proprietor, kept a "rum hole"—that is, sold intoxicants contrary to Maine law. Grandfather and Addison had sought repeatedly to have the place closed up and thereby incurred Tibbetts's rancorous enmity. He was standing in his door as we approached—a frowzy, heavy-set, unwholesome-looking person. Doane drew rein to allow his horses to drink at the water tub. I do not think that the taverner saw Theodora or myself inside the barge.

"Hullo, Jim!" he called out huskily to the driver. "On yer way back, I see. Call in a minute shall ye, while yer hosses breathe?"

This last remark seemed charged with covert significance. Doane appeared to hesitate a little but finally said to the girl on the box with him, "Jest speak to 'em if they go to start, Jen."

"Jim, I wouldn't go in," we heard her say to him in a low tone.

But he went in with the landlord and was gone five minutes, perhaps, when he reappeared and climbed hastily to his seat. We then proceeded on our way.

"Been in there to get another drink, I suppose! I despise the looks of that rogue Tibbetts!" Theodora added vehemently. "He looks nasty all through!"

I laughed, but there was cause for anxiety. Half a mile above Norway station there is a long hill, which is steep near the bottom. We had scarcely begun to descend this hill when we perceived that we were moving much too rapidly for safety. At the same moment we heard the girl exclaim to Doane, "Put on the brake, Jim! Why don't you put on the brake?"

If the half-drunken man heeded her warning, it was now already too late. The heavy vehicle had acquired such momentum that the horses must run. Theodora and I threw open the rear end door, jumped, and next moment were rolling over in the dust and pebbles of the road. We quickly regained our feet just as the "Yankee Doodle" crashed and came to grief.

Thirty or forty yards below us, Jenny Moody, who had also jumped off, was rising from the ditch looking much excited, and with an ankle sprained somewhat. But our main anxiety was at first for our honey—barge, horses, and driver had rolled down a steep bank together. The body of the vehicle was broken to pieces, and Doane lay under the forward wheels with a leg broken, much bruised otherwise, and literally smeared with honey! Both horses were also badly injured.

Of course our first duty was to the suffering man, and we went at once to summon assistance in the village and also to notify the owner of the barge and horses.

That done we turned our attention drearily to our damaged sweets. Less than a hundred boxes were rescued unshattered from the wreck, and these were covered with so sticky a coat of honey and dust, externally, as to be badly injured for market purposes.

Ah me, that was a black Wednesday! For two days we labored there and in the village, saving as much as possible of the broken honey. It was the most vexatious, disheartening work that I ever attempted, and after all we saved but sixty dollars' worth.

Naturally the Old Squire wrote to Mrs. Strong about all this, and it was an agreeable surprise to have her come to see us in the afternoon of the third day afterward, accompanied by a lawyer from Norway, whom she introduced as Mr. Shearman. Our mercantile godmother announced her purpose even before she had alighted from the buggy.

"I came to Norway early this forenoon," said she. "I have seen that driver, and Jenny Moody, and everybody connected with that smash-up. Squire, you have got just the prettiest case in law that ever was against that beery old villain who keeps the tavern down here. Mr. Shearman tells me that a liquor seller in this state can be made to smart for selling rum to a man like Jim Doane, known to be an inebriate—and coax him in to drink, too, mind you!

"We will put the screws on him!" continued Mrs. Strong exultantly. "He shall settle for every cent of damage! Lucky for us, we have all the evidence we need. That Jenny Moody is just the witness we want. She is all ready and willing to testify. Doane himself, who is now on his back in bed, admits that he drank liquor there, both going up and returning. I have inquired about the rum seller, too. He has property. We'll make him pay for that honey. You'll see!"

This was, indeed, good news for us, but the Old Squire felt a great reluctance to embark in a lawsuit, even after Mr. Shearman had assured us that we had a just case. I think that Gramp should have let the matter drop, but for our good friend, Mrs. Strong, who declared that it would be positively immoral not to stand for his rights.

As finally conducted, the suit made it necessary for us to be present at the county courtroom only once—for about an hour to give testimony. Still, it was a very disagreeable business, and I have related these details of the suit because it was the first one of the kind ever brought in that state.

A verdict was rendered in our favor against Tibbetts for three hundred dollars' damage, and he appealed to the higher court; but his lawyer, learning that a similar case in another state had recently been won by the plaintiff, after an appeal, advised his client to settle with us, as he did in March following the honey smash. One hundred dollars of the money went to our lawyer, and we wished to divide what remained with Mrs. Strong, whose reply can easily be gauged.

"Not a cent!" she exclaimed. "I have had my full pay already! The satisfaction of bringing that old rascal to book is all the fee I want."

One disagreeable result of the lawsuit, however, was that the bitter enmity of Tibbetts and his associates, as demonstrated by their seizure of our school district, would get much worse.

But even before the crash, we had been having apistic problems with Mr. Tibbetts. He kept his bees in large, old-fashioned box hives that were fully twice the size of our modern hives; their swarms were therefore very strong in numbers and correspondingly aggressive. All spring and summer the Old Squire had been at his wits' end to guard our home bees from the forays of those freebooters from across the ridge. When we discovered that a hive was attacked, the Old Squire would immediately narrow the entrance to the smallest dimensions that the bees could use, in order to give the sentinel bees a better chance to defend it. Sometimes, if the robbery was in full blast, he would close the entrance altogether with wire gauze, and when the robbers gathered outside would play on them with a bee smoker. Sometimes he would put a tent of fine netting over the assailed hive for two or three days, until the robbers gave up coming.

In August the Old Squire formally notified Tibbetts that his bees were giving us trouble and asked him whether he would not keep bees of less warlike propensities, or at least reduce the size of his hives.

Tibbetts laughed at us. It was our business to protect our own bees, he said.

That evening Addison saw an advertisement for Egyptian bees in the *Maine Farmer*. Among other advantages that the advertisement set forth was that Egyptians were never robbed by other bees. It also declared that they were very prolific and great honey gatherers.

We were surely in need of a kind of bee that would not be robbed, and so the Old Squire sent for a nucleus swarm to be sent by express, and ordered two queens to be sent by mail. They arrived promptly, and by September that season the nucleus swarm had increased to full hive strength, and two Italian colonies in which the Egyptian queens had been introduced were largely replaced by the newcomers. They wintered well.

The so-called Egyptian bees were a little larger, we thought, than Italians and much darker in color. Whether they came originally from Egypt, I do not know. They may even have been hybrids from Old

World stocks, perhaps Crimean bees, or bees from Cyprus, or Damascus, or the Sudan.

We soon guessed why they were not likely to be robbed by other bees. They were the most ferocious insects and the most vindictive touch-and-go stingers that we had ever seen. It really was not safe for the girls, or indeed for anyone, to enter the garden and pass in front of their hives without veils and gloves. There was no saying when one or more of the bees might take offense and dash at our faces.

That second season our own hives were not attacked and we had no complaint of robbing. But in early June, our neighbor, Mr. Edwards, informed us that bees coming from the direction of our farm had robbed one of his hives. Then came tidings of what can only be described as an apistic catastrophe at Tibbetts's place.

The day before, as we learned, Tibbetts had discovered that one of his large hives was being robbed. He closed the entrance, and when the robbers—undoubtedly our Egyptians—had gathered in an eager throng round it, played on them with a contrivance of his own invention—nothing less than the detached barrel of a large old musket filled with ammonia water and used as a squirt gun. The fumes of the pungent liquid suffocated numbers of the intruders and appeared to work well. At intervals, as the robber bees collected throughout the following forenoon, he continued to use the contrivance with great glee. Later, however, he found that the fumes had affected not only the invaders but many of his own bees as well.

At last, while the robbers were still attacking, Tibbetts's supply of ammonia water gave out. Suddenly all of the bees appeared to go mad. They rose in clouds, fighting madly among themselves, and fell to stinging every living creature they saw. Pouring in at a window of Tibbetts's stable, they stung a young horse so ferociously that the animal broke its halter and dashed away.

Simeon Glinds, the surrogate school agent Tibbetts had appointed last spring, had driven over for a supply of liquor and left his horse and wagon standing near the stable door. The enraged bees descended on the animal, which broke away and dashed down the road. Glinds, followed by Mr. Tibbetts, dashed out of the house to learn what the cause of the commotion was.

The bees quickly sent them scurrying for the house, but Glinds, an old tippler, who had evidently been sampling his purchase, stumbled and fell; before he could get indoors the bees had stung him so savagely that he was confined to his bed for days afterward.

Hurriedly putting on a veil, an old coat, and some gloves, Tibbetts sallied forth with a pan that contained coals and burning tobacco. He hoped to quiet the bees with the smoke, but by that time every swarm at his hives was in the air, circling and eddying overhead. Such mad gusts of bees swooped down on him that they soon drove him into the house again.

The infuriated little creatures stung everything round the place. They attacked a veal calf and badly stung it, and stung two cosset sheep about the head and nose—one of them so severely that Tibbetts had to kill it. Poultry did not escape. A large turkey gobbler was found later in the day, dead under the stable. Several hens perished. The bees set on Tibbetts's hound and chased him until the poor beast finally escaped them by taking refuge in a house a mile away.

It is not to be wondered at, perhaps, that Tibbetts, smarting from so many losses and stings, ardently desired redress from some quarter. He appeared at the Old Squire's two days later and in a towering passion demanded payment for the damage that our Egyptian bees had done. He even threatened us with extreme legal penalties for keeping them. After some argument the Old Squire offered to leave the matter to three disinterested neighbors to say what was right and ought to be done. The three referees were chosen, but Tibbetts, becoming dissatisfied, repudiated the agreement and began suit at law against us.

The case came to trial in the following May. By its novelty it excited considerable interest and amusement in that region. Testimony brought out several facts that were exceedingly damaging to Tibbetts: namely, that he had been using ammonia fumes on the bees for several hours preceding the disaster, that his own bees had done most of the stinging; and also that when we had asked him to do something about his bees, which were robbing our hives, he had laughed at us and told us to take care of our bees ourselves.

The jury—many of whom were ill disposed toward Tibbetts anyway, for his part in the schoolhouse diphtheria epidemic of the previous summer—found a verdict of one-cent damages and ordered the plaintiff pay all court costs.

With the Edwardses, whose bees our Egyptians had robbed, the Old Squire amicably adjusted the matter by presenting them with a hive in place of the one that had been despoiled. As to the Egyptian bees themselves, the Old Squire had already decided that they were too bad-tempered, and replaced them with Italians once more.

Now, however, we began to lose box honey by night. A few days after the trial, some rogue, or rogues, came into the garden and began drawing boxes out of the hives. First two boxes were purloined; then three boxes were taken, and on the night before the Fourth of July eight boxes were stolen. Addison believed that if Gramp would get a search warrant, a part of the honey might be found in one of Tibbetts's houses, at the Corners. But the only clue to the theft was boot tracks in the soft earth that were not sufficiently distinct to avail as evidence, and without clear proof the Old Squire would not set the law in motion for a few boxes of honey.

Two cosset lambs also disappeared from our pasture at about this time; and as Addison and I drove past the Corners, on our way to the mill with another grist of corn, the day after the lambs were missed, we saw Tibbetts's dog gnawing a bone beside the road.

"Take the reins a minute!" exclaimed Addison, pulling up. He then leaped out of the wagon with the whip, so suddenly, that the dog left the bone and ran off. Addison picked it up and examined it attentively. "It's a mutton bone, sure enough," he said. "It is one of the leg bones; the hoof is on it and there's enough of the hide to show that it was smut-legged, like ours. But of course we cannot prove much from it," he added, throwing the bone after the dog and getting into the wagon.

On our return, we called at the post office, which was at Tibbetts's grocery. The semi-weekly mail had come that afternoon, and quite a number of people were standing about. I went in to inquire for our folks' papers and letters, and as I came out, I saw the grocer emerging from the grocery portion of the store.

"How d'ye do, Mr. Tibbetts?" cried Addison. "I'm afraid your dog has been killing two of our lambs."

"Ye don't say!" said Tibbetts. "What makes ye think so?"

"Why, I thought it might be he; I saw him gnawing the bone of a smut-legged lamb like ours," replied Addison, with every appearance of extreme candor. "Cannot say certain of course, but I feel quite sure 'twas from one of ours."

Tibbetts looked at Addison a moment, then replied, "Wal, now, if ye can prove 'twas my dog killed 'em, I'll settle with the Squire."

"I'm afraid we cannot prove it," replied Addison and drove off. "I thought that I would blame it all on the dog," he said, laughing.

Two or three days after that, Theodora, Ellen, and Kate Edwards went out to the Corners to purchase something at the store and, instead of returning by the road, came home across lots, following the brook up through the meadows. They often took that route to and from the Corners; both enjoyed going through the half-cleared land along the brook.

Beside an old log in the meadow, where evidently someone had recently sat, they picked up and brought home with them the bottom and about half the side of one of our lost honey boxes; bits of fresh comb were still sticking to it. The rogues who took it had manifestly sat on that log while they regaled themselves.

After dark that evening, Halstead—who had turned on Tibbetts after Wealthy's death—and I carried the fragment there and stuck it up on his platform. Halstead also wrote on it with a blunt lead pencil, "To whom it may concern. This honey box was picked up on a direct line between the hives from which it was stolen and this place."

We thought that we had done a rather smart thing, but when the Old Squire heard of it, he told us that we had done a foolish one.

"Better let all that sort of thing alone, boys," he said. "Never hint, or insinuate charges against anybody. Never make charges at all, unless you have good proof to back you up. Tibbetts and his cronies are too old of birds to care for any such small shot as that. They will only laugh at you. The less you have to say to them the better."

We racked our brains for some less expensive means of trapping the offenders, and it was Addison who came up with the answer—photography!

Photography had rapidly developed from daguerreotypes, tintypes, and ambrotypes to pasteboard photographs, and Addison thought that by buying a camera we might produce some criminal "types," by burning magnesium powder as a flashlight in the night. But how to accomplish this was the problem!

All of our hives were on stands grouped irregularly within fifty or sixty feet of the corner of our east barn. Now to obtain a tolerably distinct photograph by artificial light, it is necessary that the object be within thirty or forty feet of the light. Still we resolved to take our chances, especially as the illuminating powder, a pint of alcohol, and a coil of small rubber tubing were the only additional materials that we were obliged to purchase.

Being in some fear, personally, lest the thieves might do us bodily injury, the Old Squire stipulated that we must operate from the shelter of the barn, and we chose the second-story doors to the hayloft as our base of operations.

Twenty feet from these doors a box with an open top was set on a small post five feet in height. In the box we contrived two little spirit lamps that would burn continuously, with a well-nigh invisible flame hidden entirely from view by the side of the box. Close by each lamp was placed a little pasteboard cup to contain the "flash" powder. From the bottom of each cup, rubber tubing extended to the loft. Two lamps, two powder cups, and two tubes were employed, so as to take two pictures if possible.

We set the camera—which took a picture five inches by four, at a focus of forty feet—on a stool in front of the open doors. Our plan was that if we heard anyone about the hives, Theodora should puff the flash powder into the flame of the lamp, while Addison managed the camera.

Every night for a week or more we set our apparatus at ten in the evening and watched until two o'clock in the morning, but this proved so fatiguing that we decided to watch in shifts. It was Grandmother Ruth who at length heard a slight noise outside one night. She woke Addison, Theodora, and myself, and we made equal haste to reach the window, where we found Halstead, whose turn it was to watch that night, asleep on the hay.

"Lie still!" I whispered in his ear, as he stirred. "Don't speak or move."

The night was cloudy but still, and we heard stealthy movements and a low, scraping noise near one of the hive stands.

"Ready, Doad!" Addison whispered, and pressed the button of his camera so as to hold the film exposed. "Now!" he exclaimed aloud.

Instantly a darting blue flash lighted up everything in the yard! We each caught a distinct glimpse of two persons bending over a hive, who turned their faces toward us when they heard Ad yell out. They both ran next instant and began to scale the stone wall.

"Now!" Addison exclaimed again, for he had turned a second film in the camera. Theodora blew the other tube and another flash lighted the yard brilliantly, and again we saw two men, now on the wall. Just as before, they turned their faces toward us when they heard Ad speak!

Too much excited to sleep again that night, we developed the films in our makeshift darkroom and saw, revealed by the red light, two fairly good pictures of the two men of whom we had caught glimpses: Tibbetts and Glinds. The first picture also disclosed a gun standing against the wall on the inside.

We printed two photographs and then took them to Mr. Shearman.

The lawyer had no sooner looked at them than he burst out laughing uproariously. "You are pretty cute, no mistake!" he exclaimed. "Those two rogues are clearly recognizable, and I promise you that they shall pay handsomely for all the trouble they have caused you.

"Now I will tell you what we shall do," Lawyer Shearman continued. "This is too good a joke to let die quietly. I will get warrants for the arrest of both of these men, and have the deputy sheriff watch them privately. Meantime, you print six more photographs from each of these negatives and send them down to me as soon as you can. Print plainly under each photograph the words, HONEY THIEVES AT THE OLD SQUIRE'S APIARY. I will post them in conspicuous places throughout the Corners. Everybody there will recognize these two faces at once. Oh, there will be fun, I promise you!" and the lawyer indulged in another outburst of merriment.

"If they try to run away, I will be all ready to nab them," he went on presently. "But I think that they will come to me to settle, and I promise to fix it so they are not likely to bother you again, if you choose to settle that way."

We sent the photographs to Mr. Shearman next day, and from all that is said, I suppose there was never a more lively afternoon at the Corners than that which followed his posting of them.

Beneath each photograph the lawyer had appended these words: "The above will do well to see G. B. Shearman in his office at Norway without loss of time." So the rogues called on him and humbly asked how much there was to pay, that very evening!

"Seventy-five dollars, and a dollar a pound for all the honey the Old Squire might lose hereafter," replied the lawyer briefly. "You need to thank your stars, too, that he is not the vindictive sort. Otherwise, you would probably see the inside of the state penitentiary."

The Old Squire had hoped that this experience might convince Tibbetts to close up his "grocery" and move away. However, Halse was of the contrary opinion that Tibbetts or one of his crew would try to set our barns afire once things had quieted down again.

But life never goes on quite as we plan it, or think it will. Tibbetts continued his shady commerce at the Corners, but, after entering Norway Academy that fall, we youngsters seldom ran across him. And Tibbetts, apparently content to let sleeping dogs lie, never bothered us again.

23

A Wakeful Night

MY COUSIN HALSTEAD WAS THE ONLY ONE OF US AT the Old Squire's in Maine who "walked in his sleep." If he was ill or if anything had excited him during the previous day or evening, he was very likely to start up from bed soon after he had fallen asleep and run out of his room, jabbering unintelligibly to himself; and unless some of us stopped him there was no saying where or how far he might go. When he waked, he would not know where he was or what had happened, and generally he began to shout in great alarm.

For a year or more Grandmother used to come upstairs after he had gone to bed and lock his door on the outside. But that made it necessary to let him out in the morning. Moreover, it mortified him to be thus jailed overnight, and unless his window were also made fast there was some risk that he might try to get out there and fall.

For a year after we first went to the old farm, I had the job of guarding Halstead by night—and did not like it. We shared a room together, and it was my business to wake in haste if he started to walk in his sleep, go in pursuit of him, and lead him back to bed. It was a task that involved much broken rest and occasional fracases in the dark, for when first overtaken Halstead sometimes put up a vigorous fight.

At last I rebelled, and after a patient hearing of my side of the case, the Old Squire ordained that thereafter I was to have a bed to myself.

It was then that Grandmother resorted to locking Halstead up at night; but after a year of such nocturnal imprisonment he also rebelled;

and I think that he hid the key to the lock, for it could no longer be found.

Thereafter it was the business of anyone who heard Halstead stirring about at night either to rush in pursuit or to raise an alarm. When the two girls heard him first they came to Addison's door or mine, knocked and cried, "Halse is out again!" We then attempted to recover the wanderer without disturbing the old folks in the rooms below, if possible. Often, however, there was a considerable commotion before we got him safely back in his room.

Once he greatly startled the whole house by falling down the front hall stairs and smashing the hat tree and umbrella crock below. When Addison, the Old Squire, and I reached him with a light, he had regained his feet and was rubbing his eyes sleepily. Strange to say, considering the destruction he had wrought, he was wholly uninjured. Not so much as a scratch or a bruise was on him anywhere!

On many nights when he "walked" he seemed possessed by a desire to climb out at a window that opened near the roof of the ell at the end of the hall upstairs. The roofs of the farm buildings adjoined in such a way that you could go from the roof of the ell to that of the wagon house and from that to the roof of the barn beyond; or if you were not afraid to go still higher up, you could climb from the roof of the ell to the steep roof of the house and ascend to the ridge pole, where the large, old-fashioned chimney emerged. We boys often made excursions about the roofs. But to prevent Halstead from going on them in his sleep, this end window was usually kept fastened at night, though sometimes that precaution was forgotten.

He was very subject to bad colds and at such times nearly always had an unquiet night, starting up from sleep as if in terror, often crying out wildly in a distressed and hollow voice that sounded like the last notes of a dying pig. The Old Squire had a particular name for those seizures. "The poor boy has got the horrors!" he used to say, and he often went upstairs to wake him, calm him down, and sit by him for an hour or two.

When Halstead was well and "walked" on account of exciting dreams, he generally rose suddenly, muttering low words, and stole forth as if in a tremendous hurry.

Once on a dark, rainy night he ran off along the road and reached the schoolhouse, half a mile away, before Addison and I overtook him. We had started out in our socks, expecting to catch him downstairs, but he ran rapidly down the lane. We did not like to go back for our boots and so sped after him. He appeared to keep the road without effort, but we were in the ditch repeatedly, it was so dark. That was in October; the night was chilly and the road full of puddles. We had cold toes before we got back with him, also very muddy socks. But the Old Squire was up and had kindled a fire. I remember that he made hot ginger tea for all three of us.

But by far the queerest scrape we ever had with Halstead was on one moonlight night in September—the week of the harvest moon. That time he got away before any of us was aware of his escape. Suddenly we heard his doleful outcries.

The evening had been warm and the moonlight silvery, and several of our young neighbors, planning a good time, had called on us—Tom Edwards and his sister Katherine, Edgar Wilbur and Elsie and Georgie, and the Murch boys, Willis and Ben. We played hide-and-seek about the farm buildings and garden for an hour or so, and then the more exciting game of Indians. Edgar and I with all the girls were the settlers and built a cabin of poles and dry cornstalks up at the Old Squire's "Eden," near the end of the woodland.

Willis, Ben, Tom, Halstead, and Addison were the Indians, who rushed forth from the woods and attacked us. Edgar and I were shot down and had to fall "dead" and lie there while the screaming girls were "tomahawked." Then they scalped us, to the accompaniment of frightful whoops, and set our cabin on fire. We had to lie still while it burned and the Indians retired, still whooping, into the depths of the forest. It was such a fine night that we played till eleven o'clock.

Two or three hours later, after our friends had gone home and we were sound asleep in the old farmhouse, a succession of melancholy, despairing yells roused everybody. We knew instantly what had happened. Addison and I dashed forth from our rooms and ran into each other in the narrow hall outside. Theodora and Ellen were also peeping forth, exclaiming, "Where is he?" for well they knew that voice of woe.

But the outcries seemed strangely muffled, as if a long way off. Addison and I threw on our coats and boots and ran downstairs. We thought at first that Halstead must be at the barn or out at the apple house in the back garden. The moon still shone brightly, and we dashed about, stopping to listen here and there, for the cries continued at intervals.

We soon made sure that he was not at the barn or at the apple house. Meanwhile the Old Squire and Asa Doane, one of the hired men, had come out. Grandmother and the girls, considerably wrought up, also made their appearance on the piazza. But listen as we might none of us could locate those outcries.

"Sounds as if he was shut up somewhere," Ellen said, and so it seemed to all of us. I ran to the cellar door, to see whether he were down there. Grandmother, nearly in tears, had looked there already.

"The window that opens to the ell roof is up!" Theodora exclaimed. "I noticed it when I first stepped out."

"Then perhaps he's on the roof," Addison said, as he went up and got out on the roof of the ell. "No," he called down to us. "He isn't here. But I can hear him plainer now. From here he seems to be down in the house somewhere."

"But I have looked in every room!" Grandmother exclaimed. "Except the garret," she added.

Thereupon I sped into the house and up the steep attic stairs close beside the chimney, and as I clattered upward one of those dismal, muffled yells resounded close beside me. It came through the brick work.

"Halse! Halse!" I shouted. "Are you in the chimney?"

"I don't know," he wailed. "I don't know where I am!"

I dashed back downstairs and met the Old Squire in the front hall. "Gramp, he's in the chimney!" I cried.

"My sakes! How did he get there?" the old gentleman exclaimed in wonder. "He couldn't have gone up the flue of the sitting room fireplace. It isn't wide enough." But just then we heard Addison shouting on the roof of the house outside; he had climbed on it from the ell. "Halse has fallen down the chimney!" he exclaimed, when we ran to the yard.

"Fallen down the chimney!" the Old Squire repeated incredulously. "How in the world came he to do that?"

No one could even guess how, but the fact remained that he was in there, down about fourteen feet from the top and astride a partition of brick where two flues joined. It was a large old chimney, built in the middle of the farmhouse, and a number of flues from different rooms below united higher up in one large shaft that emerged about four feet above the roof. It was nearly or quite a yard square—plenty of room to fall in, if anybody were in the way of meeting with such an accident.

As nearly as we could ascertain later, Halstead had dreamed that Indians were chasing him; escaping through the window to the ell, he had climbed to the roof of the house. It is a wonder that he did not fall, but he seems to have been in such terror that he tried to take refuge in the sooty old chimney by letting himself down into it. No other explanation could be hit on, and as for Halstead himself, he could not remember why or how he was on the roof.

But the main thing now was to get him out. He had slid down for thirteen or fourteen feet and was astride the parting between the flues. Asa went up on the roof and then the Old Squire himself ascended to the ridge pole to take stock of the situation. They told me to bring a ladder from the barn, with the idea of thrusting it down the chimney for Halstead to climb out by—for he was now awake and, except for being a good deal shaken and terrified, was as rational as ever. But when we had passed the ladder up to the roof, the Old Squire found that there was not quite enough space in the chimney for a person to climb out in that way, and the plan had to be given up.

There was then some talk of attempting to get Halstead out from below into the sitting room, but as the Old Squire had conjectured, the "throat" of the fireplace flue was too narrow.

All the while Grandmother and the girls were standing out in the yard below, looking up, in a state of dreadful concern. They feared that Halstead must have been badly hurt.

"You had better begin and take the chimney down till you come to him and work as fast as you can!" Grandmother cried.

But the Old Squire did not take so dark a view of the predicament. He told me to go down to the wagon house and bring the large rope from the tackle and blocks that hung there, and when I had brought it up he made a broad loop in the end of the rope and let it down the chimney.

"Now, Halstead," he said, speaking very quietly, "calm yourself. You need not be afraid. We will get you out safe. Take hold of this rope and stand upright on the partition between the flues."

Thus encouraged, Halstead got on his feet.

"Now," the Old Squire said, "put both your feet into the loop of the rope. Stand in it and hold on to the rope, higher up, with both hands."

After considerable delay Halstead did so.

"Now hold fast," the Old Squire admonished him. "We are going to draw you up. Hold fast now." Standing about the top of the chimney, Asa, Addison, and he then hoisted Halstead up by main strength till they had him where they could lay hold of his arms and lift him out on the roof.

Even then he was so inert from fear that Asa and I had to help him down to the roof of the ell and boost him in at the window. Halstead in fact when awake was always timid as a climber, but he climbed fearlessly enough in his sleep!

Although he had slid down the chimney for as much as fourteen feet, he had suffered little actual injury. But such a black and smutty boy as he was when at last we conducted him downstairs into the lamplight! Grandmother viewed him with utter dismay. Ellen burst out laughing. His hands, his feet, his face, and even his ears were coal black, and his nightgown beggared description.

It now became my duty to kindle a fire while Addison and the girls set a large brass kettle of water to heat for a bath; Grandmother meanwhile was laying out a change of night clothes. All in all it was nearly four in the morning before we got our somnambulist to bed again. The intention was to let him sleep during the following forenoon, but he made his appearance as usual at the breakfast table; he was looking a little sheepish.

The Old Squire looked him over with a whimsical smile. "Young man," he said, "if I were in your place I wouldn't play Indians anymore. You have too much imagination—in your sleep."

24

That Little Span of Morgans

There was once a little animal,
No bigger than a fox,
And on five toes he scampered
Over Tertiary rocks.

SO SINGS THE MOST REALISTIC OF AMERICAN POETS,
concerning the first American horse, or rather the far-off ancestor of
the horse, going back to those early days of the continent when its
great Rocky Mountain backbone was pushing upward from out the
Tertiary seas.

The zoologists tell us that this little "dawn-horse," or eohippus,
roamed the primeval uplands somewhere out in Wyoming; and at Yale
University they exhibit its small skeleton with the toes not yet changed
to hoofs, a development due, it is believed, to much hard scampering
over its rocky pastures later on.

It is not wholly clear how the dawn-horse reached the Eastern continent from the Western—for the horse that we now drive probably
came to Europe from America. Perhaps there were broad isthmuses in
those early epochs, highways of animal migration, which the ever restless ocean has since submerged.

Strictly speaking, too, the poet was in error about those five toes.
There seem to have been four only. But that is a comparatively small
matter, except to the zoologists.

Moreover, it was a very long time ago, so long that most of us are now much more interested in the various breeds, strains, and varieties of horses, as we buy and sell them, than in this little Hyrocathere of the long past—and of all these many breeds and varieties there was never, as many believe, a better one than the "Morgan horse."

The United States government, which is never overhasty or enthusiastic about anything, has of late arrived at the same conclusion, and is now establishing farms to breed Morgans for use as cavalry and battery horses.

The origin of the Morgan breed is almost as obscure as that of the little eohippus himself, but is believed to be traceable to imported Arabian blood, descending, roundabout, through a small horse called Justin Morgan, after one of his many owners, which appeared in Vermont over a century ago. We say "appeared in Vermont," for there are several conflicting accounts as to how this horse first came there. He was a dark bay, weighing considerably less than a thousand pounds, but he possessed remarkable qualities. Many traditions, now exaggerated a little, perhaps, are preserved as to the strength and spirit of this obscure progenitor of the Morgans.

Down at our old farm in Maine we learned the value of Morgan horses almost by accident, from a small horse called Hannibal, or "Han," which the Old Squire got by way of trade at Portland. In color he was a dark chestnut, with a little half-moon star in his face and one white foot.

No particular value was attached to him at first, and in December that year he was sent up to one of the logging camps to work alongside a Percheron that had lost its mate by colic. Several times that winter the foreman at the camp said to us that Han was the best worker in the teams. "Whether you know it or not, Squire, you've got a mighty good little horse there," the foreman kept saying. "He's better than any of them big Islanders, and it doesn't cost half so much to keep him."

At that time we used numbers of Prince Edward Island horses, great, clumsy, slow creatures, with inordinately shaggy legs, which had to be sheared frequently in winter to keep them from loading up with ice. The Old Squire was also experimenting with Percherons, which proved rather too tender for the Maine woods in winter.

When the horses came down from the camps that spring, some attention was given to little Han. Instead of turning him out to pasture, we put him in the stable and began driving him. He was a fast walker, a keen trotter, and, moreover, so kind and intelligent that the whole family liked him. He was spirited enough, yet the girls could drive him with perfect safety. He hated dogs, but that was hardly a failing.

In fact, little Han was an object lesson in horse flesh, and as the season advanced, the Old Squire grew interested in Morgans. Among others to whom he wrote for further information concerning them was a breeder of these horses, who lived at Middlebury, Vermont, and as a result of their correspondence, in October the old gentleman drove across country to Middlebury to see some of the Morgan stock. He took Addison and Halstead with him and drove little Han beside the Percheron.

They were gone six days and came back enthusiastic in praise of the new stock. They had sold the Percheron at Concord, New Hampshire, and brought back from Middlebury three Morgan colts and a mate for Han, bearing the lively name of Hickory; and that was the origin of our little span of "Han and Hick."

This new Morgan looked almost just like Han; they walked alike and were within twenty pounds of the same weight. Each had a little half-moon star, and Hickory also had one white forefoot.

But together the span tipped the scales at only nineteen hundred and twenty pounds, which the lumber men, as well as the farmers thereabouts, thought was too light for loads.

"Smart little horses, no doubt," they said, "but they haven't got the beef and bone for heavy loads."

During the winter, however, we found that Han and Hick could draw as much as any of the big horses and do it quicker, with less expense for corn and hay. The Old Squire decided to breed Morgans and to advocate their use in Maine, and by way of helping on the good work, Addison and I determined to take Han and Hick to the fair in September and show the whole county what Morgan horses could do.

It was customary then, as now, to have drawing matches at fairs, arranged or graded for different classes of horses according to weight. Many persons whose instincts are strongly on the side of kindness to animals now condemn such tests. Others believe that—like football games between schoolboys—such matches promote strength and pluck. At that time we did not trouble ourselves much with such questions but began training our two little Morgans to pull with "the twenty-four-hundred class," that is to say with horses weighing not less than twelve hundred each.

We loaded up a large stone-drag, which some call a stone-boat, with what we estimated at a ton and a half of rock, to begin with; and every day, just after dinner, we hitched up Han and Hick for a bout of a few minutes at that drag, along the cart road from the barns out to the fields. We chose a place where there was sand and bare gravel, since a loaded drag goes much harder over such spots than on grassy sward.

The horses were not being worked otherwise at that time, and they seemed really to enjoy those brief bouts at pulling. That was all we had them do for a fortnight before the fair; but every day we added about a hundred pounds of stone to the drag-load, and always when we took them out to hitch on to it, we led them up to the drag-load to smell of it.

Addison would then say, "Han, you can pull that easy," and I would say, "Hick, you're good for that," the same words every time; and those horses would cock their eyes knowingly and come as near laughing as horses ever do.

After they were hitched on, before giving the word to pull, Addison, who generally drove them, would pass to their heads and pat each one equally, for Morgans are sensitive little horses and jealous of attentions. In fact, all horses are so, much more, I think, than people are generally aware.

When the word to go was given, it was as good as sport to see those two horses buckle down to it. Nor would they stop till they heard "Whoa!" shouted loudly. Then they would cock their eyes to us, to see if we were pleased, and get the "nubbins" of corn and a sweet apple that they knew we had in our pockets for them.

As the load was increased, the only difficulty with them lay in their lack of weight. They had the ambition, the splendid courage, and the muscle to pull three tons of rock on the drag, but it was not easy for them to hold to the ground; they pulled themselves clear off their feet, and that bothered them.

The Old Squire used to come out every day to watch them pull, and he saw where the trouble lay sooner than we did.

"Jump on their backs, boys!" he called out to us one afternoon. "They can pull that all right. All they want is foothold. Jump on their backs. Give them more weight."

It seemed to Addison and me at first that this would merely burden the horses for nothing. But we tried it.

Both were used to being ridden, and we found at once that the Old Squire was right. Under our added weight they went off with the load at a great pace, and they seemed to like it. The extra weight was what they needed to hold them on the ground.

The Old Squire laughed heartily. "That's a jockey trick I learned when I was a young fellow, years ago," he said.

"And there's another quite wonderful thing about it, boys," the old gentleman added, more seriously. "When you ride a horse in that way, *you want to pull with him.*"

"How can anybody do that, on his back?" I exclaimed.

"But you can!" cried the Old Squire. "You can pull with your horse in your mind and sympathy.

"Jump on again, both of you, and try it," he continued. "You want to lean forward just a little and put the palms of your hands on top of your horse's fore shoulders, one on each side. Then at the word go, throw your whole mind into helping him pull. Get in sympathy with him. There's a knack of doing that. Try to catch the knack of it."

We tried this "jockey trick"—if trick it may be called—for several successive days. Readers will smile perhaps, but there is really something in it. A rider in full sympathy with his horse seems actually to communicate something of his own willpower or courage to the animal he bestrides, something that adds to the horse's energy.

We had two new sets of harnesses, and when fair time came, Addison and I were for putting these on Han and Hick, to make them look finer, but the Old Squire dissuaded us. "Keep your old harnesses on them, the ones they are used to," he said. "New harness is like new boots; it never feels just right to a horse at first."

Indeed, the old collars were about worn out and showed the stuffing through holes in the leather. It was large, old-fashioned harness, too, brass-mounted, which made these small Morgans look even smaller than they were. But out of deference to the Old Squire we kept this old everyday rig on them.

Well do I recall that windy autumn morning of the second day of the fair. The drawing match was set for ten o'clock in the forenoon. They had a new stone-drag, loaded with three tons of split granite, for the twenty-four-hundred class of draft horses; and for the twenty-six-hundred class five-hundred weight more of stone was to be added.

We had entered Han and Hick in the twenty-four-hundred class, but had their weight, nineteen hundred and twenty, on a tag tied to Han's hames. A great throng of teamsters, farmers, and others had gathered to see the pulling; they crowded round to read that tag, laughed, and said, "What are those little horses doing here?" Nobody believed they could so much as stir that three tons of stone on a gravely track. We said nothing and were in no hurry.

"Hold back a little, till we see what the rest can do," Addison said to me. The Old Squire had told us to be the last team to pull, if we could.

There were four entries of spans in the twenty-six-hundred class and five or else six in our class. Among our competitors was a certain Ed Dennett, locally noted as a teamster, with a matched span of Percherons; a farmer, named Chester Hale, with two spans of Prince Edward horses, one in each class; and Sidney Means, a horse dealer, who had entered two spans of large white horses, brought from Rhode Island.

One of the three judges of the match now mounted the drag, announced the hour, and stated the terms of the match.

Dennett was the first to hitch to the drag. His horses pulled well together, but the great weight of the load was evident from the start. His Percherons could move it no more than ten or twelve feet at one pull. He pulled at it five or six times, and each time we could see that he sought to start the drag slightly at an angle, instead of in a straight line, to gain the advantage of swinging it a little. One of the judges felt obligated to call his attention to that. Hale hitched on next, and after him the others. None of them pulled the drag for more than thirty feet at one bout, and considering the great weight, everyone seemed to think that this was good hauling.

"One entry more!" the judges then called out, looking round, and when we came forward with Han and Hick, in their old collars, there were not a few humorous comments.

"Ponies, ain't they?" one of the teamsters asked us. Beside the others they did look small, no mistake.

"What class are you in?" another teamster asked us with a grin.

"The infant class," Addison said. "Of course we know they cannot pull this," he added jocosely, "but we thought we would have a little fun hitching on with the rest."

We led Han and Hick up to the drag and let them nose it. Then we hitched on, patted them a bit (while they cocked their eyes at us), and hopped on their backs.

I believe they knew what was coming and what was expected of them just as well as we did, and when we leaned forward with our hands on their shoulders, and Addison gave the word, you should have felt those little horses gather under us! They made the gravel fly from their hoofs. The crowd had to scatter to get out of the way. A shout rose, but it was a muffled shout, for all those behind us were busy spitting out gravel.

I felt the load start; that was the main thing for us. Then away we went with it. Those brave little Morgans never flinched or stopped. On they tore, faster and faster, their hind legs as stiff as shoe-pegs, with the whole crowd chasing after, shouting and hurrahing. The faster we went, the easier the drag slid, and now we came where the ground fell off a little, and both horses went on the jump for a hundred yards.

But here one of the judges, on the run, managed to overtake us and headed us off.

"Stop! Stop!" he shouted, swinging his arms. "Pull up! We didn't ask you to haul that drag home with ye! Hold up, you two young jehus! Hold up, I tell ye!" It is the truth; we had no small ado to stop our horses. And then as they puffed, each cocked his eye knowingly.

I never saw a crowd go wilder over any event at the fair than did those farmers and teamsters over Han and Hick that morning—they had looked so small, and that remarkable exploit came so unexpectedly! Not a span in the twenty-six-hundred class could haul the drag back and that part of the match was given up.

The Old Squire stood quietly by, smiling and rubbing his hands a little. There was no need for us to say much. The people were doing all the necessary talking themselves. In that five minutes' work little Han and Hick had established the reputation of the Morgan horse throughout the home county.

25

White Monkey Week

A YEAR PREVIOUSLY THE OLD SQUIRE HAD MADE AN agreement with a New York factory to furnish dowels and strips of clear white-birch wood, for piano keys and passementerie.

At that time passementerie was coming into use for ladies' dresses. The fine white-birch dowels were first turned round on small lathes and afterward into little bugle and bottle-shaped ornaments, then dyed a glistening black and strung on linen threads.

On our own forest lots we had no birch that quite met the requirements. But another lumber man, an acquaintance of the Old Squire's, named John Lurvey (a brother of old Zachary Lurvey), who owned lots north of ours, had just what we needed to fill the order.

Lumber men are often "neighborly" with each other in such matters, and with John Lurvey the Old Squire made a kind of running contract for three hundred cords of white-birch "bolts" from a lakeside lot. Each one made a memorandum of the agreement in his pocket notebook, and as each trusted the other, nothing more exact or formal was thought necessary. The white birch was known to be valuable lumber. We were to pay two thousand dollars for it on the stump—one thousand down—and have two "winters" in which to get it off and pay the balance of the money. And here it may be said that in the Maine woods a winter is supposed to mean the snowy season from November till April.

Meanwhile other ventures were pressing. In company with a Canadian partner, the Old Squire was then getting spruce lumber down the

St. Maurice River at Three Rivers, in the province of Quebec. This New York birch contract was deferred a year, the plan being finally to get off the birch in March of the second winter, when the crews and teams from two other lumber camps could conveniently be sent to the lake, and make a quick job of it.

But in December of that second winter John Lurvey died suddenly of pneumonia. His property passed into the hands of his wife, who was by no means easygoing. She overhauled this notebook agreement, took legal advice of a sharp lawyer, and on February 21 sent us legal notification that the agreement would expire on February 28, the last day of winter, according to the calendar. The notification also demanded payment of the second thousand dollars. Her scheme, of course, was to get the money in full and cut us off, in default, from removing the birch lumber from the lot. The Old Squire himself had gone to Canada.

The notification came by letter, and as usual when the Old Squire was away, Grandmother Ruth opened his mail to see what demanded our attention. We were all in the sitting room, except Halstead, who was away that evening.

"What can this mean?" Grandmother suddenly exclaimed, and handed the letter to Addison. He saw through it instantly and jumped up in excitement.

"We're trapped!" he cried. "If we don't get that birch off next week we shall lose two thousand dollars!"

Grandmother was dismayed. "Oh, that wicked woman!" she cried. "Why, winter always means through sledding!"

"I'm afraid not, in law," said Addison, looking puzzled. "Winter ends either the first or the twenty-first of March. I think a good argument could be made in court for the twenty-first. But she may be right, and it's too late to take chances. The only thing to do is to get that lumber off right away."

Addison and I went out to the stable to talk the matter over; we did not want to excite Grandmother any further. At best, she had a good deal to worry her that winter.

"Now what can we do?" Addison exclaimed. Five or six days would be required to get the Old Squire home from Canada.

"And what could he do after he got here?" Addison asked. "The teams and the choppers are all off at the lumber camps."

"Let's take our axes and go up there and cut what birch we can next week," said I, in desperation.

"Oh, we boys couldn't do much alone in so short a time," replied Addison.

Still, we could think of nothing else; and with the loss of two thousand dollars staring us in the face, we began planning desperately how much of that birch we could save in a week's time. In fact, we scarcely slept at all that night, and early the next morning started out to rally what help we could.

Willis Murch and Thomas Edwards volunteered to work for us and take each a yoke of oxen. After much persuasion our neighbor Sylvester promised to go with a team and to take his son Rufus Junior. Going on to the post office at the Corners, we succeeded in hiring two other young men.

But even with the help of these men we could account for scarcely a seventh part of the contract, since one chopper could cut not more than a cord and a half of birch bolts in a day; and moreover, the bolts had to be removed from the lot.

But as we rushed round that forenoon, it occurred to Addison to hire a horse-power and circular saw that was owned by a man named Morefield, who lived near the woodsheds of the railway station, six miles from the Old Squire's. It was a rig used for sawing wood for the locomotives.

Hurrying home, we hitched up, drove to the station, and succeeded in engaging Morefield and his saw, with two spans of heavy horses.

But other cares had now loomed up, not the least among them being the problem of feeding our hastily collected crew of helpers and their teams sixteen miles off in the woods. Just across the lake from the lot where the birch grew there was a lumber camp where we could set up a stove and do our cooking; and during the afternoon we packed up supplies of pork, beans, and corned beef, while in the house Grandmother and the girls were baking bread. I had also to go to the mill, to get corn ground for the teams.

Theodora and Ellen were eager to go and do the cooking at the camp; but Grandmother knew that an older woman of greater experience was needed in such an emergency, and had that morning sent urgent word to Olive Witham—"Aunt Olive," as we called her—who was always our mainstay in times of trouble at the old farm.

She was about fifty-five years old, tall, austere, not wholly attractive, but of upright character and undaunted courage.

By nine that evening everything was ready for a start; and sunrise the next morning saw us on the way up to the birch lot, Aunt Olive riding in the "horse-power" on a sled, which bore also a firkin of butter, a cheese, a four-gallon can of milk, a bag of bread, and a large basket of eggs.

One team did not get off so early, neighbor Sylvester's. He was to start two hours later and draw up to camp the heaviest part of our supplies, consisting of half a barrel of pork, two bushels of potatoes, a peck of dry beans, a hundredweight of corned beef, and two gallons of molasses.

Twelve miles of our way that morning was by a trodden winter road, but the last four miles, after crossing Lurvey's Stream, had to be broken through three feet of snow in the woods, giving us four hours of tiresome tramping.

We reached the lot at one o'clock, and during the afternoon set up the horse-power on the lake shore, at the foot of the slope where the white birch grew. The white birches there were from a foot up to twenty-two inches in diameter, having long, straight trunks, clear of limbs from thirty to forty feet in length. These clear trunks only were used for bolts. We contrived a log slide, or slip, down which the long birch trunks could be slid to the saw and cut up into four-foot bolts. For our plan now was to fell the trees and "twitch" them downhill with teams to the head of this slip. By rolling the bolts, as they fell from the saw, down an incline and out on the ice of the lake, we would remove them from Mrs. Lurvey's land, and thereby comply with the letter of the law, by aid of which she was endeavoring to rob us and escheat our rights to the birch.

There were ten of us. Each knew what was at stake, and all worked with such goodwill that by three o'clock we had the saw humming.

Plying their axes, Halstead, Addison, Thomas, and Willis felled upward of forty trees that afternoon, and these were all sawn by dark. On an average, five trees were required for a cord of bolts, but with sharp axes such white-birch trees can be felled fast. Morefield tended the saw and drove the horses in the horse-power; the rest of us were kept busy sliding the birch trunks down the slip to the saw and rolling away the bolts.

By dark we had made a good beginning of our hard week's task, and in the gathering dusk plodded across the lake to the old lumber camp, expecting to find Aunt Olive smiling and supper ready.

But here disappointment awaited us. Sylvester, with the sled load of supplies, had not come, did not arrive, in fact, till half an hour later, and then with his oxen only. Disaster had befallen him on the way. While crossing Lurvey's Stream, the team had broken through the ice where the current beneath was swift. He had saved the oxen, but the sled with our beef, pork, beans, and potatoes had been drawn under and carried away, he knew not how far, under the ice.

A stare of dismay from the entire hungry party followed this announcement. It looked like no supper—after a hard day's work! Worse still, to Addison and myself it looked like the crippling of our whole program for the next five days, for a lumber crew is much like an army—it lives and works only by virtue of its commissariat.

But now Aunt Olive rose to the emergency. "Don't you be discouraged, boys!" she exclaimed. "Give me twenty minutes, and you shall have a supper fit for a king. You shall have white monkey on toast! Toast thirty or forty slices of this bread, boys," she added, laughing cheerily. "Toast it good and brown, while I dress the monkey!"

Addison, Thomas, and I began toasting bread over the hot stove, but kept a curious eye out for that "white monkey."

Of course it was figurative monkey. Aunt Olive put six quarts of milk in a kettle on the stove and, as it warmed, thickened it slightly with about a pint of cornmeal.

As it grew hotter, she melted into it a square of butter about half the size of a brick, then chipped up fine as much as a pound of cheese, and added that slowly, so as to dissolve it.

Last, she rapidly broke, beat, and added a dozen eggs, then finished off with salt and a tiny bit of cayenne pepper, well stirred in.

For five minutes longer she allowed the kettleful to simmer on the stove, while we buttered three huge stacks of toast.

The monkey was then ready. All hands gathered round with their plates, and in turn had four slices of toast, one after another, each slice with a generous ladleful of white monkey poured over it.

It was delicious, very satisfying, too, and gave one the sense of being well fed, since it contained all the ingredients of substantial food. As made by Aunt Olive, this white monkey had the consistency of moderately thick cream. It slightly resembled Welsh rabbit, but we found it was much more palatable and wholesome, having more milk and egg in it and far less cheese.

We liked it so well that we all wanted it for breakfast the next morning—and that was fortunate, since we had little else, and were exceedingly loath to lose a day's time sending teams down home, or elsewhere, for more meat, beans, and potatoes.

There were several families of French-Canadians living at clearings on Lurvey's Stream, three miles below the lake; and since I was the youngest and least efficient axman of the party, they sent me down there every afternoon to buy milk and eggs, for more white monkey. Of cheese and butter we had a sufficient supply, and the yellow corn-meal, which we had brought for the teams, furnished sheetful after sheetful of johnny-cake, which Aunt Olive split, toasted, and buttered well, as a groundwork for the white monkey.

And for five days we ate it as we toiled twelve hours to the day, chopping, hauling, and sawing birch!

We had a slight change of diet on the fourth day, when Aunt Olive cooked two old roosters and a chicken, which I had coaxed away from the reluctant French settlers down the stream.

But it was chiefly white monkey every day, and the amount of work that we did on it was a tribute to Aunt Olive's resourcefulness. The older men of the party declared that they had never slept so well as after those evening meals of white monkey on johnny-cake toast. Beyond doubt, it was much better for us than heavier meals of meat and beans after days of hard labor.

From half an hour before sunrise till an hour after sunset, during those entire five days, the tall white birches fell fast, the saw hummed, and the bolts went rolling out on the ice-clad lake.

I never saw a crew work with such goodwill or felt such enthusiasm myself as during those five days. We had the exhilarating sensation that we were beating a malicious enemy. Every little while a long, cheery whoop of exultation would be raised and go echoing across the lake, and that last day of February we worked by the light of little bonfires of birch bark till near midnight.

Then we stopped—to clear the law. And I may state here, although it must sound like a large story, that during those five working days the ten of us felled, sawed, and rolled out on the ice two hundred and eighty-six cords of white-birch bolts. Of course it was the saw and the two relieving spans of horses that did the greater part of the work, the four axmen doing little more than felling the tall birch trees.

The next day, after a final breakfast of white monkey, we went home triumphant, leaving the bolts on the ice for the time being. All were tired, but in high spirits, for victory was ours.

Two days later the Old Squire came home from Three Rivers, entirely unaware of what had occurred, having it now in mind to organize and begin what he supposed would be a month's work up at the birch lot for the choppers and teams from the two logging camps farther north.

Neither Grandmother Ruth nor the rest of us could resist having a little fun with him. After supper, when we had gathered in the sitting room, Grandmother quietly handed him Mrs. Lurvey's letter, with the notification about the birch.

"This came while you were away, Joseph," she said to him, while the rest of us, sitting very still, looked on, keenly interested to see how he would take it.

The Old Squire unfolded the letter and began reading it, then started suddenly, and for some moments sat very still, pondering the notification. "This bids fair to be a serious matter for us," he said at last.

"We have lost that birch contract, I fear, and the money that went into it. And I have only my own carelessness to thank for it," he added, looking distressed.

Theodora could not stand that another minute. She stole round behind the Old Squire's chair, put her arms about his neck, and whispered something in his ear.

"What?" he exclaimed incredulously.

"Yes!" she cried to him.

"Impossible, child!" he said.

"No, it isn't!" shouted Addison. "We've got that birch off, sir. It is all sawn up in bolts and out on the lake!"

"What, in a week?" exclaimed the Old Squire.

"All in five days, sir!" cried Addison and I.

The old gentleman sat looking at us in blank surprise. He was an experienced lumber man and knew exactly what such a statement as ours implied.

"Not three hundred cords?" he said gravely.

"Close on to that, sir!" cried Addison.

Thereupon we all began to tell him about it at once. None of us could remain quiet. But it was not till we had related the whole story and told him who had helped us, along with Addison's scheme of hiring the horse-power and saw, that he really believed it. He sprang up, walked twice across the sitting room, then stopped short and looked at us.

"Boys, I'm proud of you!" he exclaimed. "Proud of you! I couldn't have done as well myself."

"Yes, Joseph, they're chips off the old block!" Grandmother chimed in. "And we've beaten that wicked woman!"

Mrs. Lurvey, as I may add here, was far from sharing in our exultation. She was a person of violent temper. It was said that she shook with rage when she heard what we boys had done. But her lawyer advised her to keep quiet.

During the next two weeks the birch bolts were drawn to our mill four miles down Lurvey's Stream and sawn into thin strips and dowels, then shipped in bundles, by rail and schooner, from Portland to New York, and the contract netted the Old Squire about twenty-five hundred dollars above the cost of the birch.

But as I look back on it, I am inclined to think that Aunt Olive was the real heroine of that strenuous week.

The following recipe will make a sufficient quantity of "white monkey" for three persons. Put over the fire one pint of new milk in a double boiler. As soon as the milk is warm, stir in one teaspoonful of flour mixed with two tablespoon-

fuls of cold water. As the milk gets hotter, add slowly, so as to dissolve it, two ounces of cheese, grated or chipped fine. Then add one ounce of butter, a tea-spoonful of salt, a dash of cayenne pepper, and one egg, well beaten and mixed with two tablespoonfuls of cold milk or water. Let the mixture simmer five min-utes, then serve hot on wheat-bread or brown-bread toast, well browned and buttered.

26

Six Hundred Bushels of Potatoes

"THREE DOLLARS AND A HALF FOR A BUSHEL OF potatoes, and they may be five if the war goes on," a prominent dealer said recently. "This German war has outdone the Colorado potato beetle as a price raiser."

That brought vividly to my mind the time when the Colorado potato beetle, on its eastward migration, first reached the Old Squire's farm in Maine. Farmers said to one another that the days of raising potatoes were past. Paris Green, London Purple, Bug Death, and other insect poisons had not yet come into use. There seemed little use in planting a crop, if a few weeks later the pest would devour the young shoots. The price of potatoes soon rose from fifty cents a bushel—the usual price—to two dollars.

At our old farm in Maine the only way we could think of to escape this pest was to plant our potatoes at some remote clearing in the wilderness, miles from any other farm. We hoped that the pest would not cross wide tracts of woods. At one of the Old Squire's forest lots that bordered the upper course of Lurvey's Stream, there was a sunny opening where a forest fire had burned off the growth and left a plot of two or three acres of brown alluvial loam. It bore grass, and we had stacked hay there for the logging camps. We decided that that opening, seven miles away in the woods, might be safe for a crop of potatoes.

The drawback to cultivating the land was that it was so very inaccessible. There was no road to it, and on account of intervening gullies, swamps, and brooks we could not build one without heavy expense. In winter, of course, we could travel on the ice of the stream that bordered the opening.

The plan that we finally hit upon was to load a plow, a harrow, and the seed potatoes—twelve bushels—in a bateau, such as Maine lumber men often use on rivers, and to pole the craft upstream to the opening. The span of horses for plowing we led there, singly and unharnessed, through the woods.

Farmers usually allow from seven to ten bushels of seed potatoes to an acre, but by cutting off the seed ends of the potatoes before starting and leaving the butts at home, we managed to make twelve bushels serve for seeding about two and a half acres.

The land plowed easily, for it was loose new loam—fine soil for potatoes. We needed no fertilizer, and we had no weeds to contend with; the seeds of barn grass, nettle, dock, and other noxious weeds had not yet found their way to that little sylvan nook. Working there was a pleasure. After we had got the seed into the ground, all the care that we had to give to the crop was two days of hilling in the latter part of June.

And how those potatoes grew! The stalks literally covered the ground. Later, when the blossoms fruited in clusters of green potato balls, we might have gathered a cartload of them.

In September, when frosts came, the crop of luxurious pink-white potatoes finally bore out the promise of blossom and ball. One cuff of the hoe would disclose a dozen or more large, clear tubers, ready to be gathered up in baskets. Not a bug had found its way there.

When we dug them up, they lay in veritable windrows across the flat—seven hundred bushels of them, at least.

The question then rose—a question to which we had given little thought thus far—how we were to transport all of those potatoes through the woods. At that season of the year it was virtually impossible. We realized that not until Lurvey's Stream froze could we get them home, or to market. Meanwhile what could we do with them? In Maine, after the first of October, freezing nights are likely to occur at any time.

The Old Squire came up and looked the situation over. "We shall have to dig them in and leave them here till snow comes," he said, and he set our three hired men at work to dig a potato pit, or cellar, in the side of a shady bank near the stream. They prepared a kind of cavern in the dry earth and covered in the entire crop first with boughs and then with earth, shoveled down from the top of the bank.

Except for twenty bushels that we drew home on sleds in December, the whole crop lay there until the first week in March, when the Old Squire contracted to deliver six hundred bushels in Portland at two dollars a bushel.

Moving potatoes in winter weather is always a ticklish business since potatoes freeze even more readily than apples, and the slightest chill turns potato starch to sugar and gives the tubers an unpleasant sweetish taste when cooked. We would have waited until April; but it was necessary to haul them down the stream on the ice, and the ice would not hold much longer. Throughout January and February there had been a winter road on the stream, and it appeared still to be safe.

The nearest railway station was fourteen miles away. The Old Squire had reserved for the fourth of March two boxcars that had stoves in them, and as it was necessary to have the potatoes there on that day, he hired four teamsters with their teams. We reckoned that a hundred bushels was a sled load for a span of horses, and so, with our own two teams, were prepared to carry the load.

At that time potatoes were generally shipped in burlap sacks instead of barrels; each sack held a bushel and a half. The Old Squire had bought four hundred of those sacks. On the second of March we opened the pit in the sandy bank beside the stream. The potatoes had kept well; only a few of them had rotted.

We had started at three o'clock that morning, and by eight o'clock the six loads were on their way down the stream. The Old Squire sent them off, one after the other, with a distance of a hundred yards or more between them, in order not to bring too great weight on the ice at any one place.

"Keep apart," he told the teamsters. "Don't drive close up one behind another. If the head team stops, you must all stop and wait till it starts on."

But when they were about three miles on their way, at a point where the stream turns round a wooded bluff, the forward team broke a whiffletree, and, without signaling back, the driver stopped to patch it up.

Unmindful of the Old Squire's orders, those behind kept on, closing up as they came round the bend, until all six teams were not far apart.

As the drivers puttered with the broken whiffletree, they noticed that water was gushing up on the ice, and before they could either back their teams or start on, the ice slowly sank down under them and left their loads in three feet or more of icy water.

A great commotion ensued, while the men shouted and lashed their horses in an attempt to pull out. The ice cracked and settled lower still. Fortunately, the stream was only a few feet deep there, or the horses would have been drowned and the loads lost. The ice kept settling until it rested on the bottom; and there they all were, the horses up to their sides in water, the drivers wading about, and the sleds more than half submerged.

At that moment the Old Squire, Addison, Halstead, and I rode up. We had stayed behind to close up the pit, in order to keep the rest of the potatoes from freezing.

We got the horses out and then, with a long warping line, tried to pull the loads out on the firmer ice below. A bitter wind had risen, and we were all of us soon wet to our waists. It was a discouraged crowd that toiled for hours that day to save those potatoes.

At last, about sunset, we got the last of the six loads onto firm ice close to the bank where the fir woods bordered the stream. But the Old Squire, who was pretty thoroughly chilled, was about ready to give up.

"We may as well drop it and go home," he said. "It'll be zero weather before morning. These potatoes will freeze here in spite of all we can do. If we go on with them, they will freeze on the way."

But six hundred bushels of potatoes! Twelve hundred dollars' worth! It seemed to us nothing short of calamity.

"Don't you suppose, sir, that we might build a fire close by the sleds and perhaps keep them from freezing?" Addison suggested. "I read that a man in Florida saved his orange orchard that way."

Addison referred to one of the first accounts published of attempts to ward off a frost by kindling fires in the open.

"I'm afraid it will be colder here before morning than it ever is in Florida," the Old Squire replied. "And more than half the sacks are wet."

"But we might save part of them."

"Maybe," the Old Squire said dubiously. "Well, you can try. We can at least dry our feet by the fire."

There were axes with the sleds, and there were plenty of fir trees—soft wood—at hand with pitchy branches and boughs that make a hot fire. Within five minutes after the word was given, trees were crashing down and the branches being lopped off. We drew the sleds up close together, piled the green boughs on the bank to the windward of them, and made great piles of them where the heat would be wafted over the loads of sacks. When lighted, the blaze streamed up ruddily in the gathering dusk, and a mighty crackling resounded far and wide.

Cold as the night was growing, the heat to the leeward of the sleds was intense. The wet sacks were soon steaming visibly. The Old Squire, however, was still doubtful about the success of the plan.

"It's hot enough here now," he said. "But you'll have to keep this up. If you let the fires go down even for half an hour, the potatoes will freeze. You will have to work all night, boys."

"Well, we will!" said Addison resolutely.

"But you'll need food before morning, and these teams must be looked to and fed."

After some discussion the two hired men and the Old Squire went to the farm with the horses to feed them and to bring back some supper.

As the evening drew on the wind died away, and we kindled several fires on the other side of the sleds. At Addison's suggestion, too, we covered the loads with boughs, so that the hot air from the fires would be held in the interstices of the twigs.

About midnight, or later, the Old Squire and one of the hired men returned, with horse and pung. They brought some hot food from home, kept warm by hot bricks wrapped in blankets.

Finding that the potatoes were not freezing, the Old Squire took heart a little and worked as hard as any of us. It was indeed a stiff fight with the cold—an unremitting battle that lasted all night long—felling trees, lopping off the branches, and dragging them forward to renew the fires.

At daylight the Old Squire sent Halstead and me and the hired man home, to bring more food and the teams. The weather had moderated somewhat, but he told us to collect every blanket and coverlet that the old farmhouse could muster and to bring them back with us.

We returned with a miscellaneous assortment of household gear, including old coats, cloaks, rag carpets, and two disused feather beds! We covered the potatoes with them, and shortly before eleven o'clock made a second start. Thus protected and tucked in, so to speak, the potatoes safely made the journey to the railway station. Once we got them aboard the cars with the box stoves our worry ceased.

The Old Squire went to Portland by train the next morning to attend himself to the delivery of the consignment. He received the amount that had been agreed on—two dollars a bushel—but the total sum was one hundred dollars less than he had expected. For, in spite of our efforts, about fifty bushels of the potatoes at the bottom of the loads had frozen.

Afterward, too, one of the Portland dealers told the Old Squire that one or two of his customers had remarked that those potatoes seemed to have an odd, faint smoky smell that they could not account for! The dealer laughed heartily when the Old Squire told him how those potatoes got to market.

For two seasons thereafter we raised potatoes at that opening in the woods, and then the bugs found them. By that time, however, Paris Green had begun to be used, and we were able to check the ravages of the potato beetle.

27

Addison Wins the Debate

NOT MANY OF OUR PRESIDENTS HAVE BEEN WHOLLY popular while holding office. The revered Washington, alas, was roundly abused throughout his first term, and the now-sainted Lincoln was not only abused but reviled and ridiculed during the entire Civil War.

There was talk of impeachment and a removal from office, at times, during the terms of two other presidents—mostly of course on the part of opposed political factions. Andrew Johnson, however, was the only one actually brought to trial before the Senate, on charges of "high crimes and misdemeanors." He escaped conviction by the narrow margin of one senatorial vote. That vote for acquittal was cast by our senior Senator from Maine, William Pitt Fessenden, and this opened the way for one of the most exciting debates that ever came off at our old academy.

Here I may perhaps be allowed to say that these weekly debates on the part of the students were, in my humble opinion, one of the best features of our school days; but that of course was before athletics replaced the more intellectual objects of education.

Our forensic contests were held on Thursday evenings, from eight until ten, and offered us boys a fine opportunity for self-improvement. They not only gave us practice in public speaking but impelled us to look up all available facts bearing on the questions to be debated and to be clear, accurate, and forcible in statement. Two disputants were appointed on each side, and after these had made their arguments, the question was opened to the house—of other students and interested townspeople—for general discussion. Afterward the merits of the argument were decided by votes of the audience.

The regularity with which these debates were maintained was due largely to the enthusiasm of our preceptor, Mr. George F. Kennard, who was wont to call on the students early every term to organize a debating society. Throughout four years—allowing for unavoidable postponements—ninety-two debates were held and a wide range of questions discussed. Current political questions were sometimes excluded, as likely to stir hard feelings. In strict point of fact, however, no great harm ever came from debating political questions; rather it trained us to habits of self-restraint, taught us to respect the opinions of opponents, and to be tolerant and good-natured toward them. In truth it should be put down as a rule, that a student, young or old, who cannot control his temper in a debate, keep good-humored, and be courteous to those who differ from him, is just the person who needs to take part in one—till he can. If a debater loses his temper, there is but one good medicine for him—to laugh him out of his weak egotism.

In our own town, as everywhere throughout the North, four persons out of five were in favor of convicting President Johnson of "high crimes and misdemeanors," and removing him from office. It was no idle transient burst of unpopularity that stirred the people, but a deep distrust of the president.

At the academy the students were nearly all in favor of impeachment. What caused widespread bitterness and exasperation in Maine was the fact that Senator Fessenden was known to be opposed to impeachment, the same position as that taken by Senator Ross of Kansas. Both these men, acting from higher convictions of duty, stood out against the popular clamor and thereby incurred hot popular displeasure.

But this, be it remembered, was shortly after the close of the Civil War, when throughout the North, animosity against the people of the states lately in rebellion was still strong. President Johnson, too, was a strange, erratic person. People did not understand him. His personal habits were far from correct. He was harsh, violent of speech, and had assumed the role of dictator. Patriotic people feared him. He was believed to be a dangerous man who meant to undo the work of the brave soldiers who had fought four years to maintain and perpetuate the Union.

According to custom, the question that we debated was put in the form of a resolve and made to bear heavily on Senator Fessenden. It read, "Resolved that President Johnson is a traitor to his country, and that Senator William Pitt Fessenden's attitude is false to his state and hostile to the welfare of this nation."

Mr. Kennard, I recollect, hesitated about giving the debate his sanction. "Have you the self-control and fairness to discuss this question in a parliamentary way?" he asked the boys.

"Oh, yes," several of them replied, laughing. "It will not take long to decide it. We merely want to put ourselves on record here and send the result of the vote to old Fessenden. The only trouble is to get anybody to take the negative."

Not a student there wished to incur the odium of arguing publicly in favor of the president or Senator Fessenden. Finally Cousin Addison said, "I will take the negative, if you can find no one else." He was at once scheduled for it, and because the committee could find no one else, they put me on with Addison, although I was too young and too inexperienced to be of much use.

At the supper table that night, when we told the Old Squire what had occurred, he said, "Boys, you will have a hot time of it. You must keep cool and not mind what the affirmative, or the audience say.

"But I am glad that you are on the negative," he continued after some moments of thoughtfulness, but more to Addison than to me. "I am glad because I want to hear a just word spoken for Senator Fessenden."

"But do you believe he is right, sir?" Theodora asked in surprise, for our girls were nearly as much interested as the rest of us. "Isn't the president a bad man?"

The Old Squire did not reply immediately. "It has not been easy for any of us to make up our minds fully as to that," he remarked at length. "President Johnson appears to be rash and wrong-headed. He is said to drink heavily, and that robs us of confidence in his character. But I am far from sure that his policy toward the Southern states is unconstitutional.

"Of one thing, however, I am wholly sure," the Old Squire continued in a different tone. "Senator Fessenden is a man to be trusted. The public outcry against him is a cruel and a mistaken one. I have known him all his life. If Senator Fessenden believes it improper to impeach the president, I am inclined to trust his judgment. He is a greater man than those on the other side, a greater statesman."

"Thaddeus Stevens and Senator Charles Sumner urge the conviction of the president," Addison offered.

"Yes, and they are both men of great firmness and strength of character," the Old Squire replied. "But I think they became too much embittered by the war to be just to the Southern people. Thaddeus Stevens' speeches sound to me revengeful. He lacks the great-heartedness of our lost President Lincoln."

That was all the Old Squire would say that night, but he began collecting everything he could find for us as to President Johnson's life and his public proclamations after he became president, also what was then in print of President Lincoln's last utterances as to Reconstruction, and the treatment that should be accorded to the Southern people after the war closed.

Time and again that week the old gentleman cautioned us to keep our tempers in the coming debate and make use of nothing save strictly courteous, parliamentary language. "If there is blackguarding, let the others do it," he charged us. In short he coached us what he could and advised us in the matter of reserving our best and strongest arguments till the final round of the discussion. He also wrote to Senator Fessenden, informing him of the debate and of the part his grandsons were to take in it. Mr. Fessenden replied in a touching letter, which, however, did not arrive until the very evening of the debate, and was handed to Addison by the Old Squire after we were on the platform.

As if it were yesterday, I recall that memorable Thursday night. Not only the members of our debating society and all the academy students were present, the large old schoolroom was crowded and packed to the doors with the villagers and people from the entire surrounding country.

Although always present at the debates, Mr. Kennard usually preferred to have one of the students preside—to give them practice; but

on that evening he took the chair himself, fearing lest he might have a disturbance to quell.

The meeting was called to order, and our secretary, Bronson Chaplin, read the question, slowly, impressively, and in a loud clear voice. What the mood and temper of the audience were can be judged from the fact that he had hardly finished when a tornado of applause shook the room.

In accord with our rules, the disputants sat on the platform with the chairman and secretary, the affirmative on the right hand and the negative on the left. On the affirmative that night were two classmates, Abner Coburn of Waterville and Hiram Sewell of Bath. The unhappy goats in the scriptural allegory of the judgment could hardly have felt more lonesome and forsaken than did Addison and I over there on the left, as those hostile cheers rent the air. In truth, I felt pale all over. If we said too much we might even be mobbed! Addison, I remember, sat as still as a statue, with his eyes fixed on the floor.

In case of an affirmative resolve, like this, it was customary to call on the negative first, to dispute it; but there was so much pent-up excitement that night that Mr. Kennard judged it better to allow the affirmative to have its full say at once and relieve the tension, so to speak. That course seemed, at first, to favor the affirmative, but in reality it made it easier for the negative and it also gave the closing speech to us. Knowing that we had the hard end of the debate, Mr. Kennard was doing what he could for us.

With a confident smile, Abner took the floor, and his first words were, "A great war has been fought for human liberty on this continent; a great victory for freedom has been won at a cost to us of three billions of dollars and a million lives, but now a traitor sits in the presidential chair, who seeks to reverse that victory and render all this vast outpouring of blood and treasure of no avail. A traitor, ladies and gentlemen, who seeks to give that victory back to the nation's foes!"

A great outburst of cheers interrupted him with cries of, "Right you are!" and "That's God's truth!"

Abner then went on to depict the president according to the ideas that then prevailed concerning him, personally, throughout the North. He described him as a coarse, violent man, debased by bad habits. He pictured him in league with defeated traitors, himself a traitor to his high oath of office. In short, he repeated what so many thousands of the Northern people were then saying, or thinking, in all honesty. Never a speaker had his audience more entirely and heartily with him. Abner was cheered at every pause, and when he finished, the applause burst forth afresh like pent-up waters.

Master Kennard determined to let this sentiment run its full course and now, in an unprecedented move, called the second disputant on the affirmative. Hiram promptly took the floor and in tones of indignation attacked Senator Fessenden as recreant and false to his native state.

Nothing could ever at any time be said against the high character of William Pitt Fessenden. That was impossible. Hiram therefore proceeded to trace what he termed our fallen senator's present strange and amazing course, to political jealousy of Senator Sumner, Thaddeus Stevens, and other radical leaders in Congress. He drew an ugly picture of a man who allows personal spite to take root in his mind and control him to the point of disloyalty to his country, and he ended by contrasting the treachery of Senator Fessenden with the staunch loyalty and patriotism of our other senator from Maine, Senator Morrill.

There were more cheers, alternating with groans at every mention of Senator Fessenden's name. The affirmative clearly had everything its own way; and when at length Mr. Kennard said, "The negative now has the floor," a ripple of merriment ran around, accompanied by certain uncomplimentary remarks and queries of, "What will the little Johnson bubs say?" "Oh, well," others remarked, "there have to be two sides, you know. They are just taking the off side to keep up the discussion."

In order to hold the negative's best disputant in reserve, Mr. Kennard called on me first; and as Addison and I had agreed in advance what line of argument each should take, I began my small share of it with a brief account of Andrew Johnson's boyhood days in North Carolina and his journey to Tennessee, his poverty, his efforts to educate himself, his first election to Congress, his important services as a Congressman, and finally his grand stand for the Union, during the whole Civil War. I then described him as conscientiously attempting to reconstruct that Union, now that the War was ended.

It was a forlorn little effort at an argument. When I sat down, one of my classmates back in the audience tried to start applause for me by clapping his hands; but he was alone, and the audience laughed. "Well, he had to say something," I overheard one man say. "He did the best he could."

Mr. Kennard then called on Addison, who rose quietly amidst utter silence. "Mr. Chairman, ladies and gentlemen," he began, "I find an impression prevails here tonight that the negative is talking just for form's sake, just for the sake of having two sides, that we are doing so for that purpose only. Now I would be sorry to have you think that of me. I beg you to believe that in every word I say here, I am in earnest, not pretending. I consented to take the negative of this question because I fully believe that it is the side of right and justice, because [and here his voice took a deeper tone] I believe that to impeach the president on such slight grounds as those thus far shown against him would be a national calamity. I go further than that even, I believe that

Andrew Johnson is a patriotic president and in no sense a traitor, that he is doing what he thinks is his duty, under the Constitution, that he is taking the course toward the Southern states that President Lincoln would have taken, had he lived. I take the negative, too, because I fully and earnestly believe in Senator Fessenden, in his statesmanship, in his high character, because I believe these charges of spite against him are cruel, cowardly, and unworthy of the people of Maine. I believe that everyone of you who now makes these charges will live to be ashamed of them!"

There was no laughing now. Astonishment had fallen, astonishment rapidly changing to hostility and anger. Someone started to hiss, but the audience was not quite ready for that, yet.

"I do not admire President Johnson personally," Addison continued. "I am not his apologist. I believe it unfortunate that he has come to the presidential chair. He is said to be a hard drinker. That may be true. The affirmative says that he is coarse and undignified. That appears to be the fact. His public speeches show this. Admit it all. But when the affirmative goes on to intimate that he was in league with traitors and with the assassins of President Lincoln, they appear to forget that Vice-President Andrew Johnson was one of the very men whom those assassins planned to kill and that he narrowly escaped death at their hands, himself. They appear to forget, too, that at the trial of these assassins not one particle of evidence could be found that either Jefferson Davis or any of the Southern leaders had any hand whatever in those assassinations.

"I shall show you that if President Johnson is a traitor, then the late President Lincoln was a traitor, for I can prove to you that after his harsh fashion President Johnson has sought to carry out the very policy, the self-same measures toward the South that President Lincoln had planned but two days before he was murdered.

"I can also prove to you that if President Johnson is a traitor, then General Grant is one, General Sherman another, and Edwin M. Stanton another—for all three have favored and endorsed President Lincoln's policy of mercy and conciliation toward the South." Addison had got no further than General Grant's name, however, when a storm of hisses and outcries drowned him out.

"That's false!" "You can't prove it!" "You don't know what you are talking about!" "You're a young copperhead!" "Shut up!" "Sit down!"

Addison stood still and let the storm rage itself out. But the instant he attempted to speak, it burst forth again. The audience would not hear him state what General Grant or General Sherman had said. "That's false!" "Sit down!" "Sit down!" were the shouts that met him every time he tried to go on.

"Very well, then," Addison at length managed to say. "If you will not listen to what General Grant said [another tumult], will you hear what Senator Fessenden writes about it? Will you?" Hisses and cries of "No!" "No!" "He's another traitor!" cut him short.

Just then, too, a voice out in the audience was heard addressing the chairman. It was young Lieut. Col. George Bloodgood, who since the close of the war had become an aspirant for political honors in our part of the state, and who now saw his opportunity to make a speech.

"Mr. Chairman!" he shouted above the tumult. "If this young Johnson rooster has got through crowing, may I say a few words?"

"Not in order," Mr. Kennard ruled. "The negative still has the floor." He rapped sharply, but the audience, now out of all bounds, began shouting "Colonel Bloodgood! Colonel Bloodgood!" and kept it up, till after a word with the secretary and Addison, Mr. Kennard judged it best to recognize him, but remarked that it was by courtesy of the negative—at which the audience jeered!

Amid hearty applause, Colonel Bloodgood came forward and began what proved a long, set speech, denouncing President Johnson, praising his opponents in Congress, and ending finally in a most unjust, bitter, personal attack on Senator Fessenden. He occupied so much time, too, that the regular hour for closing our debates—ten o'clock—came and passed by twenty minutes. The moment Bloodgood sat down and the cheering ceased, Abner Coburn called for the question—in order to decide by vote which side had won. Of course there was no doubt as to the result. What chance had the negative?

But Addison was on his feet at the same instant.

"Mr. Chairman," he exclaimed. "The negative yielded the floor this evening by courtesy, to our visitor, Colonel Bloodgood, who has largely occupied the time. By our rules all debates finish at ten, but the negative has not concluded. I move therefore that this debate be adjourned till one week from this evening, to be continued at that time."

"Question! Question!" numbers shouted. "Settle it now!" "Bring it to vote!" "No adjournment!"

We had never adjourned a debate before; Mr. Kennard seemed slightly perplexed, but Addison, who still held the floor, took Senator Fessenden's letter from his pocket. "Ladies and gentlemen!" he cried indignantly. "I am not asking a favor for myself. But I hold in my hand a letter from Senator Fessenden, which came in this afternoon's mail. In this letter Senator Fessenden gives his reasons—very good, strong, manly, statesman-like reasons, too—why he cannot and will not vote to convict President Johnson.

"Now Senator Fessenden has served the people of Maine for thirty-five years. He is the acknowledged leader of the Senate. He has brought honor to us as a state. As Secretary of the Treasury he has managed the disordered finances of this nation with skilled ability, and up to this time not one word has ever been breathed against his integrity.

"Now are you so lost to all sense of fair play that you will not hear what he has to say to us? Will you condemn him and throw him over without a chance to say a word—a man who has devoted his life to the welfare and interests of our state?"

The indignation, energy, and scorn with which Addison hurled this demand made itself felt. Silence suddenly fell. Then someone cried, "Read the letter! We will hear the letter!"

"Ten o'clock!" "Ten o'clock!" "Time's up!"—a score of voices were shouting, and Addison repeated his motion to adjourn. A classmate seconded it, and amidst a confusion of conflicting cries it was carried.

At the end of that first evening, therefore, we of the negative had put off the hour of defeat for a week. Not much more could be hoped. We had a fighting chance left. That was about all—that and Senator Fessenden's letter.

An even greater crowd gathered on the second evening of our debate. Incensed as the people were with Senator Fessenden, however, there was yet much curiosity to hear his letter. Although a personal letter, the senator had not requested that it should be confidential, and the Old Squire decided that it might properly be read in public.

Master Kennard presided as before, and after reading the minutes of the previous meeting, the secretary repeated the question:

"Resolved that President Johnson is a traitor to his country, and that Senator William Pitt Fessenden's attitude is false to his state and hostile to the welfare of this nation."

As before, cheers followed the reading of it, with a groan at the mention of the senator's name. Thus far there was evidently no change in the sentiments of the audience.

When the tumult had subsided, Mr. Kennard stated briefly why the debate had been adjourned and called on us of the negative to proceed with our argument. Much as before, we had to face laughter and ironical remarks. Again my own small part for the evening consisted of a brief account of Senator Fessenden's early life in Maine, his public services, and his remarkably able management of the national finances during the Civil War. I occupied ten minutes and made the senator's claims to the gratitude of the nation plain, or tried to do so. The effort was listened to in grim silence and won no applause. Mr. Kennard then called on Addison, who took the floor.

"You will remember, ladies and gentlemen," he said, "that an adjournment was requested to allow a letter from Senator Fessenden to be read here. Although not intended for publication, we believe that the reading of it can do no harm." In clear, earnest tones Addison then read as follows:

Washington, DC
May 19, 1868
My dear old friend:

Amid the deluge of letters recently from those who formerly called themselves my friends, yours alone expresses unswerving confidence in me as a man and a public servant.

Standing, as I undoubtedly do, at the close of my career and on the brink of a political grave, your kind words are like a friendly hand grasping mine in the dark of the future. Truly those who have chosen to tread the dusty paths of political life find only too often that these paths lead them on to dreary deserts. Little enough have I gained for my old age save public reprobation.

The people of Maine appear to have condemned me with one accord. They seem wholly to forget that I am here on my oath as their senator and bound in honor by that oath, to vote at this strange trial according to the evidence and not according to my own preferences.

What those preferences are, I need hardly tell you. The president is a headstrong, erratic man for whom personally I have little sympathy. His quarrel with Congress is largely the result of his harsh, enormous egotism. Of that, however, little account need be taken now. He is not on trial for his personality but on a charge of high crimes and misdemeanors—a wholly different matter. On such a charge this trial is a wretched farce. There are no proper grounds for it. The man is loyal after his peculiar fashion, a devotee, indeed, to the Constitution, and a patriot of a sort. In his own rude way he is as much a patriot as Sumner or Stevens.

In voting "Not guilty," last Tuesday, I had absolutely nothing to gain and everything to lose—namely, my political reputation, the esteem of my friends and of the people of Maine, even life itself, perhaps. Incredible as it will seem to you, my life has been three times threatened during the past week. In the quiet of your farmhome you can have little idea of the madness that prevails here since this trial began. I dare not go out after nightfall lest I may be kidnapped and spirited away, till after the final vote of the Senate on the 26th of this month.

My mail is heavy with letters, demanding that I shall vote to convict the president. If I yielded to these demands, I could not return to Maine and look an honest man in the face. If the people of Maine desire a senator who will commit perjury at their bidding, either from alleged necessity or love of popular favor, let them seek someone else. I am not that man. God helping me, I shall follow the dictates of conscience under my oath of office.

Eleven articles of impeachment have been framed for indicting the president. Several of these are trivial, none of them very clear; the eleventh only embodies a charge of crime, and this one, in my judgment, remains unproven.

I have felt from the first that to convict and remove the president of the United States from his high office on charges as weak as these would be a national calamity, the far-reaching consequences of which would seriously jeopardize our republic for the future.

What dignity would go with this highest office in the land, or what respect could be felt for it, if the president can be deposed whenever the leaders of a party in a majority grow angry or dissatisfied with him?

The real point at issue, the gist of this whole quarrel between the president and Congress, is that President Johnson thinks he has the power, under the Constitution, to deal with the Southern states and restore them to the Union according to a policy of his own. On the other hand, Congress asserts the opposite view, that since the war these states are in the condition of conquered provinces, to be readmitted to the Union on such terms as Congress shall accord to them. Those who read our Constitution must take their choice which of these opposed views is right. Opinions differ widely as to this.

The late President Lincoln apparently held the view that President Johnson holds. I am far from saying, however, that the latter holds it because it was President Lincoln's view. He is too opinionated, too egotistic, to adopt any view save his own. A more aggressive, not to say offensive, man never lived; and yet he possesses qualities that have made him trusted and respected in his native state of Tennessee. The effort to impeach him has come largely from the hatred that the leaders of the dominant party in Congress feel for him on account of his bitter language and lawless manners. But these can hardly constitute high crimes and misdemeanors, nor can any of his acts be fairly construed as such.

Not much more need be said. In giving the turning vote that defeated this impeachment, it was my hard fate to be caught betwixt the upper and nether millstones of popular wrath. It closes my political career. None the less I shall do my duty as your senator, even as I know you would do yours.

Sincerely your friend,

W. P. Fessenden

An uneasy stir followed. Clearly the letter had made an impression. Addison held the letter up and looked around over the audience. "What think you, ladies and gentlemen?" he exclaimed. "Is this the letter of a man who is, as this resolve declares, 'false to the people of Maine and hostile to this nation'?"

For a moment, dead silence—then again young Colonel Blood-good sprang to his feet, shouting, "Mr. Chairman! Mr. Chairman! May I not say a word?"

"The affirmative disputants have the floor," Mr. Kennard ruled, without recognizing the interruption. Bloodgood continued shouting "Mr. Chairman!" however; and his friends in the audience began howling, "Bloodgood!" "Bloodgood!" "Hear Bloodgood!" keeping it up till, to avert a riot, Mr. Kennard judged it expedient to recognize him.

Having obtained the floor, the aspiring politician entered on another long harangue much like, if not the same, as that of the previous evening, abusing the president and ascribing a great variety of unworthy motives to Senator Fessenden.

It was noticeable, however, that the cheering was not as hearty as the week before, and that many in the room were growing tired of hearing mere abuse, instead of facts. We of the negative took heart a little, and Addison made ready to give in reply President Lincoln's policy of Reconstruction and General Grant's opinion in regard to it.

But when Bloodgood had finally talked himself out, one of those vexatious, embarrassing things occurred that had, time and again, nearly driven us academy boys to desperation during previous debates. The Reverend Elnathan Hatch, one of the village clergymen, rose and requested the privilege of saying "just one word." Mr. Hatch was one of those very good men who seem to think that his profession entitled him to be heard anywhere, at anytime, whether in order or not. Moreover he was a vague, dreamy person, with little practical knowledge of public affairs. Yet our respect for him and for the church had always led us to yield the floor to him, although having got it, he appeared never to know when to leave it.

Mr. Kennard recognized him, and with an inward groan we settled back in our seats to pass the time.

For a while it was far from certain which side Mr. Hatch was on; gradually he ranged himself on the affirmative, and then began to give us what was apparently one of his old war-time sermons against slavery and secession. Once started there was no stopping him till he had run down. We listened as patiently as possible, but as the time for the debate to close drew on, Addison and I raged inwardly. We were being smothered by talk. Senator Fessenden's letter had created an impression. If only we could follow it up with our facts, we had hopes of success.

It ended exactly as we had feared. Mr. Hatch's "one word" dragged on for more than half an hour and profoundly wearied everybody. When finally he sat down, cries of "Question! Question!" rose. "Give us the question!" "Settle it!" "Put it to vote!" "Now settle it!"

Defeat stared the negative in the face.

Then by a supreme effort, Addison again saved the situation for us. "Mr. Chairman, ladies and gentlemen!" he shouted in tones that rang through the room. "Hear me! Is this fair play? Hear me! Listen! The affirmative speakers on this question have had four hours and twenty minutes for their argument. The negative has had just thirty-six minutes against two hundred and sixty minutes. Is that fair?"

A laugh went around.

"The negative has simply been talked off the floor!" Addison shouted. "We have had no proper chance to make our arguments. On the other side speakers with political axes to grind, and others who love to hear their own voices, have monopolized seven-eighths of the time, both evenings. I appeal to you, is this fair play? Our best arguments are still to come. We have been ready to give them but have been drowned out by talk. Will you give us fair play, or not? As it is already long past ten o'clock, I move, I demand, that this debate be again adjourned, till one week from tonight."

There was such energy, such force, such indignation in his appeal, that for the first time since the discussion began, a cheer rose for the negative. Numbers cried, "That's so!" "Fair play for the negative!" The motion to adjourn was seconded and carried—and for the third time we had a fighting chance.

"Addison," Mr. Kennard said privately, as we were leaving the academy that night, "You are making a fine fight. You have set these people thinking. Have your facts ready next time. Facts are what count, when there's a chance to present them," he added, laughing. "Next time you shall have the floor."

I am afraid that none of us did much except study the question during the week that followed. Lessons received but scanty attention. Everybody was discussing the impeachment trial, and it was plain that people were taking second thoughts about it. Violent party men, like Colonel Bloodgood, were as bitter as ever against Senator Fessenden; others expressed doubt; not a few said, "I guess Fessenden meant well, whether he is right or not."

That was the frame of mind the students and the people were in during that third week of the debate. By fighting for adjournment and delay, Addison, like Fabius of ancient Roman days, had won opportunity for a calmer consideration of the facts of the case.

On calling the meeting to order the following Thursday night, Mr. Kennard remarked that two new rules had of necessity been adopted for the debate: first, that no speaker, either negative or affirmative, should hold the floor for more than five minutes at one time; second, that everyone who spoke should confine himself strictly to the question. This was done to protect the debate from long, rambling, vainglorious speeches by outsiders.

The audience saw the point, and a laugh went round.

The question was read again, but failed to evoke the storm of applause that had previously greeted it.

As the negative had the floor, Addison rose and without losing a moment of time said, "Does anyone here tonight believe that the late President Lincoln was a traitor?

"I see that you deem that question too silly to require an answer. President Lincoln's plan for restoring the Union, after the Civil War, was summed up in these simple but nonetheless great words, addressed to the South:

'Abolish human slavery. Cease your acts of war. Come back home to the Union of States. No state has ever got out of that Union, nor by the grace of God, ever shall. We have fought no war of conquest, only one of self-preservation.

'I will suffer my right hand to be severed from my body before I will sign one measure for ignoble revenge on the Southern people. I love the South as I love the North, because it is a part of the Union, a portion of our common country.'"

After quoting these noble words, Addison summarized briefly President Lincoln's plan for restoring Louisiana to the Union, then his historic proclamation to the people of North Carolina.

Parallel with these, he then summed up President Johnson's several proclamations to the Southern states, showing them to be exactly in line with the plans and proclamations of President Lincoln.

"Now I am not trying to force this audience into an unpleasant position," Addison continued urbanely. "Yet I can but point out to you that if by your votes here tonight you declare Andrew Johnson a traitor to his country, then you declare that Abraham Lincoln was one. Are you prepared to do that?" And he sat down just as the secretary called, "Time!"

Colonel Bloodgood and his friends started a groan, but several voices cried, "Oh, hush!" "Enough of that!"

Abner Coburn, for the affirmative, then took the floor and made the point that, in removing Secretary of War Edwin M. Stanton from office, President Johnson had violated a law enacted by Congress, termed the Tenure-of-Office Act, and was therefore guilty of a crime as charged by the articles of impeachment.

Following advice from Addison, I met this charge instantly, by arguing that Secretary Stanton was a member of the president's cabinet, that cabinet officers were the president's personal advisors, selected by him for that purpose and holding these positions subject to the president's approval. I quoted the opinions of six senators, and also that of the Hon. William M. Evarts, that the Tenure-of-Office Act does not by precedent, nor under the Constitution, apply to officials of the president's cabinet.

Both of us had kept within the five-minute limit. It was a fine bit of attack and defense, with honors about even.

Facts like these, however, were far from suiting the aggressive tastes of Colonel Bloodgood and his friends. The colonel was on his feet, shouting, "Mr. Chairman!" the instant I finished; and again his cronies in the audience bawled, "Colonel Bloodgood! Colonel Bloodgood!"— till at length Mr. Kennard recognized him. The colonel then resumed his personal attack on Senator Fessenden in much the same strain as on the previous evening. He appeared to delight in personal abuse of that kind and was in full blast when "time" was called for him. Then he made a mistake. "I demand five minutes more!" he shouted.

The sense of fair play among the students rebelled at that. "No, no!" was the cry. "No favoritism," and thereupon they all shouted,

"Time!" "Time!" "Down!" "Down!" till the colonel was forced to subside.

This time he had distinctly injured the affirmative. The audience felt it, though his cronies cheered persistently for some moments.

Hiram Sewell, the regular disputant on the affirmative, then took the floor; and after a few words of denunciation of President Johnson, he too made the blunder of again attacking Senator Fessenden personally, charging him with using his official position to secure military promotion for his sons. By the Old Squire's advice Addison was prepared for this with evidence from the reports of the superior officers of the Fessenden boys, showing indisputably that they had been promoted for gallant conduct on the battlefield and that one of them had been severely wounded.

This occupied but four minutes. When he sat down someone in the audience cried, "Read us that letter of Fessenden's again." The opposition began hissing, but other voices repeated, "Read the letter! Letter! Letter!" and continued calling for it till Mr. Kennard called on me to rise and read it for them.

This time the cheers clearly outnumbered the groans. The tide had turned. The affirmative felt it and grew excited. Abner Coburn sprang to his feet and again attacked the president as a traitor, but failed to produce facts in support of the charge.

In reply Addison quoted the opinions of General Grant and General Sherman to show that at the close of the Civil War both these victorious leaders had been fully in accord with the policy subsequently adopted by President Johnson toward the Southern people.

"I have already proved by facts that the president's policy is, in the main, that of the late President Lincoln," Addison concluded. "I now show that both General Grant and General Sherman held the same views." Addison still had a minute of time left, and he used it to add, "Fellow students and others, before you vote tonight, I wish to call your attention to the exact words of this question. It is not whether you consider President Johnson a model man, or a good man, or a desirable president, or anything of that kind, but whether he is actually a traitor to his country.

"Now a traitor to his country means one who is treacherous at heart and who has committed treacherous acts against her.

"In regard to Senator Fessenden, too, if you vote 'yes' on this resolve, you are saying that, on your honor, you believe that he is false-hearted and willfully hostile to his country."

Ten o'clock was striking as he took his seat, and Mr. Kennard announced that the debate was closed. The secretary then called the names of the fifty-two members of the debating society.

Forty-one voted "no," only eleven "yes."

It had been the custom to invite the audience at large to vote on the questions that we discussed, by a count of hands. Such a vote was now taken, and resulted in two hundred and sixty-eight negative, to but ninety-three affirmative.

Altogether this was considered the greatest victory in debate ever won at the old academy. The negative had gained it largely by good management, sticking closely to the facts, and adjourning the discussion until the audience had had time and was in a mood to properly appreciate those facts.

It taught us that an American audience is usually conscientious and may be trusted to vote right on any question when the facts bearing on it are adequately presented.

Very appropriate to this debate and to Addison's strategy in winning it, are the lines of a well-known poem, which, however, had not then been written:

> If you can keep your head when all about you
> Are losing theirs and blaming it on you;
> If you can trust yourself when all men doubt you,
> But make allowance for their doubting, too;
> If you can wait and not be tired with waiting,
> Or, being lied about, don't deal in lies,
> Or, being hated don't give way to hating,
> And yet don't look too good, nor talk too wise;
> . . . .
> Yours is the Earth and everything that's in it,
> And—what is more —you'll be a Man, my son!

28

Selling Eye-Sharpeners

AT ONE TIME OR ANOTHER NEARLY EVERY YOUTH who is ambitious to obtain an education and has his own way to make in the world turns canvasser for something or other in the hope of adding to his revenues. I took my turn at this diversified and often distracting occupation at the early age of fifteen, with a device called an eye-sharpener, of vast advertised promise. If I remember aright, it was the invention of a certain Doctor Grote of New York, who may have made a fortune from it—though I did not.

The invention was not called an eye-sharpener in the grand prospectus that beguiled me into becoming its traveling agent and salesman. "Eye-sharpener" was merely a nickname for it. That prospectus was headed with the seductive words:

"OLD EYES MADE YOUNG. No more bother with glasses. Spectacles discarded. Near-sighted persons equally benefited. Can be applied and used by anyone, young or old. The greatest ocular discovery of the age. Based on anatomical principles. Four brief applications daily for a few weeks will restore the eyes of the aged to the keen vision of youth. No drugs, no eyewashes. A clean, harmless mechanical device for giving the eye greater or less convexity as the individual case requires."

Then followed a technical description with diagrams of the eye and the changes resulting from age. This and much more, all concluding with the oft-repeated question, "Why bother all one's life with glasses?"

Why indeed when the price was but two dollars by mail, postpaid?

The circular also stated that agents were wanted everywhere and added that many agents were already clearing a hundred dollars a day.

The prospectus reached our old farm in Maine on a sunny day in July, and I recall that the Old Squire read it with grave attention and sat thoughtful for some moments. "I doubt if this will do what it claims," he said. "But it seems simple. Old eyes do shrink and grow flatter than young ones. This may possibly be an experiment worth trying."

But my more youthful and mercenary attention was fixed rather on that call for agents and the large profits they were alleged to realize from canvassing for it. I therefore strained my resources, scraped together two dollars and sent it, as directed in the circular, with a request for information concerning agents and what profits were allowed them.

The response came promptly in the form of a little pasteboard box containing the eye-sharpener and a letter praising my manifest perspicacity in thus early securing territory for canvassing. Our entire county was accorded to me, and a special profit of seventy-five cents on each and every sale was guaranteed to me. On receipt of fifteen dollars, a dozen of the eye-sharpeners would be sent to me at once, together with hints and instructions for canvassing—what best to say to elderly people and the quiet, respectful way in which it would be wise to approach them and introduce the subject of my call.

The Old Squire and Grandmother Ruth, I recollect, examined the new device with much curiosity. It consisted merely of an oval rubber cup of the same shape as the human eye, being designed to fit on it. The rubber of the cup was stiff and kept its shape. At the base of the cup a small rubber tube about a foot in length entered it, having at the other end a thin rubber bulb like the bulb of a cologne spray.

The directions for use were simple: "Take the cup in your left hand. Grasp the bulb in your right and squeeze it until all the air is expelled. Next cover the eye gently with the cup, holding it steadily and firmly in place. Then slowly release pressure on the bulb in your right hand. The pressure of the air seeking to enter the vacuum thus produced will draw the eye upward from its flattened condition to one of greater convexity, allowing the humors to fill the cavity and resume the youthful condition. After one minute by the clock the treatment should be renewed and repeated five times, and this daily for a month or more. Spectacles can usually be discarded in the course of a month. Cases of near-sightedness, where the eyeball is too convex, may best be remedied by reversing the treatment for long-sightedness, namely, by first adjusting the cup to the eye, then gradually squeezing the bulb, thus using the air pressure to flatten the eye."

In accord with the Old Squire's advice—he wished to inculcate New England thrift in his grandsons—we had each of us started a small account at the village savings bank. I had rather more than twenty dollars there, as witnessed in my carefully kept bank book. I boldly drew out fifteen dollars, consigned it to Doctor Grote, and received a dozen eye-sharpeners in return with some further hints and good advice about canvassing.

"I feel sure you will soon need another dozen," the doctor wrote, "and perhaps it might be safer for you to send for two or three dozen at once, since the limited number in stock is now being rapidly diminished."

I appreciated his kind interest in me, but lack of funds prevented me from availing myself of his suggestion. Next day, a canvasser with high hopes, I set off on foot.

Hours before the close of my first day's effort, however, I was in a state of bewildered wonder. How had those other agents managed to clear a hundred dollars a day! I tramped all day to sell one, and all the next day to sell two!

After getting more promises than sales, I made a cash sale at a little grocery kept by two old-maid sisters named McCrillis, at a place called Pillow's Mills, a walk of eleven miles from home. I was an hour or two effecting that sale. Those old maids were talkers. They escorted me into their little back room at the rear of the grocery store. There we talked the matter over at length and finally talked it out.

They were very large, tall, coarse-featured women about fifty years old, who had both come to wearing spectacles with silver bows. Our long conversation had included nearly everything I could tell them about myself, parentage, and present place of abode, and in return I had learned nearly as much about them, among other things that they were born in Nova Scotia and that the name of the older sister was Roxan, and that of the younger, Lovisa.

I explained carefully how the eye-sharpener was to be used, adjusted it to their eyes, and gave them both a treatment. Incidentally, I recollect what large, hard gray eyes each had. At last I received payment and got away, victorious. That, however, was the last eye-sharpener I was able to dispose of. The roseate dream of a hundred dollars a day had faded in the lowering dawn of a very drab reality.

I went out only twice after that. Planting time had come. Farm work was beginning, and the Old Squire thought I would be better employed putting in the year's crops. Thus far I was several dollars in arrears, not to mention a new pair of boots quite worn out, but the Old Squire had paid for those.

This was not the end. Reports began to follow the use of the invention. An old miller named Lovejoy, to whom I had sold one, sent angry word that the contraption had given him sore eyes. Two old housewives whose promises I had taken sent their eye-sharpeners back with messages to the effect that the transaction was off, no benefit having followed use; others I never heard from, and I hadn't the heart to call on them.

But I did hear from the two old-maid sisters at Pillow's Mills. I was driving past their store about a year afterward and, seeing one of them standing at the door, was unwise enough to bow and raise my hat.

Unwise indeed! I ought to have known better, for I noticed that she still wore her silver-bowed spectacles. For a moment she stared, then cried, "Oh, that's you, is it?" But instantly, with an air of great sweetness she added, "Do stop a minute. Sister and I would like to speak with you."

Common prudence should have bidden me to whip up, but I suppose some lingering faith in the eye-sharpener prompted me to seek confirmation of it. In spite of adverse reports, I still half believed in it. I had written to Doctor Grote and told him what folks said of it, and his indignant reply was that these ignorant and clumsy complainants had not properly applied his beneficent invention.

I followed Lovisa—I think it was she—into the store and into their back room, where we found Roxan, who at the sight of me cried, "Hah!" and, opening a drawer, snatched out the "beneficent invention"

and thrust it at me. "And now, you little lying scamp, you hand back that two dollars you took from us for this worthless thing!"

"But have you tried it?" I faltered.

"Tried it!" they both shouted. "We tried it all last winter! We squeezed and squeezed till we nearly sucked our poor eyes out of their sockets. Never did a mite of good! It hurt 'em! We had to buy new glasses. Now you pay back that two dollars!"

Truth to say I hadn't two dollars about me, and I suppose I may have cast a glance at the door. But with one long stride Lovisa was there and had put her stalwart back to it. I began to say that it was quite out of the question to think of doing business in such a way, but Roxan cut that short.

"Hand back that two dollars, or you'll get the hottest spanking ever a boy got!" she commanded and took a step toward me. I was in the toils, trapped!

"But I haven't two dollars here," I confessed.

"No more of your lies!" cried Roxan. "You had two dollars fast enough when you changed that five-dollar bill we gave you the time we paid for this miserable thing! Hand it out now and be quick about it!"

"You'll have to wait till I go home," I protested.

But Roxan's only reply was to roll up her sleeves. Lovisa was doing the same behind me. To be spanked by two old maids would be a life-long disgrace if the news got out. I hastily produced my little pocket-book, opened it, and showed them that a dollar and sixty-one cents was all that it contained. They looked hard at me for several long moments. The truth was but too apparent.

"Wal, hand it over," Roxan said at length. "And when you get home see that you send us the other thirty-nine cents." She stuffed the eye-sharpener into my hand; Lovisa opened the back-room door, and I sneaked out through the grocery store, "trimmed" but wiser.

There were reasons why I thought it best to tell the Old Squire what had befallen me. He laughed, then looked serious. "I make no doubt this eye-sharpener is a fraud," he said and handed me thirty-nine cents. "Better go back there tomorrow and give it to them."

I drove over next morning, peered in at the store door, and seeing Roxan behind the counter, walked in and put down the money before her.

She burst into a loud laugh. "Wal, I vum!" she exclaimed. "You're more honest than I thought you was!"

The incident has a sequel, which is my reason for telling so humiliating a story on myself. Nine years later, after I had left home and was employed at the office of *The Youth's Companion*, the publisher, Mr. Daniel S. Ford, handed me a circular one morning, saying, "This is a device for improving the eyesight, and the proprietor of it has written to secure advertising space in the *Companion*. He offers to take half a double column at one thousand dollars. What do you think of it?"

I glanced at the prospectus. It was my old friend the eye-sharpener, still going strong. I related my experience with it, not omitting my interview with Roxan and Lovisa.

Mr. Ford laughed heartily. "I am glad to learn this," he said. "Of course the thing is a hoax," and he tossed prospectus and offer into the waste basket. "I dare say that many papers will print this and pocket the money," he added more seriously. "But no boy or girl who takes my paper or any person reading it shall be cheated by fallacious advertisements in its columns, if I can help it."

It is a pleasure to know that the same policy of good faith toward its readers still prevails at the *Companion* office.

29

In Sermon Time

IT WAS QUARTERLY MEETING SUNDAY AT THE METHO-
dist chapel, and Mr. Colby, the presiding elder, had just begun his
sermon. The day was unusually hot for June in Maine. Every window
of the old meetinghouse, even the two little red-curtained windows
behind the pulpit, was wide open. The girls, dressed in white, flut-
tered their fans. The men mopped their brows. The odor of lilac
drifted into the chapel, in at a window, too, came a great yellow bum-
blebee and hummed and buzzed along the plastered ceiling overhead.

Our whole family was there that day: the Old Squire, Grandmother, the girls, Addison, Halstead, and I, and even our two hired
men; for although we were Congregationalists, we thought very highly
of Elder Colby, both as a man and as a preacher. Almost everyone for
miles around was there; the entire countryside was left to Sabbath quiet
and its own devices.

"And ye shall know the truth, and the truth shall make you free."
That was Elder Colby's text; even to this day I remember it. He began
his sermon with a distinct, remarkably clear definition of truth as contrasted with falsehood, error, and evil, but I heard only the opening of
that sermon, for an unexpected interruption occurred.

Everyone knows what a truly hideous outcry a horse makes when
one of its fellows bites it. Now, from the long row of sheds just behind
the meeting house came one of those agonized squeals.

Elder Colby paid no attention, for he was warming up to his great
theme. But in another moment that brazen shriek pealed forth again.

In our pew we grew uneasy, for we feared that our old Nance was raising that ear-splitting protest.

Not until the third or fourth outcry occurred did the elder show that he was disturbed. Then he stopped and said quietly, "I fear someone has hitched a horse too near another horse. Will someone kindly relieve the situation by shortening those halters?"

The Old Squire nodded to Addison and me and we stole out on tiptoe, then hurried round the building to the sheds. But when we drew near, we saw that it was no horse that was biting old Nance; Zinky Dunham, a half-wit who lived at the town farm, was pinching her side with a split stick.

Zinky's real name was Sinclair, but that had been shortened to Sinky, which had finally become Zinky. The boy had a short thick body with legs disproportionately long. His head was thickly thatched with tan-colored hair. He had a large black mole under his right eye and another on his upper lip. In some ways Zinky was not lacking in intelligence, but he had a silly sounding voice and an expression of countenance that was sillier still.

The queerest thing about him, however, was that he hopped on one foot a great deal—his left foot, too. He had begun to do so as a child, and as he grew older he continued the habit. People said that he could hop for a mile on his left foot without touching the other foot to the ground. He would clear almost ten feet at a hop and get over the ground faster in that manner than he could by running. When he was in a great hurry he nearly always hopped.

Addison, who was ahead of me, pounced indignantly upon Zinky.

"Here! Stop that!" he cried, grabbing the stick. "Stop it at once! What are you about?"

Zinky backed off a few steps.

"Now you go back to the 'farm'!" Addison exclaimed. "What are you over here at the meeting house for? You, go straight back to the 'farm'—or Elder Colby will take you in hand!"

Zinky retreated a little distance farther, and then he began to say:

"Buzzy, buzzy, buzzy bee! You come see, you come see."

As he spoke, he swung his arms wildly this way and that and wrinkled his nose.

"Keep still!" Addison ordered him. "Go home. You're disturbing the meeting!"

We hurried him away past the sheds and across the field behind him in the direction of the town farm, which was not more than a mile and a half away.

"Stivver, now!" Addison cried. "Don't you come back!"

When Zinky had gone a few steps he turned again and began to chant that silly, "Buzzy, buzzy bee."

We picked up some sticks and chased him a hundred yards farther, for we were afraid that he would follow us back and begin tormenting the horses again after we had gone into the church. He hopped out of our way, but as soon as we started back, he turned and came slowly after us, like a dog that does not wish to be sent home. He was still saying, "Buzzy, buzzy bee. You come see."

"What do you suppose he means?" Addison exclaimed impatiently.

We began to think that perhaps Zinky had come to the meeting house for some purpose and that, not daring to come in, had begun to torment old Nance in order to attract attention.

"What is it you want?" Addison said to him sharply. "What did you come for?"

Keeping out of reach of our sticks, Zinky circled round us, still repeating his, "buzzy bee" nonsense; then he ran a few steps and made motions again over his shoulder.

"He wants us to go with him," Addison said. "Had we better do it?"

We knew that the Old Squire would expect us to come back into church, but after a moment's hesitation we decided that we had better find out what the trouble was.

The moment we started to follow him, Zinky capered away, and when we broke into a trot, he started to hop. We went on at a great rate across another field, then through some bushes and a belt of woodland, and at last came out in the rear of the buildings of the Dennett Wells farm.

We heard a discordant drumming noise, and on running round to the front side of the buildings we saw old grandsir Wells thumping a tin pan and gazing up into a tall pear tree. Aloft, high on a bending branch, hung a great black mass of bees as large as a water bucket.

A colony of bees from the row of hives in the garden near by had evidently swarmed and settled in the tree. Deaf old grandsir—the only one at home that Sunday morning—had discovered them and was out drumming. According to the tradition of the time, the noise would drown the note of the queen bee and prevent the swarm from taking flight to the woods. Grandsir Wells had been out there drumming for half an hour or more and Zinky, in his wanderings about the neighborhood, had seen him and had come over to the meetinghouse with some vague idea in his head of getting help.

"Now, what can we do?" exclaimed Addison, with a glance at the black buzzing mass. "Egyptian bees, too, by the color of them!"

We knew Egyptian bees, for some time before the Old Squire had bought a swarm of them. They are savage insects and have wickedly long stings.

As soon as grandsir Wells turned and saw us, he shouted. "Help me hive 'em!" Then he hobbled indoors and brought out a new hive and a saw; he made a second trip for salt and water, with which to rinse out the hive. Addison gave Zinky the pan and told him to drum while we ran to the barn for a long ladder. Numbers of bees were darting to and fro, and before we got back an Egyptian stung Zinky's ear. Dropping the pan, the boy fled, howling, in the direction of the "farm."

Before we could climb up to saw off the limb, the swarm began to take flight, and to the tune of a deep, solemn humming moved off across a cornfield beyond the road.

At first the bees flew thirty or forty feet in the air, but they gradually settled to within nine or ten feet of the ground. They resembled nothing so much as an immense train of trailing black lace floating across the field.

Grandsir Wells kept crying in his cracked voice, "Stop 'em! Stop 'em! Drum! Drum!"

We gave chase across the cornfield. While I banged on the pan, Addison pulled off his duster. So slowly did the winged cloud move on that we easily outstripped it. The bees were so near the ground, too, that Addison could swing his duster up among them as he ran. Every bee appeared to be flying in little zigzags.

At the farther side of the cornfield we climbed a stone wall and entered a horse pasture that sloped toward woodland along a boggy brook. Grandsir Wells stopped on the other side of the wall. We guessed now that the bees were heading for some hollow tree in the woods that their scouts and spies had already selected.

So we redoubled our efforts to confuse them, for we knew that if we could knock down or capture the queen bee, the swarm, not hearing her call, would alight or turn back.

By a lucky upward throw of his duster, crumpled into a wad, Addison succeeded in bringing down into the grass almost as many bees as would fill a pint measure and among them, to our delight, was the queen. We recognized her immediately by her large size, and Addison quickly threw his hat over her. That would put an end to the swarming.

Meanwhile a new source of trouble had appeared. In the pasture were five or six colts that had been turned out for the season—the Morgan colts of the Wells farm—beautiful creatures and great pets of the family. Seeing us with the pan and thinking that we had salt or provender for them, they all came racing to meet us. Apparently they did not see or notice the bees, for they ran directly under the swarm and circled round us. While Addison was securing the queen, I tried to drive the colts away, but they persisted in circling round us. Suddenly an ugly buzz took the place of the previous soft, sibilant hum of the bees; the long, trailing swarm bunched up, rolling round like a cloud of black smoke. Perhaps it was the smell of the colts or the sight of them running about that infuriated the bees. At any rate, they settled on the animals and began to sting them vengefully. The colts set up a frightful squealing, kicking and snorting.

On the ground we were making a little bag of Addison's pocket handkerchief and trying to get the queen into it; both of us were stung two or three times, but finally we made off on hands and knees with the royal captive buzzing in the handkerchief. The bees followed us until at last we crept into a plot of brakes and, muffling the queen's buzzing with Addison's duster, lay still.

Not until then did we have time to see what was happening to the colts. The poor beasts, surrounded by clouds of bees, were galloping wildly round the pasture. At last one of them, a glossy, dark-brown three-year-old, jumped the high fence at the lower side of the pasture and disappeared into the woods. Two others jumped out on the side nearest the barns; the other three, squealing and snorting, coursed madly round and round the enclosing fence.

Most of the bees had now left us, and so we crawled to the wall and made our way to the house. There we put the queen into a bottle and tied a piece of thin cloth over the top of it. Then, at grandsir Wells's entreaty, we went back to catch the colts that had jumped the fence.

The cedar thickets below the pasture fence were humming with stray bees. Following the tracks of the colt that had first jumped the fence, we presently came upon the animal up to her sides in a bog near the brook. In trying to escape the bees she had mired herself and had at last given up her struggles to get out. She lay there, helpless, with numbers of bees still darting at her. All round her the bog was very soft; we hardly knew how to go about rescuing her. In such plight horses as well as cattle soon perish unless succored.

We thought at first of returning across the fields and pastures to the church to get help. But we remembered seeing the long rope of a horse fork in the Wells barn when we went there for the ladder; we also recollected that a yoke of working oxen had been standing at their stanchions in the barn. Addison thought that we might pass the rope round the colt's body and have the oxen haul her out.

Accordingly, we hastened back and, with grandsir Wells's help, yoked the oxen. Then, taking the rope we returned to the swamp. The old man, so greatly excited now that he shook like a leaf, hobbled after us and kept calling out advice that hampered us more than it helped us. Those irate Egyptians, too, still bothered us—they stung grandsir badly; if the oxen had not been steady, we could not have brought them near the place.

To pass the rope under the colt's body, in such a manner as not to injure her seriously when the oxen pulled at it, proved the hardest task of all; the fact that we had to stand knee-deep in the mud added to the difficulties of the job, but at last we adjusted the rope satisfactorily. We had just started to haul the colt out when Amos Wells, grandsir's son, who with his family had been at church, came hastening down to the swamp and took charge of the rescue. By that time the Sunday service was over, and the people were returning home.

We recovered the other colts with less difficulty; all of them were badly stung—most painfully so, if they suffered as we did. On the way home Addison and I counted the places where we had been stung and pulled out several long black stings left in the wounds. He had eight large red wheals, one of which was on his cheek; and I had six, including one over my left eye, out of which I could now hardly see.

The family was at dinner when we got home.

"Why, boys, where on earth have you been?" the Old Squire asked us reproachfully.

I think that for a moment the old gentleman suspected that after quieting old Nance we had gone off fishing and had had trouble with other boys. Not only were our faces disfigured but our clothes were torn, and we were plastered from head to foot with mud. We hurried to give a full account of our adventures, and as our tale proceeded the Old Squire's face softened.

"Why, you poor boys!" he cried. "You did the best you could, and no one can do more than that, either on Sunday or on any other day."

But I have often thought since that we should have done better to let those Egyptians go to the woods, for although we captured their queen, she was never able to reassemble her scattered subjects.

As for Zinky, whenever we met him during the next year or so he would clap his hand to his ear and say, "Buzzy, buzzy, buzzy bee!"

30

Hulled Corn

HULLED CORN, FRIED, WITH MAPLE SYRUP ON IT, WAS a favorite dish with us young folks at the Old Squire's. At first we had hulled corn only once a year, near the last of March, when maple syrup was being made. That, indeed, had been the family custom for three generations.

About March 20, when "the sun crossed the line" and the snow was melting fast, the Old Squire would glance across the breakfast table to Grandmother and say, "Ruth, isn't it about time to hull corn? Some of this syrup would go pretty well on hulled corn."

And Grandmother would reply, "Not today, Joseph. I'm making soap today. But about day after tomorrow.

Ashes were always leached in a large tub of lye to make soap, and sometimes we used the last run of the lye from the leach tub for hulling corn. But we all thought that this last run of lye was not so good as fresh new lye from birch ashes, leached in a little firkin that held about a bushel. This firkin had holes bored in the bottom and was set on a broad clean board having a circular crease cut in it round the bottom of the firkin to conduct the lye to a little spout at the front, where an earthen pot was set to catch it.

First we put a wisp of clean rye straw in the firkin, then the ashes, and then poured in spring water. Soon the clear, rich-colored lye began to exude at the bottom and drip into the pot. Four quarts of the lye were then poured on a peck of dry, nicely winnowed yellow "Pine Knot" corn and the whole put to boil in a brass kettle for about two hours, or until the hull started and the hard outer glaze of the kernels was eaten away.

The peck of corn finally swelled to a bushel, and it had then to be rinsed and washed clean of the hulls and afterward boiled for several hours longer, until soft enough to dish out for eating, either in milk, or fried, with maple syrup, or cold with cream and sugar.

The process occupied the most of the March day and, added to the leaching of the ashes, occasioned so much work and care that once a year was as often as we could persuade Grandmother to embark upon it.

That bushel of hulled corn rarely lasted us for more than two or three days, and often Theodora or Ellen could be heard saying, "Isn't there any way, Grandmother, that we could hull more corn at a time and keep it a while?" And Grandmother always said, "No, child. It sours and spoils very soon as the days get warmer." Ice chests had not then come into use with us. That appeared to be the final word about hulled corn—a peck of corn once a year and no more.

Addison, however, was the one among us who was always questioning old methods and cogitating new ones. And one time he burst out with, "Grandmother, I believe I could keep that corn the year round!"

"Ad, that would be fine!" Ellen and Theodora both exclaimed. But Grandmother only laughed.

Addison sat thinking it over for some moments. "Well, Doad," he said, "if you and Nell will hull another peck of corn, I think I know a way to keep it to use just as we want it, all summer."

At first Grandmother objected to having the lye and kettles in her kitchen for another whole day, but the Old Squire said, "Let the boy try, Mother. Let him try."

We had a good deal of faith in Addison. The girls set to work and during the day hulled another peck of corn, which made four heaped-up panfuls. One of these was reserved for immediate consumption, and the remainder turned over to Addison.

He carried all three panfuls up to the long ell chamber. "Now don't come spying round me," he said to the rest of us. "I don't know that I can make it work yet, and I don't want spectators."

Thereupon he shut and bolted the door leading to the staircase.

This long, open chamber was where Grandmother had her loom and formerly wove bed blankets and rag carpets. At one end stood an old stove having what was called an "elevated oven," that is, the oven was raised over the stove, at about breast height. It had been the kitchen stove but had gone out of fashion and been put away up there. When she was weaving on a cold day, Grandmother was accustomed to kindle a fire in it.

Immediately we heard Addison building a fire in that "elevated-oven" stove. Soon he made his appearance to borrow bake-sheets and tin plates from the kitchen. What he could possibly be doing with that hulled corn was more than we could guess; but we left him in peace, and he was up there, coming and going, all that day and the following evening.

At the breakfast table the next morning, however, he displayed a sample of his preserved hulled corn. It was dry as a bone and shrunken back to the size of the kernels of dry corn before hulling.

"What have you done to it, Ad ?" Theodora exclaimed. "Have you baked it?"

"No, merely dried it," he said, "just as you would dry sliced apple for winter use. I kept a slow fire and dried it. That corn can be put away now in boxes, or done up in packages. It will keep as long as you want it."

"But how is anyone to eat that dried stuff?" Grandmother demanded.

"Why, soak it out," said Ad. "When you want hulled corn for breakfast, put it in to soak overnight, just as you do beans for baking."

"I don't believe it would be good!" said Grandmother; and we all had doubts as to that.

But Addison argued that as nothing but water had been taken out of it, the flavor and goodness must be in it still and would reappear when the water was put back.

He poured hot water over a pint of it, covered it, and set it away, and at noon, lo! there were nearly two quarts of hulled corn that was as good as before it had been dried. No difference could be discerned in the flavor.

The Old Squire patted Addison on the shoulder. "Well done, my boy, well done!" he exclaimed. "You've solved the hulled corn question." And even Grandmother admitted that it might prove a good thing.

As the lye was still running, she and the girls set to work again and hulled fully half a bushel of corn, which Addison dried the next day. It was put away in the pantry and used occasionally all summer; but we had several quarts of it left over that autumn after we began attending school at the academy in the village, seven miles from the farm.

In fair weather we boarded at home, but when it was stormy, or there were evening lyceums, we often remained overnight in the village and boarded ourselves at an unoccupied house that the Old Squire owned there. At such times we took most of our edibles with us from home, and the girls got our meals.

While grubbing about in the pantry at home for food to take with us one morning, Ellen and Theodora came upon that dried hulled corn and appropriated three quarts of it, with a bottle of syrup, for every spring we were accustomed to put up a number of gallons of maple syrup in two-quart bottles, for use through the season.

The next morning at the village we had some of that hulled corn, fried, for breakfast. There were then nearly a hundred students at the academy, many of them living at a distance away. Not a few of these latter merely hired a room in the village and boarded themselves, for economy's sake. Not infrequently some of them dropped in to take breakfast with us, when their own supplies were running low.

That morning one of our classmates, named Anson Coburn, presented himself. "Just a cup of coffee," he said.

But Theodora gave him a generous plateful of the fried corn, and Addison bade him try the syrup on it.

"My!" Anson exclaimed. "But this is good! Does it cost anything?"

"Oh, no!" said Theodora, laughing.

Anson ate two platefuls. He also spread the news, and on the following morning there were five in for breakfast besides Anson. The supply that the girls had prepared ran so short that we had but one small plateful apiece.

Our callers smacked their lips. "Only one drawback 'bout this," Anson remarked. "There's not enough of it! Go home and get some more!"

"Yes, go home and get some more!" they all shouted uproariously.

Friday night, after we drove home, Addison put ashes to leach, and during the day, Saturday, the girls hulled a peck of corn. We took it with us the next time we remained over at the village, and as a consequence had seven of our fellow students in to breakfast the next morning! In fact, that peck of corn lasted but two mornings, for there were fourteen there the next morning!

When the last kernel had disappeared, they all joined hands round the table and improvised a song, the chorus of which was, "Go home and get some more."

Anson, however, mounted a chair. "This will never do!" he shouted. "We are eating these people out of house and home!"

To be frank, we were beginning to feel a little that way about it ourselves.

"Now listen," continued Anson. "Whoever comes pushing in here to breakfast after this pays for it—hey?"

"That's so!" they all said, and four or five cried, "Why not sell us some corn and syrup every morning! We will pay ten cents a quart for the corn."

Accordingly, the following Friday night and Saturday we hulled half a bushel of corn. The Old Squire had recently purchased what was called an "evaporator," then a new invention for drying apples. This time Addison used the evaporator for drying the hulled corn. It worked like a charm for that purpose—and this was the beginning of quite a little industry for us at the village, both that fall and during the terms of the year following.

The students who boarded in the village and families living near formed a habit of coming in to us in haste in the morning for a quart of hot hulled corn. Often we dealt out twenty quarts of corn in a single morning. I do not now remember how much it netted us, but it was a considerable sum, which came in very opportunely for the purchase of textbooks and other school expenses.

There were good profits in hulled corn at ten cents a quart. One bushel of dry corn, worth a dollar, will make four bushels of hulled corn, so greatly does it swell during the process, and one hundred and twenty-eight quarts of hulled corn, at ten cents, makes twelve dollars and eighty cents.

Ellen and Theodora were wont to furnish it to our fellow students all hot from the frying pan at just seven o'clock in the morning. Half a dozen of them at once would often come running in, joking and laughing, each with his or her little pail or jar, so as to carry it home hot. It never occurred to Addison, or to any of us, to make commercial use of his process for drying hulled corn.

A fine opportunity for profit was thereby lost. But less than two years ago, a Maine dealer in hulled corn adopted this self-same process, and is now reported to be making a fortune from evaporating hulled corn and selling it in pound packages like the cereal foods.

31

Treading Down the Herd's-Grass

IT WAS IN HAYING TIME, AND THE WEATHER WAS SO fair that we had mowed all the grass in the "south field." We had doubts about cutting down so much, for there were only three of us to take care of it, but the weather had cleared off bright and windy that morning, after a thundershower in the night.

"There are pretty sure to be three or four days of good, hard weather now," said Addison, or "Ad," as we called him. "Let's down with it!"

And we did. There were six acres of it, all stout grass, following clover the summer before; two tons and a half to the acre of long-stalked herd's grass, which, when dry and ready to go into the barn, is about as stiff and hard to pitch and handle, as so much wire. Any country boy who has ever "mowed away" knows what such grass is when it is pitched off the cart to him in big forkfuls.

The sun shone hot all that first day, and heavy as the grass was, it "made" well. We raked it into windrows with the horse-rake during the afternoon. The Old Squire was up Lurvey's Stream, in the Great Woods, "cruising" certain lots he owned for pine and spruce to lumber that coming winter, and Addison and I had the haying to do, with the assistance of our hired man, Asa Doane.

The next morning, as soon as the dew was off, we turned the windrows. There were about twenty rack loads of the hay. We planned to haul in ten loads that second day and ten the next.

Seven or eight tons of hay, as everyone knows, are about as much as three men ought to handle in one afternoon. It has all to be pitched over twice with fork and trodden down in the haymow; and this latter part of the work, in the case of coarse herd's-grass, is the worst, for the tramping has to be done in a hot, close barn, amid choking dust.

Until noon the second day, when we began hauling, the weather was fair, but immediately after twelve o'clock, a change was apparent. A gray haze appeared in the south, soon followed by small shreds of clouds, which increased in size. In Maine we knew those signs only too well during the warm season. Such southern rains come on suddenly.

"It will rain by five o'clock," said Addison. "And all this hay out! What's to be done?"

The only thing we could do was to swallow a hasty luncheon and begin hauling as fast as possible.

We sent word of our plight to our next neighbors, the Edwardses, and as they had finished their haying a day or two previously, they kindly sent over their two hired men, with hayrack and ox team, to help us.

We had been saving what we called the "west bay" of the barn in which to put this herd's-grass. The usual cross girders had been taken out of this bay, making one long haymow of it, fifty feet by twenty, and we knew that the crop in the south field would fill it to the "great beams" of the barn, eighteen or twenty feet above the barn floor.

When we drove in with the first load, the hired man started to pitch it off into the bay, and I undertook to stow it. Addison had remained out in the field to roll the windrows up into "tumbles," ready to be pitched upon the cart as soon as it returned from the barn.

Asa Doane was a large, strong fellow. At every forkful he flung off about half a hundred weight of that coarse, snarled hay, and I soon found that I was going to have quite as much work as I could manage, for I had to pull the hay back into the long, deep bay, tread it down in the dust and heat, and return to the front in time to take the next tough, snarly forkfuls as they came rolling down off the cart. I could not do it; no one could. My weight, indeed, was not sufficient to tread the coarse stuff down.

This first load was no sooner pitched off and the cart backed out than in drove the Edwards rack, piled high with another load. One of the men with this team had remained in the field, rolling up tumbles;

the driver was ready to throw off the hay, and they all seemed to think that I could take care of it.

Finding myself worsted, I ran into the house to see if I could not get some of the women to help me tread the hay down, but they had all gone raspberrying.

As I ran back to the barn, however, I happened to see in the lane two three-year-old colts that we were pasturing for "Uncle" Billy Murch. They were handsome brown Morgan colts, of which the old gentleman was very fond, for they were well matched, and he expected to exhibit them as a trotting pair at the state fair. He was over nearly every day looking at his pets, giving them salt or tidbits, and seeing to it that we kept the watering trough in the lane pumped full of water. He also made us put brass balls on the horns of all the young cattle, for fear they would hook those colts.

It came into my mind that I might make them tread that hay down in the mow. My need of aid was pressing. I ran out to the lane and called the colts through the yard into the barn, then led them across the barn floor and urged them into the mow. The hay was up just about level with the barn floor when I drove them in, and I put up a board to keep them from coming out. The Edwards load was half off by this time; but I pulled a part of it back, and then, snapping a horse whip in the air, I ran those colts up and down the mow. They were fine, plump, heavy colts, and the way they tramped that herd's-grass was a joy to behold.

The Edwards cart had no sooner backed out of the barn floor than in came our cart with its second load. Addison had loaded it hastily, for the sky was darkening.

"Pitch it off! Roll it off!" I exclaimed to Asa Doane. "I'll take care of it! I'll stow it now as fast as all of you can bring it to me!"

I would wait till I had half a rack load of it rolled back and distributed about a little; then I would get up on the front girders to snap the horse whip and send those colts back and forth, from one end of the long bay to the other. Eight feet are much better than two for treading down hay, and the difference between a hundred and forty pounds of boy and sixteen hundred pounds of colt was at once apparent. It was a great scheme!

Meanwhile the loads came in hurry and haste. One was no sooner pitched off to me than another was ready. We were all working as swiftly as possible. But while throwing off the eighth load, Asa Doane suddenly stopped, leaned on his fork, and began to laugh.

"Say," he drawled, "I s'pose you see that this haymow is filling up pretty fast. It is up to the front beams now. 'Tain't any of my business, but how are you goin' to git the colts down oft'n the mow?"

In the heat and hurry of the emergency I had not thought of that, and they were being elevated higher and higher with every load. In fact, they were up nine or ten feet above the barn floor already, too high for them to jump down without breaking their legs.

Asa Doane stood and laughed. "Those colts'll be up in the roof of the barn when this field of hay is in," he said.

When he drove out to the field he told Addison of the fix I was getting into with the colts, and Ad came running in to see about it.

"That's a pretty go!" he exclaimed. "What will Uncle Billy say? I don't think you ought to have taken those colts for such a job. The dust is making them cough."

"Well, they might just as well be on the great beams as where they are," said I. "Now that they are up here I am going to keep them at it till this hay is in."

"There'll be the mischief to pay if Uncle Billy finds it out!" replied Addison. He hurried back to the field, however, for the cart was waiting.

I felt not a little anxious about the situation, but the loads were coming thick and fast. As I could not get the colts down, I kept them treading and getting higher with every load. The rain did not begin until nearly five o'clock, and we hauled in eighteen big loads of that herd's-grass; there were only about two loads that became too wet to get in.

But those eighteen loads had filled that haymow quite up to the great beams of the barn. As Asa Doane had anticipated, the colts were up in the top of that high barn, with hardly room to stand under the roof. Truth to say, too, they were hot and sweaty.

The men from Mr. Edwards's went off home, laughing over it; and as for Addison and me, the more we studied the problem of getting the colts down, the more difficult it looked. We set a long ladder and car-ried up two buckets of water to them, and let them stand in the hay and eat what they wanted. In fact, we were tired out with our hard after-noon's chore, and there were the cows to milk and all the barn chores to do. It was Saturday night, and Asa Doane's night off.

While we were milking we heard Uncle Billy calling the colts. It was now raining hard, and he had come over to see that they had opportunity to get under the barnyard sheds.

"Just what shall we tell him?" said Addison anxiously.

Of course I ought to have gone and confessed. I knew it, but I did not want to have him find out what I had done. It disturbed me a good deal to hear the old gentleman out in the rain calling, "Nobby, Nobby, Nobby!" and "Co-jack, Co-jack, Co-jack!" up and down the pasture; but I kept quiet, and when at last he came back to the barn and looked for us boys, to ask about the colts, Addison and I kept out of sight.

Uncle Billy at last decided that they must have taken shelter in the woods at the far side of the pasture, as they sometimes did, and although still somewhat disappointed by their non-appearance, he went home without making any further search.

Day had no sooner broken the next morning than Addison and I were at the barn. We knew that we must get those colts down in some way even if it were Sunday. It was really work of necessity, but how to manage it and not injure the animals was something of a problem.

We went quietly to Mr. Edwards's, called out his two hired men, and held a conference. We hit upon a scheme, and to carry it out we were obliged to go to a sawmill half a mile distant and bring four sticks of timber, two by eight inches, and each twenty-four feet in length.

These we set up aslant, close together, reaching from the barn floor to the top of the haymow and forming a kind of chute. Taking halters and bits of rope, three of us then climbed on the mow and, by pushing against their sides suddenly as they stood in the snarly hay, threw down first one, then the other of the colts, and tied their legs securely, to pre-vent them from struggling. Then we dragged them forward to the top of the chute.

While we were thus employed, Addison had gone to bring the long, large rope from a set of pulley blocks, and also an old buffalo skin. Having wrapped the skin round one of the colts to prevent injury to its sides, we then let the animal slide down the chute, steadying it with the large rope passed round its body.

We were fortunate enough to get both of them down without accident, and we then untied their legs and turned them out.

The colts were in the pasture, feeding as if nothing had happened, when Uncle Billy came at eight o'clock. He looked them all over but could not find a scratch or a mark on either of them. They did cough a little for several days afterward, but he did not chance to hear or notice that.

That winter, however, in December, when the Old Squire began to take the hay out of the mow, he had some difficulty. Addison and I were away from home at the time, teaching district schools several miles away, but he wrote to us:

"I should like to know how you two boys stowed that herd's-grass hay last summer and what you did to it; you must have used a pile driver. No living man can pitch it out with a hand-fork. I have sent for a grip-fork, and I want you both to come home Saturday and help me pull out two or three tons of it with a tackle and block."

32

Addo's Queer Courtship

AT THE COUNTY FAIR THAT WAS HELD EVERY FALL near our old homestead in Maine, many prizes were offered for the best farm products. Among the awards were a first and a second prize for the best bread baked by any girl in the county under eighteen years of age.

Any kind of wheat bread was admissible, but most of the loaves entered for the prize were yeast bread. The managers of the fair appointed three judges—two men and a woman who was usually a housewife of wide experience. The men had merely to say which loaf tasted the best. They sat at a table in the committee room, cut and buttered slices of the bread, and then tasted them judicially.

The competition attracted considerable attention, and people gathered round the table to see what went on. It was a good-natured and often merry competition. Frequently some of the bystanders stepped up and asked to taste this or that loaf, the appearance of which they especially liked. Some liked one, some another loaf best. But the judges held to their own decisions. They took into account the lightness, the whiteness, and the degree of sweetness; whether the bread had risen too much or too little; whether it was baked too long or not enough.

On the whole, the judges' decisions were usually regarded as fair and just. My cousins Theodora and Ellen competed two or three times, and once Ellen won the second prize. One of our young neighbors, Georgie Wilbur, won the first prize two years in succession; the third time she competed she got the second prize. Some said that even that time the judges considered her bread as the best, but that they feared to give her the first prize three times in succession, because it might discourage the other girls and lead them to give up.

Georgie had won all her successes not with ordinary hop-yeast bread, but with that peculiar kind variously known as salt-rising bread, "patent" bread, or milk-yeast bread. At the Old Squire's we called it "mug-bread," because Grandmother Ruth always set the bread to rise overnight in a large mug.

Georgie Wilbur would probably have continued indefinitely to capture bread prizes at the fair, but her eighteenth birthday fell a few months after she had received her third award, and that of course excluded her from competing anymore. But Georgie's third and last contest was a memorable one for her.

Among the young fellows who gathered jocosely about the judges' table when they tasted the bread was a boy named Adoniram Dudley— Addo, his friends called him. He was the son of a lumber man and mill owner in one of the northern townships of the county. It was the first time that he had attended the fair. With three young friends he had come to see the sights and to have a good time, and the little group of them had drifted in to see the loaves of bread sampled and to hear the names of the prize winners. He was a tall, healthy, resolute-looking boy—plainly not one of the diffident sort. Seeing several young men step up to taste the bread, Addo approached the table and asked whether he might do so. "Certainly," one of the judges replied, and a woman standing by the table smilingly asked the boy which loaf he wished to taste.

Addo glanced at them critically. "Well, that's the best-looking loaf," he said, pointing to one of the loaves that Georgie Wilbur had brought. "It looks to me the lightest and the whitest. I'd like to taste of that if you please."

"You shall," replied the woman, and cutting a slice, she spread it liberally with butter and handed it to him.

Addo viewed it approvingly, and without more ado proceeded to show what bread is made for. Meanwhile, several of the competing girls (Georgie among them), who were grouped on a settee farther back in the room, nudged one another expectantly and pricked up their ears to hear what this young stranger would say next.

No doubt the morsel was toothsome, and very likely Addo was hungry.

"Well, that's good!" he cried emphatically to the woman who had served him. "That's tiptop. That's better than Mother makes."

"I'm glad you like it," the woman said, smiling at his enthusiasm.

"That's the best bread I ever ate!" Addo exclaimed. "If ever I get married, I hope my wife will make bread like that."

The girls snickered audibly, and the woman said jokingly, "Perhaps, then, you would like to see the girl who made this?"

"Yes, I should!" cried Addo.

"Well, there she sits!" exclaimed the woman, laughing heartily, and to Georgie's consternation pointed her out to him. By that time the judges and everyone else near the table were smiling broadly. They thought that the young man had got himself into an awkward situation and that he would probably beat a hasty retreat. Not he! After one good straight look at Georgie, he pushed through the crowd to where she sat and, to the hilarious surprise of everyone, exclaimed, "Say, I'd like to marry you!"

Poor Georgie! She was dreadfully embarrassed, and angry, too.

"Go away!" she cried desperately.

One of Addo's friends now tried to pull him away, but he resisted.

"Oh, I'm in earnest! I mean it!" he cried, still facing the much-flustered girl.

By this time Georgie was on her feet, anxious to escape. "You must be crazy!" she cried. "Why, you great blockhead, I don't even know you! Go away, I tell you!"

But Addo, looking at her with entire frankness, stood his ground. Everyone was tremendously amused—everyone except Georgie, who, with two or three of the other girls, now managed to make her way from the room. Afraid that this "loony," as she called him, could follow her, she immediately left the fairgrounds and waited outside until her parents came out to drive home.

Naturally, the young people in the neighborhood had plenty of fun with Georgie about Addo. But she refused to see any humor in the incident.

"Just because he liked that bread, to come and propose such a thing as that!" she exclaimed indignantly to the other girls. "He must be a pig!"

She had not seen the last of Addo! Less than a week later he drove into the yard of the Wilbur farmhouse. Georgie saw him through the window and would not answer his knock. Her mother went to the door at last and, when he asked for Georgie, told him that her daughter did not care to see him.

He looked very much disappointed, stood there awhile, and then asked hesitatingly whether Georgie were "keeping company" with anyone else.

"Why, no, I don't think so," Mrs. Wilbur replied, for she rather liked Addo's looks. "But you don't seem to know that girls are not pleased to have such pointed attentions paid to them in public—by strangers."

"I suppose that is so," Addo said thoughtfully. "I wish you would tell her I am sorry I plagued her—and that I will call again," he added as he went away.

After that, Georgie lived in a state of alarm lest Addo should appear again. She entreated Theodora and Ellen to be on the watch for him and to bring her word if they saw him in the neighborhood.

About a fortnight later Addo drove up to the Wilburs' in a sleigh, for by this time snow had fallen. Georgie's sister, Elsie, went to the door. Addo asked whether Georgie were at home and said that he had come to ask her to take a sleigh ride.

"Well, I'll call her," replied Elsie, who was something of a rogue. "Come in, please. She's in the kitchen. I'll tell her you're here."

Addo, smiling hopefully, followed her indoors and took a seat. He was quite unprepared for the storm that burst about his ears when Elsie delivered his message. For Georgie, after giving her sister a shaking, rushed angrily into the sitting room.

"You here again?" she cried. "You—you bread eater! Can't you take a hint? Must you have the dogs set on you before you will keep away?"

Addo backed slowly to the outer door. "I—I didn't know you were so riled," was all he said, and backed all the way out of the house.

Pink with vexation, Georgie ran back to the kitchen and, hastily wrapping up a loaf of their bread, told Elsie to take it out to Addo, who was turning his horse. She meant it to be, not a present, but a parting insult.

"Tell him I sent him that!" she exclaimed. "Bread is what he wants. Tell him that is bread. Tell him to take it and go!"

Elsie garbled the message shamelessly. "Here's a present from my sister," she said, as she handed the loaf of bread to Addo. "She hopes you will like it."

Addo, considerably bewildered, took the package and drove off. I do not know how he explained the present in his own mind. His mother afterward declared that it was his first experience as a suitor; perhaps he imagined that all girls behaved in that way and that his rebuffs were such as anyone might expect.

He carried the loaf of bread home and showed it to his mother, who also misunderstood the real meaning of the gift. They ate the bread and agreed that it was the best that ever was baked—and a hopeful indication of the young lady's real sentiments. As a result when Addo drove to the Wilburs' again, less than two weeks later, he brought his mother with him.

Mrs. Wilbur, who had been trying to play the difficult part of a benevolent neutral, went to the door and after some conversation with Mrs. Dudley invited them in, although Georgie from the background was making frantic signs of protest. Finding that the visitors were really coming in, Georgie scurried upstairs, then down a flight of back stairs, and fled across the fields to the Old Squire's, where she stayed until she was sure that the Dudleys had gone.

Meanwhile, Mrs. Wilbur had been very much attracted to her callers. Mrs. Dudley proved to be a kind, motherly person who talked a great deal about her son; and Addo, in spite of his lack of tact in wooing, was apparently a fine young man.

When Georgie returned home that evening, Elsie said to her mischievously, "Since you don't want Addo, I guess I'll try to catch him myself—if you will make some more bread. I think Addo is a pretty good sort—even if he does like bread! At any rate, I'd rather have him like bread than whiskey or tobacco."

"You're welcome to him if you want him!" Georgie retorted hotly. "But you'll have to make your own bread to catch him with."

Addo's visits to the Wilburs' continued for a year or more, and it became evident that he would not let himself be "caught" by anyone except Georgie. As time passed, Georgie obviously got to like him better, for early that next winter we saw them drive past the old farm in a sleigh together. That Georgie's liking for him grew rapidly is shown by the fact that in the following fall—just two years from the time when Addo had made his impetuous proposal at the county fair—there was a wedding at the Wilburs'.

It has proved to be a very happy marriage. Addo has made a fine husband, whose chief care has been to make Georgie's new home a pleasant one. Elsie says that he seems never to have got over blaming himself for the blunder he made in proposing marriage so precipitately and so publicly, and that he has been trying hard to make it up to Georgie ever since.

33

Halstead's Saga

Halstead Disappears

YSABEL MARIA PILAR DE CARANZA—MY COUSIN Halstead's mother—was the daughter of a Spanish merchant at Matanzas. Her mother was a Creole from Vera Cruz, in Mexico. The circumstances of her marrying Uncle Coville—Halstead's father— were peculiar.

Away back in 1850, at the age of twenty-four, Uncle Coville was captain of a schooner in which the Old Squire had helped him buy an interest, and made voyages from Portland to Cuban ports with hogshead shook, bringing back molasses, brown sugar, and tobacco. I never saw him, but he was said to have been a lively, attractive young fellow, energetic, handsome, prone to jokes and to singing sea songs, and a good dancer. Often he was a guest of Señor José de Caranza at Matanzas, and the result was that the Señorita Ysabel, then scarcely more than sixteen, fell violently in love with him, and on the evening of the sailing of the schooner she left home clandestinely to join him.

Uncle Coville told the Old Squire afterward that he had never had a thought of marrying her and had merely paid her the attentions in her father's house that a guest might be expected to pay. He was as much astonished as anyone and a good deal upset when the girl came aboard, flung her arms round his neck, and begged to go with him. She was beautiful, impetuous, and wildly affectionate. Suddenly, rashly, Uncle Coville resolved to let her come away with him and to marry her, and they were married by a justice of the peace as soon as the schooner reached Portland.

Uncle Coville's lifelong troubles began then and there. His young wife proved a creature of ungoverned impulses, emotions, and imprudences. There was no predicting what she would do if the freak or impulse seized her. They lived in Portland for a year. Uncle Coville brought our Aunt Ysabel home to the old farm but once. Later they went to live in New Orleans.

In justice to Uncle Coville it should be said that he stood by his wife, thus imprudently acquired, with steady loyalty, to the end. He accepted the consequences of his error and never complained, even to his own family.

In the spring of 1860, while Uncle Coville was away on a voyage, Aunt Ysabel left little George Halstead to be cared for in a Creole family where they had lived and went home to her people at Matanzas. Uncle Coville made no effort to have her return; he wrote to his parents that Ysabel had come to him of her own accord and that if she wished to leave him she could do so without let or hindrance on his part. Two years later she died during the cholera epidemic at Matanzas.

At the outbreak of the Civil War, Uncle Coville sold his schooner to be used as a mortar vessel for the reduction of the forts below New Orleans. A few weeks later he brought little George Halstead home to the old farm, preliminary to enlisting himself in the naval service of the government. That was the last time he ever came home. He lost his life in the naval battle at Mobile Bay on August 5, 1864.

The spring of 1869 was a backward spring. Snowdrifts not half melted away lay in the lee of the fences and stone walls. People still went out with sleighs and sleds along the icy roads. For several days the mornings had been very sharp, with the snow hard-crusted, yet broad bare spots were beginning to show in the fields and pastures. On a certain Sunday morning the sky looked mellow and mild; even before we were up we heard a robin chanting loud and clear in the balm of Gileads and two bluebirds chirping cheerily about their old nest box on a high post of the garden fence.

Addison and I had been doing the barn chores alone that morning, wondering a little and somewhat resentful because Halstead had not made his appearance to help us. On a Sunday morning, and sometimes on other mornings, he was prone to sleep over, purposely we thought. For several years he had roomed alone. Neither Addison nor I quite liked to room with him; he often talked and jabbered in his sleep and sometimes sprang up, sleepwalking.

Theodora had been out to hear the robin, watch the bluebirds, and have a run on the snow crust from one bare spot to another. She came in with cheeks aglow, just as we sat down to breakfast. "Oh, those dear little bluebirds! You ought to see them!" she cried. "They are so happy round their box. They are peeping at the hole, looking their house over, to see how it had stood the winter. I'm so glad it's spring again!

"But, oh, boys! You should hear the bees inside the hives out there under their shed," she continued. "They are roaring; they want so to get out! First, all will be as still as can be; then one bee will begin to buzz, then another, and then they all take it up together, till the whole hive roars! You can almost see it shake, they buzz so hard! Then another hive will begin, then another, along the whole row of hives. I guess they hear each other and are responding."

"That's because they smell the honey sap in the maple tops over the sugar lot," said Addison.

"What, away over in the Aunt Hannah Lot?" cried Ellen, laughing. "Do you believe, Ad, that a bee can smell so far?"

"Yes, I do," rejoined Addison. "A bee can smell sweets a mile off— and there are tons of that honey sap now, in all the maple woods of New England."

I remember looking at Addison in surprise, when he said "tons," but I now know that he was not far wrong. The sharp cold snaps of our Northern winters open millions of tiny cracks in the bark of innumerable sugar maple twigs. From these the sap slowly exudes, when spring comes, and soon there will be distilled a tiny drop of nectar, which bees dearly love, since it is the purest of maple syrup. Sometimes there was such quantity of honey sap in the big old rock maples of the Aunt Hannah Lot that we boys climbed the trees and scraped it off the limbs. Bees eagerly seek such tree tops. Often of a warm spring afternoon I have heard the maples hum with bees, like apple trees in full bloom.

Theodora turned to the Old Squire. "Couldn't we let the bees out a little while this morning?" she pleaded. "They've been shut up all winter, poor things—and they don't know it's Sunday."

"Perhaps," he said, smiling. "If it gets warmer and the wind doesn't change. But it's risky for them while there is so much snow on the ground and that long drift is in front of the bee house. They'd get tired flying home from the lot, and if they settle on snow they chill and perish almost instantly."

"Couldn't we cover over the snowdrift with dry boards," said Theodora, "so that if the poor tired bees light there they can crawl on into their hives!"

"That wouldn't be a bad plan," said the Old Squire. "We will let out two hives, by and by. After you get the chores done, boys, you may fetch some of those smooth, planed boards from the wagon house loft and lay them close together over that drift before the bee house. It will not be much work and may prove merciful to the bees, when we will let them out."

"Halse might help fetch those boards down," I said to Addison.

"That's so," exclaimed Addison. "It is time he was up and had his breakfast like other folks. Nell, run up to sleepyhead's door and rouse him."

"Maybe he isn't well this morning," interposed Theodora.

"He was well enough last night," I said. "He was tearing round in his room till long after eleven o'clock."

Thereupon Ellen went up to Halse's door. She too wanted him to get up and eat his breakfast and be out of the way, so that she could clear the table and wash the dishes.

She came hastily back downstairs just as Addison and I were going out. "Halse isn't there," she said. "He has got up and gone somewhere."

"What, gone off without his breakfast?" Grandmother said in surprise. "Why, he hasn't had his breakfast yet!"

Addison glanced toward the Old Squire but went out to the stable without saying anything, and I followed him.

A good many difficulties had arisen of late between us and Halstead, things we did not like to speak of to the Old Squire or Grand-mother, or even to the girls. All the time we were working up the year's fuel—the stove wood and fireplace wood—in the kitchen yard, Hal-stead had been in one of his bad moods, indulging in a great deal of wild talk about what he would or wouldn't do. Addison and I paid little attention to it. Halstead had an idea that he was terribly hard-worked, that he had always done more than his part at the Old Squire's, and that he ought to be paid wages, by the month. He had been harping on that strain for weeks, till we were so out of patience with him that one day, as we were splitting stove wood, Addison told him what he thought about it.

"Halse," he said, "you have never half earned your board and clothes here. You have been more trouble and expense to the old folks than all you've done was worth—twice over!"

How angry Halstead was, and how he ran on! Yet it is not worth-while to repeat what an angry boy said or what he threatened to do. We merely laughed. Time and again we had heard him go on in just that way. He was in one of his "bad fits." Generally after such a scene he would have a "good fit" and do pretty well for perhaps a month.

At the stable Addison and I went on doing the morning chores for some time and were feeding and watering the horses when Theodora came out.

She had been crying. "Oh boys!" she exclaimed. "I'm afraid Hal-stead has run away!"

Addison went on dipping out corn into the provender boxes. "It would not surprise me much," he said. "Halstead is getting to be a bad boy, and it's a shame after all the folks have done for him!"

"No, he isn't really bad," Theodora lamented. "It's just sensitivity and rattle-headedness that make him so unsteady."

"Rattle-headedness, my foot!" exclaimed Addison impatiently. "Head rattling is what he needs!"

Theodora tried faintly to apologize for Halstead. "You know he thought he had worked very hard and done more than his part, and that wages were due him," she reminded us—at which Addison and I merely snorted our indignation.

We finished the chores and went back into the house. The break-

fast table stood as we had left it. The Old Squire and Grandmother had been upstairs to have a look at Halstead's empty room and see what clothes he had gone away in. Not only his best suit was gone, but many of his other clothes. He had had a valise in his room, and it was not to be found.

The Old Squire then bethought himself to look in a desk in the sitting room where he kept a pocketbook containing money for the family expenses. Breathlessly we watched him unstrap it and count the money. Grandmother too sprang to her feet and approached him.

For a moment the Old Squire stood thoughtful, reflecting on the money I suppose, so as to be sure, then counted it again and drew a long breath. It seemed to me I had never seen him look so pale or so stern. But all he said was, "There are thirty dollars gone."

Grandmother dropped back into her chair, quite unnerved. "I can't believe it!" she sobbed. "I can't believe he would do such a thing! I know he would never steal!" We were all badly upset.

Out of the pocketbook half a sheet of paper had dropped on which Halstead had written the following farewell notice:

"I ought to have as much as thirty dollars for my work, and I took it. It was only fair. Nobody need trouble about me. I have lived here as long as I want to, and I shall never come back."

When that was read, Grandmother's tears flowed afresh.

All the while Theodora was attempting, whenever she could get in a word, to explain and palliate what Halse had done, on account of his long-standing grievance as to the value of his work and his notion that he ought to be paid wages. "I am sure Halstead wouldn't really steal," she said, over and over. "He wouldn't take money anywhere else." This was probably true.

Theodora could not better matters much, but she did her best for the erring one. "Oh, I do wish we had all been more thoughtful and kinder to him!" she exclaimed, and that bore on Addison and me much harder than we liked to admit even to ourselves.

The bees were wholly forgotten; they no doubt went on roaring for release from their hives, but in the usually happy hive of our old farm-house there was now commotion that quite eclipsed that at the bee shed. Dinner and supper passed gloomily. Grandmother and the Old Squire scarcely spoke. We had never seen them so silent. Afterward, as night fell, they sat for some time in the sitting room with the door closed, but by and by they called us in. Hitherto they had never spoken to us of our Aunt Ysabel from Cuba. But now—as if they had agreed together that something ought to be told us—first Grandmother, then the Old Squire, spoke of her and related the facts I have already told.

Halstead Falls from Grace

HALSTEAD WAS "his mother's own boy" in disposition as well as in looks. He had the same small round head, the same restless, brilliant black eyes, and the same abundant, wavy black hair. There was a faint trace of swarthiness in his complexion. He might easily have passed for a Cuban boy or a rather handsome Mexican.

He could whistle, sing, and carol like a bird—when he felt like it. Melody was born in him. For our school studies, particularly arithmetic, he had no head whatever, and he couldn't climb, unless sleep-walking, ten feet from the ground on a ladder, or in an apple tree, without growing dizzy and perhaps tumbling down, but he could play on a violin or a jew's-harp without apparent effort.

One morning following Halstead's disappearance the Old Squire drove to the railway station and learned that the runaway had bought a ticket for Portland the previous day. He had been accompanied by a fellow named Harris, well-known to us as a worthless person.

The Old Squire went to Portland and was there for several days making inquiries, but could learn nothing.

Several rumors came to our ears as weeks passed, one that Halstead and Harris had gone to Biddeford, fifteen miles from Portland. Thither the Old Squire hastened, but Halstead was not to be found. In July he learned that a youth answering to his description had shipped from Portland on the schooner *Thomas Fessenden* for Galveston, Texas. In reply to a letter sent to that port, Skipper Ludlow of the *Fessenden* admitted that Halstead had gone with him but wrote that he had deserted immediately on reaching Galveston.

For a long time Theodora believed that he would come home. Grandmother too used to dream of him, occasionally, and then look for him for days afterward.

But two years passed without a word. Later we learned what his adventures had been.

Two months from the day Halstead disappeared from the Old Squire's he was toting bunches of shingles on his back through a mangrove swamp on the coast of Texas, somewhere near the mouth of the Trinity River.

He had gone to sea, just as we had heard, on the schooner *Thomas Fessenden*, then clearing for Galveston with a cargo of slates and grindstones. The *Fessenden* was a small schooner; Halstead was dreadfully seasick, but at first the skipper was not unkind to him and refrained from ordering him aloft when he saw how timid he was about climbing.

Hardships came, however, when—disappointed in a return cargo of hides from Galveston for Boston—Skipper Ludlow determined to fetch north two hundred thousand cypress shingles from the swamps of Trinity River. Carrying bunches of shingles through the swamp to the vessel was a fearful task, but there was still a worse one allotted to Halstead.

Nearly all the old hollow cypresses in the swamp contained colonies of bees that had accumulated honey for years. Skipper Ludlow conceived the idea of filling several empty hogsheads and barrels with it to be sold as strained honey in the North. A sailor was set to fell the bee trees, and as a change from toting shingles Halstead was ordered to muffle his head in a burlap sack and fetch honey aboard. The whole swamp was soon humming with enraged bees. Clouds of them followed the dripping honey buckets, as Halstead went to and fro, and eddied furiously above his head. Despite his best efforts at muffling himself, he was stung repeatedly, and either from this or from partaking too freely of honey he became strangely affected. His entire body became swollen. His head throbbed, his vision wavered, he grew fevered and fell off the logs on his trips, wasting honey to such an extent that the skipper disciplined him; and this, together with the heat, bees, and all, quite disordered his wits.

Toward noon of the fourth day he staggered off into the woods, beyond the shingle camp, wandering aimlessly for a time, then throwing himself down to die, as he thought. In fact, he was tired of life.

All the rest of that day he lay there. Twice he heard the skipper hallooing for him, but he felt little disposition to answer. Mosquitoes swarmed over his head and red ants bit him. But he was past caring for torments and lay there through the night, expecting soon to die and be out of his misery.

Probably he was not nearly so near dying as he imagined, for he not only was alive the next morning but found that he could lift his head, and he felt hungry. Presently at a distance he heard the strokes of mallets where the schooner's crew were riving shingles. For some time he lay debating with himself whether or not to go back to the camp; he had about concluded that this was the only course open to him when a long way off he heard a rooster crow.

That decided the question of going back. He couldn't be worse off, he thought; if there were settlers anywhere near, he determined to join them. The instinct to run away was always strong with Halstead. He left behind him his wages, no part of which had been paid.

Hobbling away through the forest, he came suddenly to a bend of the river and saw a Negro boy in a boat, fishing. Halstead had passed his childhood in New Orleans among Negroes, and he readily entered into conversation with him and shared his lunch. Learning that the boy lived at a place called Anahuac, a few miles distant, Halstead persuaded the young man to take him there in his boat. They were trailing a baited hook, however, and on the way suddenly hooked an enormous catfish, which upset the little craft and nearly drowned them both.

They finally got ashore, very wet, and walked to Anahuac, then a place of greater commercial importance than at present. Here almost the first person they fell in with was a lightning rod agent named Jefferson Hanna, from Buffalo, New York. Hanna was driving four fine mules, attached to a long-bodied wagon, heavily loaded with rods and ladders. He was a character, and one afterward not too favorably known in that part of the country; at that time he had just arrived in Texas and was starting out from Anahuac to "rod" the state, a business not without its perils. Catching sight of Halstead, he pulled up his mules. "You look like a likely young feller!" he called out. "Don't ye want an easy job, riding round with me and my son Lucas?" Halstead took a look at the red-painted wagon and decided he did. Within three minutes he was hired, at fifteen dollars a month, and climbed aboard the lightning rod wagon beside Lucas.

Now, if there was one job rather than another for which Cousin Halstead was unfitted, it was erecting lightning rods on the roofs of buildings. But it was characteristic of him not to inquire what his work was to be, and neither Hanna nor his son had thought it worthwhile to tell him that their former helper had fallen and broken his neck. What Hanna wanted was a nimble youngster, to climb with Lucas and attach the rods and insulators to the ridge poles of buildings. Lucas, indeed, could climb like a squirrel. The boys had to put up the ladders, then carry the rods up in sections and attach them, after Hanna had struck a bargain with the owners.

They journeyed first to Houston, then on across country to Austin, stopping at all the smaller towns and calling at the houses of the more prosperous planters and cattlemen. Halstead's timidity as a roof man was soon apparent to his new employer, but helpers were not easily hired at low wages. Hanna therefore adopted a policy of bantering and jollying him, to get him up the ladders, jocosely daring him to climb as high as Lucas and not let Lucas outdo him. It is a wonder how he induced him to climb to a roof at all, but he jockeyed him up and down with some success for a month or more until one sorrowful morning in July, when they were near San Marcos, twenty-four miles or more out of Austin.

Here they had undertaken to rod Grace Church, a small Methodist institution owned and attended by Negroes.

Lucas and Halstead got a ladder up to the eaves of the church; then, climbing to the roof, they drew up another ladder, which they placed against the steeple, setting the foot of it astride the ridge pole. Up went Lucas, with staples and insulators, and called on the timid Halstead to fetch up the rods and points. The roof, however, was about as high as Halstead had the courage to climb. He grew giddy. Thereupon the wily Hanna, who was handing up the rods to them, began to cajole him.

"Don't look down! Don't look down!" he cried. "Look up to the sky! Look right up at Lucas. You don't want to let Lucas beat you like that! Maine boys are just as brave as Buffalo boys, I know. Steady now and up ye go! 'Red bean, yellow blow, give a step and up you go!' Keep saying that and your head will be as clear as a goose quill!"

Thus exhorted, Halstead lifted himself, trembling, up the tottery ladder, one arm full of rods. Unfortunately, the steeple was in bad condition. The platform against which the upper end of the ladder rested gave way under the added weight as Halstead ascended, and the top of the ladder was canted off. Feeling it move, Lucas caught hold of a projecting spike in the spire and held fast; but Halstead, with his armful of rods, went with the ladder and fell sideways to the roof, whence ladder, rods, and boy slid off the eaves and crashed to the ground below.

The fall broke his leg and also fractured his hip. Hanna's attention was naturally given first to his own son, who was holding on by that spike aloft. With the aid of several persons who came running to the scene of the accident, another ladder was got up and Lucas rescued from his dangerous situation.

Halstead, meanwhile, lay groaning from pain. A horse doctor who happened to be passing was the first to give him aid. Nearby lived a widow and her daughter, named Hauschild, people from Saxony, of a colony that had settled at New Braunfels. Halstead was left at the Hauschild cottage.

Hanna then drove on. He had secured his pay for the rods, and he told the three stewards of the church that he was going after a physician, but would return and erect the rods during the afternoon. No one saw him again in those parts, and Halstead never got his wages.

Of what passed during the rest of that day and night Halstead afterward remembered little. The horse doctor at last summoned a physician to assist him. Chloroform was administered, and the broken leg was set and the fractured hip treated after a manner.

It was not till the following morning that Halstead fully regained consciousness. He came to himself quite suddenly, from hearing a curious noise hard by—a clinking, chipping noise as of a hammer and chisel on stone. His eyes opened, and he found himself looking through two folding doors into a room adjoining the one in which he lay, looking straight at someone in white, who had an equally white slab of marble propped up in front of her. In one hand she held a curious little hammer, in the other a bone-handled chisel. She was cutting a letter in the marble. From where he lay the letter looked like an "H"; the stone was clearly a gravestone.

Was it an angel thus employed? Strange fantasies sped through his still semitorpid brain. "I guess I've died," he mused, for he now remembered falling off the church steeple. "I must have died. That is why I am lying here so still, and she is cutting my gravestone! Well, I don't much care," he thought. "It's comfortable over here, anyhow." Yet he felt rather curious about it, tried to look at his hands, which were under a white sheet that came up to his chin. He started to turn it down, when instantly such a terrible spasm of pain shot along his broken leg that he cried out involuntarily.

The "angel" before the stone quickly turned a very human face toward him; she was a girl in a big, all-enveloping white apron, which perhaps needs a word of explanation.

The story of the Hauschilds was a pathetic one. They had immigrated to Texas fourteen years before and taken up a large tract of farm land thirty-five miles northeast of San Antonio. There were two brothers in the family named Naum and August Wilhelm. Naum was a marble worker by trade, in the old country, and unmarried; but August Wilhelm had a wife, Frederica, and a little daughter, Hilda Frederica, aged four. They had brought to Texas the frugal habits, household arts, and homely virtues of Saxony. Agriculture was at first the pursuit in which all engaged, but as time passed the older brother, Naum, reverted to his vocation of marble worker. This he taught to the growing Hilda Frederica.

The period of the Civil War bore heavily on these colonists. There was savage fighting on the Nueces River, and among those who lost their lives there were Naum and August Wilhelm Hauschild. Lamentable hardship now fell to the lot of Frederica Hauschild and her daughter, but slowly, patiently, Hilda and her mother retrieved the worst of their losses.

As time passed and deaths occurred, their Teuton neighbors remembered the gravestones beautifully lettered and fashioned by Naum Hauschild and desired Hilda to do inscriptions for them. This she did at first merely to oblige a few friends, procuring the marble slabs at San Antonio, for she remembered her Uncle Naum's methods and knew with whom he had dealt for marble, both abroad and at Rutland, Vermont.

Soon much of her time came to be thus occupied, and she found it necessary to make fixed charges for her work. She began to feel something of her Uncle Naum's joy in his craft—the joy and the ambition to do beautiful work and make each new effort surpass the last.

It was through the doorway of her humble studio that Halstead first saw Hilda in her big white apron, and he thought she was an angel, inscribing his tombstone!

In dropping Halstead at the door of these kindhearted people fortune had indeed been good. Few would have done for him what they did, for Halstead was there three months with his left leg in a splint, quite helpless, often in great pain and an object of constant care, without a dollar in his pocket to pay either his doctor's bill or for nursing.

Every day Frederica Hauschild worked out of doors, tending her crops, while Hilda looked after the bees and between whiles cut and polished little urns, cherubs' heads, roses, and mortuary inscriptions.

Yet busy as life forced them to be, they found time to give this wanderer the best of care, minister to his many wants, and in the end pay for all without a murmur.

Not till late in October that fall was Halstead able to take his first feeble steps on his broken leg; and then it was found that, owing to the hip fracture and imperfect surgical treatment, his left leg was two inches shorter than the other and that he would be obliged to walk with a limp and perhaps a cane.

Under the circumstances it is not strange, perhaps, that he evinced little disposition to stir forth from this harbor of refuge to shift for himself. He accepted the care bestowed on him as a matter of course. It seems never to have entered the minds of the Hauschilds to turn him adrift, and throughout the following winter he sojourned with them, doing little more than hobble forth for a walk on fair days.

In one minor matter only was he of the least use or benefit. He spoke English, of which their own knowledge was still very imperfect. But now both Hilda and her mother became daily learners of English, making a merry agreement to speak no other language in the household conversation.

And how did we learn of this, the reader may ask? In an odd way and not till two years later.

Halstead Reappears

THOSE TWO YEARS, after Halstead had left us, had brought changes at the Old Squire's. Addison was now studying under Professor Agassiz at Cambridge, and Theodora was attending the second term of her two years' course at Kent's Hill Seminary. Ellen and I were at home, for the time being, alone with the Old Squire and Grandmother. Halstead, like little Wealthy, who had died, was coming to be merely a memory, a memory of failure and regret, fading from our daily lives.

Then one Thursday evening there came a letter for "Fedora" (for that was the way it was spelled), a letter in a queer pink envelope, addressed too in a hand that was peculiar. The postmark was not wholly distinct but seemed to be "Neu," and then another word that looked like "Braunfels," followed by "Tex."

Grandmother's curiosity, or else a presentiment, overcame her proper scruples; she opened the letter. For a moment she seemed unable to speak. "This is about Halstead," she then said in a voice that trembled.

Ellen dropped her paper, and I jumped from my chair. The Old Squire too started up. "Is that letter from Halstead?" cried Ellen.

"It is about him, I'm sure, for I see Halstead's name in it," faltered Grandmother. "I think a woman wrote it."

"But look at the signature," the Old Squire exclaimed.

"I can't make that out either," said Grandmother.

"Do let me see!" cried Ellen.

"Yes, child, see if you can read it," Grandmother replied.

Ellen scanned the letter. "'Couzzin Fedora,'" she spelled out. "That is the way it begins, so it must be from some relative of ours." But the next words that she deciphered seemed to contradict this surmise. "'Neffer haf I seen you and am stranger. Harlstad haf neffer tell me only little. He neffer say what for he left his home. But often now I think it not right when you not hear for such long time.'"

"Dear me, dear me!" Grandmother exclaimed. "Who is it that's writing this?" Ellen looked for the name at the end. "'Hilda Frederica.' Sounds like Dutch. Do you suppose she has thoughts of marrying Halstead?"

"Poor Halstead," Grandmother sighed.

"Poor Hilda Frederica," said I, and the Old Squire smiled.

"She is writing to us because she thinks we ought to hear from him," he said. "That sounds as if she has a good heart. But go on!"

Ellen resumed, but what followed puzzled us completely.

"'You know Harlstad not haf the mind that stand in the same place very still. Tomorrow he not be like today. Yesterday he go one way fast, today not the same mind.'"

"No doubt that is Halstead!" I exclaimed.

"'So I haf often to change my thought quick, what to do next. Soon he dislike some work and haf no patience. So I say, Harlstad, you go on far ride, ober long roads for some orders, and I keep on the work cutting the letters with my chizzel alone.'"

"Now what can that mean?" Ellen stopped to ask. "'Chizzel,' 'letters'?"

We had to give it up.

"'Next week he come back with the good heart and robb the stones hard.'"

"'Robb the stones hard!' What on earth can that mean?" Grandmother exclaimed.

Ellen spelled it over again, but we could make nothing of it.

"'So we live that time, and next week I say, Harlstad, you go to San Antonio and haul the stones that haf come from Vermont.'"

"Vermont! Stones from Vermont!" cried the Old Squire. "What can she mean?"

"'Harlstad go very lame. Often he not very strong for work. When first him I saw, I think him todt, he haf fall so deep. But my modder and I feed him and nurse him to some more strength. Long time he haf no heart. Then my modder say: Harlstad, I gif you money to go home. But he say, Never shall I go home. So I haf you written at last, when Harlstad not see me, but I not know what you may feel to me, or whether I do right.'"

"And that is all," added Ellen, drawing a long breath. "All but the name, 'Hilda Frederica Hauschild,' at the bottom."

By this time the Old Squire was silently walking the floor. "Whoever she is, that is the letter of a good girl," he said.

"But I cannot understand it," exclaimed Grandmother, wiping her eyes. "How came he to be so sick and lame?"

The Old Squire was still walking the floor. "I hardly know what we ought to do," he said. "Halstead is now nearly twenty-one."

"Oh, but I should like to see him again!" Ellen cried suddenly.

"So should I," Grandmother added fervently. "He had as tender a heart as ever a boy had!"

"What will Doad say?" Ellen queried. "This is her letter, too."

"And what will Addison say?" I exclaimed. "We must let him know."

A family council was clearly in order. Accordingly a letter was sent the next morning to Addison, bidding him come home over Sunday, and as it was but thirty-three miles from the old farm to Kent's Hill Seminary, I drove over to get Theodora the following afternoon.

She was surprised to see me. "Is anything wrong at home?" were her first words. "But I guess not by the looks on your face," she added.

"No!" I cried. "But we've heard news! You can't guess from whom!"

She looked at me strangely, her face changing color. "Not from Halstead?" she asked, suddenly divining it.

"Yes, from Halstead!" I shouted.

Theodora turned quite pale. "Good news or bad?" she asked anxiously.

"Well, he is alive," I replied. "And well, I think."

Theodora's face was a study. "Did he write to tell us that?" she asked.

"No, he didn't write," said I. "But 'Hilda Frederica' did. She is our new 'couzzin,' or going to be, Ellen thinks. It all came in a pink letter and, by the way, it is your pink letter, but Grandmother opened it. Here it is."

Theodora pounced on the letter and was still reading it and puzzling over some of the sentences all the way home the next forenoon.

During the following week Theodora wrote a long, cordial letter in reply, sending kind regards to Halstead, with no reference whatever to the past. For lack of a more definite address, the letter was directed to "Neu Braunfels." It came back several months later from the dead-letter office in Washington, stamped "Unclaimed."

A year passed. Addison was in his second year at Cambridge. Theodora was finishing her course at the seminary and considering whether or not to accept a position as teacher in a proposed new school for Indian girls, far out in what was still Dakota Territory. And then another pink letter came.

This time it was Grandmother's pink letter, instead of Theodora's, and it was postmarked San Marcos, Texas, instead of Neu Braunfels. On being opened, however, it was found to contain merely a photograph of Halstead. Evidently it had been sent by the kind and constant "Hilda Frederica," who had received no answer to her former letter to us. This last missive wrought deeply on Grandmother's feelings again, as well as Theodora's, and set the Old Squire—who had not been very well that spring—earnestly pondering how we could best recover our lost kinsman.

Theodora and he were also having many long talks together concerning the Indian school, whether it was best for her to go so far from home into a new country. The work of educating Indian girls in the West had from the first appealed very strongly to Theodora. The great distance from home and the privations and hardships certain to attend the effort led us all to dissuade her, but she held to her purpose.

That spring I was trying—with many small worries—to manage the old farm alone and did not know all that was planned in the house. One day the Old Squire joined me out in the east field and after looking round awhile said, "I have been disgracefully lazy this season. Everything has been put on your shoulders, and you've done finely. But my conscience begins to prick me a little; I am going to take hold again and give you a breathing spell.

"Theodora is going to leave us," he continued rather sadly. "I hardly know how we shall get on without her, but she thinks it is her duty to go. We have been talking it over for some time. I don't like to have her take such a journey alone, so I want you to go with her; and I want you both to go round by the southern route, through Texas, and see Halstead, if you can find him, and see what we ought to do for him.

"We did pretty well with our lumber last winter, you know," the Old Squire added. "So I guess we can afford it. I want you both to see Halstead and learn what he is doing and with whom he is living. I will take hold again while you are gone, and if I find I cannot manage I will write to you for advice." His eyes twinkled.

Of course I was glad enough to have a fine long trip out into the great world, though I had no very strong desire to see Halstead. Small-minded as it sounds, I had never quite got over those disagreements of our boyhood. But if the head of the family said go and provided the funds for the trip, I was more than willing to set off; and set off we did four days later, the Old Squire entrusting the sum of three hundred dollars to us, in addition to expenses, to be used in Halstead's behalf, if we deemed it advisable. If we found him an invalid, I was to fetch him home.

It was the first time that either Theodora or I had been farther south than Philadelphia. We spent one day in Washington, half a day at Richmond, thence journeyed on southward to New Orleans, where we spent another day, sightseeing, and finally reached San Antonio, Texas, eleven days from home. From San Antonio we went by the mail stage up to the pretty German town of Neu Braunfels, and there the quest for Halstead began. The signature to Theodora's pink letter had been merely "Hilda Frederica Hauschild," and we had been unable to guess as to her location. Yet somewhere at or between Neu Braunfels and San Marcos we hoped to find her.

At Neu Braunfels we inquired in vain and at San Marcos were equally unsuccessful. There were Hildas and Fredericas by the dozen, but none of them proved to be the one we sought. We first made sure that the Hauschilds did not reside in the place, and then, during the next two days, we drove out along the roads, leading into San Marcos making inquiries as we went.

About eleven o'clock of the second day we passed a small church with a spire and near it the house of a Negro family. Here a little black pig by the wayside set our mustang horse on the jump. I had him well in hand but let him run for a bit along the level road, Theodora holding on and laughing.

While thus in full career, we came to a pretty white cottage among peach and plum trees, the low veranda in front overrun by a crimson rambler rose, and on the portico, right under the drooping festoons of roses, stood a fair, middle-aged woman in a blue gown. I didn't notice her myself, being fully occupied with our riotous nag, but Theodora saw her, and some intuition prompted her to cry, "Pull up! Pull up! I do believe this is the place!"

I brought the runaway to a standstill; almost before we came to a halt Theodora was out and hastening back to the cottage. When I reached it, after hitching to a wayside tree, she was at the cottage steps, where a much younger woman had appeared, little more than a girl, indeed, with fresh prepossessing face and abundant flaxen hair. In her hand was an odd little mallet, and she too had on a blue frock, protected by a great white apron.

"Do pardon me," Theodora was saying as I approached, "but is your name Hauschild, and is there a young man here you call Halstead?"

"Ja," the elder woman said, smiling, but the girl in the door behind her suddenly dropped the little mallet, and her blue eyes opened wide.

"We are his cousins from Maine," Theodora began to explain but had scarcely spoken when the younger woman cried, "Oh, it is that you are Fedora! I knew you as soon as you I saw!"

"And you are Hilda Frederica?" Theodora asked.

"Yes, yes," and then the two grasped each other's hands and after a look in each other's eyes, kissed quite as if they had been long-parted friends instead of strangers who hardly knew each other's names!

The elder woman's greeting was scarcely less cordial than her daughter's, and then Theodora introduced me as another cousin from Maine.

"And Halstead?" we both asked. "Is he here?"

"He haf drive to San Marcos this day," Hilda Frederica replied. "He will return by early the afternoon."

They pressed us to remain, so heartily, so much as a matter of course, that we were glad to do so, nor shall I soon forget the gentle, unaffected kindness of those newly made friends. They made their pretty little cottage so wholly free to us that cousin Theodora and I felt at home in it from the first moment we entered the door.

Afterward they showed us Hilda Frederica's workroom and the tools of her craft, along with a specimen of her recent work and some new slabs of Parian marble that had lately come from overseas. It was our first understanding of what the quaint word "stones" meant, as used in Hilda Frederica's letter to Theodora.

Quite as a matter of course, the mother of Hilda set lunch for us under the shaded porch, overhung by that wonderful crimson rambler rose; and then, as we broke bread together for the first time, she and her daughter told us about Halstead and how he was first brought to their cottage after his fall from Grace Church steeple, also of his lameness. Of the care they had been obliged to give him and other trouble he had made, they said little, Hilda merely remarking gently that "Harlstad haf the mind that change soon. But he haf the goot heart, at sometimes," she continued with an honesty that made me laugh, while Theodora blushed. "And now he do much the better," she added.

As it came time for Halstead to return from San Marcos, Hilda and Theodora planned a surprise for him by having us sit out of sight in the stones room till after he entered the house.

Presently we saw him approaching and, peeping from the window, had a good view of him as he drove past the cottage to the little barn in the back yard. He had changed considerably and had now a faint little black mustache that emphasized his dark complexion and black hair. Much as he had suffered, he had grown handsomer too.

Erelong he came in, walking with a limp. "Whose little white-eyed pony and buggy is that in our barn?" were his first words—and how familiar his voice sounded!

Hilda laughed. "Neffer could you guess whose!" she replied.

"Who's here?" he cried, after a moment's silence.

Without replying Hilda brought him to the stones room, where Theodora and I stood just inside the open door. He saw us then and started violently.

"Oh Halstead, I am so glad to see you again!" exclaimed Theodora and, rushing forward, grasped his hand while I chimed in with, "How d'ye do, Halse? I'm glad to see you!"

He turned very red, staring first at one then at the other of us. "Where . . . where did you come from?" he cried quite roughly, then as suddenly, broke down and, dropping into a chair, put both hands to his face and sobbed convulsively.

Theodora sought to calm him, but it nettled me, as it always had, to see him behave so weakly. Hilda, however, had flown instantly to his side, with a piteous glance, and something in the gentle hand she laid on his shoulder made me think of what Ellen had said, at home, when she had first read that pink letter. Theodora glanced at me eloquently. The same thought, I fancy, had come to us both, that honest little Hilda's affection might do more for our errant cousin than all the efforts of our family at home.

Halstead Finds Peace

As the Old Squire had entrusted the sum of three hundred dollars to Theodora and myself to be used if needed, we asked Mrs. Hauschild how long Halstead had been helpless and how much trouble he had caused. Both she and her daughter were very loath to speak of this at first, exclaiming repeatedly that they would accept no money!

Bit by bit, however, we drew from them certain facts of their curious experience with our young kinsman. After his first helpless winter they had begun to take thought as to what he might do to aid them in earning a living. It occurred to them that he might be able to cultivate a small field of canaigre root, then beginning to be raised in Texas for tanning leather. Very gently the subject was broached to him, and, as Halstead assented, an acre of land was prepared and the canaigre planted. Thereafter for an hour at a time, as he felt able to work, it was to be his task to tend this crop, without interference from anyone. A hoe was bought with which he was to "hill" the plants and weed the field.

But canaigre is a kind of dock, and there is also a weed in that region which resembles it. After Halstead had been cultivating his field about a month it was discovered that he had cut up the canaigre and "hilled" the weeds, thereby hopelessly ruining the prospects of a crop for that season!

Thereafter they set him to riding their mule and cultivating the cotton until he mistreated the creature and was kicked by it and made an invalid once more for two months.

Mrs. Hauschild still held to her homely confidence that "efferry-pody iss goot for somedings" if only it can be discovered.

A small mill for extracting the oil from cotton seed had been started about five miles from their place, and, as it was really necessary that Halstead should do something in self-support, an easy job was found for him at this new mill. Hilda was to carry him to his work with Grutch, the mule, every Monday morning and bring him home Saturday night. He remained there a week and three days, then came hobbling home afoot on Thursday night—discharged. He had begun to complain that the work was too hard and that he was doing more than his share. Then the owner of the mill had told him to take what was due him and go home.

During the winter that followed he was of little, if any, service to the Hauschilds. He was painfully lame, and Mrs. Hauschild dared not trust him to tend Grutch at the barn, lest there might be further doctor's bills. Yet we could not learn that one impatient word was ever said to him.

The bees had laid in great stores of honey for two years, and this was followed by a prolific swarming year when they multiplied rapidly. Several of Hilda's fifteen hives sent forth young swarms in one summer, which had all to be hived. A sharp eye had to be kept on them to prevent the young broods from flying away to the forest; the thrifty women attempted to have Halstead watch the bees and assist in hiving the swarms. He was also set to hoe in little patches of buckwheat and alfalfa about the apiary.

Anyone who had previously known Halstead, as we did, would have hesitated to send him near a beehive! He was one of those persons whom for some reason bees are prone to attack. At the Old Squire's he could scarcely enter the garden, where the bee shed was, without getting stung, and the first time he attempted to assist Hilda in hiving a swarm, first one, then another, and then a dozen or more bees darted at his face. Afterward Halstead could not work within fifty yards of the row of hives without trouble. The plan of making a bee farmer of him had therefore to be given up.

After this last failure the Hauschilds were at their wits' end for months, yet they appear never to have quite lost their calm faith that he might be found good for something.

Hilda was taken ill with measles and convalesced somewhat slowly. Just previously she had finished a job of marble work for a settler's family, fifteen miles out of San Marcos. The stones were for their only son, who had been drowned in the Colorado River, and they desired them set on the anniversary of his birth. Not to disappoint the customer, Hilda hired a kind old black horse from a neighbor and sent Halstead to deliver the gravestones.

He returned the next day at noon, in a fine mood. On his way he had exhibited Hilda's beautiful handiwork at a number of places and obtained two orders for stones. What was better still, he appeared animated by a new idea that he could assist Hilda to polish marble and learn to cut it.

It was the first helpful effort in which they had ever seen him evince the least interest. Hitherto he had been "dumm" when work was mentioned. Both Hilda and her mother gave ear in pleased astonishment.

They baked him a special cake that night and praised his act heartily. A long dormant ambition to be of some use in the world stirred in him. He asked permission to go out again to obtain orders, and a little later the kind old horse was purchased for him to drive.

Curious indeed and far borne are the influences of ancestral traits and occupations. Looking the matter up of late, I find that on the Spanish side of Halstead's Cuban descent there were two noted sculptors in the Caranza family. Can this new interest that he took be traced to some inherited liking for marble or some hereditary aptitude for marble work?

There had waked in Halstead the first real interest or aptitude that he had ever felt for anything like work, the first prompting to industry, the first stir of an ambition to accomplish something in the world.

Pleasanter days now dawned at the Hauschild cottage. From the outset of this, his new departure, Halstead showed a certain befitting tact in soliciting orders for marble work and adopted a properly serious mode of address. Under Hilda's good-humored instruction he learned to cut inscriptions in both varieties of marble in which she worked.

Theodora and I listened to the story in wonder and thankfulness, thankfulness not unmixed with self-reproach that at home we had so far fallen short of the patience and tact evinced by these kindly Saxon hearts. We had done what we could—so we had thought—but they had done better and had succeeded where we had failed.

While I was caring for our little mustang the next morning Halstead came to the barn and asked me how we had learned where he was.

"Oh, a little bird brought us the news," I replied, not caring to betray Hilda's secret letters. "Didn't you want us to know?" He did not reply, and then I explained that Theodora was on her way to Dakota and that we had come round through Texas to make him a visit. "The Old Squire wanted very much to hear from you," I added. "So did Gram and Ellen, and Theodora always hoped that you would come back."

He noticed that I did not mention Addison and said, "I suppose Ad wouldn't speak to me if he met me."

"Not so bad as that! But you know he has pretty strict notions of what is right. He will be glad as anyone to know that you are succeeding out here in Texas, and you don't know, Halse, how it will please the Old Squire and Gram."

We remained another day, and then Theodora astonished me by announcing, "I am going to stay here in Texas a year."

"What! Give up Dakota?" I exclaimed.

"For a year," she replied. "I believe I ought to stay here awhile. Halstead is doing well now, but you know how suddenly he changes and how hard it always was for him to hold to one thing long. I'm afraid one of his 'bad moods' will come on and spoil everything. Perhaps if I am here, I can help to keep him steady." She thought she might secure a position as a teacher at San Marcos, or at Neu Braunfels.

So on the fourth morning I bade her farewell, handed over the Old Squire's money to her, to be used at her discretion, and set off alone on my long journey home. I found it almost as hard to say good-bye to Halse as to her. Hilda and her mother too had come to seem like warm friends.

Nine days later I was at home again with my cheering news about Halstead. Within a short time a letter arrived from Theodora saying that she had been offered a position as instructor in a school at

Austin, thirty miles from San Marcos, and that this circumstance would enable her to spend her Saturday afternoons and Sundays with Halstead.

Throughout the summer no week passed without its letter from Texas. In September Halstead himself—at Theodora's suggestion, perhaps—sent Grandmother a letter full of affection, confiding a secret to her that the dear old lady kept with true New England fidelity. Halstead was still doing well, Theodora's letters assured us, and she also hinted at certain things in a special letter to Ellen.

In the week before Thanksgiving we were formally notified of a wedding at the Hauschild cottage. Hilda and Halstead were married, and presents, congratulations, and good wishes passed. Grandmother longed exceedingly to be there and see her new granddaughter, but distance forbade. The Old Squire sent a substantial gift in token of the family appreciation of what had been done for Halstead.

After Theodora's departure for Dakota, letters came regularly from Hilda. From them we continued aware that Halstead—though still Halstead, at times—was doing reasonably well. Journeying to take orders for marble work, with occasional hours of using the chisel and mallet himself, offered that variety of occupation congenial to his love of change.

Some years went by, and when at length a little new face—an infant Halstead—made its appearance at the rose-embowered cottage still another phase of Halstead's disposition disclosed itself. Hitherto he had seemed to have no special fondness for small children and disliked their outcries. But from the first moment of little Halsy's birth, he became the most doting of young fathers!

He could scarcely bear to have the child out of his sight. If he were at the stable and heard the baby cry, in he would come, limping hurriedly, full of solicitude. For hours he sat talking of the child's future, and of what great things he meant to do for him when they got rich in the marble business.

The youngster was not in the least like Halstead. Not only had he inherited his mother's light hair, blue eyes, rose-pink complexion, and calm temper, but he had other characteristics still more unlike his father—characteristics that raised quite a happy commotion among us at the old farm in Maine when Hilda sent the little fellow's first ambrotype picture to Grandmother.

No sooner had Grandmother put on her glasses, opened her letter, and inspected that ambrotype than she cried out, "How much he looks like Joseph!"

And he did, even at less than two years old. We all saw the resemblance to the Old Squire, saw it at a glance: nose, eyes, brow—a faithful little reincarnation! Grandmother sat and doted on that picture; Ellen too hung round, laughing and peeping at it over Grandmother's shoulder. "Oh, but he is such a dear little fellow!" they cried. "And he's my great-grandson!" Grandmother added solemnly. "Joseph, the Lord has spared us to live to be great-grandparents!"

"And only think of it!" Ellen cried mischievously to me. "You're an uncle-cousin now, and I'm an aunty-cousin!"

In the sitting room that evening I surprised the Old Squire covertly inspecting that little ambrotype with an odd, fond look in his own blue eyes.

During one of the summer vacations that she spent in Texas, Theodora informed us that Halstead was becoming a fairly responsible citizen. "Occasionally he is a little discontented for a few hours and wants a change," she wrote. "But the fits are shorter now. Hilda has only to send little Halsy to him, with her mallet in his hand, for Halstead is firmly convinced that the boy is going to make a great sculptor one of these days and will carve heroic statues for all future Texas! 'We will have a big studio for him,' he often says to Hilda and Mother Frederica. 'We will send for the best marble in Italy.' Perhaps they will, for their business is a good one, and they are doing well.

"I really think Halstead is all right now," Theodora continued, "and I am indeed thankful that we tried to help him through his wild, weak boyhood. If we hadn't, he might have gone off, heaven knows where. But what Halstead really needed was to have his bad traits of character held in check by someone like Hilda till his better traits had time to outgrow them, and getting away from Addison, whose superiority became a millstone round Halstead's neck and brought out his worst, was a good thing to have happened to him."

All of this was indeed gratifying, and as the years went by, we began to think of our kinsman as a successful citizen of the great, growing state of Texas.

Three times he came East to visit us at the old homestead, once with his wife and little Halsy. The Old Squire and Gram were still living the second time he came, and the sight of Hilda and the promising young Halstead was one of the genuine pleasures of their last years.

34

When the Self-Sender Walked Home

THE UNITED STATES HAS VERY APTLY BEEN TERMED the Land of Self-Made Men. Large numbers of its most famous and successful people have been born, if not in poverty, in at best but very humble circumstances and have risen to eminence mainly by their own unaided exertions.

It is said that in some of our colleges from one-fourth to one-half of the young men who have been graduated have paid their expenses with money they have earned by their own labor.

At Bowdoin College, when the writer was a student there in the mid-seventies, the sophomores and upperclassmen would inspect the new freshmen at the opening of the college year, in September, with a view to taking them into the societies, and the like. A common question concerning each was, "Who sends him?"—the answer being usually, "His folks," or "Sends himself." There was, it is true, an immediate caste or grade, in part assisted by parents or friends, but about thirty percent of the one hundred and eight students there then were self-senders, pure and simple.

How this runs since 1880 I am not well informed, but believe the percentage to be less, as it naturally would be, with the increase of wealth in the country. The subject is not wholly pertinent to my present homely narrative and is introduced merely as a prelude to declaring my own caste there; I was a self-sender, and at times a wildly distressed one. In truth, the undergraduate whose bills are honored by the paterfamilias, and who has only to attend to athletics and the curriculum, has and can have no idea of the exigent mental attitude of the self-sender; he is quite another being.

Eminent educators have held, I believe, that more than compensating advantages come to the student who has his own way to make, in the habits of thrift and self-reliance thus fostered; but I have never yet met a bona fide self-sender who would fully endorse this view, much less one who would voluntarily subject himself to such a discipline.

But it is a fine topic for the self-made man and others to expatiate on to the young, thirty years later, when they have all become prosperous, and after a good dinner. It requires about that amount of perspective to be really enjoyable.

My own idea is that the uncertainty, worry, fret, fear, envy, and other ignoble emotions that periodically agitate the self-sender's mind rather more than offset any good that accrues to him from his scrimping and self-reliance. But cases and temperaments differ, no doubt. Some boys have better heads for managing these things; some bear the pressure of debt with equanimity and a calm confidence in the future. One of my college-mates, I remember, was always smiling, always happy, always whistling, and caroling like a bob-o'-link, though he owed everybody from two old aunties at home to Gripus at the college bookstore; and he who could owe Gripus and yet be happy must needs have been panoplied with more than Horatian armor of triple brass. But the men of later years don't know Gripus; we did.

Various were the expedients to which we aspirants for academic honors and a liberal education were sometime reduced. One of the sternest methods of self-help that I remember among my student acquaintances was that practiced by a freshman, whom his classmates called "Calhound," from his mispronunciation in a class debate of the name of the celebrated Southern statesman.

During the winter term Calhound would disappear for two or three hours, immediately after morning recitation and again after prayers at four o'clock in the afternoon.

For a long time his classmates did not know where he went, or what he did; but near the close of the term it was discovered that he

had taken a contract to cut wood, by the cord, for the use of locomotives, at a railroad station a mile and a half away. He received a dollar a cord and cut about a cord per day, and at the same time he kept up in his studies with his class.

He completed his contract and cut fifty cords of wood during the term, for which he received fifty dollars. While at work with his ax, he would have his Latin or his algebra propped open on a stump hard by, and after a hard bout at a thick log, he would sit down and master a passage, or an example, jotting the translation or the solution on a large, white chip, which his well-applied ax had thrown out of a scarf.

And I am glad to say Calhound took very good rank that term in his class, and at the end of it he had become quite a giant, in muscle, and was a picture of manly health.

Another student, whose means of earning money were exceedingly meager, used to "board himself" in his room. During one fall term of fourteen weeks, he felt that he could spare for the whole term but seventeen dollars for food, a sum that certainly did not admit of many luxuries.

Squashes were very plentiful and cheap that season, and he came to the conclusion that there was a great deal of nutrition in a mealy Hubbard squash. His stove had a little oven in the top of it, in which he baked half a squash at a time.

A spoon with salt and pepper and now and then a ball of butter that his mother sent him, completed his culinary and dining outfit, for he took his squash in the shell and followed it with a hearty draught of water at the pump.

He actually got through that term at the rate of a dollar a week for food, which left him three dollars of the seventeen he had set apart for that purpose, and with the three remaining dollars he bought a Smith's *Classical Dictionary*. I hardly need add that he achieved success in life. He is now a prosperous publisher.

In my own case, the joys of college life were frequently devastated by financial crashes that I had not the skill or the sagacity to forestall and stave off; or rather, I did stave them off too long and held on till the bottom fell clean out.

One such overtook me near the end of the fall term of my sophomore year. At the beginning of 1874, I had sold a serialized novel, *Tom and Ruth of the Chatham Four Corners*, to *The Lewiston Journal*, thus raising a comfortable nest egg. Subsequently, however, all my small monetary expedients had gone wrong. An incautious expenditure in furnishing my room (No. 2, Appleton Hall) began the trouble. Bad luck with two or three ventures for gain followed on. I had been agent for an inexpensive sewing machine during the summer vacation—a light machine, operated by a crank; I carried the sample about the country, in a valise. In September, I entrusted my sample and three other machines to a sub-agent who was to sell them on a commission. But now—in November—I learned that he had sold the three machines and decamped with the proceeds and had left my sample machine and valise at Yarmouth railway station. A small speculation, too, in stovewood and dried apples, at the old farm up in Oxford County, which I had deemed a sure thing, had come to naught from the accidental burning of the building in which they were stored.

In brief, my whole *ménage* had collapsed. I was bankrupt. Even my steward and fellow student of the boarding club was after me, with suspicion on his brow. Him I satisfied by leaving my sophomore books with Gripus, on an advance of six dollars. My last dollar was then in and naught remained but to foot it home via Yarmouth, to reclaim the "sample" sewing machine—my only available asset.

Ah, what a bleak morning that was! Bitterly cold with the ground hard frozen and beginning to spit snow. Yet even the hard, whitening earth and cold gray heavens were less bleak than my financial sky.

After a last vain effort to mortgage my half of the room furniture to my chum who was a crafty financier, I crossed the campus—not then adorned by the Art Building and Memorial Hall—to Gen. Joshua Chamberlain's cottage. A distinguished Civil War hero and former governor of Maine, he was then the college president, and my object in calling was to obtain his permission to withdraw before term closed and seek the sanctuary of home. Thus the hard-run fox as a last resort seeks refuge in the burrow of cubhood. I had the promise of the district school in the home neighborhood, and the Old Squire's farmhouse was good for unlimited board, till new schemes could be hatched.

Briefly I recounted my condition to the general's keenly appreciative ear, and having heard it, he made not the least objection to my immediate departure. He agreed with me, *nem con*, that home was the best place for me. With laughter, but a cordial handshake, he wished me a pleasant walk up the country and regretted the state of the weather!

Dear, kind old Professor Packard had noted that I was in trouble the day before and had made it in his way to join me as I left the recitation room. Encouraged too far by his sympathy, I told him how I stood. But when he had grasped the full significance of my revelations, even his warm heart was chilled. In all his experience of indigent sophomores, he had never met one so utterly devoid of resources. He acknowledged with regret that he knew not what to advise me.

I have a vague faith still that "Billy" (Prof. William Smythe, professor of the algebra and calculus and who, college tradition says once ciphered himself up at midnight from the bottom of the college well into which he had inadvertently fallen) might have figured it out for me in terms of x, y, and z, if only I could have taken refuge in one of his equations; but the old arithmetician was ill in bed that week, lying now very infirm, and so missed the chance of a lifetime to perform one final, famous feat in those abstruse mathematics that he loved so well and long. Could he have rescued me that morning—and I have always half believed he could—not far below George Washington himself ought he now to be sitting in Miss Helen Gould's new Hall of Fame.

But no help came to me, either from the chair of moral philosophy, revealed religion, or mathematics; and buttoning up my old overcoat, I set off along the railroad track to face the snowstorm and walk to Yarmouth, thirteen miles, there get my abandoned sample sewing machine, and then walk home, forty-seven miles from Yarmouth, sixty in all.

It soon became hard walking on the ties, for snow was now falling fast, but I reached Yarmouth by noon and recovering my property, on which, luckily for me, there was no storage charge. I sat down in the station to eat a meager bit in the way of a lunch that, mindful of emergencies, I had privately conveyed to my pocket from the club breakfast table. Then for an hour or two I attempted to do a little sewing machine business in Yarmouth village. I hoped to sell my sample machine and thus be able to take the evening train home. But it wasn't a good day for it: the women cut my story short, snappishly; an "agent" of any sort was *persona non grata* that bleak afternoon. Later, I tried to dispose of the machine in several stores and at a hardware shop—quite in vain. No one would even look at it; there did not seem to be a smile, nor a bit of geniality that day, in the whole place.

I had staked a good deal of time on hopes of selling my sample machine in Yarmouth; and now, at two of the short winter afternoon, found myself face to face with the necessity of reaching home that night, for I had money neither for food nor lodging.

For three or four miles I plodded along the railroad; then as the snow was deepening on the track, I diverged to a highway off to the left of the line. Here by good chance, as I at first thought, I was immediately overtaken by a man alone in a large pung, driving a fat, strong

horse. He wore a broad-brimmed hat and blue-drab cloak; he proved to be a Shaker elder, returning from Portland to the Shaker village at New Gloucester.

"Will thee ride, friend?" he asked with grave kindness. "Thank thee, I will," said I, and immediately conceived rosy hopes of accompanying him home, spending the night with the Shakers, and even selling them my sewing machine. I had heard that these good people do not charge wayfarers for a night's lodging and food. Accordingly, I set myself to beguile the way and amuse the elder with lively conversation. But I must have overdone it, I think. For some reason, which I never quite understood, the elder suddenly froze to me. Possibly it was from learning that I was a college student. He waxed grim and became as mum as an oyster. I tried him further with two humorous stories, but he never cracked a smile to them; and soon after, coming where the road to the Shaker village diverged from the main road, he pulled up for me to get out.

Thereupon I asked him point-blank to let me go home with him, overnight. But "Here is where our roads separate, friend," was all the answer he vouchsafed me.

By this time it was dark, and being both hungry and cold, I applied recklessly, at the first house I came to, for lodging and supper, and then at the next house and the next; but the people were all inhospitably inclined.

There were eight inches of snow by this time, the footing getting more difficult every hour, and I resolved to apply at every house till someone took me in.

The next human habitation, however, was fully half a mile farther on. It stood back from the road, and I could see neither tracks about it nor light within, but I plodded to the door and knocked. There was no response, but I heard a cat mewing dolefully inside. It was a small, low house, with a shed and a little stable adjoining. I knocked again and yet again, without result, but still the cat mewed on, piteously. Finally I tried the door; it stuck at the top but was not locked. I pushed it open and shouted, "Hullo! Anybody at home?"

All dark and still, but I heard the patter of the cat's feet. I stepped in. It seemed not very cold inside, but the air was dank and had an odor of household laxity, or senility. I had a match and struck it. The outer door opened into a low room nearly bare of furniture, with soiled, green-figured paper on the walls. There was a fireplace and ashes but no spark of fire. A little blue tin match safe stood on the mantel shelf, also an iron candlestick with an inch or two of tallow candle. In the match safe were four or five matches and stubs of matches. When I had lighted the candle, the cat came and rubbed against my legs.

There were three doors opening out of the front room, one to the chamber stairs and one into a little kitchen in the rear. The third I could not open; it appeared to be stuck fast in its casement, or else buttoned or propped on the other side. I knocked at it and called out again, then came to the conclusion that the house was one from which the inmates had recently moved and taken most of the furniture. The appearance of the kitchen also confirmed this surmise. It contained little save a rusted, much cracked cooking stove, choked with ashes. In one corner stood an empty flour barrel, having a large white cloth spread over the top of it and a gummy, warped old cake-board on top of that. In the shed leading to the stable were chips, litter, and a few sticks of wood.

After several failures, I kindled a fire in the stove and warmed myself a little, for my feet were wet and it was chilling, bleak weather. Snow drove against the windows, and altogether the night was so bad that I determined to remain there till morning, if not ordered away, by the proprietor. But hunger was nearly as imperative with me as cold, and after getting the old stove warmed up, I searched the premises again for food stuff, going down cellar—where there was not so much as a frozen potato—also to the shed and stable and upstairs to the low open chamber. The only edible that could be discovered anywhere was a little husk trace with five small dry ears of sweet corn, hung on a nail in a rafter of the chamber roof. Thus it had escaped the mice, though the small rodents appeared to have been making frantic efforts to reach it.

Appropriating the court trace, I went back to the kitchen and began parching the kernels for my supper, and I left the poor cat—a little, lean Maltese tabby, with eyes the largest part of her—shut up in the chamber to look for the mice. The cat had been tagging my every step, getting under foot, ever after I had entered the house.

Dried sweet-corn kernels, when toasted, swell up to full size and are not very difficult to chew. My hunger prompted me to roast and eat every kernel of the five ears, and afterward I thawed a handful of snow in a tin basin by way of a solvent. Altogether it was as frugal a meal as even a self-sender has ever made, I fancy.

Fatigue, after my long, hard day exposed to the cold wind and snow, soon asserted itself. There was one old basket-bottomed chair in the front room. Placing this in the warmest corner, I filled the stove with the last of the wood, then took off my damp boots, opened the old oven door, and thrust in my feet. Afterward, drawing my overcoat about me, I leaned back with my head against the wall, to take things easy till morning.

Very soon I was asleep, but voices that sounded like those of boys or youngsters waked me not long after; I also heard sleigh bells. A sleigh in passing appeared to have stopped near the house; I heard the occupants talking low and snickering. Suddenly four or five tremendous blows, as if from an ax or club, were struck on the clapboards of the house near the door, and a voice shouted, "Wake up, Granny! Wake up!"

For the moment I imagined that the rogues had peeped in at the uncurtained back window of the kitchen and by the faint gleam from the stove had taken me for an old grandsir, sitting there with my feet in the oven. Presently several missiles, stones it is likely, from the stone wall near the road, were thrown on the roof and rolled off with a great clatter, and I could still hear the scamps sniggering.

By way of a counter demonstration, I caught up the big white cloth from the flour barrel and, wrapping it around myself, head and ears, stalked to the outer door, which I threw wide open, and uttered a horrible groan! What with the snow on the ground and a moon under the storm clouds, there was sufficient light to render objects dimly visible. Two of the rogues were standing in the yard near the wall, and I think that they actually took me for something spookish. One of them uttered an odd sort of exclamation. They beat a retreat to their sleigh and drove off.

It was still snowing and so cold that I made haste back to my warm stove oven and chair; I was apprehensive lest the young roisterers might raise a party and return, bent on investigating the supernatural. My dread of that, however, did not prevent me from soon falling asleep again, my head propped in the angle of the wall, on the chair back, and my feet in the oven as before.

I waked several times, I remember, but my final nap must have been a long one. There was broad daylight when I roused last. Indeed, it was much later than I supposed, being nine or ten o'clock I am sure. The sky was still clouded, but the storm had ceased. The stove and kitchen were cold as a tomb. I pulled myself together, washed my face in snow at the front door, tidied up, and made ready to sally forth from this harbor of refuge. But I was gaunt from hunger and made yet another search for something with which to stay the sense of inner emptiness. I found a squash in the stable and had thoughts of attempting to bake it in the stove, having first cut it into slices.

While canvassing this expedient, however, I heard a noise in the front room and hastily looking in saw the door—the one I had found fastened—shaking, as if someone were removing a bar or a prop on the other side. Even while I stared, it opened and there issued forth a very tall and wild-looking old female in a long yellow bed-gown, and it is no exaggeration to say that the skin of her face and hands was quite as yellow as the flannel of the gown! But her hair was as white as an albino's and fully as voluminous. Indeed, there was a most uncanny quantity of it. It frowsed out and hung down her shoulders and in front over her arms, quite to her waist. She had an old tin teapot in her hand and came directly toward the kitchen door where I stood, rooted and dumb with wonder as to how this could be!

What was stranger, I saw that she did not seem to see me, though apparently looking straight at me. Her eyes appeared to have a mottled gray crust on them, which I now presume to have been cataracts. On she came and I backed back into the kitchen, then spoke. "Is this your house, marm?" I exclaimed, not knowing what else to say. But she paid no heed and came on, I backing away till I was directly between her and the little window. Then she stopped short, having caught sight of something against the light. Turning her head and strange white hair down and to one side, she peeped and peered at me, like a hen in the dark, out of the corners of her nearly sightless eyes.

"I see ye!" she then cackled out. "I kin see ye there. Who be ye? Be ye Sally Dennett's man, or be ye Bijah Libbey?"

"No, marm, I'm a stranger," I said. "I thought this house was empty. I came in on account of the storm."

"Whart?" she bleated. "Be ye Bijah?"

I repeated that I was a stranger.

"Wha-a-art?" she cried, taking a step nearer me.

It was plain now that she was deaf also, as well as blind—deaf as a post.

"Whart? Whart be ye a-saying?" she cried again, and put out one of those awful skinny yellow hands to feel me over.

Ah well, I was young then and had had not breakfast and not much supper; partly for that reason, perhaps, my stomach gave a sudden turn. Snatching up my valise, I bolted out of that house, gained the highway and deep as the snow was ran for as much as half a mile—till I felt better.

It was an old beldame granny who lived there alone. She had been abed in that room all night, while I was ranging over her house and parching her trace of sweet corn! The poor, deaf, blind old creature had heard nothing of my invasion. It was too scandalous even for a sophomore; and I never dared tell any of the fellows about it.

My only consolation and hold on self-respect lay in the thought that I had discomforted the louts who had stopped there at midnight to torment her, but it is doubtful if she heard even the stones on the roof.

Plodding on drearily enough for an hour or more, my luck took a turn for the better. A woman driving a white horse in a pung set full of stone pots overtook me, a large, fleshy, comfortable-looking, middle-aged woman with three big brown hair moles on her lip and cheek. I suppose I cast a longing look at the vacant seat and warm buffalo robe, for she pulled up after passing, looked around, and presently asked me if I would like to ride.

I did not keep her waiting while I considered whether I had another engagement, for my feet were already wet again.

Remembering my ill success with the Shaker elder, I determined to go easy in conversation and did not talk much. Besides I was cold and faint. But conversation did not lag; this woman was herself a talker, and before we had gone a mile I had learned that she had been to the "village" that morning, that she had sold a hundred and twenty pounds of butter, that butter was twenty-six cents a pound and eggs twenty cents a dozen, and that her hens were laying well, also that she had told George, her husband, that he was welcome to all the farm crops came to, if she could have the butter and eggs.

But *mox anguis recreatus*. Having gained breath and warmth under her comforting buffalo skin, I took thought and, putting my best foot forward, turned the conversation on sewing machines—not then so hackneyed a theme for an agent's eloquence as now.

Unsuspecting woman! She little imagined how desperate a man she had been warming back to hope and guile under that cozy robe. In twenty minutes I had sold her my sample machine for seventeen dollars, delivered the goods, and got my money!

By good luck, too, her homeward route took me within a mile of the Empire Road railway station, which I reached in time to take the afternoon train home.

Once more on my native heath, I settled to pedagogy and studying for ten weeks, and meantime sold eight sewing machines. So that in March I was able to rejoin my class, in funds again for the rest of the year.

35

The Mystery of Quog-Hoggar

Katherine's Secret

MANY OF THE PLEASANTEST MEMORIES OF MY BOY-
hood at the old farm in Maine are associated with two of our young
neighbors, Thomas and Katherine Edwards, who lived just across the
west field from the Old Squire's place.

In those days the Edwards farm was well tilled, unencumbered, and
prosperous. There were three hundred acres of tillage, pasture, and
woodland, with a well-built two-story house and two large barns.
Unfortunately, their father, Jotham Edwards, was one of those unsuccessful farmers of whom New England has not a few: men who struggle on all their lives, acquire a mortgage for temporary relief, and who,
when they die, leave nothing except the mortgage to those who come
after them.

Tom, after quarreling with a schoolteacher, had left home at the
age of eighteen. In time he became a civil engineer, first in the oil
regions of Pennsylvania and afterward at Baku on the Caspian Sea,
where he helped the Swedish brothers Nobel to develop the petroleum
industry in that distant quarter of the world. He married the daughter
of a rich Parsee merchant, who could be induced neither to come to
America herself nor to allow Tom to come. Maine knew him no more
for many years.

Katherine, his sister, was, in many ways, a remarkable girl—good-
looking and a bright, keen student at school, and moreover she had a

practical turn of mind and a strong sense of filial duty and great loyalty to her home. Largely by her own efforts, she had graduated from the state normal school and obtained a position as instructor in another normal school at a good salary. But at the age of twenty-one, after her father's unexpected death, Katherine resigned her position, bade farewell to all prospects of advancement as a teacher, and came home to take up the burden there. It was she who lifted the mortgage from the unremunerative farm by industriously drying and selling the apple crop from the neglected old orchard for several years in succession— thus insuring a home for her mother and an infirm old aunt. Meanwhile she tried to run the farm with hired labor. But unfavorable seasons ensued; prices for all farm products were low, and even farmers who did their own work were hardly able to make a living.

So she turned to one of the quaint little industries of her girlhood, by means of which she had at times earned considerable sums much needed for clothes and school books. This industry was gathering, drying, and pressing wild herbs for sale to druggists. Cohosh, pennyroyal, peppermint, spearmint, comfrey, skullcap, lobelia, old man's root, snakehead, catnip, and many other herbs supposed to have medicinal virtues grew in the nearby woods and fields and could be sold at a fair profit.

Gathering herbs was a craft, if craft it may be called, that had come down to Katherine from her octogenarian grandmother, Anice Edwards, who had been a noted herb doctor, and who in the latter years of her life had taught Katherine not only how and at what time of year to gather and cure herbs but also where they grew—information that she jealously kept secret. There were in our neighborhood few places where herbs grew that Katherine had not visited by the time she was fourteen years old.

Now Katherine decided to gather her herbs on a larger scale than she had gathered them in her girlhood. But, alas, there were also other cullers of samples abroad. Bedotte, a certain soft-spoken, old French-Canadian "doctor"—commonly called "the sin smeller" because of a sharply upturned nose—made his medicines from wild herbs, and seemed to discover them as if by instinct. Then an old couple living at the Corners not far away had taken up the business, having heard that

Katherine was doing well at it. Toward these three old neighbors she harbored no resentment; she even told them how to prepare and where to sell what they gathered. Among them all, however, they so depleted the herbs that little enough was left for her. Katherine found almost all the familiar places ravaged in advance of her visits, especially since the affairs of the home farm occupied so much of her time and attention that she was unable to go herb gathering oftener than twice or three times a week. During the second summer, therefore, she abandoned the old places altogether and went to Quog-Hoggar.

Quog-Hoggar lies three miles to the northwest of our old home neighborhood on the farther side of a long ridge of land known as Coleman's Whale Back. The Old Squire's father, the first settler in our part of the country, once described it in this manner:

"When the Creator made the world and put things in shape for us here below, He had a lot of odds and ends left over, quogs and bogs and scrogs and crags, that He didn't know what to do with or where to put them to get them out of the way. So He went over t'other side of Coleman's Whale Back and dumped them all down together and left them just as they fell."

From what we knew of Quog-Hoggar we were quite ready to agree with the old pioneer's notion. There were three or four square miles of it, the most higglety-pigglety jumble of tangled swamps, rock ledges, deep black muck holes, clay banks, bare gravel hills, and black fir woods that it is possible to imagine. No one except Pony—during the time she attempted to develop a goose farm—had ever attempted to take up land there. No one indeed ever went there if he could help it. Years before, a hunter named Nowell had become lost and perished there, and for that reason the place was sometimes called Nowell's Misery; but Quog-Hoggar was the name it generally went by. The word seemed to fit it well. A large and often stagnant brook, the outlet of a muddy pond at the northerly corner of the tract, meandered through the place—a brook that anyone trying to cross Quog-Hoggar was constantly meeting in the most unexpected places. Folk said you would cross that brook six times before you got across Quog-Hoggar! Where the brook finally went or whether it ever left Quog-Hoggar at all, no one seemed accurately to know. One farmer on the farther side declared that the brook itself got lost in the swamp and flowed round and round till hot weather dried it up!

One day in October after the leaves had fallen my cousin Addison and I undertook to trace the course of the brook. I shall never forget that tramp. Sometimes we were up to our knees in mud, sometimes we had to cut ourselves loose from alder and clematis thickets with our jackknives. Twice we were as good as lost. But we stuck stubbornly to the brook, though that was far from easy, for it flowed into many sloughs and little muddy ponds, the shores of which were grown higher than our heads with rushes, cattails, queen of the meadow, goldenrod, thoroughwort, elecampane, and other towering weeds, some of which I never saw anywhere else. Whenever we came to high ledges or gravely hillocks, we climbed them and tried to take our bearings. We should never have started without a compass. Once we grew utterly discouraged and would have gone back as we had come had we been sure we could have found our way.

At last after we had been traveling nearly eight hours we came late in the afternoon to a soft bog, along the far side of which there was a long white ledge that resembled a dam. It was through a cleft in that ledge that the brook made its way and thence flowed down a densely wooded gorge for half a mile to a pond several miles long, at the farther end of which we saw cleared land and farm buildings. We were now out of Quog-Hoggar and after following the pond shore to the farms were able to take the highway homeward. During the day we had seen a bear, several deer, dozens of muskrats and hedgehogs, numerous meadow hens and herons, and the biggest water snake I ever set eyes on—a monster seven feet long, we thought. Until then neither of us had been in the swamp farther than a partly cleared meadow that bordered it on the east, where there was a hay barn. So after following the brook through we considered ourselves as geographical authorities on Quog-Hoggar. But that was seven or eight years before Katherine began going there for herbs.

A person needed courage to enter so wild and sinister a tract, but Katherine's jaunts collecting herbs in girlhood had given her confidence and experience. She found her way first to one, then to another of the little wild meadows and open spots along the brook where boneset, comfrey, cohosh, and veratrum grew. The swamp bore so ill a

name that no rival herb gatherer followed her to those places. In the course of a year or two she began to improve on nature and make the place more productive by taking a hoe with her and transplanting herb roots to favorable spots on the banks of the brook or round the open sloughs, where there was dark rich earth. She had in mind a project for converting Quog-Hoggar into a wild herb preserve and acquiring a legal title to the entire tract.

Naturally Katherine said nothing to others of her plan or of her visits to the place; she did not tell them even to her mother and still less to her Aunt Columbia, who was somewhat of a neighborhood gossip.

On her jaunts Katherine was wont to hitch up Bim, a horse she used for marketing, and drive past the homes of certain of her neighbors, then along the little-traveled road beyond to a point where a grass-grown "winter road" diverged from it and led through woods for half a mile or more to the meadow where the old hay barn stood; she would leave the horse in the barn to wait for her to return, laden with herbs from Quog-Hoggar. So careful was she not to have those trips known that if she saw or met people on the road she used to drive on past the place where the winter trail diverged and come back to it later.

Near neighbors as we were, I knew nothing of her enterprise for a long while, though in other matters Katherine and I had much in common, for we were the last two remaining at home of the little group of young folks who had grown up there together. All my cousins—Halstead, Addison, Theodora, and Ellen—had gone their different ways in life, and only I, a recent college graduate, was left to help the Old Squire carry on the homestead—while also attempting to carry out my brave resolve to live by the use of a pen.

I learned about Quog-Hoggar accidentally one evening after a long day's work in September. Just as I was closing the stable doors for the night I saw a light coming along the path across the fields from the Edwards farm. As it drew near the shadowy bearer proved to be Aunt Columbia. She was much disturbed.

"Kate's gone and hasn't come home; we're dreadfully worried about her," were the old lady's first words.

"Where did she go?" I asked, not at all startled, for I knew Katherine's resourcefulness.

"We don't know," Aunt Columbia replied plaintively. "She drove off with Bim this forenoon. We haven't seen her since."

"Drove to the Corners, did she?" I asked.

"No, she took the west road up by the Murches and Wilburs."

It did seem a little strange that Katherine should be away so long if she had gone that way; for after passing our neighbors' farms the west road did not lead to much except Quog-Hoggar. Still I was far from feeling anxious.

"I guess it's all right, Auntie," I said. "But you go home. I'll get my supper, and if she doesn't come by nine, blow the horn. I'll come over, and we will see what is best to do."

Promptly at nine o'clock I heard Aunt Columbia blowing the dinner horn. As quick as I could I lighted a lantern, hitched up, and drove round by the road to the Edwards farm.

Katherine had not come. Her mother and Aunt Columbia were greatly worried. "Bim's so skittish I'm afraid he's run away and thrown her out," Mrs. Edwards said.

Neither of them knew for what purpose Katherine had driven away, but her mother said to me in a low tone, so that Aunt Columbia could not hear, that Katherine had gone that way several times lately. "She brings home lots of herbs," Mrs. Edwards continued. "I think she went for more today, and what I'm afraid of is that she's been going into that awful Quog-Hoggar for them."

I recollected instantly that Addison and I had seen cohosh, spearmint, elecampane, and other herbs growing abundantly there, and I remembered Katherine's troubles with rival collectors. "That is just where she went!" I thought, and now misgivings beset me, for I knew what a bewildering and really dangerous place it was.

"Oh, she will come back all right," I said to her mother just to cheer her. "Don't worry. I'll drive over that way. Probably I shall meet her."

The more I reflected as I drove along the more certain I felt that Quog-Hoggar was where Katherine had gone herb gathering, and when I came to where the winter trail diverged from the highway I got out and, taking the lantern, looked for wheel marks in the grass. There they were, fresh and distinct. Turning in, I followed the trail slowly, for it was rough, as far as the meadow in the woods. When within a hundred yards of the old hay barn I heard a horse whinny—the whinny of a horse in a lonesome place when he heard another horse coming, I knew that it was Bim. Katherine evidently had left him there and had not come back. In the dark I came near running into her little driving wagon, which stood in front of the barn door; behind the seat was lashed a large sack of herbs. Bim was in the barn. Katherine had taken him out of the shafts and hitched him to a post. It looked as if she had been off and returned once with herbs and then had gone for more.

Thinking she might be near, I "sohoed" first softly and then louder, but got no response except dismal echoes and a derisive hoot from an owl.

It was so lonely a place that I was sorry I had not taken a gun. The region was so unfrequented that it had become a sort of wild animal preserve. What I most feared, however, was not that animals had attacked Katherine but that she had either got lost or, while gathering boneset or cohosh, had leaned out too far over one of those soft black sloughs and fallen in. The thought of her smothered in one of those repulsive places was indeed disquieting.

I shouted again and yet again. If she were within half a mile and living, I felt sure she would guess that someone had come searching for her and would reply. The darkened swamp gave back no response, however, except from the owl, whose hooting there in the night sounded sinister and mocking. It was not easy to decide what to do. Beyond doubt Katherine had gone back after more herbs, but where? Quog-Hoggar was a big tract. I thought of driving back to the home neighborhood for a dog to put on her track. But no one living near us kept a hound; the only dog thereabouts was an old collie of little use for tracking. Nor would any of the men then at home know enough of the swamp to aid me greatly. Since I was there, I concluded to strike out alone and begin to search at once, for every moment might be precious.

Hitching my horse, I set the barn doors open so that the animals should be company for each other. A rusty hay fork with one broken tine was lying on the barn floor. Taking the fork in one hand—it was better than no weapon at all—and the lantern in the other hand, I started. My plan was to push into the swamp, shouting at times as I went, till I came to Quog Brook and then follow the stream for a mile or two both ways: north and south. Never shall I forget that night trip into Quog-Hoggar!

A Night in the Swamps

THERE ARE PERSONS who have so good a sense of direction that they can keep a straight course through thick woods by lantern light, but I am not so endowed. In ten minutes after I had entered Quog-Hoggar that night in search of Katherine I had little idea which way I was going, whether west, north, or south. Curiously enough it was the owl hooting in response to my hullos that kept me headed toward Quog Brook. Every time I stopped to shout in the hope of getting a response that dismal bird replied, "Hoot, hoot, hoo-oot," off in the woods to my right. If, as seemed likely, the owl was sitting quiet in a tree, I knew I was moving toward the brook.

After a short time I came to several long soft sloughs bordered with rank weeds higher than my head. There frogs were clamoring, muskrats were plunging into the water at sight of my lantern, and mosquitoes were biting rabidly. Beyond that chain of treacherous bogs were numerous craggy hillocks and gravel knolls overrun with poison ivy and other creeping plants. From the top of one of them I again hulloed repeatedly, but merely set another owl hooting farther away.

Two deer that had lain ruminating on the other side of the hillock bounded off, "whistling" shrilly, as I stumbled toward them, and another large creature beside a rock among the vines growled softly and sprang away as I passed. I walked round two other bogs, and by that time the owls had tired of replying. Two meadow hens were now uttering their metallic squawks, and ducks were "quacking" on a pond nearby.

I climbed another rocky hillock, pushed through tangled cedar and clematis, and coming to more sloughs, began to fear that I might share the fate of the hunter Nowell, whose "misery" had become a tradition. Then quite unexpectedly I came out on the brook and nearly walked off the bank into it, for now, to add to my other troubles, my lantern was burning dim; setting off so hastily, I had not thought to refill it. To go on without a light seemed impossible. Though I knew I had not walked much more than a mile, I was afraid I could not grope my way back and concluded that I might have to remain where I was till daylight.

Not to give up entirely, I followed along the bank of the brook by the now fast-expiring light of the lantern, hulloing again and yet again. Suddenly I heard a distant "coo-ee" from far down the brook to southward. It was Katherine I knew instantly, for that was the way she often responded to a hail across the fields between our two farms. I think I never experienced a sense of greater relief. What the matter was or what had kept her so late I could not imagine, but I hullooed again and received a second response; then I caught the echoes of several far-borne sounds as if she were attempting to say something to me.

Thereupon for some minutes I made what haste I could along the bank in her direction and then shouted again. To my astonishment an answering "coo-ee" came from a considerable distance off to the left in the direction of the old hay barn. Katherine appeared to be making her way through the swamps back to the place where she had left her wagon and Bim, and I guessed now that that was what she had shouted to me to do and I had not understood.

I turned and, shaking a little oil from the bottom of the lantern into the failing wick, started to make my way back across Quog-Hoggar. Before I had gone far my light went out entirely. The night was dark, and if I had had difficulties before, I had double the number now. I feared that I should never get through the swamp, and indeed it is likely that I should not have escaped till daylight had I not stopped every few minutes to hullo and get an answering hail from Katherine. I learned later that she had a trail of her own across the swamps that she was able to follow even at night. Having no such aid, I was so long beating about among the sloughs that Katherine lighted her lantern and came to meet me. The tables were turned somewhat to my disadvantage: I had come to find Katherine, and now it was she that came to find me.

When at last we met in the fir growth near the first of the sloughs, I could see that she was almost equally astonished and amused. No doubt I cut a queer figure, grasping that old hay fork in one hand and a dark lantern in the other. Withal I was muddy, had lost my hat, and had torn my coat. She laughed a little as she held up her lantern, and her first words were, "Well, well, well, what are you doing here at this time of night?"

"That is what I was about to ask you," I retorted. "What are you doing here in Quog-Hoggar of all places at this time of night? Did you imagine I came here for fun?"

Katherine regarded me a little more seriously. "Did you really come here to look for me?" she asked.

"Herb gathering is all right, Kate," I said, "but your friends are entitled to some consideration. Aunt Columbia and your mother are frightened half to death about you. What in the world kept you so late?"

"I'm sorry," Katherine replied humbly, yet not very contritely, for she was still inclined to smile. "It was kind of you. But really what were you going to do with that old one-tined hay fork? Not putting up hay in Quog-Hoggar?"

Clearly Katherine was laughing at me. "Well, I am glad you're safe," I said with as much dignity as my disheveled appearance permitted. "And, since it's past eleven, perhaps we'd better hitch up and drive home. You can explain to your folks."

To that bit of scolding Katherine did not reply—not until I had helped her to hitch up Bim and had gone to untie my own horse. "Of course I owe you an explanation," she said then. "Nobody in the world except you, I'm sure, would have taken trouble to come out to look for me at this time of night. You are the one neighbor who has always been helpful and showed an interest in my luckless affairs. I am going to confess right here that I heard you hulloing all the while and that I guessed it was you."

"Then why on earth didn't you answer?" I exclaimed in astonishment.

"I did once, but not very loud, and after that there was a good reason why I did not shout again."

"This is all rather mysterious," I said.

Again Katherine hesitated. "Just now I don't want to tell you why I stayed so late," she said at last. "Let it go that I was busy and got belated. Afterward when I started for home I met with an adventure that delayed me still longer."

"Oh, all right," I said perhaps a little stiffly.

Katherine again assured me that she felt far more grateful for the trouble that I had taken than she had been able to say and that she hoped I would believe her.

We set off for home; I drove Bim, and Katherine led my horse by one of the reins. When we reached the Edwards place Aunt Columbia and Katherine's mother came rushing out with a torrent of anxious questions, which Katherine answered evasively. I did not stop to go indoors, but after helping her to put her horse into the barn went home.

I will not deny that I was curious to know what had happened to her. It seemed to me that she had been excited about something all the way home. But after what she had said I did not care to pry into her affairs. I learned the following evening too that she had gone back to Quog-Hoggar at nine o'clock the next morning and had not returned till six o'clock in the afternoon. Apparently there was something more in the wind than mere herb gathering; but four months passed before I learned anything further. This is Katherine's story as I heard it then.

After driving over to Quog-Hoggar that afternoon she had gone to a place far down the brook where comfrey and boneset grew abundantly. There were so many bogs to cross that in order to keep her feet dry she had put on rubber boots. In the course of an hour or two she had gathered a large sackful, which she brought back to her wagon, and then she had set off to get another.

From going about so much alone in swamps and thick woods Katherine had learned to move as cautiously as a woodsman. She rarely cracked a dry stick underfoot or shook a bush in passing, and it was her custom, particularly while exploring new places in Quog-Hoggar, to go forward a few yards and then stop to listen and peer round, for it is only in that way that a person is likely ever to catch sight of the larger birds or animals.

She had reached the brook and while listening a moment after crossing it was sure that she had heard a gritting sound close by. The place was among black alders overrun by clematis, and peeping through the festoons, she saw an otter crouched on a fallen tree trunk that lay partly in the brook; the little creature was eating something. It had just emerged from the water, all wet and shining, and had neither seen nor heard her. What it had was a mussel, or freshwater clam, and as she stood there it slid off the log and brought up another, which it contrived to open, though not without much audible gritting of its teeth on the shell.

When she whistled the otter disappeared like a shadow and took refuge beneath the bank of the brook, and as she went on past the log she saw that the animal had made a meal there. Numerous freshly opened shells lay along the log and in the water beneath, and clinging by a fiber to the lustrous white nacre inside one of them, she discerned a pearly globule as large as a small bullet.

Katherine knew at once that it was a freshwater pearl, and going tiptoe down the log, she picked it up. She had some little knowledge of pearls and surmised that it was of considerable value. She realized too that there might be others. She got down from the log into the brook, and finding that there was a numerous colony of clams beneath the overhang of the bank, she took the knife that she carried for cutting herbs and began digging them up and cracking them open on the log.

After cracking open and exploring the contents of forty or fifty mussels she was rewarded by finding another pearl, not so large as the first yet very pretty. Later in the afternoon she found an oblong pearly slug and another little pearl, no larger than a mustard seed. It was muddy work, but the sight of the large, beautiful pearl that the otter had exposed kept her at work. She examined it more than once with growing interest, speculating what it was worth and whether there might not be others equally large somewhere along the brook. In fact pearl hunting proved so fascinating to her that it was not until the sun had dipped below the treetops and the brook bed had darkened that she thought of going home. Even then she lingered to explore the channel a little way and to crack a few more shells—and at the last moment she found another small pearl.

Dusk was falling, and realizing now that it was high time for her to go, she climbed out of the brook and started home, but she had taken only a few steps when a noise in the brush close by made her pause; some animal appeared to be coming directly toward her. Immediately a little black creature no larger than a small pig emerged from the thickets scarcely ten yards away. It set up an odd whimpering cry, and at almost the same moment a much larger black animal emerged, stopped, sniffed the air and growled.

Katherine knew that they were a bear and her cub, and although black bears generally are quite harmless, she was a little afraid of this one on account of the cub. What a hunter who lived near us had once said occurred to her: if you are unarmed and a bear stands sniffing, clap your hands smartly; the unusual noise will almost always frighten it away. But Katherine clapped her hands so vigorously that the cub whimpered in alarm, whereupon the mother bear growled again and rushed forward in an ugly temper.

Katherine backed away nimbly, but the thick brush impeded her. After a few steps she backed into a thicket of small firs, the lower boughs of which trailed on the ground. Unable at once to free herself and noticing that one of the firs was five or six inches in diameter, she grasped the branches and climbed hastily to a height of seven or eight feet, as far up as the trunk would support her weight. She shook the boughs considerably in climbing, and that circumstance perhaps still further disturbed the bear. In truth she had scarcely time to get out of the way when with the cub whimpering at her heels the bear came quite close, still growling. For some reason the creature did not seem inclined to move off, but growled every time Katherine stirred or shook the bough.

Not a little annoyed as well as alarmed, Katherine concluded that nothing was left for her to do except remain there and keep as still as possible until the bear was pleased to go away. Her position in the tree was not wholly comfortable yet it was not insupportable, for her feet rested on the branches close to the trunk. That was the queer state of affairs when she heard my first shouts. She guessed it might be me and "coo-eed" once in answer. But on hearing her shout the mother bear rushed forward close beneath where she was standing and snarled so menacingly that Katherine thought it imprudent to call out again lest the suspicious beast rise on her hind legs and try to pull her down. But when I came as far as the brook and hulloed so many times there, the bear appeared disturbed and presently made off with her cub in an opposite direction. It was then that Katherine had ventured to hail me again and, getting down from her insecure perch, had set off for the hay barn.

I suppose she was a little mortified at being treed by a bear and did not care to have me know it. Moreover, if she had told me about the bear she would have been obliged to explain why she had lingered so long at the brook, and she did not care to have anyone know what she had found, at least not for the present.

It was with that odd incident that Katherine's quest for pearls in Quog-Hoggar began. The season was now early August when Maine streams are usually low. Providing herself with a hatchet, tweezers, and a stout knife, she went back there every day for a week and began a more thorough search of the mussel beds—a kind of hunting that proved so attractive that for a time she wholly gave up gathering herbs. Fortune seemed at last to have tossed a morsel of its beneficence in her direction, and she wished to make the most of it.

Katherine Shares Her Secret

DURING SEPTEMBER and October Katherine visited Quog-Hoggar quite as she pleased, and no one was the wiser for her discovery of pearls. Equipped with rubber boots, garden rake, hatchet, tweezers, and oyster knife, she overhauled the clam beds along the entire course of the stream. On nearly every afternoon she spent there she found at least one pearl, and some of them were of good size.

Almost all the brooks and rivers of the United States from Maine to Texas contain mussels or clams in which pearls are occasionally found. No form of life is more widely diffused than these various specimens of pearl-bearing mollusks. In some regions they abound; in others they occur but scarcely. Oddly enough Quog Brook in that sinister, forbidding, and man-forsaken marsh proved unusually prolific in pearls.

Of course she did not publish the discovery abroad—to people Quog-Hoggar with pearl hunters! She went on with her quest and kept quiet about it; she did not even tell her mother or her Aunt Columbia. When the ice formed in November, she had followed the brook through all its devious windings from Mud Pond to Loon Pond, into which it finally found its way, and pretty thoroughly ransacked every mussel bed. It was characteristic of her that at every bed she left a few mussels for "seed" in order that they might again replenish the brook and sometime perhaps produce more pearls.

What pearls she found she laid aside at home, and the way I came to know about them was from being able by chance to help her to dispose of them. I had had a hard summer's work at the old farm, and shortly before Thanksgiving I made up my mind to visit Addison for a few days at New Haven, where he was an instructor in zoology, and then perhaps go to New York to look for a publisher. The evening before setting off I went over across the fields to stop in at the Edwardses' for a few minutes and tell Katherine that I was going away.

"Well, I hope you will have a nice trip," she said as I was going out. "Tell Ad how much we should all like to see him again. And did you say you would perhaps go to New York?"

"I think I may," I replied. "Any errand I can do for you?"

Katherine hesitated. "Maybe," she said. "If it wouldn't be too much trouble. I've just thought of something; come back a moment, please"—for we were at the door—"I don't want to talk of it out here."

We went back to the sitting room, and Katherine shut the door. Her mother and Aunt Columbia were in the kitchen. I had said good night to them, and they thought I had gone. Katherine glanced at the window shades to make sure they were down; then she brought forth from a locked drawer in the old-fashioned bureau a folded chamois skin, which she spread out on the table beneath the lamp. On it were all the pearls that she had collected from Quog Brook—sixty-two of them! Some were scarcely larger than bird shot, but fifteen were much larger; and there were six truly beautiful ones, two as large as small bullets, very lustrous and pearly white. Those two were perfect spheres, but some of the others were pear-shaped and otherwise deformed. There were also three or four slugs, or baroque pearls, as jewelers term pearls of irregular shape.

"Well, Kate!" I exclaimed, and I suppose I stared, for I noticed that she was regarding me with amusement.

"You know what they are?" she said.

"Pearls!" I cried. "No doubt of that. Beauties too! Why, those are valuable!"

"I do rather hope so," said she. "And what I should like awfully to have you do for me if you will is to take them to New Haven with you and let Addison see what he thinks of them, and then maybe carry them to New York and see what they will fetch. I don't quite like to trust them to the jeweler at the village here."

"You don't want to keep them and wear them then?" I asked.

"Dear me, no," said Katherine, laughing. "I am too poor to put on pearls. I have too many expenses to meet."

We stood there for some moments, looking them over and counting them while Katherine told me how and at what places in the brook she had found the prettiest ones. Then, hearing her mother calling to her from the kitchen, she hastily bound up the package, and I put it into my pocket. "It is better that Aunt Columbia and Mother do not know about it," she said, smiling. "Auntie, you know, just cannot keep from talking, and a word dropped might send a dozen idle people over there searching, and they really wouldn't find anything there now except my seed clams, for I have cleared the brook out pretty thoroughly."

I fully agreed with her. "Not even Ad shall know where you found them," I said.

"Oh, we can trust him!" she exclaimed, and then I took my leave.

When I showed the packet to Addison at New Haven, he was interested at once, for he had searched for pearls several times himself before leaving home—in Lurvey's Stream and in smaller brooks—but without much success.

"Where did you find these?" was his first question.

"In a certain place," I replied, at which he regarded me with a humorous grin. Then I told him who owned the pearls and that I was anxious to sell them.

Addison looked at them again and examined several with a magnifying glass. "Most of these have little value, I think," he remarked. "Worth five, ten, or fifteen dollars apiece perhaps. But there are two here that will bring good money. They are perfect spheres, very lustrous, have a fine tint, and are remarkably large ones."

We took them to the college laboratory and weighed them. The larger two weighed eighty-seven grains, or nearly twenty-eight carats; the other weighed eighty-three grains, but you could hardly tell the two apart.

"Set with a diamond these would make a beautiful ring or a lovely pin," Addison remarked. "I think they will sell well. I'll go to New York with you," he added. "We must do the best we can for Kate. She deserves it if ever a girl did. Think what she has done at home to keep things going!"

We went to the city next morning, and before taking the pearls to a famous jewelry firm that Addison thought was likely to pay the highest prices, we decided to call at another place, a very showy shop on Broadway, and get an opinion there. Our experience is worth recording as an instance of the caution that it is necessary to use in disposing of gems. The salesman to whom we made known our business at once called another person, presumably one of the proprietors, from the back of the shop, and then while they were examining the pearls another man joined them. They asked a great many questions—where the pearls had come from, when they were found and how long ago. The last question was evidently put to find out whether we had shown the pearls to other dealers. Addison and I said little except to reply briefly as we saw fit and at last to ask whether they wished to purchase and what they would give us.

After telling us that the present market for pearls was very poor and trying in vain to find out what we knew of the value of pearls, one of them offered three hundred dollars for the lot. Addison folded up the packet. Thereupon one of the others remarked that possibly after notifying a certain good customer who had left an order with them for a pearl pendant, they might do a little better. Would we leave the packet with them overnight till they could consult with the customer?

"I'm afraid we can't do that," Addison replied, and we came away. "I wouldn't leave those pearls there an hour," he said to me, laughing. "I wouldn't even let them be taken to a back room for examination."

"You don't think they would be stolen?" I exclaimed.

"No, but there might be substitution of inferior pearls. And what could we prove if we left undescribed pearls with them overnight? Nothing."

We then proceeded to the dealers whom Addison had first had in mind and asked them to examine and value the pearls. A dry little man, evidently an expert, took the matter in hand and was about an hour in examining, testing, weighing, and scrutinizing the larger pearls under high lights.

"I have to make my report to the house," he said at last. "Call at three o'clock this afternoon." But he did not ask us to leave the pearls.

Somewhat to my astonishment Addison asked to have the packet put into the firm's safe for us, and the man carelessly assented as to a matter of no consequence.

"That's the difference between a reputable house like this and a nest of gem sharps," Addison remarked as we came out. "No funny business done here. The pearls are a good deal safer with them than in my pocket on Broadway."

A member of the firm met us when we called at three o'clock. It was as Addison had conjectured regarding the pearls. With the exception of the two large ones the collection was of no great value, not more than seven hundred dollars for sixty pearls. But for those two he named a price that astonished me, though Addison appeared to expect it.

"I have never seen finer pearls from freshwater mussels," the dealer remarked. "I hope you will find others and bring them to us."

To state the exact sum paid us would give a wholly erroneous idea of the value of freshwater pearls as generally found, even when they are as large as those two. It was their unusual luster and tint that determined the price. Curiously enough one of the pair was from the clam that Katherine had surprised the otter in the act of eating.

When I got home four days later, I hastened across the fields to acquaint Katherine with her good fortune and tell her what Addison and I had done. I had thought the sum the jeweler had paid was too much money for me to carry round in my pocket, and so on my way home I had deposited the check, which was to order, in Katherine's name with our local bank and had taken a certificate of deposit in the form of a passbook for her.

She saw me approaching and came out a little way to meet me so that Aunt Columbia need not hear what passed. I felt so merry that I could not resist a little stage play, and so I smoothed the elation from my face and pulled it as long as I could.

"Yes, we sold them," I said. "I hope you will not be too much disappointed. We took them to more than one place. At the place where we went first, they offered us three hundred dollars. Is that anywhere near what you expected?"

"Why, yes," Katherine replied hesitantly. I could see that she was just a little disappointed but determined to be satisfied. With great difficulty I kept my face sober.

"Then we went to another place where Addison said they would be sure to treat us fairly, and there they offered us rather more. They paid us with a check that I deposited at the village bank as I came along. Here's your passbook," and I handed it to her, opened at the figures.

Katherine glanced at it, and I saw her eyes widen. Then she laughed incredulously. "You're joking!" she exclaimed. "You made those figures yourself!"

"Draw on the bank and see," I replied. "Yes, Kate, we got all that!"

When you have worked hard for small gains year in and year out, an unexpected windfall lifts your spirits strangely.

"Can this really be true?" exclaimed Katherine exultantly. Then she thought of Addison and me. "I ought to share it with you!" she cried.

"Share nothing!" I exclaimed. "Do you imagine we would take anything just for doing you a neighborly turn?"

But Katherine was already thinking of the thousand wants in their home. We had turned and now stood facing the weather-beaten, unpainted farm buildings with their leaky, sagging roofs. "Now I will make our home more presentable!" she cried with sudden exultation.

And she did. Within a year you would hardly have known the place. Indeed, I could have almost envied her the possession of so much ready money, for that was not a very prosperous year with us at the Old Squire's. I was almost tempted to abandon writing for pearl hunting myself, and as a matter of fact did several times overhaul the mussel bed up Lurvey's Stream in the pools below Sister's Falls and the Little Sister. But only a few seed pearls and slugs rewarded my delving. In my case the otters, minks, and crows must have swallowed all the fine ones!

36

The Young Birds Come Back

IF THERE IS A LONESOME PLACE IN ALL THE WORLD—
when Thanksgiving Day comes—it is an old homestead where the
young people have grown up and gone, leaving two old people
behind to live alone.

That was the case for a year or two, at our old farm in Maine. Addison was now a professor at Yale, when not journeying to various parts
of the world to gather geological collections. Theodora had finished
her course at the Kent's Hill Seminary and gone to teach at an Episco-
pal mission school for Indian girls in the Dakota territories. Ellen,
whose first fiancé, Thomas Jefferson Cobb, had drowned in the Kennebec, eventually married a farmer and had also moved to the Dakotas.
Halstead, who had shocked us by making a hasty and seemingly unwise
departure from the old farm at the tender age of nineteen, had found
himself, after a rocky start, and established a successful business in
Texas. I, myself, had moved to Boston a year after finishing college to
write full time for *The Youth's Companion*, and was so struck with my
career that I hardly thought of anything else.

So, quite in the natural order of things, it had come about that the
Old Squire and Grandmother, after having a houseful of young people
for years, found themselves alone.

Happy, quiet, blessed lonesomeness, some might say, but Grandmother and the Old Squire were not that sort. It was like death itself to
them to feel that they were no longer needed by those they had worked

so hard to bring up, but who had now taken flight, without a thought, as it seemed, of the old nest or of the old birds.

Looking back, it is not easy to understand how we could have been so thoughtless of them, but we had felt all along that we had been a great tax on the old people, coming home as we did for our upbring-ing, and that they must feel relieved to have us off their hands and able to care for ourselves. We did not realize how sadly they missed us.

It was Kate Edwards who first set us thinking. Kate had lived at the farm across the fields from the Old Squire's and had grown up with Theodora and Ellen. At seventeen she, too, went from home for a time, but after her father's death, had returned to run the farm and care for her mother. "Do you know," she wrote in her letter to Theodora, "that Aunt Ruth and Uncle Joseph"—meaning Grandmother and the Old Squire—"are terribly lonesome, nowadays, over at your old place? They don't seem as well as they used to be, either, and you've no idea what a still, solemn, lonesome place it has come to be. I almost dread going over there, it is such a contrast to the merry household it was, when you were all at home. It seems like a graveyard, it is so still. None of you were at home last Thanksgiving, you know. Aunt Ruth shed tears when I called that afternoon, and you know she isn't one of the crying kind. The Old Squire tried to turn it off with a joke about an old robin's nest, but I could see that he was just as lonesome as she was. Hadn't you better try to come home, Dora, this next Thanksgiving? I really think you ought to."

Theodora wrote to Addison about it and enclosed Kate's letter, and after a while Addison wrote to me. "Perhaps we had better try to get down there, Thanksgiving time," he said. "Doad writes that Grand-mother and the Old Squire are mighty lonesome and that they're not very well. Doad is going to come on East, if she can get away, and she has written to Nell to join her on the way. We had better all try to go, I guess, and, say, you write to Halstead and get him started."

That was in September 1880. We wrote back and forth several times about it, and I got Halstead to promise to go. It would cut a large slice off Theodora's annual wages as teacher to come east, but she decided to do so. We finally planned to arrive all together and surprise them on Thanksgiving Day. We agreed to meet in Portland, go up by train in the forenoon, and drop in on them just as they were sitting down to dinner, for we knew, or thought we did, that Grandmother always had an abundance of food on Thanksgiving Day.

We met as agreed—a joyous meeting, for we had seen little of each other for several years—and then went up by train together to the home station. There had been an hour and a half to wait in Portland; and as an afterthought, at the last moment, the girls bought a few packages of nuts and sweetmeats to take with us. More thoughtful than Addison and myself, too, Theodora and Ellen had brought many nice little presents for Grandmother. It was a fine Indian summer day. We hired a surrey at the station, six miles from the old farm and, to make our arrival a complete surprise, drove round first to the Edwardses' place, whence, after putting up our team, we stole across the fields with our packages to the line-wall bars and reconnoitered the home buildings.

"I guess they've sat down to dinner, already," Halstead said.

We sneaked across the west field, got into the wagon house by the back door, and then went on tiptoe through the wood house to the kitchen door, which was closed. Stealthily Addison turned the knob, opened it a crack, and we peeped in. The kitchen was warm, but very still and did not seem at all as on former Thanksgivings. The door into the dining room was open; the table, a little one, was set in there, and we could just see Grandmother on one side of it and knew that—out of sight—was the Old Squire on the other. They were eating their lonesome Thanksgiving dinner, or trying to, neither of them saying a word.

For a long minute we peeped, without hearing either of them speak. It was so pathetic that Doad's eyes filled with tears, and Addison drew back from the door, looking very uncomfortable.

"I say," he whispered, "isn't that doleful?"

The place wore such a saddened, subdued air that we did not have the heart to rush in, uproariously, as we had at first agreed, and stole back to the wagon house to lay some new plan.

"Let's go to the door, one at a time," Addison said at last, "and sing or whistle or say something as we used to, so that they will hear us first and come out. Halse, you go ahead. "You're the best singer among us. Go just outside the kitchen door and sing 'Dixie.' They'll know you by that the moment they hear it."

Halstead's early childhood had been passed at New Orleans, and even after he came north to live with us at the Old Squire's he always pretended to sympathize with the South.

Halstead limped cautiously to the door, while the rest of us kept back out of sight. Instead of singing "Dixie," however, he burst forth with "The Bonnie Blue Flag That Bears the Single Star" and had scarcely caroled the first stanza when the door was pulled open and we heard the Old Squire crying out, "You dear boy! Why, where in the world did you come from!" By this time, too, Grandmother had her arms round his neck. They drew him in, and then on toward the dining room, without a thought that any of the rest of us were out there.

"You go next, Nell," whispered Addison. "What will you sing?"

"Oh, I know my part," said Nell.

"I will steal to the kitchen sink and begin to rattle the dishpan. That was always my job."

She shut the door after her, but had not been clattering the tinware many moments when we heard Grandmother cry out, "Why, Ellen! When did you come?"

Still they did not suspect there were more of us outside, for Halstead and Ellen said not a word of our presence; and after awhile Addison and Theodora sent me to the door, to declaim "Spartacus to the Gladiators," since it was one of the long-standing family jokes on me that I had once—when I had the mumps—been heard declaiming "Spartacus" in my sleep!

I had got no further than, "Ye call me chief, and ye do well to call him chief who for—" when out rushed the Old Squire and grabbed me, laughing like a boy, and Grandmother was close behind him.

They suspected now that Addison was somewhere round and, rushing forth to the wagon house, surprised him and Theodora just scudding out of sight through the door into the west barn. They had no chance to play their two parts; Theodora was to blow the old dinner-horn that hung by the kitchen door and Ad was to drum on a milk pail, as was his wont when going to milk the cows in the morning. There was no forgetting Theodora's performance on that old horn; it blew hard, and she always elicited a peculiarly ragged blare. That, too, was one of the family jokes. They came back from the barn and surrendered, hilariously.

It touched our hearts, our consciences also, to see what joy this homecoming of ours had brought, but when Halstead rather inconsiderately cried, "What have you got for Thanksgiving dinner?" Grandmother's countenance fell suddenly.

"If I had only known you were coming," she lamented, "I would have had a fine one. But with only Joseph and me I didn't prepare much this year. We don't, either of us, care much for large dinners. So I only cooked a little, just for him and me."

"Yes, your grandma and I don't eat many kinds of food, now," the Old Squire explained.

In fact, one small chicken, a plate of cookies, and a little lonesome-looking custard pie were all we saw outspread; the table seemed to be mainly tablecloth! Contrasted with what we remembered, when we were at home and had a host of company besides, this was indeed a change! Then there was always a goose, a turkey or two, or three chickens, besides a big plum pudding, four kinds of pie, with cake, fruit, preserves, maple syrup, cheese, honey, nuts, and numerous other dainties. Such a roar of voices and laughter, too, as made the old house shake! But now—till we came—you could have heard a kitten mew up in the attic! That silence, indeed, was the most eloquent contrast of all.

There was plenty in the house, however: honey, cheese, canned fruits, eggs, too, that distressed housewife's ever-ready refuge in times of emergency. With the girls helping, the table was soon lengthened out and set again, making quite a brave show of Thanksgiving cheer.

After dinner, when we had gone out to look the old place over and were at the apple house in the north orchard, Addison gave the rest of us a queer look and said, "This never will do, you know. How are we going to fix things here? Which of us can come home and take hold? One of us must. Which?"

It was not an easy duty to face. Theodora was pledged to that mission school for the present. And the way Halstead and Ellen were situated, too, gave them little chance of escaping their new responsibilities. To me, I confess, it appeared to be a great sacrifice, at least I thought so at first, for my job looked good to me; but to ask Addison to give up such a promising scientific career as had opened before him seemed an endless pity and a loss of great opportunities.

We stood there in the old apple house and looked at each other in a perplexity that was well-nigh distress; for some minutes, we said scarcely a word. Each knew just how the others felt. None of us wanted to do it.

"But it's of no use to haggle over it," Addison said at last. "Think what the Old Squire and Grandmother have done for us. Took us in when we were about as good as homeless and orphans. Brought us up. Worked and slaved and planned to have us go to school and make a good start in life. And now we have scattered and haven't so much as looked back, once! You can all see that they're getting old. They will soon need care. What is worse, they feel lonely and deserted. This isn't a thing we can hire strangers to do. Which one of us is going to come home here, take the old farm, and put things through? That's the question we must face, and we had better face it now. Shall we draw lots for it?"

Still we looked at one another and for some minutes did a lot of hard, uncomfortable thinking, without many words. We tried to see one another's necessities, impartially, without personal selfishness.

Everything considered, it grew plain to me that I could do it with the least self-sacrifice, and after a long breath I bade farewell to my

Bean Town life and said, "I'm the 'chick' for the coop. This, I see, is my job, but you must all promise to come home once in a while and help make things go."

"Yes, yes, yes," they all said eagerly. "We will come."

"But you shall come every Thanksgiving, and as much oftener as you can," I stipulated, saving what I could from a hard bargain. "You shall not go off about your own business and forget me and never come near. You shall keep the old place in mind."

They promised faithfully and sincerely.

So before leaving the apple house that afternoon we settled it that way, and shook hands on it all round as we went out; and that evening, in the sitting room, we talked it all over with the Old Squire and Grandmother and arranged the preliminaries of my going home to take up the burden of life at the old farm in Maine.

I have never regretted my decision. One of the most pleasurable results of that home-going was the new lease on life and joyousness it gave those dear, old people to whom we owed so much. Again there was something for them to live for. With what fresh interest they advised my efforts at farming! What practical points and details they gave me out of their wealth of past experience! They even rose ahead of me to look after the dairy, the bees, the poultry, and the garden.

Again the Old Squire read the farm journals for improved methods of cropping and for contending with insect pests in the orchard; and again—one autumn morning—we heard Grandmother making the old spinning wheel whir up in the attic, to produce a stock of wool yarns for winter socks. When the Old Squire heard that familiar sound, he cocked his ear, laughed outright, and clapped me on the shoulder.

But the greatest joy to them, I think, was to see and feel that the dear old place, where they had labored so long and hard, was not to relapse, fall into decay, and pass into the hands of strangers, as has happened to so many New England homesteads, but that it was to be kept up, go forward, and remain the home of their descendants.

We all believe that this second homecoming of ours added fifteen years to their lives, for they lived in good health till long past ninety. What was better than mere years was that they kept hopeful and optimistic, and to the end were ready to aid in every good effort.

C. A. STEPHENS: THE MAN
AND HIS WORK

IN HIS 1976 BIOGRAPHY *THE WORLD OF C. A. STEPHENS*, Ronald G. Whitney says of Charles Asbury Stephens:

Who was C. A. Stephens?

Few now living can tell you but once upon a time he was one of America's most beloved storytellers. In the years between the Civil War and the 1920s his name was a household word to millions.

"Prodigious" is the only adequate word to describe his literary output. Over 2,500 short stories, 31 full length books, and a host of articles and pamphlets flowed from his prolific pen.

But perhaps his best known books today are those which he wrote about life on the old Squire's farm "away down east in the Pine Tree State" by the shores of the placid Pennesseewassee. Those books are still sought after by thousands of people and have given him enduring fame and a secure niche in the Parthenon of American literature.

Above all, C. A. Stephens was the most authentic interpreter of the old rural way of life which gave American society many of its basic values. Throughout his stories, from beginning to end, we have one of the best, most accurate portraits of our pre-urban culture which so carefully nurtured those values. One of the reasons why our cities are so sick is because we have not been able to translate those rural human values into relevant urban terms. We must recover those insights if our urban world is ever to be a good place for human existence.

C. A. Stephens was a greatly gifted gentle genius with universal vision and sparkling imagination. The spell he wove with his pen still lingers like the soft afterglow of a summer sunset. His beautiful, nostalgic stories, so full of the light of reality, still retain their power to enthrall.

We shall not see his like again.

One of the questions I had when I began studying Stephens, was whether his Old Squire stories were fiction or nonfiction. Both Ford and Stephens gave the impression that they were nonfiction. That is clearly not the case. Many stories are quasiautobiographical, but characters, incidents, and locations have been changed and amalgamated for artistic (as well as legal) purposes. Several versions of some stories exist, with different consequences occurring, or identical actions being attributed to different characters. Several characters even have multiple fates. (We present the most optimistic here.) Five major differences are that the beginning of the story line has been bumped up a decade, from the mid-1850s to the mid-1860s; the Old Squire and his wife are based on Stephens' maternal grandparents, but named after his fraternal grandparents; the Old Squire's children have been killed off in the war, which they were not; the Old Squire's farm (which burned down in 1885) actually belonged to a relative whose daughter, Christine (Stephens' second cousin), became Stephens' first wife; and the cousins, who were based on real people, though not all cousins, are presented as living in one place, which they did not.

The Old Squire stories are prosocial in nature, stressing hard work, individul responsibility, the value of education, entrepreneurial risktaking, a social responsibility for helping others, and a strong belief in democracy. C. A. Stephens' strengths, as demonstrated in this series, include intimate familiarity with the subjects he writes about, a great ability to explain things clearly and simply, a childlike sense of enthusiasm, a wonderful sense of humor, and a strong narrative ability.

Unfortunately, Stephens also produced lots of dross and many of his stories haven't aged well. This, of course, doesn't mean his good stories aren't good, just that there are fewer than we'd like. Also, structure was not one of Stephens' strengths, and his literary reputation probably declined because he never assembled his best Old Squire stories into a damatically complete—with beginning, middle, and end—

one-volume overview (His increasing preoccupation with gerontlogical research may have led to this mistake.) As I began listing and annotating Stephens' work, I realized such a volume could be produced: *Stories from the Old Squire's Farm* is the result. The grandchildren arrive (although why they, except for Halstead, didn't stay with their mothers is never explained), grow up, go into the world, return for a reunion, and decide one must remain to provide company and care for the grandparents. In completing this collection, Eric-Jon and I chose, from more than one thousand published (and unpublished) works, Stephens' most important stories (in the sense of being excellent reads, important information sources about the times, and/or critical to plot development). Fourteen are reprinted for the first time, one has never been published, and only a few are taken from existing collections, which all are, incidentally, out of print. *Stories from the Old Squire's Farm* is enjoyable reading for all ages, and provides, next to *Tom Sawyer,* the best view of coming-of-age in rural nineteenth-century America I have ever encountered.

Basically the two of us made five contributions to Stephens' work. We provided a unified framework for the stories, transforming them into what could be considered an episodic novel. We pieced together separate story parts (on five occasions) to produce needed bridging material, or to produce, in our judgment, a more complete story. We incorporated, on six occasions, as Stephens' himself did, autobiographical nonseries stories (two) or parts of stories (four) to portray important periods of, or episodes in, the development of the Old Squire saga. We pieced together, as independent short stories, the best manuscripts of each episode, from existing variations. Finally, we developed a comprehensive timeline and common fate for characters—remember Stephens wrote these stories over a period of sixty years—and smoothed out inconsistencies.

During his life, C. A. Stephens (changed from "Stevens" to avoid embarrassing relatives) published eighteen books of fiction (mostly collections and short story fix-ups) and five books of nonfiction (based on personal research into aging). Since his death in 1931, six books of fiction, several reprints, and a book of recycled stories have appeared. The total number of stories Stephens wrote, for *The Youth's Companion* or elsewhere, will probably never be known because he didn't keep records and wrote anonymously and under several pen names. However, he claimed the number exceeded 3,000 short stores. (And, Bowdoin College has thirty-four boxes of mostly unpublished manuscripts, a number of which are, in my judgment, excellent.)

In addition, Stephens' Boswell, the quirky Louise Harris, published five books of nonfiction about *The Youth's Companion* and Stephens' life. These provide valuable information, but are somewhat unreliable, lack important specifics, and are disorganized. (She is to be commended, however, for assembling at Brown University, at great effort, the largest collection of Stephens' material in existence.) A more reliable source of information, though still incomplete, is Ronald G. Whitney's little known biography *The World of C. A. Stephens* (1976).

Born in Norway, Maine, on October 21, 1844, C. A. Stephens was an only child who grew up on several farms in the area. He graduated from Norway Academy, spent one year at Kents Hill, and entered Bowdoin as a sophomore in 1866. He became a writer for several reasons: success in selling stories during a poverty induced junior-year sabbatical; advice from Elijah Kellogg, a popular Maine writer; and failure to find a job during a midwestern trip he took in 1869, shortly after graduation.

He moved to Boston and was immediately successful. In January 1870 he sold two stories to *The Youth's Companion*, one of the two most influential children's magazines of the time. Its editor, Daniel Sharp Ford, was impressed by Stephens and the quantity and quality of his stories. He put Stephens on an annual salary in 1871 and under exclusive contract in 1874. (Stephens repaid him by becoming the magazine's most popular and prolific writer.) Ford, who didn't like to travel, used Stephens as an extra pair of legs and eyes, sending him on an almost continuous series of grand tours for thirty years. From 1884 to 1887, however, Ford paid Stephens to remain home and attend Boston University Medical School so that the magazine could acquire a staff physician to write scientific articles. Finally, just before his death in 1899, Ford planted the seed for the quasiautobiographical Old Squire series with Stephens, most of whose writings were quasiautobiographical anyway.

Indeed, the quasiautobiographical nature of the series is probably best illustrated by Stephens' failure to take the next logical step in developing his series: having the narrator marry Katherine, whom he has been sweet on for years, thus producing a second generation of adventurers. But Katherine, the neighbor, seems to have been modeled on Christine, the second cousin, whom he married in 1871. The marriage was not a happy one even though it produced two daughters and, apparently, Stephens could not bring himself to even write fictional stories about that relationship. So Nicholas is portrayed as an old bachelor, and the next generation of adventures that he reports on occurs on an isolated farm in Canada with cousin Ellen's children.

In the 1890s Stephens began pioneering research into gerontology, an effort that consumed increasing amounts of time and capital. But even though business reverses forced the publishers of *The Youth's Companion* to reduce costs by taking him off their payroll from 1916 to

C. A. STEPHENS' HOME AND LABORATORY WERE THE SUBJECT OF MUCH CURIOSITY, EVEN AS TO THE NUMBER OF ROOMS. SOME SAY IT HAD SEVENTY, OTHERS FORTY. BUT IT CANNOT BE DENIED THAT IT WAS AN ARCHITECTURAL WONDER, FULL OF GABLES AND TOWERS, ROUND CORNERS AND METAL WALLS. THE BUILDINGS ARE NO LONGER STANDING.

1925, he loyally continued writing exclusively for them until the magazine failed in 1929. Indeed, his death on September 22, 1931, may have been hastened by the financial pressure he was under. Ironically, by the time Minnie, his second wife, and her mother had died, several hundred thousand dollars in book royalties had accumulated. The money and the house were left to Norway Hospital, which declined to take the expensive-to-maintain house and laboratory Stephens had built. Therefore distant relatives had the impetus to contest Minnie's will. And, also, in consequence, most of his personal and business records and many of his manuscripts were lost or destroyed when Minnie's trustees sold the structure in the early 1950s to raise additional funds for the proposed hospital (and the house was then demolished).

In conclusion, Stephens still has much to offer. In America, between the end of the Civil War and the onset of the First World War, Sarah Orne Jewett (also from Maine) and C. A. Stephens were the twin colossi of serious and popular short stories.* Even today, tourists wander the hills of Pennesseewassee during the summer to soak up Stephens' atmosphere, and a former custodian of the Maine writer's room at the Maine State Library has told me they still receive more requests for information about Stephens than any other author. Indeed, the *New York Times* has written that C. A. Stephens is "one of the best loved and least known of American storytellers." Once you have read this book, you will understand why!

Dr. Charles G. Waugh

*Jewett even seems to have satirized Stephens in her short story "The New Methuselah," *Scribner's*, 7 Apr., 1980, pp. 514–24, and included in Richard Cary, ed., *The Uncollected Stories of Sarah Orne Jewett*, 1971.